Inside trueSpace4

Frank Rivera

New Riders

201 West 103rd Street, Indianapolis, Indiana 46290

INSIDE TRUESPACE4

Copyright © 1999 by New Riders Publishing

International Standard Book Number: 1-56205-957-2

Library of Congress Catalog Card Number: 98-89436

Printed in the United States of America

First Printing: February, 1999

00   99   4   3

EXECUTIVE EDITOR
Chris Nelson

ACQUISITIONS EDITOR
Laura Frey

DEVELOPMENT EDITOR
Linda Laflamme

MANAGING EDITOR
Sarah Kearns

PROJECT EDITORS
Clint McCarty
Caroline Wise

COPY EDITOR
Cliff Shubs

INDEXER
Rebecca Hornyak

TECHNICAL EDITOR
Alain Bellon

SOFTWARE DEVELOPMENT SPECIALIST
Craig Atkins

PROOFREADERS
Maribeth Echard
Elise Walter

LAYOUT TECHNICIANS
Liz Johnston
Jo Anna LaBarge
Louis Porter, Jr.

TRADEMARKS

All terms mentioned in this book that are known to be trademarks or service marks have been appropriately capitalized. New Riders cannot attest to the accuracy of this information. Use of a term in this book should not be regarded as affecting the validity of any trademark or service mark.

Adobe, the Adobe, After Effects, Photoshop, and Premiere are trademarks of Adobe Systems Incorporated.

WARNING AND DISCLAIMER

Every effort has been made to make this book as complete and as accurate as possible, but no warranty or fitness is implied. The information provided is on an "as is" basis. The authors and the publisher shall have neither liability nor responsibility to any person or entity with respect to any loss or damages arising from the information contained in this book or from the use of the CD or programs accompanying it.

Contents at a Glance

TABLE OF CONTENTS

FOREWORD

When trueSpace1 arrived in 1994 as the first integrated 3D authoring tool for MS Windows, it caused a sensation and received many coveted industry awards. Since then, numerous competitors have arrived on the scene with varying degrees of success. Many of these programs cost hundreds (or even thousands) of dollars more than trueSpace, but none of them have received comparable press reviews. The current version, trueSpace4, pushes the envelope firmly into the realm of very high-end, while maintaining its trademark ease of use.

trueSpace began its development on the Amiga PC in 1985, so the current version, trueSpace4, is actually in its eighth generation! During all these years, Caligari Corporation has relentlessly pursued two seemingly contradictory goals.

The first goal is manifested in the elegance and functionality of the trueSpace user interface. Caligari has pioneered a number of innovations in its user interface design with the firm belief that real time, perspective, direct manipulation of 3D objects would enable the user to be more productive than the traditional user interface based on multiple windows, dialog boxes, slider and numerical entries. The interface further frees the user to create because it is self-evident each tool indicates its function visually.

Our second goal is to deliver to the mainstream user the power of a high-end solution at a fraction of the cost. Virtually every trueSpace4 review stresses that we have indeed achieved this goal. With great modeling tools, bones, and radiosity rendering, trueSpace4 truly redefines the categories of high-end and mid-range.

No one is more qualified to demonstrate the power of trueSpace than Frank Rivera. Frank has followed trueSpace's progress since its Amiga days, and with time has achieved a level of mastery few others can match; this is true not only of trueSpace, but also of 3D design in general. His art is well-known and respected in the trueSpace community, as is his long-standing activism and pioneering work in many different media.

We at Caligari Corporation have proudly showcased his art often, most recently in our advertising campaign for trueSpace3. The pages of this book demonstrate again and again not only trueSpace's high-end capabilities, but also Frank's amazing talent. This book presents a most valuable gift to the entire trueSpace community.

Roman Ormandy
Caligari Corporation

ABOUT THE AUTHORS

Frank A. Rivera is a software engineer with a love for CG. With several low-level graphic libraries developed for TopSpeed Corporation under his belt, he brings his knowledge from the technical end of Today's 3D tools to the creative end. Frank creates imagery in MH3D, Softimage3d, Lightwave, Lightscape, POV, and his personal favorite trueSpace. Frank has a small 3D media studio in Roselle, New Jersey, and has lectured on effective lighting, inverse kinematics, and scene design. Frank's 3D work has been published in *Science Fiction Weekly, Publish Magazine*, trueSpace3 packaging, and a multitude of industry periodicals. Frank has been a key demonstrator for Caligari at Siggraph 97 in Los Angeles, California, and Siggraph 98 in Orlando, Florida. Frank can be reached via email at **LOGICBit@aol.com** or **Frank@LOGICBit.com**.

Alain Bellon, a native of Ganymede, one of the better moons of Jupiter, has lived most of his life on planet Earth. He is a physicist with serious interests in relativity theory, cognitive science, philosophy, computer science, psychology, mathematics, metaphysics, and martial arts. In his spare time he enjoys doing 3D design, animation and, of course, plug-ins for trueSpace. With this range of interests, it is not surprising that Alain's hero is Leonardo DaVinci (along with Richard Feynman, Sir Isaac Newton, Roger Penrose, and David Copperfield). If you have met an alien before, you know there never is a dull moment if you are with Alain. He will make objects float in midair, as he is also a skilled illusionist. Or perhaps he will draw you into a deep conversation regarding the most profound ideas, his latest theory of human behavior, or a highly convoluted practical joke. He favors small and tranquil meetings with friends over noisy social environments, unless he is performing magic for a crowd. When he grows up, he intends to go back home to Ganymede and visit the Jupiter suburbs. Alain has developed several outstanding plug-ins for trueSpace: ThermoClay2, SpaceTime Morph, 3D Energy, Fluid Reality, Quark Layers, and more. To find information, visit his home page at **http://www.MenteMagica.com** or write to him at **neuronal@netservice.com.mx**.

Terry Cotant is the Software Evangelist for Caligari Corporation. Aside from "spreading the word" about trueSpace to every individual on the face of the Earth, Terry is responsible for managing third-party plug-in (tSX) relations, and is part of the marketing and tradeshow planning teams. Terry was responsible for the production of the Caligari trueClips3 and pluSpack1 CDs as well as the new truePartner Catalog. Recently, Terry has signed on as Technical Editor for the new *trueSpace* Magazine. Before coming to Caligari, Terry worked for Kmart Corporation's World Headquarters as a UNIX system administrator and Informix Database Administrator for large-scale systems. Terry also had his own company, selling trueSpace bundled with highly optimized "trueSpace workStations" that were designed for using trueSpace in a digital studio. Terry can be reached via email at **terry@caligari.com**.

Arnold Gallardo has been using trueSpace for four years. He has extensively researched radiosity for the last two years by using both commercial and academic versions of radiosity. He is currently researching the viability of radiosity as a replacement for photography in the pursuit of image synthesis.

Tom Marlin has worked in the computer industry since the 1970s in a number of management, marketing, and technical positions. He is an accomplished publisher, producer, writer, game/Web designer and 3D artist/animator, with several successful commercial textures collections and game titles to his credit. Tom has used trueSpace since the first version was released and uses the program to create his renowned photorealistic art. He is president of Marlin Studios, a graphics and animation studio and publisher/developer of commercial graphics software. You can reach him at **tmarlin@marlinstudios.com** and visit **http://www.marlinstudios.com** to see more of his work and the company's texture collections.

Jeffrey W. Wall, M.D. lives and works in the Kansas City area. His wife fails to understand his passion for 3D graphics. He can be reached at **www.animavitae.com** or at **wally@kc.net**.

Oliver Zeller became intrigued with 3D Computer Graphics shortly after coming to New York City from Australia over six years ago. At the end of 1994, he stumbled across trueSpace 1 and has used trueSpace ever since. In 1996, he became Resource Specialist of America Online's PC Graphic Arts, 3D Rendering SIG. Oliver Zeller's artwork can be seen in numerous books, magazines, and exhibitions. Apart from other freelance work, he has also written for *3D Design Magazine* and is a Contributing Editor for *Serious 3D* and *trueSpace* Magazines. You can contact Oliver via email at **pcroliver@aol.com** or drop by his Web site, The 3D Graphics Outpost at **http://users.aol.com/pcroliver**.

ACKNOWLEDGMENTS

Frank Rivera:

First, I would like to thank you, the reader. Without an audience, I would have no reason to write this book. I would also like to thank Tom Marlin, Jeffrey Wall, M.D., Terry Cotant, Arnold Gallardo, and Oliver Zeller; the contributions that you have made to this project are invaluable. Your professionalism, dedication, and expertise are without measure. Thank you, Terry, for thinking of me when Macmillan first approached you with the idea for this book. Thanks to Tom; you've always been one of the most respected trueSpace users, ready to answer any questions regardless of whether they come from a novice or a professional. Thank you, Jeff, for your support and for sharing your lighting techniques with us in this book. Your 3D illustrations are morbid and a little disturbing, but they are fantastic. Thanks, Arnold, for agreeing to come in late in the game and to take on one of the most technical chapters in the book. A special note of thanks to my friend Oliver. I don't know whose phone bill is higher, yours or mine, but the late-night cram sessions really helped. Thank you for all of your support during the toughest times in this project, for going well beyond the call of duty, and for helping out with the CD content and the appendixes.

Thank you to the Plug-In developers Axion, Binary Reality, Blevins, Brenden Hack, Michael Gallo, Primitive Itch, Quantum Impulse, Urban Velkavrh, and White Dragon Studios. Thanks to all of the artists who contributed artwork to the color panels of this book. Thank you to Artbeats, VCE, and Adobe Systems for providing demos of your great products.

Thank you, Laura Frey, for asking me to do this book and for being there every step of the way with this project. You were there encouraging me and showing me that although this was a rather daunting undertaking, in the end, it was all worthwhile. I always knew that you were only a phone call away, eager to help any way you could.

Thank you, Linda, for helping to pull it all together and for your patience and guidance. You made my erratic broken thoughts somehow come together to form coherent sentences. Let me thank you on behalf of the readers.

Now for my technical editor Alain Bellon, what would I have done without you? You had the toughest job of all. Checking for technical accuracy and verifying the most intricate steps of this dance we call 3D art was a challenge. If I missed anything, you caught it; you were my safety net. Thank you for not letting me fall. I also want to thank you for creating what is in my opinion the most significant addition to my trueSpace tool set. I thank you for the plug-in ThermalClay. It has literally changed the way I model in trueSpace.

Roman Ormandy, CEO of Caligari, also deserves a special note of thanks. Taking time out of your busy schedule at Siggraph 98 to meet with Macmillan Publishing and me showed that you not only felt this project was worthwhile, but you were also confident that we would do a good job. I especially want to thank you and the Caligari staff for always being on the list during the Beta cycle; it was nice knowing that you guys were in the trenches with us, not only developing the product but also sharing with us your thoughts and ideas. It was a wonderful experience.

A special thanks goes to Pavol Elias for taking time to answer our questions during the writing of this book and for bringing important issues to my attention. Thank you, Aimee Jones, for keeping the lines of communication between Roman and me open, and for all of your help at Siggraph 98. Another special thanks to Mauricio Almeida, 2D illustrator extraordinaire for creating the storyboards and the character development sheet used in this book. Thanks to Arie, Steven, Leo, Steve, and Robert. It was great hanging with you guys at Siggy 98.

I would like to thank the members of the TSML and the Beta team, without whom this software would probably not be possible. You're a great bunch.

Thanks to Angel and Turk for understanding why I couldn't kick your butts in Tekken while I was writing this book.

The most important thanks go to my wife Penny and my daughter Briana. Penny, thank you for eight wonderful years, and for understanding that I had to lock myself up from dusk to dawn without complaining. I know that waking you up every morning at 4 a.m. hasn't been easy, but again, you never complained. Thank you, Briana, for adding little spurts of levity during those long periods in front of the computer monitor and for being a great daughter. I love you both; you are the most important people in my life.

It has become a tradition for authors to thank their pets these days, so I thank my dog for walking himself and letting me know when he was done and I thank my cat for sitting on my keyboard at the worst possible moment.

Once again, I thank you for reading my book. I wish you all well.

Yes, Carole, the book is finally done.

Arnold Gallardo:

First of all, I would like to acknowledge Frank Rivera and Jeffrey Wall for giving me the opportunity to share my enthusiasm for the field of radiosity to tS users and for believing in me. I hope that I did what was expected of me.

I would like to thank Laura Frey for her enormous help, patience, and understanding. I thank her for giving me an overview of the whole writing process. Thank you, Linda Laflamme, for editing and helping me develop the chapter into a coherent level. I also would like to thank Alain Bellon for the late-night discussions on the IRC about my chapter and about radiosity in general. I would like to thank him for the different perspective he brought into the chapter.

I also would like to thank my family for believing that this can be done, especially my mother for helping in the editing of my first draft and correcting grammatical errors, to my brother who read it even if he is not interested in it, and my father who helped me obtain CG reference materials.

I also would like to thank all the people who reviewed and looked at my first draft. Thanks to you all for your time and effort in reading it and in your feedback about it.

Last, I would like to give enormous thanks to Pavol Elias of Caligari Corporation for solving my problems with my SCNs and for his insight into how radiosity works inside trueSpace 4.0. Some of the exercises and demonstrations in my chapter would not be possible without his help and assistance.

Terry Cotant:

I would like to thank Frank Rivera and Laura Frey for selecting such a great team of trueSpace artists, and allowing me to be part of it all. Also, many thanks go to my wife Jenny and sons Brandon and Luke for endless amounts of encouragement and inspiration, and allowing those endless nights and lost weekends. Not to go unmentioned, I would like to thank Roman for his grand vision, and the rest of the outstanding team at Caligari for doing such a fantastic job and being great team players. Last, a thank you to my grandparents, who got me started in this computer 'biz when they bought me that little black Timex/Sinclair computer (too) many years ago.

Oliver Zeller:

Thank you, Frank and the gang at New Riders, for giving me the opportunity to write for this book.

Big thanks to Bob Hayes, Julie Hill, and Phil Bates at Artbeats for supplying several great clips for this book, and for your helpful and kind support.

Also, thanks, Brendan Hack, for creating a long-awaited Gaussian Blur filter for trueSpace and surprising me with a special version for the book.

New Riders

New Riders would like to thank the tireless spirit of Frank Rivera and incredible editing talent of Linda Laflamme for making this book possible. As always, Linda, it was a pleasure.

TELL US WHAT YOU THINK!

As the reader of this book, *you* are our most important critic and commentator. We value your opinion and want to know what we're doing right, what we could do better, what areas you'd like to see us publish in, and any other words of wisdom you're willing to pass our way.

As the Executive Editor for the Graphics team at Macmillan Computer Publishing, I welcome your comments. You can fax, email, or write me directly to let me know what you did or didn't like about this book—as well as what we can do to make our books stronger.

Please note that I cannot help you with technical problems related to the topic of this book, and that due to the high volume of mail I receive, I might not be able to reply to every message.

When you write, please be sure to include this book's title and author, as well as your name and phone or fax number. I will carefully review your comments and share them with the author and editors who worked on the book.

Fax: 317-581-4663

Email: **graphics@mcp.com**

Mail: Executive Editor
              Graphics
              Macmillan Computer Publishing
              201 West 103rd Street
              Indianapolis, IN 46290 USA

Introduction

Inside trueSpace4 is about visualizing and creating 3D imagery in trueSpace. Inside trueSpace4 is not another manual. You won't find every option or every panel explained within these pages. What you will find is a hands-on book that illustrates how to

- *Model by using a variety of tools*
- *Model characters by using different methods*
- *Animate objects*
- *Animate characters by using bones*

It also discusses visualization, good lighting, camera and cinematography techniques, texture properties and how they affect what we see, atmospheric effects and how to visualize a special effect before committing to it, and creating radiosity solutions. It concludes with how to create a short film and what's involved, how to get your work viewed by the masses, and how to create your own 3D media studio.

Inside trueSpace4 comes bundled with

- A lite version of trueSpace4
- Demos of the very best trueSpace plug-ins available today
- Over 300 textures you can use royalty free

All images in the color plates were created by using trueSpace. With this book and a little imagination, you can create stunning imagery. A complete beginner can create images of startling beauty and quality. An expert will find trueSpace's power and ease of use a good fit because trueSpace was developed around the way an artist likes to work. Many professional graphic artists use trueSpace to create images that were previously possible only with very expensive computer systems.

INSIDE TRUESPACE4 CHAPTER BY CHAPTER

Chapter 1 begins with a brief rundown of some of the new features in version 4. If you have trueSpace4 and are familiar with its suite of tools, I suggest you jump right into Chapter 3.

Chapter 2 is a 3D primer for those of you new to 3D. For those of you who are familiar with 3D imagery and for those of you who want to create images right away, skip to Chapter 3.

Chapter 3 begins with modeling in trueSpace and prepares you for Chapter 4, "Character Modeling."

In Chapter 4, we look at using different tools and methods for modeling characters from simple primitives, modeling segmeted characters by using deformation techniques, modeling a full-body humanoid from metaballs, modeling the female form from a single primitive, and modeling hands.

Chapter 5 is a discussion of surfacing and surface-texture properties and what makes a good surface texture. At the writing of this book, the new shaders weren't fully implemented, so you won't find any step-by-step tutorials, but I have included some surface formulas (metals, china, glass) in Appendix B to help you get started.

In Chapter 6, Tom Marlin explores the creation and management of your own texture collection. Tom has authored several seamless texture CDs, so I can't think of anyone better to explain how it's done.

Chapter 7 is an animation primer. Here we look at what it takes to create a simple animation, how to make objects follow a path, and how to use basic bones to animate inanimate objects.

Chapter 8 is a brief rundown of the keyframe editor and how to edit keyframes and object hierarchies by using the Object Tree.

Chapter 9 covers advanced bones techniques, skeletal animation, and the muscle and tendon tools. We will explore creating a bone structure for characters, how to edit joints and tendons, and flexing a character's muscles.

In Chapter 10, we use the bone structure we created in Chapter 9 to animate a character we created in Chapter 3. We look at creating a walk cycle and changing that walk cycle to reflect the character's mood.

Chapter 11 looks at your rendering options, the difference between radiosity and ray tracing, and the rendering panel options. This chapter is only a precursor to Chapter 15, "Radiosity."

In Chapter 12, Jeff Wall, M.D. (I like to call him Doc), discusses lighting techniques. The foundation of every 3D image is built on good lighting, so you will probably refer back to this chapter often.

Chapter 13 explores atmospheric effects with Oliver Zeller. Oliver also discusses many plug-ins, such as lens, flares, and glows, that are available for trueSpace.

In Chapter 14, Oliver Zeller and I discuss previsualizing special effects. We use an animated sequence from an upcoming short film we are creating as an example.

In Chapter 15, Arnold Gallardo discusses radiosity and its use in trueSpace.

Chapter 16 looks at cameras and cinematography, and applying them to scenes you create in trueSpace.

In Chapter 17, we discuss creating a short film, storyboarding techniques, and managing complex scenes.

In Chapter 18, Terry Cotant discusses the creation of your own 3D media studio and the hardware and software involved. Terry is responsible for a lot of the visuals you see coming from Caligari, as well as the visuals for the siggraph shows.

EXTRA GOODIES

In the back of the book, you will find appendixes filled with game-creation tips, surface formulas, and tips on getting your work viewed, and a glossary of 3D terms. You will also find a CD filled with plug-ins, third-party programs, two games with graphics created in trueSpace, fire and explosion animations, over 300 textures and images, and so much more.

To save time and to maximize the value of this book, we have made every effort not to reiterate the information found in the trueSpace documentation. Although it wasn't possible to avoid repetition, you will find that a majority of the information within these covers builds upon concepts that were merely introduced or lightly covered in the documentation.

KEEP IN TOUCH

If you have any problems getting the same results as those described in this book or you just want to tell me what you think of the book, contact me via email at **Inside-trueSpace@LOGICBIt.com** or visit the *Inside trueSpace* Web site at **http://www.logicbit.com/Inside-trueSpace**.

PART I

INTRODUCTION

CHAPTER 1

WHAT'S NEW, FEATURES AT A GLANCE

by Frank Rivera

With version 4.0, a whole new world has been opened for new and old trueSpace users. trueSpace4 is faster, stronger, and more flexible than previous releases, and as Caligari states, it's "born to accelerate." The company isn't kidding, either; trueSpace4 takes advantage of hardware acceleration and multiple processors. trueSpace4 also has a new powerful render engine that supports radiosity and ray tracing for the highest-quality imagery. Now even existing studios, hobbyists, and production centers can enjoy trueSpace's seamless modeless environment specifically designed the way an artist likes to work.

You will come to appreciate the power of trueSpace's tools and the simplicity of its interface throughout the course of this book.

trueSpace4 is a major upgrade that contains a number of powerful and exciting new features. In this chapter, we will take a brief look at what's new for:

- The trueSpace interface
- Modeling
- Animation
- Rendering

MODELING

trueSpace has always been a great modeler. Its ease of use and intuitive tool set make it a favorite 3D package for the traditional artist making the transition from 2D to 3D. Version 4 has some new features designed to help the modeling process, and has a totally brand-new way of modeling through a new tool called NURBS.

NURBS

NURBS enables you to form smooth surfaces from polyhedrons by a technique that can only be described as "melting" (see Figure 1.1). A NURBS surface can also be animated by using the Point Edit tools. An ideal method for creating organic forms, NURBS is covered in Chapter 3, "Modeling."

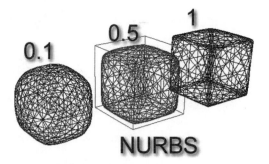

FIGURE 1.1   *An example of a NURBS object with different tension settings.*

SELECTION TOOLS

You can now select multiple objects by pressing the Ctrl key and clicking on an object. You can also use the new Lasso, Rectangle, and Free-Hand tools to select multiple faces or vertices. These awesome selection tool additions are covered in Chapter 5, "Surfacing."

CUSTOM POLYGON CREATION

trueSpace4 now has the capability to draw custom polygons directly on an object's mesh, as well as the capability to create new vertices and edges. You can even copy, slice, or bevel polygons. These new tools enable you to model freely, creating any shape you want. If you choose, you can model by adding edges and sweeping surfaces. They are a major step forward from the previous method of modeling (with limited point-editing tools and Boolean operations).

ANIMATION

In the past, trueSpace has been overlooked as a production tool in the area of character animation. This is no longer the case with the addition of Bones and function curves to trueSpace's animation tool set.

BONES

Skeletal animation is now possible in trueSpace with the addition of Bones. trueSpace bones enable you to create and animate more naturally and realistically. The Bones tool is superb and allows you to have full control over polygon selection, muscles, and tendons. trueSpace's inverse kinematics is now integrated with Bones, providing a very easy-to-use and powerful set of tools. In upcoming chapters, we will make objects swim, dance, and walk with Bones (see Figure 1.2). I also cover making your character's muscles bulge.

Bones are covered in Chapter 7, "Animation," and Chapter 9, "Advanced Bones."

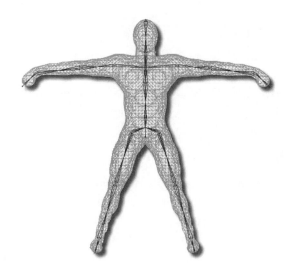

FIGURE 1.2   *An example of a bone structure being applied to a character you will build from meta-balls in Chapter 4, "Character Modeling."*

FUNCTION CURVES

The KeyFrame Editor (KFE) has been improved with the addition of function curves (see Figure 1.3). You can now fine-tune animations via direct manipulation of splines for realistic and accurate character animation. Function curves are covered in Chapter 8, "Secrets of the KeyFrame Editor."

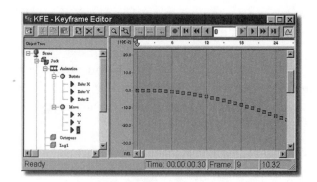

FIGURE 1.3   *Function curves have been added to the KeyFrame Editor.*

Render Engine

trueSpace4 now includes a high-end render engine capable of producing stunning photorealistic images. The render engine is based on Lightworks Pro by Lightworks Design. Following are some of the new features this render engine brings to trueSpace.

Hybrid Radiosity

Radiosity provides for the ultimate realism in computer-generated images. trueSpace4 seamlessly integrates radiosity with ray tracing. Radiosity is the perfect addition to trueSpace, enabling you to create images with spectacular realism. In addition, you can create realistic soft shadows with a penumbra effect by using area lights in conjunction with radiosity. Radiosity is covered in Chapter 15, "Radiosity."

Figure 1.4   *trueSpace4 has the capability to create imagery using radiosity and ray tracing.*

VOLUMETRIC LIGHTING

Volumetric shading enables you to create environments that appear to be filled with fog or smoke. The volumetric lighting effects in trueSpace4 are accurate, including the volumetric shadows, and provide consistent results. Volumetric lighting effects are covered in Chapter 13, "Atmospheric Effects and Advanced Lighting."

PROJECTOR LIGHTS

You can use projector lights to project images or animations onto other illuminated objects. Projector lights are covered in Chapter 12, "Lighting in trueSpace."

GLOWS AND FLARES

You can introduce glowing effects and lens flare artifacts into your images with trueSpace4's built-in glows and lens flares.

PER-FACE UV MAPPING

This new tool will change the way you texture map complex objects. You will no longer have to build objects from smaller parts because each surface will have its own UV projection and texture. trueSpace4 now supports the capability to assign a UV projection method to individual or groups of faces. Of course, this is in addition to the planar, cylindrical, spherical, and cubic UV mapping tools. We put this tool to the test along with the Lasso and rectangular selection tools in Chapter 5, "Surfacing."

SHADERS

trueSpace4 now has some serious material shaders (see Figure 1.5). The new, improved tool is composed of four component shaders:

- Color
- Reflectance
- Transparency
- Displacement

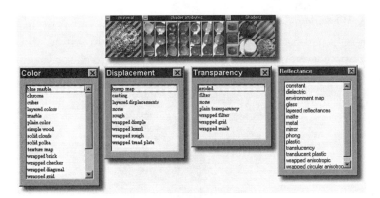

FIGURE 1.5   *trueSpace4's shader panels and list boxes.*

trueSpace4 also supports background, foreground, and post-processing shaders. In addition to these shaders, trueSpace includes an Anistropic reflectance shader for mimicking metal effects, such as brushed metal. You now have the ability to layer different shaders in trueSpace4. You can combine the effects of two or more shaders to create incredibly realistic-looking surfaces and effects. At the time of this writing, Caligari was adding the capability to create custom shaders, so check Caligari's Web site (**http://www.caligari.com**) and the *Inside trueSpace* Web site (**http://www.inside_truespace.com**) for patches and updates.

Appendix B contains some interesting surface formulas for items such as china, silverware, and glass. Before you start experimenting with this great tool, check out Chapter 5, "Surfacing," which discusses the properties that make up a good surface.

ADAPTIVE ANTIALIASING

Adaptive Antialiasing performs antialiasing only on the areas that require it. This option applies antialiasing only on areas that need it the most, freeing up valuable render cycles at render time. trueSpace still supports Oversampling.

3D WIDGETS AND MENUS

trueSpace4 now sports a new interface. It's a true 3D interface for working in a 3D environment—what a concept! The tools are right where you're working, in the actual environment. This means no more moving the mouse to a menu, back to the workspace, back to the menu, and back to the workspace. It's a productive and visual way to work. The tools are available when and where you need them.

By using 3D widgets and menus (see Figure 1.6), you can perform modeling functions, adjust the camera's point of view, or edit light settings directly from your workspace without having to leave the workspace to click a menu item.

FIGURE 1.6   *An example of the new trueSpace navigation widget.*

3D widgets and menus haven't replaced the tried-and-true 2D interface permanently; it's still there if you need it, or if you don't have a 3D accelerator card. You can use both interfaces, if you like.

NOTE

To enable the Global panel, the 3D Widgets option must be checked in the Preferences panel. It is toggled on by default.

THE 3D GLOBAL PANEL

When in Solid Render mode, you can access and change environment settings from within the workspace by right-clicking in the trueSpace4 workspace (3D widgets must be enabled). With the Global panel open (see Figure 1.7), you can change its position on screen by right-clicking in the location where you would like it to be placed. With the Global panel, you can

- Set object collision properties.
- Adjust real-time render settings.
- Change the visibility of cameras and lights.
- Modify deformation lattices.
- Specify physics and IK properties.
- Choose between either a 3D or 2D Global panel.
- Alter the grid size and visibility.
- Switch between the 2D and 3D interface and enable the visibility of the Help Bar.

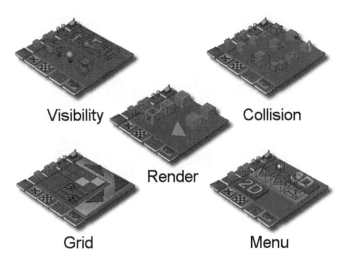

Visibility   Collision

Render

Grid   Menu

FIGURE 1.7   *An exploded view of the five states of the 3D Global panel.*

To close the Global panel, click the X icon in the Global panel.

The 3D widgets and menus are designed to be used in Solid Render mode using either 3DR, OpenGL, or Microsoft's D3D APIs, but they can be used in Wireframe mode as well.

The quality of the real-time rendering in trueSpace, especially transparency, is much faster. Direct3D acceleration is almost five times faster compared to trueSpace3. trueSpace4 also supports anti-aliased lines, that is, if your card supports it.

OTHER IMPROVEMENTS

In addition to these improvements, trueSpace has also added two new powerful features that aid game designers and speed up rendering.

PYTHON SCRIPTING

trueSpace now supports Python scripting (see Figure 1.8). You can create custom behaviors for characters, custom animation, modeling effects, and prototype games with the built-in script editor. The scripts you create have access to the all internal functions for maximum flexibility.

NOTE

An interesting thing about the Global panel is that when it is set for 3D space, you can rotate your eye around the panel and see it from any angle. This comes in handy if you are having trouble seeing its associated 3D icons.

NOTE

If you're in the market for a good inexpensive video card, check out Diamond Multimedia's FireGL 1000 pro. There has been some talk about the cards not functioning with trueSpace4 and Direct3D, but that is not the case anymore. Diamond Multimedia has a free BIOS upgrade on its Web site that eliminates any bugs that may have existed in the past. Check out **www. diamondmm.com**.

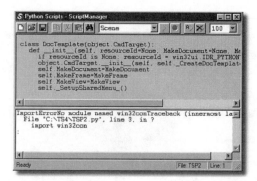

FIGURE 1.8   *trueSpace4's built-in Python script editor.*

MULTITHREADED

trueSpace is now a serious production tool. The new rendering engine now supports multiple threads on multiple processors; all that is required is Windows NT. I have personally tested this feature with a quad 400MHz Xeon ALR, and have found it remarkably fast and reliable.

SUMMARY

trueSpace4 isn't a package to be taken lightly by its competition—its modest cost and long list of features are outstanding. No other 3D illustration *and* animation package includes radiosity, lens flares, volumetric lighting, bones, metaballs, NURBS, Spline polygons, scripting, and multiprocessor support for under $1,000. In fact, trueSpace is the first 3D animation package to include radiosity as part of the package itself.

In this book, we will explore some of these new features, but for those of you new to 3D, join me in the next chapter. There we will prepare ourselves for what's to come.

GETTING IN THE RIGHT STATE OF MIND

by Frank Rivera

Thinking with images is called visualization. It is a powerful thinking tool that enables us to use our minds to simulate the real world and probe abstract ideas. There is, for all practical purposes, no limit to what we can visualize.

We use visualization as a tool for thinking and expressing ourselves. It helps us solve problems, realize new designs and processes, and speculate our choices. There is no denying that our minds are graphically orientated. We are obsessed with images.

*3D imagery is used today for scientific visualization, for medical research, and to create virtual worlds, computer games, sci-fi illustrations, and entertaining movies. Much more is **possible because** we're not limited to any genre, storyline, or style.*

3D is a fairly technical art form; however, if you are new to 3D, you can take comfort in the fact that the jargon and techno-babble are exactly that, babble. What counts isn't whether you can quote the definition of an Isosceles or NURBS, but rather the ability to create and express yourself with the tools. When all is said and done, it's your imagery that speaks for you, not how well you can memorize the definition of lofting or radiosity.

In our world, we are surrounded by objects that take up three-dimensional space—rocks, trees, and the chair you're sitting in. We are equipped with senses that enable us to interact in this three-dimensional universe of ours. With our sense of touch, we can experience the texture of the objects around us. With our ears, we can locate sounds in 3D space that may be a threat. With our eyes and brain, we take in a flood of information and color. We further use this information to determine the distance an object is from us, its mass, and even the temperature of its surface.

NOTE

This chapter is not intended to give you a blow by blow of the trueSpace interface or every nuance of its tool panels, but rather to familiarize you with some of the common and basic aspects of 3D and trueSpace, as well as to get you into a 3D state of mind.

Our senses, like fine instruments, collect and record the information around us. There is no doubt we developed these senses in order to survive, but we can also reap the benefits of the wonderful experience of absorbing life's beauty.

In this chapter, we will look at

- Three-dimensional space
- The 3D universe according to trueSpace
- 3D basics

Before we can understand how to use trueSpace to model the world around us, we first must understand how we perceive this world with our own senses. If you are already familiar with 3D concepts, I suggest you skip ahead to the next chapter.

VIEWING THE WORLD AROUND US

Before the Renaissance, accurate linear perspective wasn't used in art. The Renaissance marks a period when European artists started to understand the natural phenomenon of *linear perspective* and its use as an aid in illustrating reality.

PERSPECTIVE

The way we see our world in regard to perspective can be defined by two major factors:

- Parallel lines converge at a vanishing point on the horizon.

- Objects that are farther away look smaller than those that are closer.

Technically, these effects are caused by the fact that the light rays traveling from the object's outer edges to our eyes converge more than the rays traveling from the objects that are near. This means the outline of objects farther away are drawn (so to speak) on our retinas smaller than those objects that are near. The space between objects, the width, length, and height are also affected in this way. Let's look at some key elements that describe a perspective view.

- **The horizon line:** If we removed every object from view as far as we could see, we could then turn around 360 degrees and view the entire horizon. This is described as the circle around us. In Greek, it's called the bounding circle, which means *horizon* to you and me. Even though the horizon is round, it is usually depicted as a straight line because we see only a short segment.

- **Vanishing point:** The vanishing point is a point on the horizon toward which we are looking and toward which all the parallel lines parallel to our line of sight converge. Figure 2.1 illustrates this best.

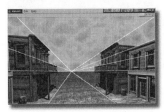 

FIGURE 2.1 *The images on the left depict a line of sight down the street from a window. The images on the right illustrate a line of sight down the street from ground level. The horizon line is always at eye level, no matter from what perspective you are viewing the world. The images on the bottom depict each of the images' vanishing points.*

- **Viewpoint/point of view (POV):** The viewpoint is the point at which the viewer views the scene. Where you're sitting right now is your point of view, also called a viewpoint.

- **Line of sight:** The line of site is the line between the viewpoint and the vanishing point.

- **Picture plane:** The picture plane is an imaginary plane that is perpendicular to the line of sight and that stands between the viewpoint and the scene being viewed.

- **Visual rays:** Perspective depends on the concept that when we look at an object, every point on its surface sends a visual ray in a straight line to our eyes. These rays converge on us exactly like the lines drawn along parallel edges of an object converge on a vanishing point, as depicted in Figure 2.2.

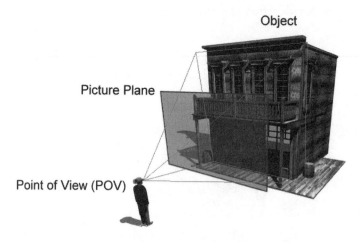

FIGURE 2.2 *In this image, the cowboy is the point of view. The lines running from the POV to the building represent the visual rays. The plane between the POV and the object being viewed is the picture plane (what is seen by the viewer).*

Although these parallel lines we have been talking about help us illustrate the real world, they also can cause what we see to become distorted.

- **Foreshortening:** A form of distortion that occurs when we look at an object from an angle close to the horizon line. Foreshortening occurs because the parts of the object that are closer to us look larger than those farther away, as well as the fact that the parallel lines of the object converge on the horizon over a short distance. Figure 2.3 illustrates this effect.

FIGURE 2.3   *The figure on the left illustrates foreshortening, whereas the figure on the right does not. Note that this is not because our line of sight is nearly perpendicular to the object's parallel lines.*

The European artists of the fourteenth through the sixteenth centuries aren't done yet. Let's look at some more elements with regard to perspective.

Occlusion

The *occlusion* depth cue is one of the most apparent and easiest to understand. Objects that are closer to us partially block our view of the objects that are farther away. This blocking effect is called occlusion. In Figure 2.3, the right foot of the character on the right partially covers the character's left leg.

Texture also plays an important part in how we perceive perspective.

Texture and Depth Perception

Patterns appear denser as they recede into the distance. This effect is caused by the fact that objects of the same size look smaller the farther away they are (see Figure 2.4).

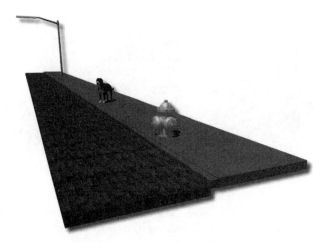

FIGURE 2.4   *As the road recedes into the distance and the bricks appear farther away, the pattern they create tends to appear denser.*

Leonardo da Vinci gave us so much more than *The David*; he also was the first to describe the phenomenon of atmospheric perspective, which he called *aerial perspective*.

AERIAL PERSPECTIVE

Another key to depicting three-dimensional reality is the fact that our eyes perceive distant objects as less clear and more monochromatic than objects that are near. Near objects look sharper and more focused than those that are far away. Distant objects also look blue for the same reason the sky looks blue. (No, God didn't render it that way.) The sky looks blue because blue light is scattered by the atmosphere far more easily than the other colors of the spectrum, primarily because of its short wave length. So, it should be obvious that if we are looking through more atmosphere, the objects in the far distance would take on a blue hue. You can add an aerial perspective type of effect to the scenes you create in trueSpace by using trueSpace's atmospheric tools, such as Fog and volumetric lighting—two subjects covered in later chapters. Another area where Leonardo da Vinci has contributed to how we perceive perspective and illustrate the illusion in 2D is with the art form known as *chiaroscuro*.

LIGHT AND SHADE

In addition to perspective, another essential technique for creating the illusion of depth in a two-dimensional image is *chiaroscuro*, the modeling of forms with areas of light and shade.

With this technique, objects do not have clear outlines but appear to emerge from the darkness, as though slowly being revealed by a light. Dark shades of gray blend gradually across the object where the light's impact decreases, until they reach the edge of a light or dark area. The shadows cast by lit objects are also rendered in varying shades of gray. The parts of the shadow that are closest to the object are usually the darkest. As it becomes affected by ambient light, the shadow becomes lighter the farther from the object it gets.

Chiaroscuro is also used in 3D by taking into account color, intensity, light direction, and the object's surface properties. The subject of light and surfacing is covered in later chapters.

We have taken a brief look at how we perceive our world, but now let's look at viewing the world in trueSpace.

VIEWING THE WORLD THROUGH TRUESPACE

For the artist of the Renaissance, the creation of realistic paintings involved a laborious process of sighting along perspective grids. Today, this problem is easily avoided because trueSpace automatically solves for the correct perspective view of the objects in your scenes. We started this chapter by discussing perspective, and it's a good idea to do the same here.

PERSPECTIVE VIEW

The Perspective view is how the workspace is presented to you in trueSpace by default, and it is the most flexible of the four views. In the Perspective view, the point of view, or "eye," can be positioned so that your line of sight is pointing in any direction. Another method of viewing the world through trueSpace is with a camera object.

A *Camera view* is the POV from a selected camera, object, or light. The orientation of the line of sight is in regard to the selected object's z-axis (we cover cameras and the z-axis in a later chapter). This view can be moved, rotated, and scaled either with the Eye Navigation tools or by manipulating the selected "camera" object itself.

A Perspective view won't always do the trick when constructing your scenes, so Caligari has provided us with three orthogonal views.

ORTHOGRAPHIC VIEWS

Ortho means straight or at right angle to. An *orthographic view* is one in which all that is viewed is perpendicular to the picture plane (no perspective). In trueSpace, these are the Front, Left, and Top views. In these views, the parallel lines in the model do not converge on a vanishing point but remain parallel, and objects of the same size look the same size no matter what their distance from the viewer is.

- **Front view:** Your line of sight is looking down the world y-axis.

- **Left view:** Your line of sight is looking down the world x-axis.

- **Top view:** Your line of sight is looking down the world z-axis.

FIGURE 2.5 *Orthographic and Perspective views available in trueSpace.*

In the Front, Left, and Top views, the view can be moved and scaled, but not rotated. Figure 2.5 illustrates the four views in trueSpace.

You're not limited by a single orthographic or perspective view in trueSpace.

MULTIPLE WINDOWS

trueSpace has the capability to view the worlds you create in multiple views by using multiple windows. The New Window tool, found only on the main window, can be used to open three additional windows in either Camera, Perspective, Front, Left, or Top views. Each of these additional windows has a set of standard Viewpoint Navigation, View Select, and Render tools. These windows also function as workspace because they can be used for object manipulation, animation, and rendering. As stated previously, the orthogonal views can be moved and scaled, but not rotated. These smaller view windows can be moved by clicking on the upper-left corner of the window and dragging, and they can be resized by clicking and dragging the edges or corners. You are not limited by how small these additional windows can be scaled to, but you are limited to a maximum size equal to one quarter of the screen resolution.

Now that we have windows to view our world, let's examine how objects are displayed in these windows.

DRAW MODES

trueSpace4 has four ways of displaying objects: bounding boxes, wire frames, solid, and photorealistic. Here is a synopsis of each.

- **Bounding Box mode:** Temporarily displays bounding boxes for objects. This greatly decreases redraw time when positioning the eye or camera view.

- **Wire Frame mode:** Objects are drawn as transparent wire frames consisting of vertices, edges, and faces. Wire Frame mode is very useful for point editing.

- **Photorealistic mode:** In this mode, an object's surface attributes can appear smoothly shaded, textured, bump mapped, or transparent. Also visible are the environment attributes, such as fog, volumetric lighting, and lens flares. Enable ray tracing, and reflections and refractions are also visible.

- **Solid mode:** Objects are shaded and textures are displayed. The effects of lights on a scene are also rendered in real time.

NOTE

When I speak of draw modes, I'm referring to how environments and the objects within the scene can be displayed in the workspace.

NOTE

trueSpace4 takes advantage of Microsoft's Direct3D (D3D), Intel's 3DR, and OpenGL.

Because we are on the subject of solid mode, let's look at how objects can be viewed in this mode.

NOTE

Because ray-traced images can be time-consuming and because ray tracing isn't usually used during the build process, the option is disabled by default. You can enable it by right-clicking on any Render tools to open the Scene Render Options panel.

SOLID VIEW MODES

The objects you create in trueSpace can be viewed in five modes (see Figure 2.6):

- Solid
- Transparent
- Transparent Wire Frame
- Wire Frame
- Solid Wire Frame/Outline Solid

The ability to view your objects in all but Wire Frame requires you to be in Solid mode. You can select from one of three solid mode engines: Microsoft's Direct3D (D3D), Intel's 3DR, or OpenGL.

FIGURE 2.6   The five view modes available in trueSpace4. We revisit these modes in Chapter 3, "Modeling."

- **Solid:** You can see your object completely rendered as a solid.
- **Transparent:** Enables you to see through objects.
- **Transparent Wire Frame**: Transparent rendering with visible wire mesh, enabling you to see through object.

- **Wire Frame:** View your objects in wire frame form.

- **Outline Solid/Solid Wire Frame:** Your object's wire frame is superimposed on its solid depiction.

SOLID RENDER APIS

If you have a video card that supports either Intel's 3DR, Microsoft's Direct3D, or OpenGL, you can have trueSpace display everything in the workspace as a solid that you can manipulate in real time as you work. Let's briefly review these three solid render APIs.

DIRECT3D SOLID DISPLAY

If you have a 3D accelerator card that supports Microsoft's Direct3D, you may want to use Direct3D (D3D) as your primary solid render display mode. This mode provides fast feedback for scenes with fewer than 1,000 polygons and offers Bilinear Filtering for improved texture map display. Here are some facts you should be aware of in regard to your video card and Direct3D.

To use this mode at a resolution of 800×600 with a two-byte color depth (16-bit), your video card will need at least 4MB of video RAM. At a resolution of 1,024×768 with a two-byte color depth, your video card will need at least 8MB of video RAM. Texture maps are stored in video memory of the video accelerator. If the card runs out of texture map memory, trueSpace4 will automatically switch to 3DR Solid Display mode.

Right-click on the D3D Solid Render Display button to open the D3D panel. Here you can select Bilinear Filtering, Perspective Correction, Dithering, and Transparency.

- **Bilinear filtering:** A feature of many hardware Direct3D accelerator cards. The cards that support this feature remove the pixel artifacting caused when texture maps are viewed up close. The use of bilinear filtering might reduce the display performance on some cards.

- **Perspective Correction:** Displays perspective with a higher level of realism. For example, foreshortening is displayed correctly in Solid mode.

NOTE

The Options Panel is used to set such Solid mode attributes as smoothness, textures, enabling the solid grid, and displaying the background image in the workspace.

NOTE

To check whether hardware acceleration is enabled, select Help, About. At the bottom of the credit screen on the right, you will see the name of the API you are using. If it isn't visible, hardware acceleration is not enabled.

WARNING

Using the 3D Paint tool in D3D mode causes erratic, unpredictable behavior. Caligari is aware of this issue and expects to have it resolved in the next patch. For the latest news, patches, and contests, visit Caligari's Web site at **http://www.caligari.com**.

NOTE

trueSpace will use hardware acceleration in D3D mode only if your video card supports D3D in a window. If your video card supports full-screen D3D only, trueSpace4 cannot take advantage of the hardware acceleration. trueSpace4 does not support hardware acceleration at the one-byte (8-bit) color depth. If you use trueSpace4 in 256 colors, Direct3D will run in software emulation.

- **Enable Dithering:** Simulates a higher color depth by creating smooth gradients between colors.

- **Transparency:** Three levels of transparency are supported. Level 1 allows the use of sprites for the best performance. Level 2 supports sprites only if the scene does not contain transparent objects, including widgets. Level 3 uses transparent triangles if transparent objects exist in the scene. The triangles are Z sorted. This is the slowest of the three levels.

OpenGL Solid Display

To use this OpenGL Solid Display mode at a resolution of 800×600 with a two-byte color depth (16-bit), your video card will need at least 4MB of video RAM. At a resolution of 1,024×768 and with a two-byte color depth, your video card will need at least 8MB of video RAM.

You can open the OpenGL Property panel by right-clicking the OpenGL Solid Render Display button.

- **Bilinear filtering:** A feature of many hardware Direct3D accelerator cards. The cards that support this feature remove the pixel artifacting caused when texture maps are viewed up close. The use of bilinear filtering might reduce the display performance on some cards.

3DR Solid Display

Use 3DR Solid Display mode if you don't have a 3D accelerator card and want to work in Solid mode. trueSpace's Solid Render mode has some advantages. You can see the impact lights have on objects in your scenes in real time. Object orientation is practically always apparent, as opposed to Wire Frame mode where an object's orientation can be difficult to see. Object surface attributes are visible to an extent, which mean less guesswork on your part. Object construction is easier, especially when using deformations and sculpting.

WIRE FRAME DISPLAY

I do all my modeling in the Wire Frame Display mode. It is the fastest of all the modes and is ideally suited for point editing. Clicking the Wire Frame tool while in one of the solid modes disables that mode. Clicking the Wire Frame tool while in Wire Frame mode refreshes the active window.

Some of the advantages of the Wire Frame mode are

- Faster feedback
- Easier object axes manipulation
- Easier viewing and selection of objects behind other objects

Now that you understand how trueSpace displays your work, let's look more closely at what it's displaying and how objects are visualized in 3D space.

3D SPACE

Programmers use the *Cartesian coordinate system,* which is a mathematical method of describing points and lines in space. In this system, points on a two-dimensional surface are located by using two perpendicular axes—x (horizontal) and y (vertical)—which cross each other at a point defined as 0. In geometry, the x-axis typically represents width, and the y-axis represents height. Each point along the axis can either be positive or negative. The location of any point in two-dimensional space can be defined by two numbers, which are x, y coordinates.

Points in three-dimensional space use a third axis called z. The z-axis is perpendicular to both the x- and y-axes and represents depth. Figure 2.7 illustrates this by using a grid and a cube object.

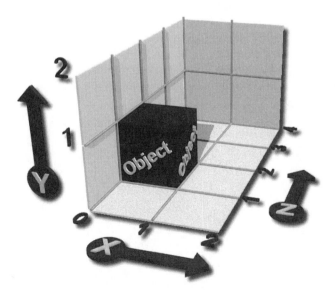

FIGURE 2.7   *The Euclidean geometry model. By adding a z-axis, we can describe the size and location of the cube.*

NOTE
Regardless of the current coordinate system, if OrthoNav is enabled, object navigation temporarily switches to Screen coordinates for navigation within orthographic views Top, Front, and Left.

Not all 3D programs use the x-, y-, and z-axes to represent width, height, and depth. Some use the x-, y-, and z-axes to represent height, width, and depth, respectively. This is also true in trueSpace, depending on the coordinate system used, a subject we will cover next.

COORDINATE SYSTEMS IN TRUESPACE

The single greatest challenge to modeling in trueSpace for a beginning 3D artist is the navigation of 3D space as displayed on a 2D monitor.

Moving an object in 3D space is called a *transformation*. A transformation can take place within three coordinate systems:

- Object coordinates
- World coordinates
- Screen coordinates

- **Object:** Navigation is constrained to the local axes of the selected object. Using Figure 2.8 as an example, from the Perspective view, moving the object along its x-axis would move the object either toward you or away from you. On the other hand, if the object were moved along its y-axis, the object would move either left or right. Moving the object along its z-axis changes its elevation.

- **World:** Navigation is constrained to the orientation of the World axes. The World x-axis runs along gridlines from the top right to the bottom left of the screen, and the y-axis runs from the top left to the bottom right. The z-axis runs at 90 degrees from the XY reference grid, as shown in Figure 2.9.

- **Screen:** The x-axis runs horizontally, the y-axis runs vertically, and the z-axis runs perpendicular to the plane of the screen, as shown in Figure 2.10.

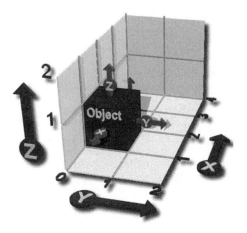

Object Coordinates

FIGURE 2.8   *In the Object coordinate system, the left mouse button moves the object along the object's x- and y-axes, whereas the right mouse button moves the object along its z-axis. This can be up, down, away from you, or toward you, depending on how the object's axis is orientated.*

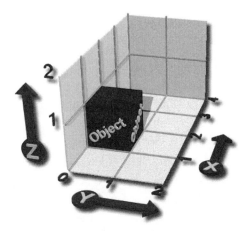

World Coordinates

FIGURE 2.9   *In the World coordinate system, the left mouse button moves the object along the World's x-axis (forward and backward) and y-axis (left and right), whereas the right mouse button moves the object along its z-axis (up and down).*

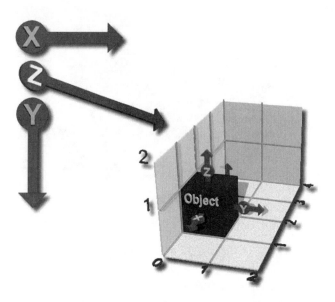

Screen Coordinates

FIGURE 2.10   *In the Screen coordinate system, the left mouse button moves the object along the screen's x-axis (horizontally) and y-axis (vertically), whereas the right mouse button moves the object along its z-axis (into the screen).*

A great way to conclude our brief discussion of coordinates and axes is with object navigation.

OBJECT NAVIGATION

NOTE

If OrthoNav is enabled in the Preferences panel, all navigation within Orthographic views is constrained to the Screen coordinates system.

The Object Navigation tools are used for selecting, moving, rotating, and scaling basic objects, objects of a hierarchy, and UV mapping space. Here are the basic tools and some notes on their use. Keep in mind that object navigation is directly related to the coordinate system being used, so for this discussion, navigation will be discussed by using the default World coordinate system.

OBJECT MOVE

The left mouse button controls movement along the x- and y-axes by mouse movement parallel to the x- and y-axes. The right mouse button controls movement along the z-axis.

The Object Move tool defaults to the World coordinate system, and if OrthoNav is enabled, object navigation will temporarily switch to Screen coordinates during navigation within any of the orthographic views—Top, Front, or Left.

NOTE

Right-clicking on the Object Move, Scale, or Rotate tools opens the Coordinates Property panel, where a coordinate system can be selected for the current tool or you can constrain transformations to specific axes.

OBJECT SCALE

The left mouse button controls scaling in the x- and y-axes parallel to the x and y mouse movements. The right mouse button controls scaling along the z-axis. Depressing both mouse buttons scales the selected object equally along the x-, y-, and z-axes. Objects always scale from their own axis which may not be positioned in the center of the object.

The Object Scale tool defaults to the Object coordinate system, and if OrthoNav is enabled, object navigation will temporarily switch to Screen coordinates during navigation within any of the orthographic views—Top, Front, or Left.

OBJECT ROTATE

The left mouse button controls rotation around the x- and y-axes perpendicular to mouse movements along the x- and y- axes. The right mouse button controls rotation around the z-axis. An object always rotates around its own axis, which may not be positioned in the center of the object.

NOTE

When you first open trueSpace, you are presented with a grid. This grid is referred to as the XY reference grid.

The Object Rotate tool defaults to Object coordinates, and if OrthoNav is enabled, object navigation will temporarily switch to Screen coordinates during navigation within any of the orthographic views—Top, Front, or Left.

EYE NAVIGATION

In some cases, moving an object to get a better view isn't desired. The Eye Move, Eye Rotate, and Eye Scale tools can be used to modify your viewpoint/point of view (POV). Here is a quick overview of each of the tools.

EYE MOVE

The Eye can be moved within all three coordinate systems, but your mouse buttons work differently, depending on which coordinate system you use.

- **World and Object coordinate systems:** Left-clicking and dragging the mouse causes the Eye to move over the XY reference grid. Right-clicking and dragging the mouse causes the Eye to change elevation over the XY reference grid.

- **Screen coordinate system:** Left-clicking and dragging your mouse vertically moves the Eye vertically, whereas a left-click and drag of the mouse moves the Eye horizontally. You can zoom in by using the right mouse button.

EYE ROTATE

Although the coordinate system controls for Eye rotation may appear the same as for the other navigation tools, they have different meanings.

- **World coordinate system:** The Eye orbits the World system's center, regardless of whether the eye points directly at it.

- **Object coordinate system:** The Eye orbits the active object's center, regardless of whether the Eye points directly at it. If no object is active, the Eye orbits the World system's center.

- **Screen coordinate system:** The Eye pans and tilts about its own axes.

EYE SCALE

The Eye Scale tool or zooming in can be equated to changing the focal length of a lens; this is discussed more in depth in Chapter 16, "trueSpace Cinematography." Eye zoom is independent of any coordinate system and moves along an axis perpendicular to the screen.

A BRIEF LOOK AT THE trueSpace INTERFACE

We have covered view modes, perspective, and navigation; now let's look take a brief look at the trueSpace interface.

Icons have one of three states:

- Inactive (raised): An inactive tool icon looks like a raised button. An icon in this state indicates that the tool is currently off or not selected.

- Active (depressed): An active tool icon looks depressed and is shaded blue-gray. An icon in this state indicates that the tool is selected or currently on.

● Not applicable (ghosted): A ghosted tool icon is shaded gray, indicating that the tool is unavailable or not applicable.

To select a tool, left-click its icon. If the tool has a control panel, it will open automatically. Right-click the tool's icon to open its property panel, if one exists. You can select variants of the selected tool by left-clicking the icon and holding the mouse button.

To close a panel, right-click in any gray area in the panel and drag your mouse outside the panel. When you see an "X" appear across the entire panel, release the mouse button.

The menu bar initially appears at the bottom of the screen. You can position it at the top by selecting the TopMenu item in the File menu's Preferences panel.

No discussion of the trueSpace interface is complete without a brief mention of the newest interface additions to trueSpace: 3D widgets.

3D WIDGETS

3D widgets are a new way of interfacing with trueSpace. They are intuitive and remarkably easy to use. They perform the same task as the traditional elements of buttons, panels, and sliders. This makes the interface part of the 3D workspace.

Some of the advantages of using 3D widgets and menus are

● You don't have to worry about coordinate systems or the x-, y-, and z-axes because the widgets always position themselves in 3D space to clearly indicate their function.

● 3D widgets and menus maintain a constant size, regardless of screen resolution.

● 3D widgets take advantage of 3D hardware acceleration.

3D widgets and menus haven't replaced the tried-and-true 2D interface permanently; it's still there if you need it or if you don't have a 3D accelerator card. You can use both the 2D and the 3D interface, if you like.

Now let's look at what the interface enables you to do: Construct objects in trueSpace.

3D OBJECT CONSTRUCTION BASICS

Fundamentally, to create 3D imagery you create a wireframe representation of an object or objects that are arranged together to create a scene. It is these objects to which texture maps and surface properties are applied. Depending on the properties you assign the objects and their shapes, the objects will absorb or reflect the light in the scene.

There are many ways to construct an object in trueSpace, and we will look at some of the more powerful methods later. For now, let's look at some of the basic techniques, starting with the fundamental building blocks.

PRIMITIVES

Generally, objects in the real world are constructed from basic components, which is typically how you create objects in trueSpace. Called primitives, the basic components in trueSpace are as follows (see Figure 2.11):

- Cone
- Cube
- Plane
- Cylinder
- Torus
- Sphere

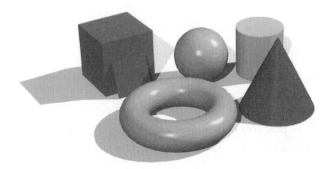

FIGURE 2.11   *An example of the six primitives in trueSpace.*

Each of the six primitives has a property panel that you can access by right-clicking on the icon of the primitive. Left-clicking on a primitive tool will create an instance of the primitive at the center of the XY reference grid.

Creating objects from primitives has its advantages—it's easy and fast. Don't let their simplicity persuade you into thinking that they have little use. Most objects you construct in trueSpace will start from a primitive or set of primitives (see Figure 2.12).

FIGURE 2.12   *This squeeze toy was constructed from basic primitives glued together.*

The Glue tools are used for grouping objects together and for defining relationships between objects in a hierarchy. These relationships define how the individual objects in a group behave during animation. After an object has been constructed in a hierarchy, the object can be edited as a whole by using other tools. Objects constructed into a hierarchy can be dismantled by using the Unglue tool.

The Boolean tools are also used to create objects from primitives and other objects. The Boolean tools are used to carve one shape from another and to fuse two or more shapes together.

Another important tool used to create objects in trueSpace is the Spline Polygon tool.

SPLINE POLYGONS

trueSpace's Spline Polygon tool enables you to create freeform 2D shapes that can be extruded (swept) to form a 3D shape. The object in Figure 2.13 was created by using the trueSpace spline tools.

FIGURE 2.13   *The simple object in this image was created by using trueSpace's Spline Polygon tools.*

A spline polygon is created by clicking in the workspace to add spline nodes with an intermediate number of interpolated points in between. Spline polygons are created from the Top or Perspective views, and all points are placed at ground level. You can even save the shapes you create with splines in a library for later use, but more on that later. Right-click the Spline Polygon tool to open the Spline Property panel. After exiting spline mode, the shape is frozen and can no longer be manipulated as a spline in a 2D fashion.

The Sweep tool is used to extrude surfaces from objects. Let's take a look.

EXTRUSIONS

Another method of constructing an object in trueSpace is by extrusion. Extrusion is performed with the Sweep tool (see Figure 2.14). The axes for swept objects is located at the center of the original polygon swept, and the axes are oriented with the World axis.

FIGURE 2.14   *The text on this box was created with the Text and Sweep tools. This is an extremely simplified use for the Sweep tool. In the modeling chapter, we will look at creating rope, bent pipes, and wrought iron fences with the Sweep tool. By the way, the textures (all 300 of them) mentioned in this image are included on the resource CD.*

ALTERING AN OBJECT'S SURFACE

Texture maps can be applied to objects to change how the observer interprets the object's surface (see Figure 2.15). Selecting an image file to apply to an object in trueSpace is done with just a few mouse clicks.

FIGURE 2.15   *The effects of a texture applied to an object can be dramatic. Which of the two objects looks squeezable now?*

TrueSpace4 currently supports the BMP, TGA, JPG, PNG, TIF, and AVI file formats. The AVI format can be used to apply an animated texture to an object's surface.

COMING ATTRACTIONS

In the upcoming chapters, we will use these construction methods to model the human form, hands, cameras, and a cute little character that we will animate. In addition, we will take a close look at trueSpace's Bones feature to animate inanimate objects and characters. We will also look at having your character's muscles bulge. All these tutorials have a few things in common.

ABOUT THE TUTORIALS IN THIS BOOK

The tutorials in this book use the OrthoNav option found in the Preferences panel and the Object coordinate system. I have refrained from using multiple windows during the exercises to reduce tool and display lag times.

To avoid alienating those of you who do not have 3D accelerator cards and those who do not model using any of the 3D menus or widgets, I will refrain from using them in the tutorials. Keep in mind that each of the tasks in the tutorials can be accomplished with the 3D widgets and menus, and in most cases, the 3D menus and widgets make the task easier.

Also, with regard to my illustrations used in the upcoming exercises, I will use Wire Frame mode to illustrate what is going on. Again, I don't want to alienate those of you who do not model in Solid mode.

If you want to use the widgets or follow along in Solid mode, by all means, please do. The same techniques apply; it's all a matter of preference and whether you have an accelerator card.

THE TRUESPACE MANUAL

Familiarizing yourself with trueSpace is the first step in your journey. Reading the manual and following its tutorials will help you immensely and will shorten the learning curve. Understanding what trueSpace can do starts with the manual. You don't have to sit down and read the entire manual from cover to cover, but you should be willing to look up a tool or command in the manual when the time comes. When I say familiarize yourself, I mean get to know the basics of how the software works, from loading scenes to rendering simple images.

TAKE THE TIME TO OBSERVE

Remember to look up from your manual, this book, and trueSpace occasionally. Learn how to observe. Observing the world around you will help you better understand how light behaves, how textures make surfaces appear, how objects are physically constructed, and the natural beat of life itself. Take some time to watch how people walk and interact with one another, how children play, and how birds dart from branch to branch. You will soon find that once you start on the road to becoming a 3D illustrator/animator, you will never see the world the same again.

UNBOTTLE THOSE CREATIVE JUICES

Contrary to popular belief, everyone is creative. Some folks just need a little inspiration, and others need to let go of the notion that what others think is important. Inspiration—that's the easy part. Everyone has their own way of seeking inspiration. Some people watch sci-fi movies; some take a drive in the country. If you find yourself having trouble being creative, it is most likely because of intimidation, not because you lack skill. Don't be afraid of new ideas or new ways of thinking. If you spend a lot of time thinking about what others will say about your idea or artwork, your creativity will get bottled up. Who cares whether someone thinks your idea is absurd or your technique isn't the accepted method? Exploring new ideas and new ways of thinking are the essence of creativity and the path every genius follows. It was once thought that exploring space, electronic circuitry, and moving pictures was absurd.

SUMMARY

You are probably eager to get started creating in trueSpace, but go slowly. Don't take on too much at one time. Be prepared to use patience and perseverance to learn these new skills.

What you create in trueSpace is a direct reflection of how you see the world. The best resource 3D artists have is their eyes.

PART II

MODELING

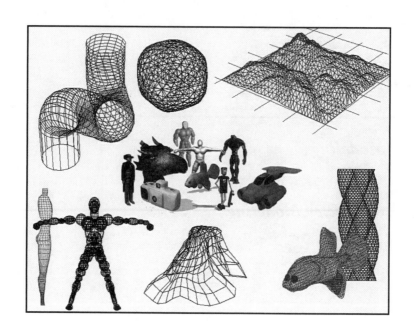

C H A P T E R   3

MODELING

by Frank Rivera

Modeling in 3D space can be equated to sculpting with clay. Just as a sculptor's studio is stocked with a full complement of instruments to form clay, trueSpace4 has a variety of tools that can be used to model your objects. Each of these tools can be used alone or to complement one another. An added bonus is that most of the modeling operations are keyframable.

What you won't find in this chapter is everything covered in the trueSpace manual or basic examples of what the tools do. Instead, I will demonstrate how to create actual objects by using each of these methods and, in some cases, I will use them in conjunction with one another. This isn't a tome to trueSpace4; it's a production guide. On that note, let's get productive.

In this chapter, we will cover

- The modeling environment
- Selecting vertices, edges, and faces
- Extruding surfaces
- Modeling with the Sculpt tools
- Modeling with the Deformation tools
- Modeling with metaballs
- Modeling with NURBS
- Modeling and mesh density

THE trueSPACE MODELING ENVIRONMENT

The best place to start is with the trueSpace work area. Take a look at a few of the environment settings as they relate directly to modeling in trueSpace4.

SOLID-RENDER AND VIEW MODES

If you're like most people, you purchased trueSpace because of its intuitive, modeless interface. To help you visualize the objects in the work place, Caligari added five object view modes to this award-winning interface in version 4. In addition, the new solid-mode rendering objects are shaded, and the effects of lights on an object are visible in real-time. For solid rendering, trueSpace4 supports D3D, OpenGL, and 3DR.

In solid-mode rendering, you can view objects in your scene in one of six object view modes.

- Hide all objects in view
- Draw all objects as wire
- Draw all objects in view as outline-transparent
- Draw all objects in view as outline-solid
- Draw all objects as transparent
- Draw all objects as solid

NOTE

Hardware acceleration is not supported in the 8-bit color depth; therefore, trueSpace4 will run in software emulation on an 8-bit system.

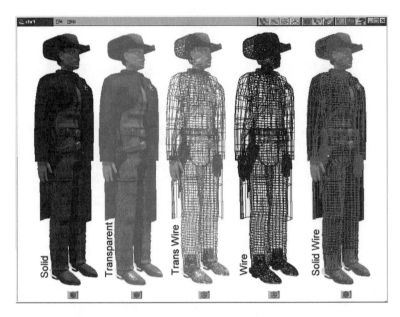

FIGURE 3.1 *The five object display options of solid-render mode.*

WIDGETS AND MENUS

trueSpace4's new 3D menus and widgets allow you to execute commands directly from within the workspace without having to seek out a tool on the toolbar. This means fewer interruptions in your workflow.

With the 3D widgets and menus, you can set an object's collision detection properties, view the object as a NURBS object, alter the axis of the object, change the display mode, and use the sweep tools on the object's selected surfaces. The interface is part of the 3D workspace and is fully accelerated by 3D hardware.

With the 3D widgets, you no longer have to worry about coordinate spaces or x-, y-, and z-axes because the widgets always position themselves in 3D space and clearly indicate their function and maintain their size regardless of screen resolution.

Don't panic; the 2D buttons, panels, and sliders are still present as part of the 2D interface. If you prefer to use just the 2D interface, you can deactivate the 3D widgets and menus from the Preferences panel. For added flexibility, you can use both the 2D interface and widgets simultaneously. You do not need to model in solid-render mode to take advantage of the 3D widgets. The widgets and 3D

NOTE

To avoid confusion and to avoid alienating those of you who do not model by using any of the 3D menus or widgets, I will refrain from using them in the following text. As I cover the different modeling methods, keep in mind that you can accomplish each of these tasks with the 3D widgets and menus. In most cases, the 3D menus and widgets are easier to use.

For the illustrations in the exercises, I will use Wire Frame mode. Again, I don't want to alienate those of you who do not model in Solid mode.

If you want to use the widgets or follow along in Solid mode, by all means, please do. The same techniques apply.

menus can be used in Wire Frame or any of the solid-render modes—OpenGL, D3D, or 3DR.

Working with widgets and 3D menus is easy. To enable 3D widgets, open the Preferences panel and check the 3D Widgets option. To open an object's 3D menu, right-click on the object. To access the 3D Global panel, right-click anywhere in the workspace not occupied by an object. The Global panel will appear at that location. To move the panel, simply right-click elsewhere. Don't hesitate to use the widgets and 3D menus. They are a powerful new feature that fit right in with trueSpace's award-winning modeless interface.

That briefly covers some of the environment options related to modeling. Let's look at some of the tools.

SELECTING VERTICES, EDGES, AND FACES

trueSpace4 certainly isn't lacking methods of selecting an object's vertices, edges, or faces. The Lasso, Rectangle, and Free-Hand selection tools offer a variety of ways of choosing sets of faces for manipulation by the Point Edit, Paint Face, and UV Projection Per-Face tools.

Selected vertices, edges, or faces can be saved to a file and reloaded later on. When one of the selection tools is active and there is a selection on the object, this selection can be saved as a .cob file. When the object is reloaded, the selection is restored.

- **Free-Hand:** Use this tool to make multiple selections of vertices or faces by dragging your mouse over the desired faces. Free-Hand selection allows selecting faces either by clicking on the surface of an object or by dragging over the surface to select all faces that are crossed by the mouse pointer. Unlike selection tools (Lasso and Rectangle), the default mode for Free-Hand selection adds a new face to the previous selection instead of replacing the existing faces.

- **Rectangle:** This tool enables you to select multiple vertices or faces by enclosing the desired faces or vertices in a rectangle.

- **Lasso:** Use this tool to select multiple vertices or faces by enclosing the desired faces or vertices in a lasso. The advantage of the Lasso tool over the Rectangle tool is you can select surface areas that would be difficult to select with the Rectangle tool. With the Lasso tool, you have the freedom to select more precisely by drawing freely around an area, whereas the rectangle might select areas you do not want included.

NOTE

Edges and vertices can be loaded only while the Point Edit tool is active. Faces can be loaded anytime, and the new selection can be used by any relevant tool (Point Edit, Face Paint, UV Mapping Per-Face).

If two or more objects are selected when the Glue As Sibling tool is used, all selected objects are glued as siblings. If the Lasso or the Rectangle selection tools are entered while the Point Edit Edges tool is active, the lines of interconnected edges can be selected.

You can further define how vertices, edges, and faces are selected by right-clicking any of the select tools (Lasso, Rectangle or Free-Hand) to open the Selection panel. The Selection panel has three buttons that enable you to choose whether you want to add, select a subset, or remove selected vertices, edges, or faces from the current selection. The panel's Backside option allows the inclusion of vertices on the other side of the object's contours. The Highlight option changes the color of internal vertices or faces during the drawing of the lasso or the rectangle selection tools. The last option is a popup you can use to specify the color of the Lasso and the Rectangle tools.

NOTE

When writing this book, I found that the way edges, faces, and vertices are selected has changed from version 3, as well as with each new beta of version 4. So, if your working copy of trueSpace4 and its manual say you must hold the Ctrl key to select multiple faces, edges, or vertices, I apologize. If history is any indicator of what's to come, Caligari will surely change it again.

To manipulate the selected vertices, edges, or faces, you have to access the Point Edit panel. This is an awful place to put the controls, in my opinion, and you will see what I mean in just a second. At the very least, the arrangement means that you have to use two panels to edit vertices, edges, and faces: one to select them and one to manipulate them.

MANIPULATING SELECTED SURFACES: THE POINT EDIT PANEL

Once you have selected the vertices, edges, or faces, you can rotate, scale, or move them by using the Point Edit panel's controls. The panel also has its own vertex, edge, and face selection tools, as well as some other interesting utilities. Open the Point Edit panel by right-clicking the Point Edit Context tool, and follow along (see Figure 3.2).

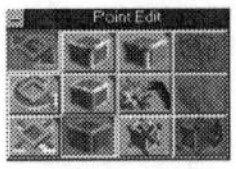

FIGURE 3.2 *The Point Edit panel.*

> **NOTE**
> You can change the coordinate system or limit the axis to any given plane via the Coords panel by right-clicking the Point Move, Rotate, or Scale buttons.

> **NOTE**
> To select multiple vertices, edges, or faces when in one of the Point Edit panel's four modes, simply select a new vertex, edge, or face. To unselect a surface, click it again. Selected surfaces are identified by a color change.

- **Point Move:** Enables you to move the selected surfaces within the active coordinate system.
- **Point Rotate:** Enables you to rotate the selected surfaces.
- **Point Scale:** Allows you to scale your object along any plane. By holding both the left and right mouse buttons, you can scale the selected surfaces equally in all three planes.
- **Point Edit Vertices:** The first of the Point Edit panel's methods of selecting an object's vertices, edges, or faces. To select a vertex, activate this option and click directly on the intersection of two vertices.
- **Point Edit Edges:** To select an edge, click directly on it.
- **Point Edit Faces:** To select a face, click its center.
- **Point Edit Context:** When active, this allows you to pick either a vertex, edge, or face, depending on where you click your mouse. To select a vertex, click directly on the intersection of two vertices. To select an edge, click directly on it. To select a face, click its center.

- **Weld Vertices:** Welds the selected vertices together. If a face or one or more edges is selected, then the vertices attached to those surfaces are welded together. Later in this chapter, I use the Weld tool to create a pyramid primitive.
- **Erase Vertices:** If an edge or face is selected, the associated vertices along with the selected edges or faces will be deleted from the object.

- **Slice Object:** Subdivides an object parallel to a cutting plane. One edge, cross section, or face must be selected for this button to be active. The slicing plane will scale to fit the entire object, hence the name "slice." To keep the selected edge sets, use your right mouse button. You can then apply any of the Point Edit operations on the selected surface after you have finished the slice operation.

- **Separate Selected Part of Object:** Detaches any selected surface from an object. After separation, the Point Edit panel closes.

- **Flip Faces:** Reverses the normal of the selected face.

BUILD A PYRAMID PRIMITIVE

trueSpace presently offers only six primitives to modelers:

- Torus

- Sphere

- Cone

- Cylinder

- Cube

- Plane

From time to time, I need a pyramid primitive, and creating one takes just a few mouse clicks. The first two methods are the most obvious. Simply add a cone primitive to the scene with a latitude of 2 and a longitude of 4 or add a cylinder primitive with a latitude of 2, longitude of 4, and a top radius of 0.01. The third method uses the Weld Vertices tool.

1. Add a cube primitive to the scene.

2. Open the Point Edit panel.

3. Using the Point Edit Edges tool, select three or four edges of the top face, or select the top face by using the Point Edit Face tool. Any will do and will yield the same result. The point here is there is always more than one way to accomplish something in trueSpace4.

4. Select the Weld Vertices tool, and you have your pyramid.

Well, that's about it for manipulating edges, faces, and vertices. The next step is to create new ones on your objects.

THE POINT DRAW TOOLS

New to trueSpace4, the Point Draw tool set enables you to draw new vertices, edges, and faces on an object. These faces can then be extruded from the original object to create complex shapes. The new polygon can form a new face inside an existing face or it can cross existing edges. Once a shape has been started, clicking on the starting point closes the polygon. If the polygon is closed and it forms a new face, the face is automatically selected, and the point-editing tools can be used on it. Internal parts of the polygons that cross edges can be selected by clicking on any vertex or edge inside the polygon to allow the use of the Sweep tool family. By right-clicking on the Polygon Draw button, the Point Draw panel is opened, revealing five additional options for making new vertices, edges, and faces (see Figure 3.3).

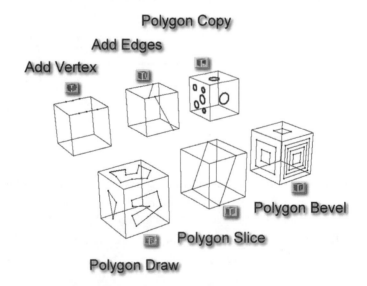

FIGURE 3.3   *A look at the six Point Draw tools.*

- **Add Vertex:** Creates new vertices when you click on edges.

- **Add Edges:** Creates new edges on vertices or edges and requires two mouse clicks to define an edge.

- **Polygon Copy:** Creates a regular polygon on a face under the cursor. You can specify the number of sides via the Poly Modes panel, but you cannot use the Subtract, Union, or Intersect options in the Poly Modes panel.

- **Polygon Slice:** Cuts the object with a plane defined by three points on edges or vertices of the object. The first point will either create a new vertex on an edge or select an existing vertex. The second point selects an existing edge starting in the first point or cuts the face. The third point cuts the object in the vicinity of the first two points along the plane defined by all three points.

> **TIP**
>
> Pressing the Ctrl key when adding the third point for Polygon Slice will instead cut off the whole object. The fourth point selects part of the object that is on the same side of the cutting plane.

- **Polygon Bevel:** Creates a new face inside the selected face. The beveled face will not have the usual loft associated with such an operation. This tool creates only the initial polygon edges. You have to use one of the Sweep tools to extrude the surface.

What can you build with these fun new tools? Quite a bit, as you will see in the projects that follow.

AWAY WITH THOSE SUPERFLUOUS AND REDUNDANT POLYGONS

Now that you've learned how to add faces, edges, and points to an object, what happens if you get carried away? Removing any unnecessary faces, edges, or points from an object is a simple matter (see Figure 3.4).

1. Add a plane primitive to the scene and place it so that it does not intersect with your object.

2. Right-click any of the Boolean tools to open the Boolean panel and enable the Delete Edges option.

3. Boolean subtract the plane from your object.

This will also undo any triangulation applied to your object.

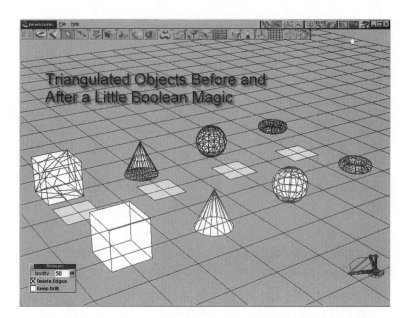

FIGURE 3.4   *You can remove unwanted polygons and reverse the effects of the Triangulate Object tool by Boolean subtracting a single plane primitive from the object.*

MODELING BY EXTRUDING SURFACES

Extruding surfaces is one of the most common methods of modeling. It is also the most covered subject in 3D books, and just about every one of those books demonstrates the art of sweeping surfaces by extruding text. Enough, I say! The next exercises do not extrude text but demonstrate how to use the Sweep tools to model actual objects. To start, I will use the basic tool to form simple shapes. From there, I will add a twist to create rope.

A quick note before we begin: The Sweep tool has a single panel that both the Sweep and Tip tool share. To open the Sweep panel, right-click the Sweep tool. In this panel, you define the number of segments to add with each sweep. The next few exercises use the default value of 1. The Sweep tools, like the Lasso and Rectangle selection tools, work in conjunction with the Point Edit panel—that is, you can't move, scale, or rotate the swept surface until you specify the surface translation method in the Point Edit panel.

BENT METAL AND TAILPIPES

From water, gas, and sewage pipes to wrought iron fences and tailpipes, the Sweep tool makes short order of your modeling needs (see Figure 3.5).

1. Switch to the Perspective view and add a cylinder primitive to the scene.

2. Open the Point Edit panel. Enable the Point Rotate button and Point Edit Faces button.

3. Select the top face and sweep it once.

4. Switch to the Left view and rotate the selected face clockwise along the z-axis about 20 degrees.

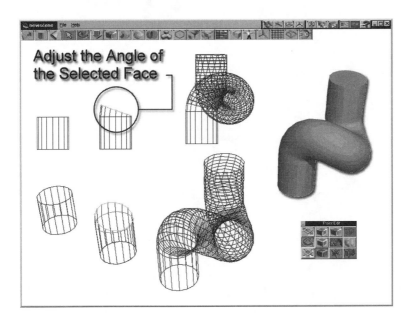

FIGURE 3.5 *Using the Sweep tool to create bent pipes.*

5. Select the Point Move tool and align the right edge of the selected face with the right edge of the cylinder. Continue sweeping the face, adjusting the angle of the selected face when needed.

Repeat the last two steps as often as necessary to get the desired shape. To create a wrought iron fence, add a cylinder with a latitude of 2, longitude of 5, and a top radius of 1 (see Figure 3.6).

FIGURE 3.6   *A wrought iron fence created with the Sweep tool.*

WATER BEADS, SPLATTERS, AND PUDDLES

To add beads of water to that '57 Chevy you just modeled or to add a frosty look to that can of Coke on the window sill, beveled polygons are just the trick.

1. From the Perspective view, open the Poly Modes panel via a right-click of the Regular Polygon tool.

2. Set the side count to 20.

3. Add one circle to the scene by clicking and dragging your mouse.

4. In the Poly Mode panel, enable the Union New Polygon with Selected Polygon button.

5. Add several more circles to the scene. Be as creative as you like. If the shape doesn't seem to be working out, you can simply remove the previous circle with the Undo tool.

6. When satisfied with the overall pattern, select the Bevel tool.

7. A bevel of 0.18 and angle of 45 degrees is a good starting point.

This is a simple use for the sweep tools; let's look at a more challenging object.

ROPE AND TWISTED WIRE

Rope and twisted wire can sometimes come in handy and are surprisingly simple to create (see Figure 3.7). The first few steps are identical to the steps for creating water beads.

1. From the Top view, open the Poly Modes panel via a right-click of the Regular Polygon tool.

2. Set the side count to 20.

3. Add one good-sized circle to the scene by clicking and dragging your mouse.

4. In the Poly Mode panel, enable the Union New Polygon with the Selected Polygon button.

5. Add two more circles to the scene but place them so that the finished shape resembles that of a three-leaf clover.

6. Switch to the Perspective view.

7. Sweep the shape's top face once.

8. Open the Point Edit panel and enable the Point Rotate button.

9. Rotate the selected face along the z-axis about 1 to 2 degrees.

10. Sweep the selected surface to the desired length.

A good length of rope can come in handy. Create a rope and save it for later use. Next time you need it, you can load it up and deform it to any shape by using trueSpace4's Bones tool.

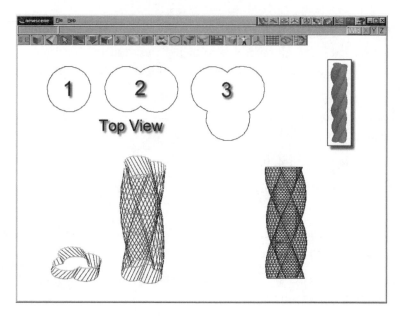

FIGURE 3.7 *Sweeping a shape created with the Regular Polygon tool to form a rope.*

MODELING WITH THE SURFACE SCULPT TOOL

You can create some unique and interesting landscapes in just a few minutes with the Surface Sculpt tools. Before we jump into the actual terrain and landscape creation, we should briefly review the Surface Sculpting tool set.

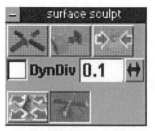

FIGURE 3.8 *The Surface Sculpt panel.*

The Surface Sculpt tool is one of trueSpace4's three surface deformation tools. (The other two are Deform Object and Deform by Stand Alone Object.) The Surface Sculpt tool can be used to deform the surface of an object, and it works best with objects that have been quad divided. The denser the mesh, the smoother the surface deformation appears.

Surface Sculpt works in two modes: Sculpting and Scope Adjustment. In Sculpting mode, you deform the surface of an object by moving and adjusting the crosshairs. The Scope mode is used to change the orientation of the sculpted deformation and to move the deformation to other areas of the object.

The Surface Sculpt panel itself is comprised of five buttons and a check box. From the left, they are:

- **Erase Deformation:** Erases the current deformation.

- **Copy Deformation:** Copies the present deformation to another area of the object's surface.

- **New Surface Deformation:** Allows you to select another area of the object to sculpt.

- **Dyn Div:** Dynamic Division; Automatically subdivides the selected sculpted surface. Helpful for smoothing those jagged edges.

- **Scope Mode:** Shows the control handles for changing the scope and position of a deformation. In other words, it enables you to reposition the selected sculpted surface to another area of the mesh.

- **Sculpt Mode:** Enables the creation and editing of a sculpted surface.

Selecting the Sculpt mode toggles Scope mode off and vice versa.

TERRAIN AND LANDSCAPES

To grasp how the Surface Sculpt tool works, we will use it to model mountain terrain (see Figure 3.9).

1. Switch to the Perspective view and add a plane primitive to the scene.

2. Quad divide the plane primitive four times to create a 256-face plane. You can smooth divide the plane later to produce a smooth, dense mesh with less-faceted surface features.

3. Open the Surface Sculpt panel and enable the New Surface Deformation button.

NOTE

A macro path is automatically constructed during Sweep operations. You can save the path by opening the Path Library panel, typing a meaningful name in the field, and pressing Enter. You can save the path of the sweep operations only while the Sweep tool is still active. The Path Library can be found in the Navigation group.

NOTE

The sculpting tool is based on the object coordinate system with its z-axis perpendicular to the crosshairs.

WARNING

Once you start a new deformation, you cannot delete the previously created deformation.

NOTE

Each handle of the crosshair can be pulled or rotated to reshape the selected deformation along any of the three axes.

WARNING

Don't waste your time keyframing the Scope Mode changes. That is moving the position of a sculpted surface to another area of the mesh as described previously with the Scope Mode button in the Surface Sculpt panel. Although vertex manipulation can be animated, trueSpace will animate the Scope Mode changes only if keyframed and played back while the Surface Sculpt panel is open. Once you select the Object tool, say good-bye to the animation. Don't let this discourage you. Surface Sculpt is a powerful modeling tool with no equals in flexibility and ease of use.

4. Select one of the vertices. It's not important which one for now—any will do. A green crosshair will appear for the selected point.

5. To create mountains and valleys, drag your mouse up or down while holding the right mouse button.

6. Once you have your mountain or valley, you can copy it to another surface of the object. Enable the Copy Deformation button and specify a new location by clicking on another vertex of the object. Repeat the copy operation until you are satisfied with the results.

7. This technique will create an unnatural uniform pattern. To add some randomness to the terrain, select a vertex and create a slight depression. Copy the newly created deformed surface to some of the other areas of the object. Remember, by switching to Scope mode, you can also add some randomness. Create a new deformation and move the deformed surface to any location on the object's surface. Repeat step 7 until satisfied with the results.

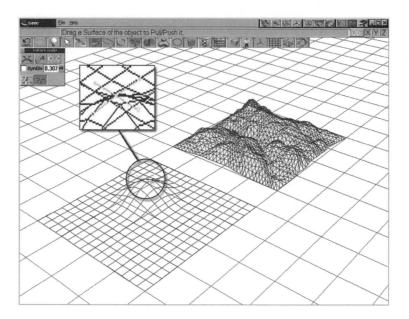

FIGURE 3.9 *A demonstration of the Surface Sculpt tools and modeling terrain.*

Modeling mountain ranges can be fun, but it's not as exciting as the next few exercises, so on to deformations.

TIP

If you need to create landscapes in a hurry, check out Vision Inc.'s PrimitivePlus plug-in. PrimitivePlus can create great-looking terrain in just a few mouse clicks and is packaged with trueSpace4. After creating your landmass, smooth it out with the ThermoClay demo on this CD for some great land-scapes.

MODELING AND THE DEFORM OBJECT TOOL

The Deform Object tool is powerful and versatile. With it, you can achieve smooth organic shapes by deforming primitives. Once again, we will look at the tool and its options before building something with it.

GETTING FAMILIAR WITH CROSS SECTIONS

I usually start with the panels associated with the tool, but this time I think we should ignore them for now and try an exercise on managing cross sections.

Modeling by deforming objects is a common practice and is an effective way to create interesting complex shapes from a single primitive. Later in this chapter and in Chapter 4, I will use trueSpace's object deformation tools to model complex shapes from a single primitive. I can do such things in trueSpace because trueSpace allows me the freedom to deform an object with an assortment of tools, and, secondly, I understand how to create, delete, and manage cross sections. So, to use the deformation tools effectively, you have to get to know how to manipulate cross sections. Let's get familiar with cross sections.

1. Add a cube primitive to a new scene and switch to the Perspective view if you haven't already done so.

2. Click the Deform Object button to open the Deformation Nav panel. You will notice that the Local Deformation button is selected by default and the cube is covered with cross sections identified by the green planes intersecting the cube.

3. Using the left mouse button, click anywhere in the workspace not occupied by the cube. Drag the mouse in any direction. Depending on the direction you drag, it will either add or subtract cross sections to the object.

4. Select one of the corner cross sections and pull it in any direction.

5. Select the Object tool. This will close the Deformation Nav panel, leaving nothing but the deformed cube visible. Reopen the Deformation Nav panel again. You will notice that the cross sections are all still intact.

6. Left-click anywhere in the workspace and try to add or decrease the number of cross sections.

You can't, can you? The reason you can't is because I had you deform the surface of the cube by pulling on one of its corners in step 4. Once an object is deformed, you essentially lock the number of cross sections. This isn't a limitation; it's a feature. If you need to add more cross sections, simply delete the existing cross sections by pressing the Delete key on your keyboard. Reopen the Deformation Nav panel and adjust the number of cross sections as you did in step 3.

Experiment a bit by adding and removing cross sections to a number of different objects. The point of this exercise isn't simply to familiarize yourself with adding and deleting cross sections but to help you develop the habits of working with cross sections. Great things can be accomplished with this tool once you have grasped the nuances.

THE DEFORMATION NAV PANEL

A left-click of the Deform Object button opens the Deformation Nav panel (see Figure 3.10). This panel is comprised of seven buttons, a check box, and an entry field. From the left, here's what each does:

FIGURE 3.10   *The Deformation Nav panel.*

NOTE

You can change the coordinate system or limit the axis to any given plane via the Coords panel by right-clicking either the Pull/Push, Stretch, or Twist buttons.

● **Pull/Push:** When selected, enables you to move the control node or cross section within the active coordinate system.

● **Twist:** Enables you to rotate the selected node or cross section.

● **Stretch:** I prefer to call this one "Scale." Clicking this button allows you to scale (stretch) your object along any plane. By holding both the left and right mouse buttons, you can scale the selected node or cross section equally in all three planes.

- **Deformation Along a Plane Perpendicular To:** Lets you select or create cross sections perpendicular to the x-, y-, and z-axis, respectively.

- **Local Deformation:** Enables you to select the nodes of the available cross sections. To select a node, click one of the cross sections. The selected node will be identified by a green cross-hair.

NOTE

Remember that all the exercises in this book were created with OrthoNav checked in the preferences panel and use the Obj coordinate system.

- **Dyn Div:** Dynamic Division; subdivides the area influenced by the deformation. Use the associated entry field to specify the density of the subdivision. The higher the number, the more subdivisions will occur. The range of values (ROV) is from .001 to 1.

THE DEFORMATION PANEL

We aren't done yet; we have one more panel to look at. The Deformation panel holds the Deform Object tool's feedback options. Open it by right-clicking the Deform Object button.

The Deformation panel has four options—Real-time, Handles, Outline, and Draw—that can be enabled or disabled. Draw's options are selected via a drop-down menu.

- **Real-time:** If the option is checked, you will see instant feedback of the actual surfaces being manipulated as you deform the object. Otherwise, only an approximation will be displayed.

- **Handles:** Displays the actual control handles and points. Each can be manipulated independently.

- **Outlines:** Displays the individual cross sections.

- **Draw:** Determines how the object's wire frame is drawn. You have two choices: Deformed or Object. The latter displays the entire object as you deform its surface, whereas Deformed displays only the vertices being affected.

Now that we have covered the tool and its options, get ready to model something with it. I hope you are fond of fungi.

MODEL AN ORGANIC FROM A SINGLE SPHERE PRIMITIVE

The Deform Object tool is one of my favorite modeling tools. Before the introduction of metaballs and NURBS, it was the only way to create organic objects. For this demonstration, we will model a mushroom from a single sphere primitive (see Figure 3.11).

FIGURE 3.11   *The finished mushroom.*

1. Open a new scene and switch to the Front view.

2. Add a sphere primitive to the scene with a Latitude of 8 and a Longitude of 12 and quad divide it twice. If you are unsure how to change the Latitude and Longitude setting, right-click the Add Sphere button to open the Sphere panel. Right-clicking the Add Primitive buttons opens a panel that can be used to control the density of the primitive's mesh. After changing the values, the next primitive added to the scene will use the new value.

3. Open the Deformation Nav panel and enable the Stretch and Deform Perpendicular to z-axis buttons.

4. Only one cross section will be visible, identified by the color green. One cross section isn't enough to deform the sphere into the shape desired, so

press the right mouse button and, while dragging the mouse, add cross sections until each of the 16 latitudes that make up our sphere is covered by a control mesh.

5. Disable the y- and z-axis buttons. Select the center cross section and scale it along the x-plane to about the width of the stem of our mushroom. Panel B of Figure 3.12 illustrates this.

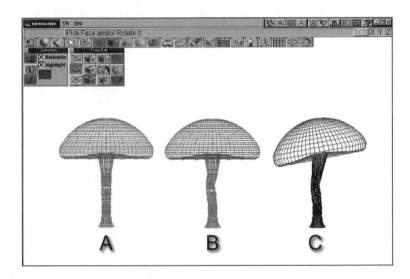

FIGURE 3.12   *Deforming a sphere primitive to form the stem of a mushroom .*

6. Working your way down from the center, select each of the next control points and scale it to about the same size as the previous one. An approximation is enough because the stem of a mushroom isn't perfect. As you work your way down the sphere, switch between the Left and Front view windows.

7. Select the cross section just above the top of the newly created stem and scale it to the same size. Remember to switch to either the Left or Right view window as you scale the cross section.

8. Enable the Pull/Push button in the Deformation Nav panel and enable the y-axis button in the Coords panel. Move the selected cross section up into the cap of the mushroom.

9. Re-enable the Stretch button and select the cross section at the bottom of the mushroom cap. Scale it and the cross section above it just enough to give the bottom of the cap a rounded edge (see Figure 3.13).

FIGURE 3.13   *More character is added to the mushroom by tilting its cap and adding a little bend to its stem.*

10. Enable the Pull/Push button in the Deformation Nav panel once more. Select any of the cross sections of the stem and pull or push along the x-plane until it is off-center. This will create a slight curve. Select the adjacent cross sections, and pull or push them along the x-plane to complete the smooth curve of the stem.

11. The final touch would be to have the cap of the mushroom atop the stem kind of off-kilter as mushrooms often are. Switch to the Left view and select the Object tool. This will close the Deformation panel. Open the Point Edit panel by clicking the Point Edit Context button.

12. Right-click the Rectangle Selection tool to open the Selection panel. Check the Backside button. Enable the Select Using Rectangle tool and enclose the cap of the mushroom with the rectangle. Enable the Point Rotate button in the Point Edit panel. Using your right mouse button, add a tilt to the mushroom cap. Switch to the Front view and tilt the cap a bit in the opposite direction.

This exercise was a simple demonstration of what can be created with the Deform Object tool. In the next chapter, we will combine this tool with some of the other modeling tools to create characters.

MODELING WITH METABALLS

Metaballs were introduced in trueSpace3 and are great to use for creating seamless characters and objects with smooth surfaces. Metaballs enable you to create objects by using a special set of primitives, similar to modeling with standard primitives. Each metaball primitive you add to your scene, however, has an adjustable *volume of influence* that determines how it blends with other primitives you place near it. A simple way to explain how metaballs work is to say that the primitives used to construct the metaball structure blob together. By adjusting the volume of influence of each of the metaball primitives, unique, seamless, smooth shapes can be created. Think of it as modeling with virtual Silly Putty™.

Before we model with metaballs, let's look at the features of the Metaball Options panel. The Metaball Options panel is where you set how much feedback you want, placement offset, and the final mesh resolution (density) when the tool is exited. The Metaball Option panel can be opened by right-clicking the Metaball tool button.

- **Conversion:** This combo box has three settings for determining the level of interactivity between metaballs. These settings control the construction of the metaball surface, what Caligari calls the "live skin." Objects created from metaballs have a high-poly count, which can cause the display to lag behind when positioning the primitives. This can become frustrating, and to combat this, Caligari has provided three options to tweak the mesh density to a reasonable number without the awful lag time:

    On Move is the default mode and updates the screen as you manipulate the object's surface in real time.

    On Demand works great if you have a slow machine or the mesh has become too dense for real-time display to be reasonable. If your display is lagging behind, this option will eliminate real-time screen updates of the object surface.

    On Release updates the display only when the object has been moved and the mouse button is released. This mode gives good feedback without out the dreaded lag time.

- **Navigation Res:** The resolution of the metaball object's mesh during the edit process. The range of the parameter is 20 to 250.

- **Render Res:** The resolution of the mesh when rendered. The range is 20 to 250.

When the volume of influence is selected, you cannot select another metaball. Deselect the Edit Volume of Influence button.

- **Use X Offset for Prims:** When this option is selected, any newly added metaball primitive is placed adjacent to the previously selected metaball primitive.

Before writing a tutorial on modeling with metaballs, I investigated how the subject was approached in the past. I didn't find much material, and what I did find didn't provide any good examples. This was a surprise because so much can be modeled with metaballs. In the following discussions, we will look at some real-world objects modeled with metaballs and the techniques that can be used to achieve the desired results, but first here are a few tidbits you should be made aware of.

A metaball's volume of influence cannot be smaller than the metaball itself and has no effect on the metaball, only its neighbors. If you give a metaball a positive volume of influence, neighboring metaballs will become largely influenced and will tend to bulge together. If you give a metaball a negative volume of influence, the metaball will subtract surface area from surrounding metaballs.

CREATE A FISH

Designing a great-looking fish is easy with metaballs (see Figure 3.14). All that is required is a group of ten metaball sphere primitives. Modeling with metaballs isn't an exact science; an approximation is all that is usually needed, but exact numbers are a big help in some cases. So, where necessary, I will provide the specific scale of the metaballs to create the desired shape. We will begin with the head and work our way to the tail and fins.

FIGURE 3.14   *The fish in this image was created by using metaballs.*

1. Open a new scene and switch to the Front view.

2. Right-click the Metaball tool and uncheck the Use X Offset for Prims option. This causes the next metaball primitive added to the scene to appear in the location of the previously selected metaball.

3. Open the Metaball Edit panel and add a metaball sphere primitive to the scene.

4. Open the Object Info panel via a right-click on the Object tool.

5. To create the head, enter the values 3.4 in the x-axis size field, 1.2 in the y-axis size field, and 2.0 in the z-axis size field. This will give you a starting point for your fish.

6. Add another metaball sphere primitive to the scene. The second metaball will inherit the size, shape, and location of the previously selected metaball. Place the newly created metaball's lower left quarter over the first metaball's upper right quarter as depicted in Figure 3.15, number 2.

7. Add a metaball to the scene and enter the values 2.07 in the x-axis size field, 0.91 in the y-axis size field, and 1.91 in the z-axis size field. This will be the start of the abdomen, metaball 3. Use Figure 3.15 as a guide.

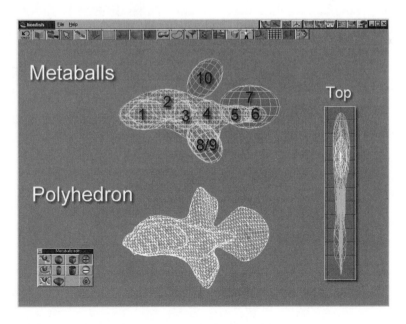

FIGURE 3.15   *The ten metaball spheres required to build our fish.*

8. Add a fourth metaball sphere primitive to the scene and place its left edge one third inside the previous metaball as shown in Figure 3.15.

9. The tail is made up of three metaballs, each a different size. To create metaball number 5, add a metaball sphere to the scene with a size of 2.144 in the x-axis size field, 0.574 in the y-axis size field, and 1.236 in the z-axis size field. Align its left edge with the right edge of metaball 4.

10. To create metaball 6, add a new metaball sphere to the scene and scale it five to ten percent smaller than the previous one. Place its left edge around one third of the way into metaball 5.

11. The final part of the fish tail is a large and thin metaball sphere scaled to 4.071 in the x-axis size field, 0.228 in the y-axis size field, and 2.843 in the z-axis size field. Align its left edge with the left edge of metaball 5. Align its horizontal center with the top of metaballs 5 and 6 as depicted in Figure 3.15.

12. To create the lower fins, add another metaball sphere primitive to the scene. Scale the new metaball equally to half its present size. Increase the metaball's volume of influence until the fin protrudes from the fish's body. Select the Rotate Metaball Primitive button in the Metaball Edit panel. Using the right mouse button, rotate the metaball about 40 degrees clockwise and place its top edge where the bottoms of metaballs 3 and 4 meet. Figure 3.16 illustrates the position of the fins.

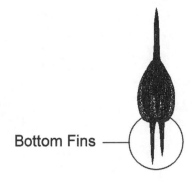

Bottom Fins

FIGURE 3.16 *A closer look at the lower fins.*

13. Switch to the Left view. Copy the fin and place it on the other side of the fish. Use the right mouse button to rotate each of the fins' bottom edges out from the body.

14. For the final fin, copy one of the lower fins. Rotate it counterclockwise about 90 degrees and place its lower edge at the top of metaball 3.

15. It's important to note that each metaball's location affects its neighbor, which affects its neighbor, and so on. Therefore, a little tweaking of the metaball positions will be necessary to get the desired shape. You can select the Object tool at any time to view the object's skin. To tweak the metaballs, simply reopen the Metaball Edit panel and select any of the Move, Rotate, or Scale buttons to continue where you left off.

16. For the final phase, we will deform the fish fins. Open the Deformation Nav panel. A dialog box will appear informing you that you are about to convert the metaball structure to a polyhedron. Go ahead and convert it. The number of cross sections defaults at two (identified as green lines). See Figure 3.17.

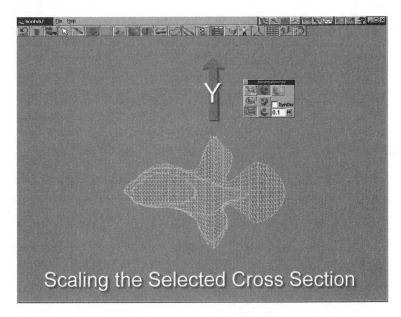

FIGURE 3.17   *Using the Deformation tools to shape the fins of a fish.*

NOTE

Caligari identifies each of the cross sections as perpendicular to either the x, y, or z planes. For the sake of simplicity and to avoid confusion, in some cases I will refer to each as it appears onscreen. I will use the terms "horizontal" and/or "vertical" where appropriate.

17. To add more cross sections, select the Deform Perpendicular to x-axis button. Holding the right mouse button down, increase the number of cross sections until you have one cross section running through the center of both the top and bottom fins.

18. Select Stretch in the Deformation Nav panel and right-click it to open the Coords panel. Disable the y- and z-axes. This will allow you to stretch (scale) the cross sections along the x-axis in a controlled manner.

19. Select the center cross section and scale it until the top and bottom fins acquire the desired shape. Season to taste.

If you are having a little trouble getting the same results as illustrated, don't despair. It takes a little practice to create the shapes you want. Here are a few tidbits to nibble on.

Altering a metaball slightly affects the surrounding metaballs to different degrees. This can be visible when placing one metaball outside a group of metaballs as you did previously in the fish tutorial. You may have noticed that the fish suddenly changed shape even though you were manipulating a metaball outside the fish's body. This can make accurate metaball modeling of complex objects difficult and frustrating.

If you were experiencing problems with the fish tutorial, here are some things you can try. Keep in mind that everyone gets slightly different results with metaballs due to its live skin feature and the inability to enter a numeric value for the volume of influence.

- *Take your time.* This is a skill that comes slowly at first. You will be cranking out cool organics in no time after you get the hang of it.

- *Adjust the volume of influence in small increments.* After adjusting the volume of influence, a slight repositioning of the metaball may be required.

- *Start with the general shape of the object.* Next, add the metaballs that will define the details.

- *Don't be afraid to start with a new metaball.* Sometimes this is the best approach when the metaballs (live skin) simply won't group to create the desired effect. This is especially true when working with limbs that extend from the organic.

You will find a complete, textured model of our fish on the CD that accompanies this book. The file is named chapters\chptr03\fish.scn.

Okay, with a metaball fish under your belt, it's time to create a nonorganic with metaballs. We will return to organic object construction with metaballs later in this chapter.

MODEL A STAR FIGHTER

The ORCA II star fighter we will model is a little more challenging but it isn't that much different than modeling a car or keg of beer (see Figure 3.18). To keep the focus of the exercise on "having fun," I have provided a reference image in the following illustrations to guide you during the modeling process.

FIGURE 3.18   *The finished ORCA II.*

1. Open a new scene and switch to the Top view.

2. Open the Metaball Edit panel and add two rounded cube primitives to the scene.

3. Select one of the cubes and scale it to a quarter of its present size.

4. Disable the x- and z-axis buttons in the Coords panel. Moving the cube along the y-plane, place the smaller cube so that most of its geometry is outside the larger cube as depicted in Figure 3.19.

5. Add another rounded metaball cube primitive. The newly created cube will inherit the size, shape, and location of the previously selected metaball. Move the newly created cube along the y-plane until most of its surface exits the larger metaball cube's lower edge. See Figure 3.19, panel C.

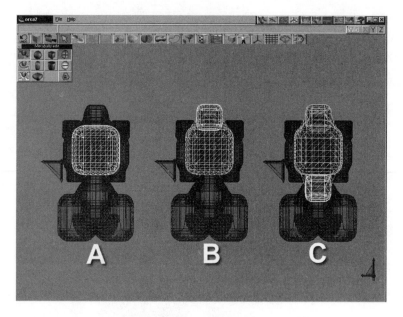

FIGURE 3.19   *Modeling the cab of our star fighter.*

6. Select the Scale Metaball Primitive button in the Metaball Edit panel and disable the x- and z-axis buttons in the Coords panel.

7. To create the whale tail fin's shaft, scale the selected cube along the y-plane to twice its present size.

8. Select the larger cube and add a metaball cylinder to the scene. I had you select the larger cube prior to adding a metaball cylinder to the structure because if you add another primitive while a stretched metaball is selected, the new metaball inherits the scale of the selected primitive.

9. Enable the Rotate Metaball Primitive button in the Metaball Edit panel. Disable the y- and z-axis buttons in the Coords panel. Rotate the cylinder

along the x-plane 90 degrees. Place it so that its center is aligned with the larger cube's left side. This should cause the cylinder to bulge from the larger cube's left side.

10. Add another metaball cylinder primitive to the scene. Align its lower edge with the top edge of the previously selected cylinder. Reduce its volume of influence as low as possible.

11. Add another cylinder and align its top edge with the center cylinder's bottom edge. Reduce its volume as you did with the previous cylinder.

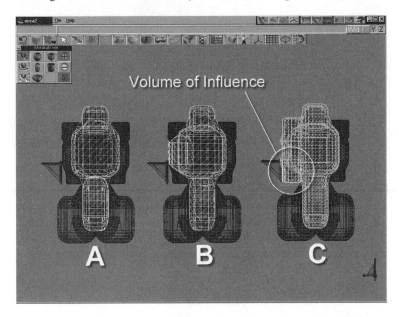

FIGURE 3.20   *Adjusting the volume of influence to shape the hull of our star fighter.*

12. For the whale tail, reselect the original cube and add a rounded metaball cube to the scene. Align its left edge with the center of the metaball structure. Move the cube along the y-plane until a third of its geometry extends past the elongated cube that makes up the tail's shaft.

13. Switch to the Left view. In Figure 3.21, you will notice that the tail fins and shaft sit lower than the reference image. To correct this, simply enable the Move Metaball Primitive button and disable the x- and z-axis buttons in the Coords panel. Select the tail and shaft and move each along the y-plane into position.

14. Enable the Scale Metaball Primitive button. Select the metaball cube that represents the tail fins and scale it along the y-plane as depicted in Figure 3.22, panel B.

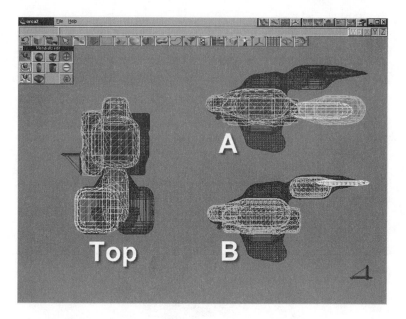

FIGURE 3.21   *Creating the wings of our star fighter.*

15. To create the cab, we will need to add a rounded cube metaball primitive to the metaball structure. But first, remember to select a primitive that has not been scaled or rotated; otherwise, the newly created primitive will inherit those traits.

16. Scale the newly created cube in the form of a barrel. This will create the belly of our star fighter, as well as the cab's canopy.

17. In my version of the star fighter, I chose to add a stabilizing fin underneath the vehicle. To create the fin, add another rounded cube to the structure and scale it to about half its present size. Switch to the top view and reduce the cube's width by scaling the cube along the x-plane about 90 percent. Switch to the Left view and rotate the cube with the right mouse button 15 degrees. Figure 3.22 illustrates these steps.

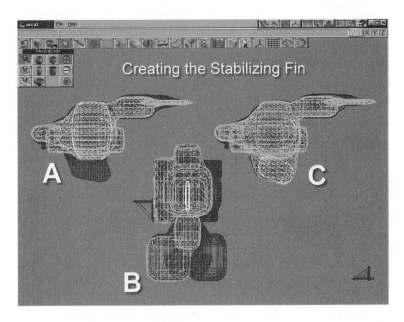

FIGURE 3.22   *Creating the stabilizer wing of our star fighter.*

18. To complete your project, select the Object tool to view the metaball object in all its glory. To tweak the shape, simply reopen the Metaball Edit panel to manipulate the metaball primitives that make up the metaball structure.

19. If you are satisfied with the results so far, switch to the Top view. Add a cube primitive to the scene and scale it equally along all three of its axes to a size equal to the volume of the metaball object.

20. Align the cube primitive's left edge with the center of the metaball object's center. Boolean subtract the cube from the star fighter. A dialog box will appear asking you to confirm your decision to convert the metaball structure to a polyhedron. Answer yes.

21. Mirror the metaball object and rotate it into position. Glue the two halves together. See Figure 3.23.

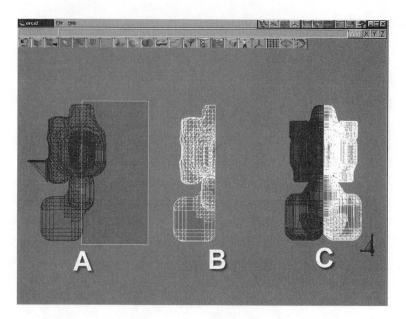

FIGURE 3.23   *Using a Boolean operation to create a perfectly symmetrical star fighter.*

You will find the complete model of our star fighter model ORCA II on the CD that accompanies this book. The file is chapters\chptr03\orca.scn.

Well, we have managed to create a simple organic as an introduction, a car for the car buffs, and a spaceship for all the *Star Trek* fans out there. What I would like to cover next is a little more complex. Whip out the marshmallows because we are going to model the fire-breathing dragon from a short story I wrote titled "Ryhme" (see Figure 3.24).

FIGURE 3.24 *A dragon from the land of Ryhme.*

MODEL A DRAGON

Modeling a dragon was a lot of fun for me. Modeling organic shapes with metaballs is very similar to modeling with clay. The medieval fire-breathing creature we will be modeling next is relatively simple to make.

We will first model the dragon's skull and upper jaw.

> **NOTE**
>
> When modeling organics with metaballs in trueSpace4, it is important to note that the more metaballs used to model the object, the better control of the surfaces you will have.

1. Open a new scene and switch to the Left view.

2. Open the Metaball Edit panel. The object we are about to model will be made up of many metaball primitives. This will increase the number of polygons in the scene and may cause the screen refresh to lag behind. To minimize this effect, open the Metaballs Options panel via a right-click on the Metaball tool. Set Conversion to On Release, Navigation Re to 25, Render Res to 50, and disable Use X Offset for Prims.

3. To create the skull, add a metaball sphere primitive to the scene. Scale the sphere along the y-plane to half its present height.

4. Place another metaball sphere above the first sphere. Enable the Rotate Metaball Primitive button and rotate the new sphere along the z-axis about 10 degrees. Add another sphere to the structure and rotate it 10 degrees along the z-axis as well. Panel A of figure 3.25 illustrates their positions.

5. To create the upper jaw, add a sphere primitive to the structure. The newly added sphere will inherit the previously selected metaball's scale, rotation, and location. Reshape the sphere so that it's close to its original form.

6. Scale the sphere equally along all three planes to a third of its present volume. Place it below the spheres that make up the skull a distance equal to three of these spheres. Once you have placed the first sphere that makes up the upper jaw, add another four spheres and place them so that they outline the shape of the jaw. Panel B of Figure 3.25 illustrates this.

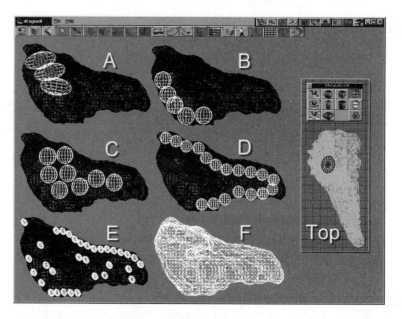

FIGURE 3.25 *Modeling the dragon's head with metaballs.*

7. To provide the filler for the skull, add seven or eight metaball spheres to the structure. The spheres can be moved later to positions that work best, but for now just place them in a tight group as depicted in panel C of Figure 3.25.

8. The outline of the jaw can be created with slightly smaller spheres. Add a sphere primitive to the structure and scale it equally along all three planes to half its present size. Starting from the spheres that make up the bottom of upper jaw, add about 18 of these smaller spheres. Place them so that they outline the jaw and skull of our dragon, as illustrated in panel D of Figure 3.25. The metaball structure should now have the basic shape of the dragon's head and upper jaw. All that is left to do is add spheres of different sizes to the areas that require more bulk.

9. To finish the dragon's skull and upper jaw, switch to the Top view. Starting from the top, select the spheres that were added as fillers in the previous steps; move them along the x-plane to shape the head. The head should appear wide near the back of the skull and should taper gradually as you work your way down the object. You can adjust the volume of influence (VOI) of each of the metaballs to help fill out the object, but make sure not to overuse the metaballs' VOI to define the overall shape. The more metaballs you have, the better control over the shape you will have. Switch to the Left and Front views as often as needed to assist in the placement of the metaballs. For a better view, you can open two smaller view windows.

10. Once the skull and upper jaw have been modeled, copy the object and mirror it. Rotate it into place and glue the two halves together.

11. Before you create the other metaball objects that will make up the other segments of the dragon, add a cube primitive to the scene. The cube has nothing to do with the model; we just need to select another object in the scene prior to adding a new metaball structure. Otherwise, any metaball primitives you create will be added to the selected object's metaball structure. You can delete the dummy cube later.

12. Model the lower jaw, neck, and throat as separate metaball structures (see Figure 3.26). Each can be modeled with just a few metaball spheres because these areas don't require a lot of

NOTE

Remember you have to model only one half of the dragon's skull. Once you are satisfied with the results, you can copy, mirror, and glue the two halves together.

NOTE

The dragon is modeled out of four distinct metaball objects. The reason for this is we can texture map each of the surfaces easily. Objects created from metaballs tend to have a very dense mesh, making such tools as Paint Faces impractical. Therefore, when modeling with metaballs, a little planning can save you some time when texture mapping such an object.

A trick I often use is I model the entire object as a whole. When I'm satisfied with the results, I make several copies of the metaball object. I then edit each, removing the metaball primitives that are not required for the particular segment I'm working on. I repeat the process with each of the copies. When done, I end up with a segment of my object created from metaballs. I can now texture map each separately and glue them together with nonvisible seams. Because each metaball affects its neighbor, this technique works only with objects that are created from many metaball primitives.

detail. You can texture map each by using different image maps and UV projection.

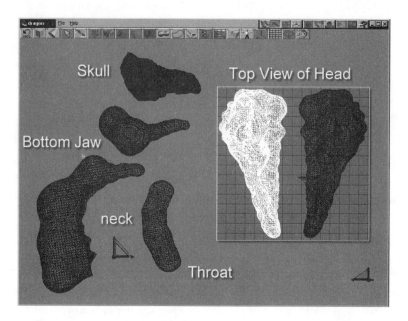

FIGURE 3.26   *An exploded view of our dragon.*

You will find the complete model of our dragon on the CD that accompanies this book. The file is chapters\chptr03\dragon.scn. I have also included a complete metaball structure of the dragon's head for you to mold into your own dragon.

Although these models were easy to construct, metaballs can be used to create complex objects. In the next chapter, "Character Modeling," you will use metaballs to model a pair of hands and the human form.

UNDERSTANDING NURBS

We have all seen or heard the acronym NURBS (Non-Uniform Rational B-Splines), but do you know what it means? What are NURBS, anyway? As a modeler, you're probably content just knowing the tool is available, but for those of you who are considering diving into Python scripting or writing your own plug-in, an introduction to what makes a NURBS surface is in order.

The good news is that the following discussion requires no prior understanding of the underlying mathematical theory for NURBS. In order of importance, let's look at each of the words that make up the acronym.

RATIONAL

The key characteristic of a NURBS curve is that its shape is determined (among other things) by the positions of its control points. The control points are joined with connecting lines whose shape or curve has a direct relationship to the weight of the control point.

These points have a four-dimensional representation (x, y, z, w). Why is a three-dimensional control point represented by four dimensions? The extra coordinate allows for the exact representation of conic curves (circles, parabolas, hyperbolas, and ellipses); basically it allows more control over the shape of these and other curves. The fourth coordinate, w, represents the weight of the control point. The control points carry a weight of 1.0, meaning that they all have equal influence on the shape of the curve. Increasing the weight of an individual control point gives it more influence, thus "pulling" the curve toward that point (pinching at the vertex). Curves that are defined with a weight coordinate w for each control point are called *rational* curves.

B-SPLINE

First off, what's a spline? A *spline* is nothing more than a curve. By combining several splines together, you can create a smooth surface called a *patch*.

There are five types of spline surfaces:

- **Linear:** Linear splines have flat surfaces. That is, the lines connecting the control points are flat.

- **Cardinal:** Cardinal splines pass through the control points, unlike linear splines, which meet at the control points. Each control point has only one tangent control.

- **Bézier:** This type of curve is probably the most widely used. The lines pass through each of the control points like Cardinal curves do, but each control point has two tangent controls. This allows the weight of the curve at the vertex to be adjusted from either side.

- **B-Spline:** In a B-Spline, the curve does not pass through its control points, called *knots*, but rather skirts them, making smooth curves. The drawback with this type of curve is the control points are a distance from the curve, making work with this type of spline difficult.

- **NURBS:** This type is like a B-Spline, except each of the control points has its own weight. Remember a curve with its own weight coordinate w is a rational curve and, in this case, a Rational B-Spline.

NON-UNIFORM

Because every control point has a weight, some control points can affect the shape of the curve more strongly than others. That's where the Non-Uniform comes from.

trueSpace NURBS aren't truly NURBS but are closer to some sort of surface-smoothing function. This isn't an issue because you can model anything with trueSpace NURBS.

MODELING WITH NURBS

With Caligari's implementation of NURBS, you can create a NURBS object by *converting* a polyhedron object. When an object is converted, the underlying geometry of the polyhedron becomes the *control mesh* of the NURBS object. The underlying control mesh can have any of the following operations applied to its surface:

- Sweep
- Weld
- Erase
- Lathe
- Any of the Point Edit tools
- Tip
- Bevel
- Slice
- Quad Divide
- Standalone Deformation
- Deform Object
- Sculpt

It can also be the operand of a Boolean operation. As an added bonus, all the vertex manipulations performed on the underlying control mesh can be keyframed. This tool is wonderful for creating smooth surfaces. Let's look at some of the features of the NURBS tool and the NURBS Option panel.

The NURBS button has two modes that relate to the selected object. If the selected object is a polyhedron, enabling the Create NURBS button converts the polyhedron to a NURBS object. Nonsolids cannot be converted to NURBS. If the current object is a NURBS object, you can switch between the NURBS representation and mesh by disabling the Create NURBS button.

To open the NURBS Option panel, right-click the NURBS Object button. The panel's four options are

- **Build:** This combo box has three settings for determining the level of interactivity. These settings control the construction of the NURBS surface and are active only when the control mesh is being edited (point, face, or vertex tools). Otherwise, these modes are inactive.

    On Move is the default mode, and it updates the screen as you manipulate the objects surface in real time.

    On Demand mode works great if you have a slow machine or the mesh has become too dense for real-time display to be reasonable. If your display is lagging behind, this option will eliminate real-time screen updates of the object surface.

    On Release mode updates the display only when the object has been moved and the mouse button is released. It gives good feedback without the dreaded lag time.

The next two options are extremely important and will determine the overall shape of the selected surfaces of your NURBS object.

- **Density:** Defines how dense the mesh will be; the range is from 0.1 to 1.0. This parameter influences the number of faces and vertices of the NURBS object. Figure 3.27 illustrates the influence Density has on your NURBS object. I always start with a setting of 0.3 and go from there. This isn't gospel; you will soon find what best works for you.

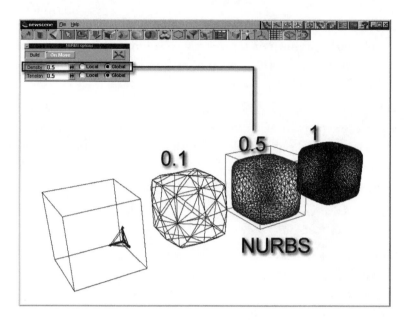

FIGURE 3.27   *Adjusting the density of the triangles and their effect on the NURBS surface.*

- **Tension:** Defines the surface attraction to the control point (weight); the range is from 0.1 to 1.0. The Tension setting doesn't influence the number of triangles of the surface, just the weight (pull) of the selected face, vertex, or point of underlying polyhedron on the NURBS surface. Figure 3.28 depicts the influence this parameter has on your NURBS object. Use less tension for a rounded surface.

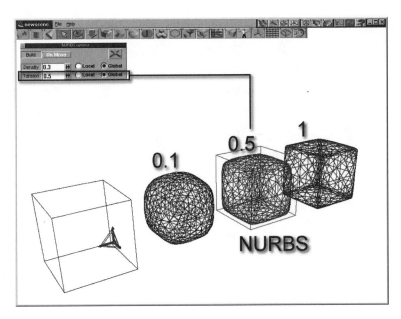

FIGURE 3.28 *Adjusting the tension of the underlying control mesh and its effect on the NURBS surface.*

- **Local/Global toggles:** Enables you to define whether a change in density or tension should affect the whole object (Global) or just the selected vertices (Local).

- **Destroy NURBS Object:** Destroys the control mesh and extracts the NURBS. A dialog box will appear asking you to either choose to keep the NURBS object or to revert to the control mesh. If you like what you created, click Yes. The control mesh will be removed, leaving the NURBS object behind. If you choose No, the control mesh will be left behind. If you applied operations, such as sweep, to any of the control mesh's surfaces, they will still be intact.

Before we start modeling something from NURBS, let's look at how the Tension setting and Point Edit tools can be used to shape and form a NURBS object.

1. Switch to the Perspective view and add a cube primitive to the scene.

2. Enable the NURBS Object button to create a smooth cube made up of triangles. The underlying polyhedron mesh is still

NOTE

Caligari extracts the NURBS when attempting to do a Boolean operation or sculpt the surface. You have to confirm this operation prior to extracting the NURBS surface and destroying the underlying polyhedron control mesh.

there; to view it simply disable the NURBS Object button. It is this underlying structure that you manipulated to create the NURBS object's shape.

3. If you haven't already done so, re-enable the NURBS Object button. Select the Point Edit button. This displays the NURBS surface and the underlying polyhedron, which I will call the control mesh from this point on.

4. Open the Point Edit panel. Enable the Point Edit Faces and Point Scale buttons. Select the top face of the control mesh. As you move the cursor over the control mesh, the nearest face's edges change color.

5. With one of the control mesh faces selected, open the NURBS Option panel. Set Tension to Local. To adjust the tension, either enter the desired value in the Tension entry field or select the small arrow button that sits right of the entry field. Move your mouse either left to decrease the value or right to increase it. Decrease the tension to 0. The NURBS mesh should look like a gumdrop.

6. Set Tension to Global and increase its value to 1. This squares off the NURBS mesh. Decrease Tension to 0. The NURBS mesh is now a round, putty-like shape.

7. Select the Sweep tool. Set Tension back to Local, and increase it to 1. Sweep the selected face again this time, leave the Tension at 1, and select the Bevel tool. Increase the bevel until it almost comes to a point.

Continue to experiment, add points with the Tip tool, and sweep and scale faces while adjusting the tension of the selected faces.

This exercise might seem a little lame at first, but it has three purposes. First, it introduces you to a new way of modeling. Second, exploration of the tool set is vital if mastering trueSpace is your goal. Third, it demonstrates the power of combining different tools in the modeling process.

Now that the preliminaries are out of the way, let's create an actual object with this new tool.

MODEL A SPORTS CAMERA BODY

I prefer SLRs, but you can't beat a sports camera for those fun, wet days. Let's try to make one. The model is relatively easy to construct and requires only a basic knowledge of how a sports camera should look (see Figure 3.29).

FIGURE 3.29   *Waterproof camera modeled with NURBS.*

1. Switch to the Top view and open the Object Info panel. Switch the World and Object fields to Milimtrs (millimeters).

2. To create the basic body of the camera, add a cube primitive to the scene. Scale the cube primitive to 1200 in the x-plane, 5050 in the y-plane, and 2000 in the z-plane fields.

3. Add another cube primitive to the scene and scale it to 1600 in the x-plane, 1900 in the y-plane, and 1600 in the z-plane fields. This will be the compartment that houses the lenses and mechanicals. Center this cube with the cube that represents the basic camera body. Place its right edge just inside the right edge of the larger cube. The left edge should stick out beyond the larger cube's left edge. Switch to the Left or Front view and be sure to center the smaller cube between the camera body's top and bottom edge. Switch back to the Top view.

4. To create the view finder, add a cube primitive to the scene and scale it to 1000 in the x-plane, 1200 in the y-plane, and 1000 in the z-plane fields. Center its left and right edges inside the camera body cube. Switch to the Left view, and place its bottom edge just below the top edge of the camera body.

5. No new camera makes it into today's marketplace without some sort of ergonomic feature, so let's add a nice rounded grip. Switch to the Top view. Add a cube primitive to the scene and scale it to 1700 in the x-plane, 1700 in the y-plane, and 1700 in the z-plane fields. Place it so that its top edge

NOTE

The Object Info panel has several fields for entering numeric values for object location, size, and rotation. These fields can also accept numeric expressions, as well as constant values. In the case where you would like to move an object to a new location along the x-axis, simply append a +25 or -25 to the value in the x-plane field.

sticks out of the top edge of the camera body. Center the cube's left and right edge with the left and right edge of the camera body. Switch to either the Left or Front view, and center the cubes within the left and right edges of the larger cube that represents the basic camera body.

6. Close the Object Info panel and Boolean union all the cube primitives together (see Figure 3.30).

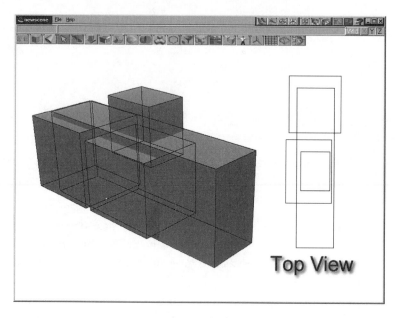

FIGURE 3.30 *Creating the basic shape of the NURBS sport camera from four cube primitives.*

7. Open the NURBS Option panel and set Density and Tension to Global with Density at 0.5 and Tension at 0.7. This should give you a nice smooth-looking camera body. We're not done yet. Although the camera body is smooth, it is still too blocky. We will round off specific areas by adjusting the tension of some of the faces.

8. Select the Point Edit context button. The underlying control mesh should now be superimposed on our NURBS surface. Open the Point Edit panel and enable the Point Edit Faces and Point Scale buttons.

9. Switch to the Perspective view. Select the front face of the camera where the lens will go. As you move your cursor over the control mesh, the faces your cursor is beneath will change color.

10. Extrude the surface by using the Sweep tool. Scale the selected face equally in all three planes to about half its present size. This operation tapers the front end of the lens housing. Remember, to scale equally, hold both the left and right mouse buttons simultaneously while dragging your mouse.

11. For the next step, we will round off the view finder. Set Tension to Local and select the top face of the view finder. Set Tension to 0.0.

12. The top edges of the camera body have a sharp look to them. To smooth them out, select both the top faces on each side of the view finder and use 0.0 for their Tension. Don't panic if the side closer to you rounds off dramatically; this is perfect for the shape we want.

13. We should smooth out the ergonomic grip we added earlier. Select the front face of the ergonomic grip, and set Tension to 0.0. This blends the grip into the camera body for a comfortable fit (see Figure 3.31).

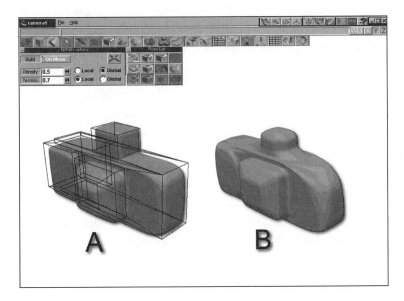

FIGURE 3.31 *By adjusting the control mesh's Tension setting, subtle curves can be achieved with the NURBS tool.*

14. You can continue to tweak the tension of the control mesh to your liking. When you are satisfied with the results, extract the mesh created from NURBS by selecting Destroy NURBS Object in the NURBS Option panel. You can now Boolean subtract out the view finder and an area for the lens. You can add a flash, add a strap, or texture map the camera. Be as creative as you want.

NOTE

The new NURBS surface inherits the dominant texture of the original. You can use the Paint Object, Paint Face, Paint Vertex, and Paint Over tools on a NURBS surface but not on the underlying Mesh.

15. Open the Object Info panel and switch the World and Object fields back to meters.

I have included the NURBS sports camera (NURBS mesh intact for your inspection) on the CD that accompanies this book. The file is named chapters\chptr03\camera1.scn.

NURBS modeling is an art form in itself. If you don't quite grasp it at first, don't give up. The learning curve *is* short. Practice forming the underlying structure from simple cube primitives as we did with the camera and tweak the faces of the NURBS object to create smooth surfaces.

MODELING AND MESH DENSITY

Modeling is one of the toughest skills to master in computer graphics. To do it correctly and, more importantly, to do it efficiently, takes a skilled artisan. It's easy to get carried away when modeling in trueSpace. To this day, I still find myself headed down that creative byway spending lots of time working out some little detail that only I will know is there. I usually snap out of it before I go too far.

Many newcomers to trueSpace, and 3D in general, have a misconception that the denser the mesh, the better the object will appear onscreen. This isn't true, and the object usually doesn't make it into the project because it is too complex and doesn't fit its role within the scope of the scene.

We are all guilty of creating objects that would bring a quad 200 megahertz Pentium Pro ALR to its knees. Let's look at this problem visually.

Load up the Camera.scn scene located in the Chptr03 folder on the CD that accompanies this book. When we created the sports camera with NURBS, we specified 0.5 for Density. Increase it to 1.0. At this setting, the mesh is too dense to be practical. Reset Density to 0.5 and gradually decrease it until the mesh becomes blocky. Looking at the camera in this blocky state may not seem like a good model at first, but it's just as good as the mesh with the higher density. The determining factor is its role in the scene in which it will be placed. If the camera will be sitting on a desk and will not have the focus at any time, then a low-poly-count model would be best. If the camera would eventually become the focus of the scene, then a mesh with a higher-poly count is probably best. This doesn't mean you should increase the mesh density dramatically—just to the point where the model looks its best with the fewest number of polygons.

SUMMARY

In this chapter, we discussed modeling with an assortment of tools and managed to create smooth organic shapes, metal objects, and fungi.

Modeling in trueSpace is an entertaining way to pass the time and can be very rewarding. You now have a solid foundation. With a little experimentation, you can build upon the rudimentary skills learned in this chapter to create complex objects that can be texture mapped and animated.

Join me in the next chapter where we will put these basic techniques to use creating characters in trueSpace4.

CHARACTER MODELING

by Frank Rivera

Character modeling is by no means a new art form. Michelangelo Buonarroti modeled The David *in the 15th century with nothing more than a few primitive tools and a colossal block of marble. Although 500 years have passed since the completion of* The David, *the approach to character modeling hasn't changed, just the tools.*

In this chapter, I will not focus on one method of modeling characters or theories on how to create a great character. The purpose of this chapter is to expose you to the tools and techniques that will enable you to create characters in trueSpace. All that is required are trueSpace's basic tool set and a little imagination. As you will soon see, a complex character can be sculpted from a single-cylinder primitive.

The following lessons are divided into character segments; for example, the lesson on building the Cybernetic Marine is broken up into modeling the head, arms, legs, and torso. I feel this method is an ideal way to illustrate just how easy it is to create characters in trueSpace by breaking up larger projects into manageable chunks. You will begin with a simple character and slowly build toward the more complex models. There is a lot to cover, so let's get started.

In this chapter, you will learn how to model

- A simple segmented character

- Hands

- A superhero from spheres

- The human form with metaballs

- A cybernetic character from simple primitives

- The female form from a single-cylinder primitive

MODELING FRANKENSTEIN'S MONSTER

Well, not quite. The character you will model is not the classic horror monster, but Franky, his teenage son who loves to skateboard. Take a look at Figure 4.1.

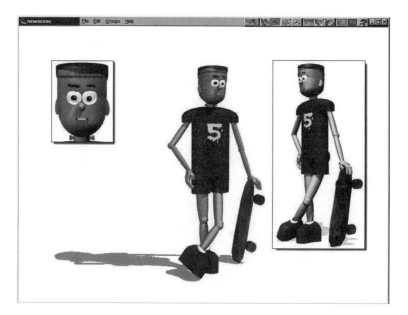

FIGURE 4.1 *Franky, the skateboarding terror.*

A character like Franky can be modeled in just a few minutes by using nothing more than a few cylinders and spheres, and he is easy to animate.

CREATE THE HEAD

The first step is to make the little skateboarding terror's head. The head is nothing more than a cylinder and two spheres.

1. Create a new scene and set the main view to Front.

2. Add a sphere and a cylinder primitive to the scene.

3. Disable the x- and z-axis buttons in the Coords panel. This will enable you to move the object along the y-axis with confidence and precision.

4. Select the cylinder and place its bottom edge at the center of the sphere.

5. Create another sphere and align its center with the top of the cylinder. Please note that you should feel free to rotate, zoom, or move your point of view with any of the Eye tools (Eye Move, Eye Rotate, or Zoom) to align any of the object segments.

6. Select the Scale tool and scale the selected sphere along the y-axis until it barely sticks above the cylinder. This will give the top of the skull a flat but natural look, as illustrated in Figure 4.2.

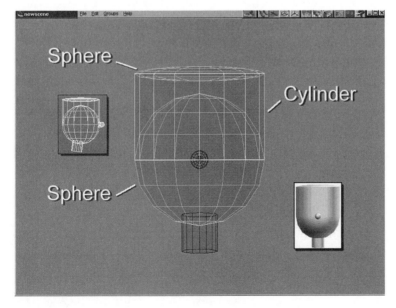

FIGURE 4.2 *Modeling the head with a sphere and cylinder.*

7. To create the neck, add another cylinder to the scene and scale it equally along all three axes to the desired size.

8. The eyes and ears are nothing more than two pairs of spheres. Scale them along their x-axis, rotate them, and place them into position.

9. To create the nose, Select the Glue As Sibling tool and glue the two spheres and cylinder together that make up the head. Copy the object and scale it down to nose size. Rotate it into position and the head is done.

MODEL THE TORSO

Modeling this character's torso involves two spheres, a cylinder, any one of the Glue tools, and a little Boolean magic.

1. Open a new scene and switch to the Front view.

2. Add a cylinder and sphere to the scene.

3. Move the center of the sphere to the top of the cylinder. Glue the cylinder to the newly created sphere with the Glue As Sibling tool. This sphere will become the character's shoulders.

4. From the Left view, scale the object along the x-axis to half its default width.

5. Navigate down the object's hierarchy with the Object Navigation tool. When the sphere is selected, detach it from the hierarchy with the Unglue tool. See Figure 4.3.

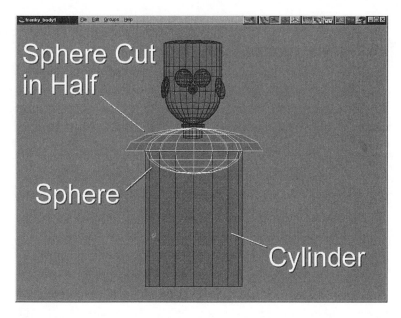

FIGURE 4.3 *Modeling the torso from two spheres and a cylinder.*

6. Add a cube primitive to the scene. Scale the cube primitive equally along all three axes until the cube is larger than the sphere.

7. Move the top of the cube to the center of the sphere in the current view.

8. Boolean subtract the cube from the sphere by first selecting the sphere and enabling the Object Subtraction tool. Your cursor will change to a glue bottle indicating that the Object Subtraction tool has been activated. Select the cube primitive to complete the operation.

9. From the Front view, scale what is left of the sphere along the x-axis just enough to fit a pair of arms under each shoulder.

CREATE THE ARMS

We are moving along nicely; we've managed to create the character's head and his torso. How does the song go? The head mesh is connected to neck mesh, the neck mesh is connected to the chest mesh...

1. Open the Object Info panel. Create a sphere and scale it along all three axes until the sphere is about 0.30 along the x- and y-axes and 1.50 along the z-axis. The sphere should be about half the length of the torso. Place the sphere where the character's biceps should be.

2. Add another sphere to the scene, scale it equally along all three axes until its equator is no larger than the diameter of the newly created biceps, and align its bottom edge with that of the biceps. This will be the character's elbow.

3. Glue the biceps to the elbow with the Glue As Sibling tool and copy the object. Rotate the copy clockwise until the two smaller spheres are aligned with each other. The copy will be the character's forearm. Having the two smaller spheres overlap each other eliminates visible seams during animation.

4. If everything looks good in all three views, glue the forearm to the bicep. This is now one of the character's arms. Copy it and move the copy under the other shoulder. When placing the arms, place them so that they look proportionately correct. You can Boolean subtract any visible parts that stick out from the shoulders later. Take a peek at Figure 4.4 if you need a visual guide.

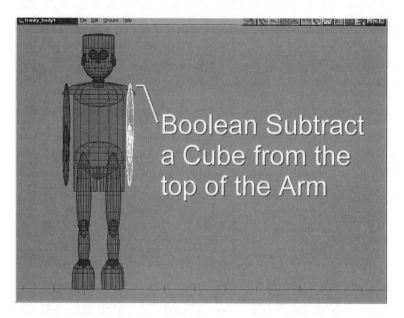

FIGURE 4.4   *Remove the pointed ends from the arms with a little Boolean magic. The legs are created in the same way as the arms.*

MODEL THE LEGS

The legs are created from four spheres just like the arms; repeat the preceding steps, converting the biceps to the thighs and the forearms to the character's calves. Keep in mind that legs have more mass than arms. Don't model them exactly as you did the arms—make them beefier. If you prefer, copy one of the arms and scale it up to size.

CREATE THE FEET

To create the character's feet, you will cut a sphere in half with a Boolean operation and extrude it to the desired shape.

1. Add a sphere and cube to the scene.

2. Scale the cube along all three axes until it encompasses the sphere. Check all views to ensure complete coverage. Move the top of the cube to the center of the sphere and Boolean subtract the cube from the sphere.

3. Change to the Perspective view, and select Eye Rotate located on the title bar. Rotate the scene so that the newly created flat end of the sphere is visible (selectable).

4. Select the Point Edit tool and move the cursor over the flat area of the sphere until the flat face becomes selected (its edges will change color). Figure 4.5 illustrates this change.

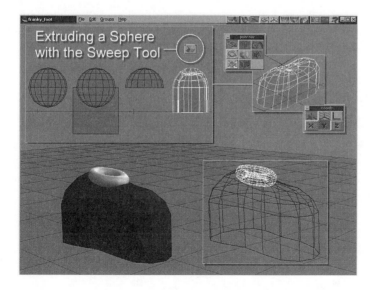

FIGURE 4.5   *Creating the character's foot with a sphere, a little Boolean magic, and the Sweep tool.*

NOTE

If the Sweep tool is used on an object that has been texture mapped, the newly created faces may have to have the appropriate UV projection applied to these areas to avoid possible texture smearing.

5. Extrude the selected area with the Sweep tool. Switch to the Left view and continue pulling the extruded surface along the y-axis until it reaches an appropriate thickness for chunky Frankenstein shoes.

6. Move the shoe under the character's leg. Add a torus primitive to the scene and place it about ankle height. Scale the torus to fit around the character's ankle and glue it to the shoe. Copy and mirror the shoe, and then place the copy under the other leg.

You will find the complete model of Franky on the CD that accompanies this book. The file is named chapters\chptr04\Franky.scn.

You may have noticed that I did not cover how the hands were created. That's because hands are such an important part of character creation that I think we should look at several methods of modeling them.

Modeling Hands

For a character animator, the ability to model hands is important. Not only do they enable your characters to manipulate other objects, they are also a great tool for communicating an action or feeling to the viewer. To better illustrate this fact, look at Figure 4.6. At first, the character appears to be speaking, but add a pair of hands and the expression takes on a new meaning.

The Simple Method

I have included Figure 4.6's simple set of hands on the CD that accompanies this book. The file is called chapters\chptr04\SmplHnds.scn. It's a great scene for working out gestures by using only eyes and hands to communicate. Try enlarging the pupils for a terrified look. With a little experimentation, you can portray just about any gesture you can think of.

FIGURE 4.6 *At first, this simple character appears to be calmly speaking. Add a pair of hands, and the message he conveys changes dramatically.*

Although hands are complex structures, a general-purpose set can be modeled by using simple primitives. It isn't as tough as it seems; look at the exploded view of a simple hand in Figure 4.7. The fingers are composed of two cylinders. Each cylinder segment has a sphere at each end to accommodate the rolling of the joints without any visible seams. The palm is nothing more than a flattened sphere. This isn't new ground we are covering here. This example was created in much the same way Franky was. Primitives glued together is the simplest method of constructing complex objects.

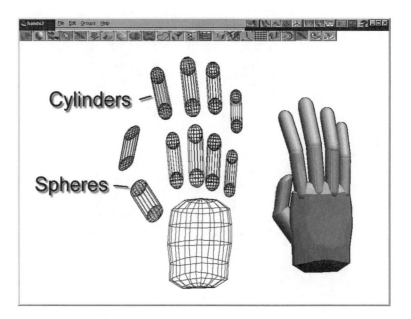

FIGURE 4.7   *This is a very simple model. Each finger has only two segments.*

THE METABALLS METHOD

Although simple, puppet-like hands are useful in many situations, some projects require more realistic models. To create these, metaballs are the tool of choice. To begin the challenging and rewarding task of modeling a realistic hand, examine your own hands.

Hands are made up of five fingers or fourteen segments. From the index finger to the pinky, each of the four fingers has three segments. The thumb has two that are visible. You will use this blueprint to create the basic shape from metaballs and then use Alain Bellon's ThermoClay (Quantum Impulse) plug-in to smooth out the surfaces.

Modeling with tS4's metaballs is similar to modeling an object from basic primitives, except you use the five special metaball primitives. I will refer to these metaball building blocks as *meta-primitives*, a term coined by E.W. Swan.

Before working with metaballs, get to know the Metaball Options panel. Objects created from metaballs have a high-polygon count, which can cause the display to lag behind your cursor's movements when positioning the meta-primitives. To combat this, Caligari has provided the Metaball Options panel. To access this panel, right-click the Metaball button. You can use the available options to tweak the mesh density to a reasonable number to allow smooth meta-primitive placement without the awful lag time. (For more detailed info on the Metaball Options panel, please review Chapter 3.)

ASSEMBLE THE FINGERS

The best way to understand metaballs is to see them in action.

1. Begin by opening a new scene and switching to the Top view. Open the Metaball Edit panel.

2. Add a rounded cube to the scene. Scale the rounded cube along the y-axis to about one and a half times its default length. This will act as the palm of the hand. I'm going to model the left hand because I can hold it out in front of me while I use the mouse to build the object.

3. Starting from the left, create the pinky by adding a rounded cylinder. Rotate the rounded cylinder 90 degrees from its original position along the x-axis. Scale it along the y-axis to twice its original height, and place it to the left of the palm. Adjust the rounded cylinder so that its center is lined up with the top of the palm. This is segment one of the pinky.

4. While the first segment of the pinky is selected, add another rounded cylinder to the scene; this will create a rounded cylinder of the same shape, rotation, and scale. The new cylinder is segment two. Scale it along the y-axis to half its present size. Place its bottom at the top of the first segment and add another rounded cylinder to the scene. Again, the newly created cylinder inherits the shape of the previous rounded cylinder (segment two). Place its bottom edge at the top edge of the second segment.

To create the other fingers, you can repeat steps 3 and 4, but before you do you will have to adjust the Volume of Influence setting of the second and third segments on each of the fingers. (For more details on using the Metaball Volume of Influence option, please review Chapter 3.) If you don't, each of the fingers will influence its neighbors, creating a hand that looks like candlesticks melted together. To avoid this, set each of the fingers' second and third segments' Volume of Influence as tight as possible to the metaball's mesh.

NOTE

You can select the Object tool at any time to close the Metaball panel and display the overall metaball object's shape. When you're done viewing your creation, reopen the Metaball panel and select one of the Move, Rotate, or Scale buttons to continue where you left off.

Objects created with metaballs tend to have a blocky polygonal look to them unless you render at a very high resolution. Raising the resolution, however, increases the number of polygons, which tends to make the object difficult to animate or shape. If the hands aren't going to be viewed up close, you can probably reduce the render resolution of the metaballs without fear of their blocky nature becoming noticeable.

If your hands will be viewed up close, there is an alternative to the resolution solution. You can use ThermoClay to smooth out the hands' surfaces. ThermoClay is a simple-to-use spline interpolation program that can smooth just about any object, even those with holes. Simply put, ThermoClay conserves areas with a lot of detail by maintaining their main shape, while smoothing areas of less detail. Here's how to use ThermoClay and metaballs to create realistic-looking hands for your characters.

1. Convert the metaball object to a polyhedron. This is important because ThermoClay processes only one object at a time. Because a metaball object is made up of meta-primitives, the object must be converted to a single object. (Objects that consist of many subobjects glued together in a hierarchy must be converted to a single object, as well.) To convert the metaball object to a polyhedron, select the Object tool to close the Metaball panel, and then select the Deform Object tool. A dialog box will appear; answer Yes to Perform the Conversion.

2. Open the ThermoClay plug-in. If you have not installed this terrific plug-in, please refer to the readme.txt file on the CD that accompanies this book. The ThermoClay files are located in the plug-ins\Quantum folder.

3. Set the Number of Passes to a Tension of 0%. Deselect the Subdivide option; you don't want to increase the object's polygon count. Melt the object by pressing the Melt button and repeat as often as needed. I prefer to view the progress on each pass so I choose to do one pass at a time. Figure 4.8 shows some sample results.

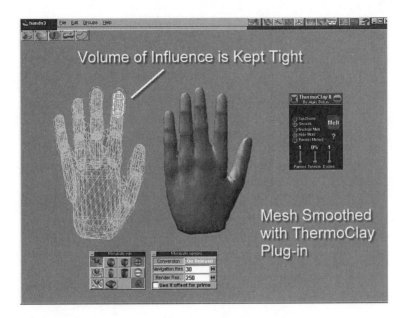

FIGURE 4.8   *Creating realistic hands is easy with a few meta-primitives and a little help from ThermoClay.*

THE NURBS METHOD

You have modeled simple hands by using primitives glued together in a hierarchy and modeled realistic hands with metaballs and ThermoClay. Now try a third method: NURBS.

NURBS gives you two options. You can combine primitives by using Booleans, and then convert the results into a NURBS object. This method isn't very good for up-close shots, however, because it leaves visible seams (see Figure 4.9). Alternatively, you can model the hands from a single cube primitive and convert the finished shape to a NURBS object. The latter yields a better result, so I'll focus on this method.

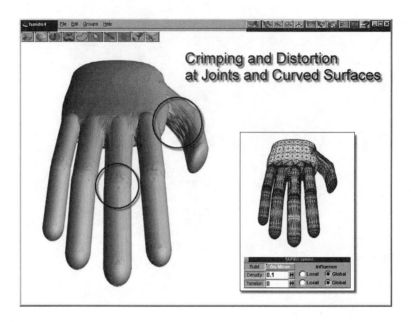

FIGURE 4.9 *Creating hands from segmented objects "Booleaned" together and converted to NURBS creates a crimping effect at the joints. NURBS look better when created from solid objects.*

NOTE

By right-clicking any of the primitive buttons, you can define the resolution of the next primitive of that type that you add to your scene.

Modeling a hand from a cube primitive requires no more work than compiling a hand from a bunch of separate objects glued together.

1. Open a new scene and switch to the Front view.

2. Add a cube primitive to the scene and quad divide it twice.

3. Add another cube primitive to the scene. Place its top edge exactly at the bottom of the first segment from the top of the quad-divided cube as shown in panel A of Figure 4.10.

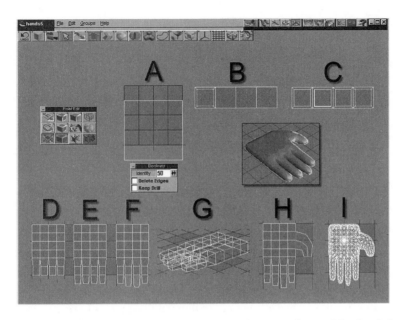

FIGURE 4.10   *Modeling hands from a single cube requires fewer steps than modeling hands from many objects glued together.*

4. Right-click the Boolean tool to open the Boolean panel; uncheck Delete Edges. Boolean subtract the cube from the quad-divided cube. This should leave you with a cube with four segments along the x-axis as depicted in panel B of Figure 4.10.

5. Open the Point Edit panel and select Point Edit Faces.

6. Select the face on the left and apply Sweep to the selected surface.

7. Enable the Point Scale button and reselect the left face. Scale the selected face just a bit equally along the x-, y-, and z-axes, as depicted in panel B of Figure 4.10. Select the next face, sweep it, and scale it in the same manner as you did the first. Repeat the same actions for each of the four fingers.

8. Select each of the inner faces and sweep each twice. Panel E of Figure 4.10 illustrates the result.

NOTE

You can scale any object equally along all three axes by holding the left and right buttons simultaneously while dragging your mouse. Remember to enable the x-, y-, and z-axis buttons.

NOTE

Remember in Chapter 3 that I mentioned you can select multiple faces, edges, or vertices by simply reselecting additional faces with the appropriate Point Edit tool.

9. Select each of the faces at the end of the fingers and scale each just a bit equally along the x-, y-, and z-axes as you did the first time around. You should now have four fingers, but they are all the same length. We can fix that by reselecting the faces at each fingertip and then switching to the Top view and pulling each along the y-axis until the fingers of the hand look proportionally correct in length. Use panel F of Figure 4.10 as a guide.

10. To create the thumb, switch to the Perspective view and rotate the scene as depicted in panel G of Figure 4.10. From the right side of the object, select the second face from the rear. Press and hold the Ctrl key and select the third face. Switch to the Top view and sweep the selected faces.

11. Enable the Point Rotate button and rotate the selected faces clockwise about 20 degrees. Sweep the selected faces again and rotate them at their new position another 30 degrees as illustrated in panel H of Figure 4.10.

12. Select the NURBS Object tool to complete the operation.

You can tweak the surface with the Point Edit tool by reselecting the NURBS tool to see the underlying mesh. When done, simply reactivate the NURBS button to view the changes.

You can find a NURBS hand model on the CD that accompanies this book. The name of the file is chapters\chptr04\NurbHnd.scn.

Working with NURBS is kind of like putting up a tent from the inside. In Chapter 3, we managed to build a sports camera with NURBS by constructing the basic framework and using the tension of the underlying structures to form the finished shape. In this exercise, we used a brute-force method of getting the shape we wanted. The method you use is totally up to you; what is important is that you are aware of the different types of objects that can be modeled with NURBS.

MODELING A SUPERHERO FROM SPHERES

We began this chapter by exploring how to create a simple cute character by using the glued primitive method, but is this technique good for anything else? You bet it is. The method isn't limited to 98-pound weaklings like Franky; you can model a superhero character from nothing more than a bunch of sphere primitives (see Figure 4.11).

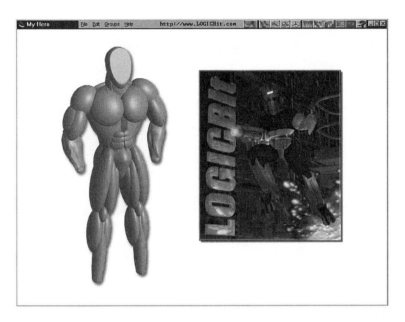

FIGURE 4.11 *The human form can be modeled with nothing more than spheres.*

This tutorial is an important step in your journey to becoming a proficient character modeler in trueSpace. It will focus on how primitives—in this case, sphere primitives—are used to create larger objects that are more complex. Secondly, and I can't stress this enough, it's a perfect way of learning how to visualize organic object construction. Frankly, if you can model organic, you can model anything.

Bipedal or quadruped organic objects can be modeled with spheres. After all, these types of organic objects are nothing but bags of water, which lend themselves to sphere modeling.

You can group spheres and Boolean them together to make complex muscle masses. You can then animate the organic in tS4 with Bones, Inverse Kinematics, or Forward Kinematics—but that's a story for Chapter 10, "Character Animation."

When modeling the human form, I recommend keeping a good book on the subject close for help. If you can't get hold of one, a comic book with images of over-exaggerated muscle-bound heroes will do fine. I used a *Captain America* comic book as my guide to the male human form.

MODEL THE CHEST

Can you make out all the spheres in Figure 4.11? The torso is the toughest object to build and is as good a place to start as any.

1. Open a new scene and switch to the Front view.

2. Add a sphere primitive and use Smooth Quad Divide on the sphere once. If the sphere primitive's default settings have been changed, please reset them to a latitude of 8 and longitude of 16. You can verify these settings by right-clicking the Add Sphere button to open the Sphere panel.

3. Open the Deformation Nav panel and enable the Stretch and Deform Perpendicular to z-axis buttons. Only one cross section will be visible, identified by the color green. One cross section isn't enough to sculpt the sphere into the shape desired, so press the right mouse button and, while dragging the mouse, add seven visible cross sections. (I say visible because the top and bottom of the object also have cross sections; they just aren't visible. You can select either by clicking in their general area.) You should have three cross sections above the center, a center cross section, and three below that.

4. Sculpt the sphere into an upside-down teardrop shape by selecting each cross section and scaling (stretching) it along the x-axis. Repeat the same actions in the Left view. When you are satisfied with the result, select the Object tool; this will close the Deformation Nav panel and complete the deformation operation.

5. The human form is narrower when viewed from the side than from the front. From the Left view, scale the object along the x-axis until the teardrop shape resembles an egg (see Figure 4.12).

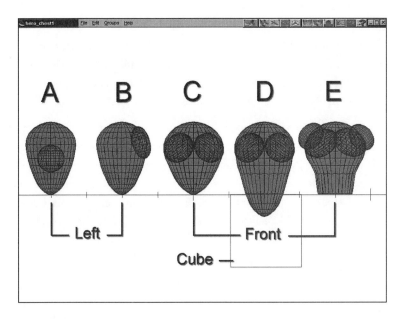

FIGURE 4.12   *Sculpting a sphere into an upside-down teardrop shape with the Deformation tool.*

6. From the Left view, add a sphere to the scene and apply Smooth Quad Divide to the sphere once. Reduce the sphere's size until it covers the four center segments of the egg-shaped object. Panel A of Figure 4.12 illustrates this.

7. Scale the sphere along the x-axis, decrease its width by about 25%, and increase its length by the same amount. Rotate the sphere so that the top is just left of its center. Move the sphere to the right side of the egg-shaped object and position it so that each of the sphere's poles come in contact with the egg-shaped object's right edge. See panel B of Figure 4.12.

8. Switch to the Front view; the sphere should be located in the center of the egg-shaped object. Move the sphere so that the left edges of both objects line up with one another. Enable the Rotate Object tool and use the right mouse button to rotate the sphere clockwise about halfway between its present position and one quarter of a turn, between 1 and 2 o'clock.

9. Line up the sphere's right edge with the egg-shaped object's center. Copy the sphere once and mirror it. You will have one sphere on top of the other, except the mirrored copy will be rotated in the opposite direction, somewhere between 10 and 11 o'clock. Line up the mirrored sphere's left edge with the egg-shaped object's center. See panel C of Figure 4.12.

10. From the Front view, select the egg-shaped object. Open the Deformation Nav panel. Select the Deform Perpendicular to the z-axis button and press the Delete key on your keyboard. This will erase any previously defined cross sections. Reopen the Deformation Nav panel and enable the Deform Perpendicular to the z-axis button and the Pull/Push button.

11. Add five visible cross sections—one cross section in the center and two above and below. Click the bottom of the object to select the cross section at the object's south pole. Pull the cross section down along the y-axis until the egg shape looks more like a top. Grab the first visible cross section and pull it down along the y-axis until the top shape returns to an egg shape. You can use panel D of Figure 4.12 as a guide. Select the Object tool; this will close the Deformation Nav panel and complete the operation.

12. Add a cube primitive to the scene and position the top edge just above the lower four segments of the egg-shaped object. Boolean subtract the cube from the egg-shaped object. What you are left with is the basic shape of the torso as depicted in panel E of Figure 4.12.

13. For the shoulders, add a sphere to the scene and quad divide it once. Scale the sphere along the x-axis just a bit. Rotate the sphere counterclockwise so that the top is just right of its center and place it on the right side of the torso just above the pectoral muscles. Copy the sphere and mirror it. Move the copy to the other side of the torso as illustrated in panel E of Figure 4.12. All there is left to do is add some abdomen muscles, a task I will leave up to you. I would have to suggest that you grab some comic books as a reference to the human form. If all you need are some visuals of the human anatomy, you can't beat the price. Art books on the human form are also a great guide, but the books can be expensive. If you're worried about being seen at your local bookstore thumbing through comic books, don't be. Most comic book collectors are adults. I also use plastic toy figures for modeling references. Can you think of a better excuse to go to the toy store? Hey, I'm doing research here!

Modeling the human form can be tricky. The curves that define our shape are subtle. You will develop an eye for creating these types of shapes with a little practice. Don't get discouraged if the torso looks like balloon art; moving the objects slightly so that they flow into one another is usually all that is needed.

MODEL THE ARMS

To create the upper arm, you will need three spheres for the biceps, one sphere for the elbow, and a sphere for the forearm. Alternatively, you can scale the torso (teardrop shape) to size, which works out nicely in place of the forearm. Start by creating the muscle mass that makes up the biceps.

1. Add three sphere primitives to a new scene and switch to the Front view. Stack each sphere one on top of the other and apply Smooth Quad Divide to each once.

2. Scale each of the spheres along the x-axis to half its original width. Fan the three spheres out slightly and elongate the center sphere a bit larger than the other two along the y-axis.

3. In the Left view, rotate the center sphere slightly so that its top is left of its center (leaning to the left). Position the bottom to about the location where the other two spheres' center line is. In other words, the bottom of all three spheres should overlap. Glue all three spheres as siblings to one another. This will be the character's biceps.

4. To model the forearm, add a new sphere to the scene. Scale it along the x-axis until it is about the width of the biceps. Scale the selected sphere along the y-axis until it is roughly twice its original height.

5. Open the Deformation Nav panel and enable the Deformation Perpendicular to z-axis button. Using the right mouse button, add three cross sections. Grab the bottom cross section and scale it inward to give the sphere a tapered look. Do the same in the Left view. To give the forearm a look of strength, you can use the Object Deformation tools, Surface Sculpt, or the Point Edit tools to pull at the surface to remove the smooth shape of the sphere. You may remember doing this in Chapter 3 when we created the landscape. The arm is illustrated in Figure 4.13.

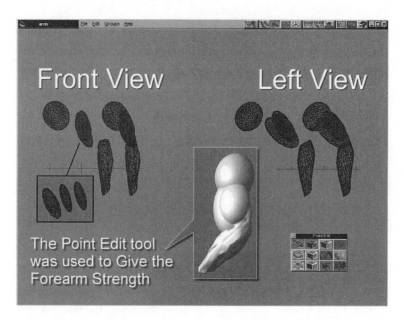

FIGURE 4.13   *The biceps, forearm, and shoulder are modeled from spheres.*

6. To create the shoulder, switch to the Front view and add a new sphere to the scene. Next, flatten the sphere a bit by scaling it along the y-axis. Rotate it clockwise so that its left side is higher than its right. This will act as the character's shoulder muscle.

MODEL THE LEGS

One of the superhero's legs can be fashioned from seven spheres—three for the thigh, one for the kneecap, two for the calf, and one for the shin. Start with the thigh.

1. Load a new scene and switch to the Front view.

2. Add three spheres to the scene. I will refer to these as the outer thigh, the center thigh, and the inner thigh. If you are pressed for time, you can use a copy of the biceps you created earlier and scale it to the desired size.

3. Glue all the spheres together and scale them along the x-axis to about half their original width.

4. Scale the spheres along the y-axis to a size one and a half their original height.

5. Unglue the spheres and spread each alongside one another along the x-axis.

6. The first sphere from the left will be the outer thigh of the left leg. Select the outer thigh, and scale it along the y-axis slightly larger than the other two spheres. You can use Figure 4.14 as a guide.

7. Select the inner thigh (the first sphere from the right), and scale it a tad smaller than the center sphere along the y-axis.

8. Select the center thigh and scale its width a little smaller than its cousins along the x-axis.

9. Switch to the Left view and select the outer thigh. Rotate the outer thigh along its z-axis about 10 degrees. Select the inner thigh and do the same.

10. Switch to the Front view, and, working with the x-axis only, place the outer thigh's right edge at the center of the center thigh. Place the inner thigh's left edge in the center of the center thigh. Figure 4.14 illustrates the final result.

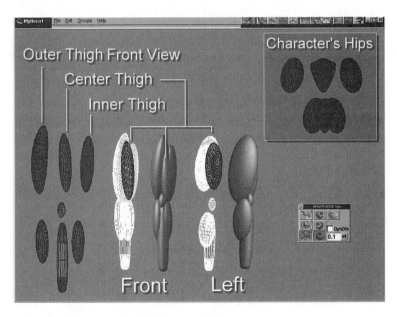

FIGURE 4.14   *An exploded view of the character's left leg.*

11. To create the character's shin, copy the center thigh and scale it along the y-axis to about the height of the outer thigh modeled earlier. Boolean subtract a cube primitive from the top and bottom of the sphere and apply Quad Divide to it. Move the top of the sphere to the bottom of the center thigh.

12. To create the kneecap, add a sphere to the scene and scale it equally along all three axes to about one sixth the size of the shin and move it into position.

13. Creating the calf muscles is a cinch. From the Front view, make another copy of the center thigh and scale it to half its original size along the y-axis. Line up its top edge with the shin's and place its right edge at the shin's center. Copy the sphere and place its left edge at the shin's center.

14. To create the character's hips and buttocks, add three spheres to the scene. Place two of the spheres alongside one another with just their edges overlapping. This will become your character's buttocks. Place the other sphere's center where the two buttocks meet. Reshape the center sphere into an upside-down teardrop, as you did to create the Superhero's chest. Glue all three of the objects together and scale along all three axes until you reach the right proportions.

You will find the complete Superhero model on the CD that accompanies this book. The filename is chapters\chptr04\MyHero.scn.

This short exercise demonstrated how a superhero can be modeled from simple sphere primitives. In this case, the seams actually enhance the muscular look of our hero. This isn't always the case, though, so we will look at some other methods of creating humanoid characters.

MODELING THE HUMAN FORM WITH METABALLS

NOTE

I have placed a black silhouette in the upcoming figures to help you visualize the shapes being formed with the metaball primitives.

You have probably all heard the hype. Seamless characters can be modeled with metaballs, but you probably never saw one created in trueSpace. Well I'm going to let you in on a little secret: You, too, can model seamless characters in trueSpace by using metaballs (see Figure 4.15).

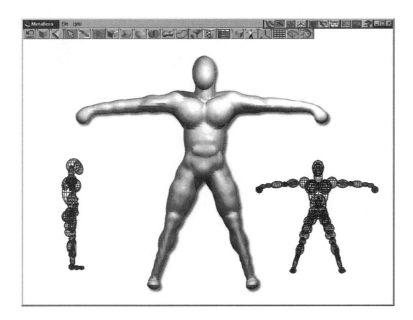

FIGURE 4.15 *Modeling the male form with metaballs.*

Modeling the human form by using metaballs is a tough nut to crack if you have never modeled the human form before, but it's not impossible. The only prerequisite is you must be patient.

SHAPE THE TORSO

Caligari's implementation of metaballs is simple yet effective. Modeling the human form from metaballs is no different than modeling with spheres. Let's take a look.

> **NOTE**
>
> Before tackling this project, you may want to review "Modeling with Metaballs" in Chapter 3.

1. Open a new scene and switch to the Front view.

2. Open the Metaball Options panel and set Conversion to On Demand. This will let you view the underlying metaball structure. Set Navigation Res to 25. Set the Render Res to 120. Disable the Use X Offset for Prims option. This will render the metaball object with a clean, tight, smooth look. Disable the Use X Offset for Prims option.

3. Open the Metaball Edit panel and add a metaball sphere primitive to the scene. Open the Object Info panel via a right-click of the Object Tool button.

4. For this character, I will begin with the upper torso. Scale the metaball sphere primitive to 5.313 in the x-axis field, 3.933 in the y-axis field, and 6.727 in the z-axis field. Panel B of figure 4.16 illustrates the desired shape.

5. To create the character's pectoral muscles, add a new metaball sphere primitive to the structure. The newly added sphere will inherit the shape, rotation, and location of the previously selected metaball primitive. Scale the sphere to 3.587 in the x-axis field, 2.479 in the y-axis field, and 3.587 in the z-axis field. Place the sphere so that it covers the larger sphere's upper quadrant as depicted in panel A of Figure 4.16.

6. Add another sphere to the structure and place it in the upper right quadrant of the larger sphere.

7. Add a new sphere to the structure and scale it to 2.779 in the x-axis field, 2.874 in the y-axis field, and 4.789 in the z-axis field. This will be one half of your character's abdomen. Align its center with the bottom edge of the larger sphere. Align the left edges of the new sphere with that of the larger one as illustrated in panel C of Figure 4.16.

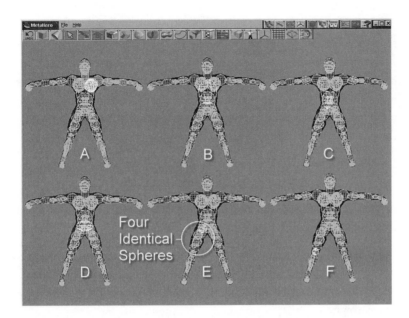

FIGURE 4.16   *Creating the human form with metaball sphere primitives.*

8. Add another sphere to the structure and align the new sphere primitive's right edge with the right edge of the larger sphere.

9. To create the waist, add a sphere to the scene and scale it to 4.930 in the x-axis field, 1.619 in the y-axis field, and 2.903 in the z-axis field.

MODEL THE LEGS

To model the legs, we will start with the buttocks. After all, that's where the legs start.

1. Add a sphere to your metaball structure. Scale it to 2.617 in the x-axis field, 3.383 in the y-axis field, and 3.218 in the z-axis field.

2. Every object has a center of gravity. In the case of the human form, it's around our waist area. To create the sphere that will become our character's center of gravity, add a sphere primitive to the scene and scale it to 4.930 in the x-axis field, 1.619 in the y-axis field, and 2.903 in the z-axis field. Place the sphere so its center line (running horizontally) rests just above the newly created buttocks.

3. The thigh is constructed from five individual metaball sphere primitives, four of which are the same size as depicted in panel E of Figure 4.16. Add a new sphere to the structure, and scale it to 2.542 in the x-axis field, 2.542 in the y-axis field, and 2.542 in the z-axis field. Place its upper half over the lower half of the sphere used for the waist. Moving outward from the object's center, add three more spheres, aligning each sphere's top edge with the previous one's bottom edge.

4. For the knee, add a sphere and scale it to 1.138 in the x-axis field, 0.316 in the y-axis field, and 0.922 in the z-axis field.

5. For the calf, add a sphere and scale it to 2.138 in the x-axis field, 2.160 in the y-axis field, and 3.584 in the z-axis field.

6. For the shin, add a rounded cylinder to the structure and scale it to 1.112 in the x-axis field, 1.411 in the y-axis field, and 5.662 in the z-axis field. Rotate it out from the body in line with the spheres that make up the character's thigh.

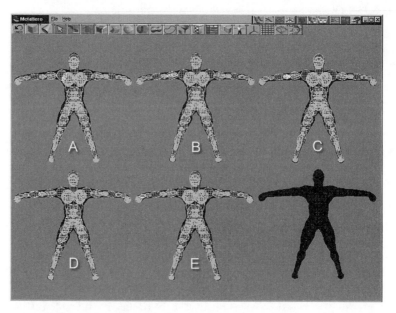

Figure 4.17 *Modeling the arm of a human character with metaballs.*

7. To create the other leg, disable the y-axis button in the Coords panel. Select each of the spheres that make up the leg, and, starting with the buttocks, work your way down. As you select each of the spheres, add another sphere

to the structure. The new sphere will inherit the scale and rotation of the previously selected primitive, so all you have to do is move the new primitive along its x-axis into position to form the other leg. With the y-axis button disabled, you can position each primitive with precision. Here is a quick way to rotate the spheres so they line up correctly: As you move each sphere into position, add a minus sign in front of the number located in the y-axis Rotate field. This will mirror the rotation of the spheres along their y-axis.

MODEL THE ARMS

Time to move on to the shoulders and arms.

1. To create the shoulder, add a new sphere to the metaball structure and scale it to 3.029 in the x-axis field, 3.155 in the y-axis field, and 3.060 in the z-axis field. Panel A of Figure 4.17 depicts its placement.

2. The biceps are constructed of two metaball sphere primitives. To create a bicep, add a new sphere to the structure and scale it to 3.341 in the x-axis field, 3.155 in the y-axis field, and 2.292 in the z-axis field. Align its right edge with the left edge of the shoulder. Add another sphere, but this time scale it to 3.151 in the x-axis field, 1.686 in the y-axis field, and 1.032 in the z-axis field. Center the new sphere with the previous one as illustrated in panel B of Figure 4.17.

3. For the elbow, add a sphere to the structure and scale it to 1.077 in the x-axis field, 0.901 in the y-axis field, and 0.884 in the z-axis field as illustrated in panel C of Figure 4.17.

4. The forearm depicted in panel D of Figure 4.17 is a sphere scaled to 3.481 in the x-axis field, 2.043 in the y-axis field, and 1.783 in the z-axis field. Align its right edge with the left edge of the bicep spheres.

5. The lower forearm and wrist are two spheres scaled to 1.846 in the x-axis field, 1.326 in the y-axis field, and 1.186 in the z-axis field. Panel E of Figure 4.17 is an example of their placement.

You will find the complete Metahero model on the CD that accompanies this book. The filename is \chapters\chptr04\MetaHero.scn.

MODELING A CYBERNETIC MARINE FROM SIMPLE PRIMITIVES

The next character to create is the USCM model 660, U.S. Cybernetic Marine (see Figure 4.18). You will use the same basic primitives as you did in the last few lessons, but this time around you will wield tS4's Object Deformation tools the way they were meant to be.

FIGURE 4.18   *To construct the U.S. Cybernetic Marine model 660, all you need is some basic primitives, the Object Deformation tools, a little Boolean magic, and a lot of attitude.*

Traditional artists often start with the head when creating the human form, but you may have noticed that I tend to start in the most unusual places. That is simply because I don't have to worry about scale. If I create a limb that is disproportionate to the torso, all I have to do is scale the object to fit—a luxury traditional character artists don't have. This approach enables me to concentrate on the most difficult areas in my design first.

By tackling the hardest part first, I draw on my enthusiasm for the project to build the difficult parts. If I fail in achieving what I set out to accomplish the first few times, it's okay—I'm still enthused. If it can't be done, then I haven't spent too much time tinkering with the idea. Once I'm over the big hurdle, however, I get excited all over again because the rest seems like a cakewalk. This approach is a great way of keeping the novelty in what you are doing, and we all know that enthusiasm for what we are doing is one of the ingredients in success.

Okay, enough of the pep talk; let's look at the tools you need. You will be using the Deform Object button and one of the two panels that are associated with it. The Deformation Nav panel is where all the grunt work is performed, but I want to cover another panel before we get started. Right-clicking the Deform Object button brings up the Deformation Panel. (It's an odd name, I know; perhaps Deform Options would have been a better choice.) The Deformation Panel is where you tweak how trueSpace4 will display feedback to you. This is a handy panel if you will be working with an object with a high-poly count. We will be increasing the resolution of our meshes in the next few tutorials so I will go over this panel briefly. The panel has four options that can be enabled or disabled, one of which is available via a drop-down menu. At a glance, they are RealTime, Handles, Outlines, and Draw.

- *RealTime:* Provides instant feedback of the actual surfaces being manipulated as you deform the object. If the option is not checked, trueSpace displays only an approximation.

- *Handles:* Displays the object's actual control handles and points. Each can be manipulated independently.

- *Outlines:* Displays the object's individual cross sections.

- *Draw:* Determines how the object's wire frame is drawn. You have two choices: Object or Deformed. The former displays the entire object as you deform its surface, while Deformed displays only the vertices being affected.

As I cover the material in the next tutorial, you may want to adjust these settings to suit your taste. I usually change these settings only when the object I'm working with has a high-poly count and is causing the feedback to lag behind. In most cases, I prefer to use RealTime, Handles, Outlines, and Object feedback whenever possible, but you might want to experiment with these settings to find what best works for you. For some helpful tips on using the Deform Object tool, please review Chapter 3.

NOTE

Caligari identifies each of these cross sections as "perpendicular to" either the x-, y-, or z-axis. For the sake of simplicity and to avoid confusion, I will refer to each as they appear onscreen. I will use "horizontal, x-axis" and "vertical, y-axis" where appropriate.

NOTE

You're probably asking yourself why not just create all the cross sections in one shot and start deforming the object? I didn't suggest that method because if you attempt to deform the sphere without first decreasing its volume, you will end up pulling your hair out by the roots. This can be real fustrating; check out the small window in Figure 4.19 to see the unacceptable result of the "one-shot" method.

MODEL THE LEGS

The most difficult objects to create for this character are the lower limbs, so I will begin with the thigh and calf.

1. Open a new scene and switch to the Front view.

2. Add a sphere to a new scene and apply Smooth Quad Divide to it twice.

3. Open the Deformation Nav panel. The Local Deformation and Pull/Push buttons are activated by default. Number of Cross Sections defaults to 2. The cross sections are identified as green lines: One runs perpendicular to the z-axis encircling the sphere's equator, and the other makes its way perpendicular to the x-axis from pole to pole.

4. Select Stretch in the Deformation Nav panel and right-click it to open the Coords panel. Disable the y- and z-axes, allowing you to stretch (scale) the cross sections along the x-axis in a controlled manner.

5. Select the center cross section; if you're successful, it will change color. Scale the cross section until it is about half its original width. Use Figure 4.19 as a guide. To further help you visualize what you are trying to accomplish, I have superimposed the finished mesh over the sphere in the figure.

6. Switch to the Left View and scale the cross section as depicted in Figure 4.20.

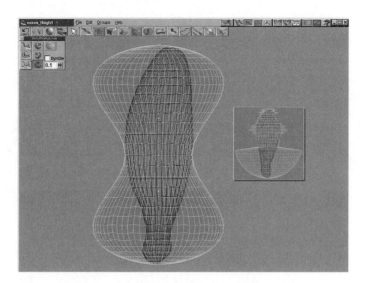

FIGURE 4.19   *Front view with superimposed mesh of desired shape.*

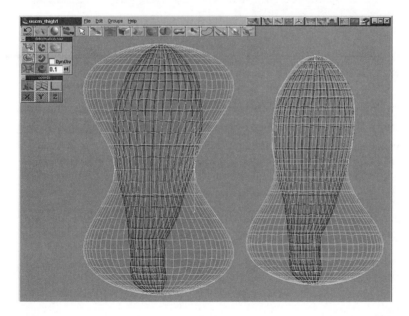

FIGURE 4.20   *Left view, the superimposed mesh of desired shape is used to help you visualize the target shape.*

By deforming your object, you lock the number of cross sections available to you. Once an object has been deformed with the Deform Object tool, the number of cross sections is locked. You can delete the cross sections by pressing the Delete key on your keyboard, which in turn closes the Deformation Nav panel. If you change your mind, simply reopen the panel and add as many cross sections as you like. You can repeat these steps as often as the job dictates.

For the next step, the single horizontal cross section won't do. You need one cross section for each set of vertices that lie horizontally.

7. Reopen the Deformation Nav panel and notice that you now have the default two cross sections again. To add more cross sections, select the Deform Perpendicular to z-axis button. Holding the right mouse button down, increase the number of cross sections until you have one cross section for each set of vertices that lie horizontally. You will end up with somewhere in the neighborhood of 30 cross sections. If you have more, that's okay.

8. Continue scaling each of the cross sections along the x-axis as you did earlier. Switch between the Left and Front views until the desired shape is reached. You may also use the Pull/Push tool in the Deformation Nav Panel to position the selected cross section along the x-axis just right. Figure 4.21 depicts the finished shape.

You can go back and tweak a cross section at any time if you make a mistake: Press the Undo button to restore the last cross section moved or scaled to its last position or scale.

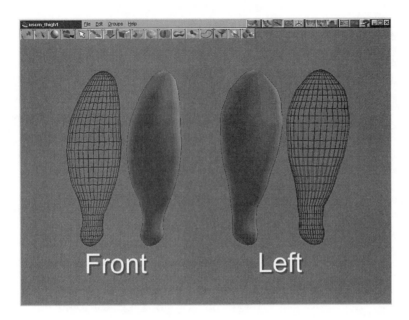

FIGURE 4.21   *The Deform Object tool is ideal for modeling organics and can be used to achieve a variety of unusual shapes.*

To create the rest of the leg, all that you need is to model the calf. Modeling the calf is no different than doing the thigh; therefore, you can use the same technique. Remember that the calf should taper at the ankle in the left and front views. The length is roughly the same as the thigh from end to end. Use Figure 4.22 as a guide to modeling the calf. For the knee, you can use a simple sphere as I did.

NOTE

The Deform Object tool has cousins. They are the Standalone Deformation tools. Their purpose and examples of their use will be explored in the animation chapters.

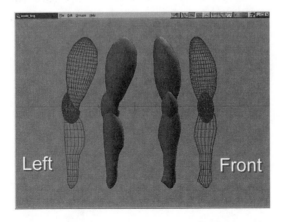

FIGURE 4.22   *This character's organic shape was achieved with tS4's Deformation tools.*

Pop quiz: What does pressing the Delete key accomplish?

A. The object is deleted.

B. The cross section is deleted and the Deformation panel closed.

C. The operation is undone.

D. All of the above.

If you answered B, you are correct. To finish the foot, you need some more cross sections, and the only way to add cross sections once the object has been deformed is to delete the existing ones.

CREATE THE FEET

In the next step, you will use the same tools to create the character's foot. The feet are a little tricky because normal-looking feet on a large character don't look right. What I opted to do was to create feet that were broad at the toe and heel and tapered up to the ankle. This approach worked out well; not only did the feet look like they would support such a huge mass, they fit the character. Here is how to create a pair of your own.

1. Add a sphere and a cube primitive to a new scene from the Front view. (Sound familiar?)

2. Scale the cube slightly larger than the sphere and move the cube's top edge to the center of the sphere.

3. Boolean subtract the cube from the sphere. You should end up with half a sphere—like I really had to tell you that.

4. Apply Smooth Quad Divide to the sphere once.

5. Open the Deformation Nav panel and switch to the Top view. Select Deform Perpendicular to y-axis and Stretch in the Deformation Nav panel.

6. Select the cross section in the center of the sphere and scale it along its x-axis until it looks like the left foot in Figure 4.23. To help you see the overall shape, the right foot is a copy of the finished foot. Once you are satisfied with the result, press the Delete key.

7. Reopen the Deformation Nav panel and add six cross sections to the object in the y-axis or horizontally from the Top view as depicted in Figure 4.23. Scale each of the cross sections to the desired shape.

8. Switch to the Front view and scale the cross sections along the x- and z-axes. It's okay to experiment, so dream up your own cool design for a cybernetic foot. When you are satisfied, copy and mirror the foot. Figure 4.24 shows the finished foot in all three views.

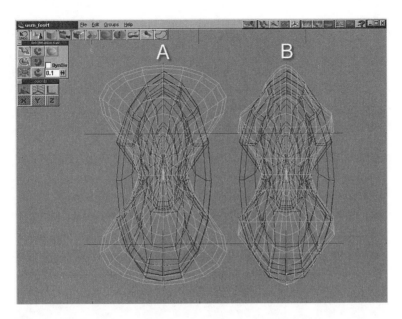

FIGURE 4.23   *On the left is the first step in deforming our sphere into the character's foot. Remember to reduce the volume of the object before deforming the object. On the right is a view of the foot after the deformation process. Notice the extra control points.*

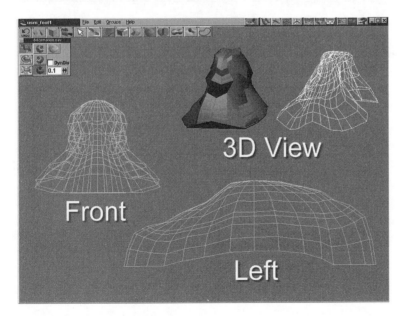

FIGURE 4.24   *The completed foot from all views.*

MODEL THE TORSO

It's amazing what can be created with a simple primitive and the Deform Object tool. Let's move on to the torso, which is composed of deformed cylinders and spheres. Toss in a few Boolean operations, and you are off to a good start. Figure 4.25 is a closer look at the deformed primitives used to make the Cybernetic Marine's torso.

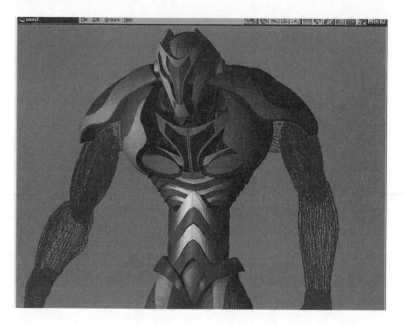

FIGURE 4.25   *The torso is nothing more than a few deformed cylinders and spheres.*

THE CHEST AND SHOULDERS

For our next trick, we will Boolean subtract portions of a sphere to get the shoulder and chest area. The Spline Polygon tool will help you define the shape that will be subtracted from the sphere. The Spline Polygon tool enables you to create any freeform shape you want, and with the Sweep tool, you can create cookie cutters out of those shapes.

1. Open a new scene and switch to the Top view.

2. Left-click and then right-click the Spline Polygon tool to open two panels: Draw Path and Spline. In the Spline panel, click the Very Smooth Corner button. In the Segments field in the Draw Path panel, enter 10 (the default value).

3. In the Top view, create a kidney or bean shape.

4. Select the Object tool to complete the operation and close the spline.

5. Using the Point Edit Context tool, click the center of the spline polygon; its edges will change color.

6. Switch to the Perspective view. You might have to use the Eye Move tool to zoom out so you can see the entire kidney-shaped spline.

7. Click the Sweep tool once to create a kidney-shaped cookie cutter like the one in Figure 4.26. Select the Object tool to complete the operation.

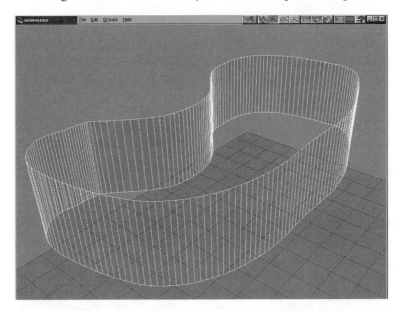

FIGURE 4.26   *The Spline Polygon tool created the kidney shape, from which the Sweep tool created a cookie cutter.*

8. Switch to the Left or Front view and scale the object along the y-axis. Switch to the Top view and verify that all three Navigation Axes buttons are activated. Holding both the left and right mouse buttons, scale the object in all three axes equally to a reasonable size.

9. Add a sphere primitive to the scene and apply Smooth Quad Divide to it once. Copy it and scale it slightly smaller than the original in all three axes. This should give you one sphere inside another.

10. Boolean subtract the inner sphere from the outer one.

11. From the Top view, select the cookie-cutter object created with the Spline Polygon tool and position it so that the curved half covers half of the sphere as depicted in step two of Figure 4.27. Check the Left and Front views to ensure that your cookie cutter is larger than the sphere in the y-axis. Boolean subtract the cookie cutter from the sphere. Figure 4.27 illustrates the result.

12. Copy and mirror the newly created object. Glue the two together as siblings just to keep them together for easy placement. You now have the upper portion of the pectorals, which make up a large part of the chest cavity. You can use a copy of the same object for the shoulders to save time.

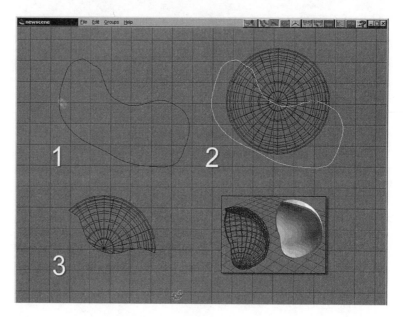

FIGURE 4.27   *The three steps to create one side of the chest cavity of our character.*

I fashioned the breastplate in much the same way. I added a sphere to the scene and then made a cookie-cutter object with the Spline Polygon and Sweep tools.

The lower portion of the pectoral muscles are flattened spheres that have had a cube primitive Boolean subtracted from one side to give the character a machined look. After you have fashioned the breastplate and pectorals (upper and lower portions), place the left and right upper pectoral muscles on each side of the breastplate. Move the lower portions of the pectorals muscles just underneath the upper two. Use Figure 4.25 as a guide. If necessary, unglue the two upper pectorals I had you glue together earlier so you can move each individually.

THE ABDOMEN AND RIBCAGE

The chest area wouldn't be complete without a ribcage, so let's take a look.

1. Open a new scene.

2. Add a cylinder primitive to the scene and apply Quad Divide once.

3. From the Front view, decrease the cylinder's height along the y-axis to about one third its default size.

4. Open the Deformation Nav panel and select the Deform Perpendicular to the X-Axis button. Disable the X- and Z-Axis buttons in the Coords panel. You will be using the default values, so go ahead and grab the center cross section.

5. Select the Pull/Push button in the Deformation Nav panel and lift the cross section until you get a nice smooth curve, as illustrated in Figure 4.28. Select the Object tool to complete the operation.

This is the key to creating both the ribcage and abdomen: The same object is used, just at different scales and painted alternate colors. The abdomen's segments are left all the same size, glued together, and scaled 20% along the y-axis. For the ribcage, one of the abdomen sections was reciprocated along the z-axis and copied, with each copy scaled a tad smaller than the last.

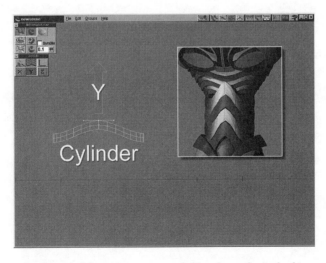

FIGURE 4.28   *The ribs and abdomen segments were fashioned out of a single object and copied.*

MODEL THE ARMS

Old USCM 660's arms are fashioned out of spheres in much the same manner as the superhero was modeled. In fact, you can place the superhero's arms on the Marine if you like.

1. In a new scene, add three sphere primitives.

2. From the Front view, stack each sphere one on top of the other. Apply Smooth Quad Divide to each once.

3. Scale each of the spheres along the x-axis to half its original width.

4. Fan the three spheres out slightly. Elongate the center sphere slightly larger than the other two by scaling it along the y-axis.

5. From the Left view, rotate the center sphere slightly so that its top is left of its center. Position the bottom to about the location of the other two spheres' center lines. Glue all three spheres as siblings to one another to be the character's biceps (see Figure 4.29).

6. Add a new sphere to the scene. Scale it along the x-axis until it is about the width of the biceps in both the Left and Front views. Scale the selected sphere along the y-axis until it is roughly twice its original height.

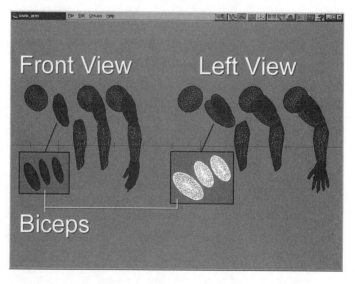

FIGURE 4.29   *The character's arms are fashioned from five spheres.*

7. To create the forearm, open the Deformation Nav panel and select the Deformation Perpendicular to Z-Axis button.

8. Using the right mouse button, add three cross sections. Grab the bottom cross section and decrease its width to give the sphere a tapered look. Do the same in the Left view.

9. From the Front view, add a new sphere to the scene and flatten it a bit by scaling it along the y-axis. Rotate it so that its left side is higher than its right. This will act as the character's shoulder muscle.

CREATE THE HEAD

Fabricating the head shouldn't be a mystery. You're going to use the same techniques as you have right along.

Figure 4.30 is an exploded view of the head. The overall shape is a deformed sphere massaged into a teardrop. (Remember, we created a teardrop shape for the superhero.) I rotated the teardrop object 180 degrees along its y-axis and copied it several times. I split one in half with the Boolean Subtraction tool and a cube primitive, and then elongated it and used it as the character's neck muscles. I employed another copy of the teardrop object for the overall shape of the head. For the chin, I punched out the center of the teardrop object with a cookie cutter (courtesy of the Spline Polygon and Sweep tools). I put a smaller copy of the teardrop object and a small sphere in the removed area to enclose the skull. For the eyes, I placed a small sphere painted flaming red just below the skull sphere. A cylinder creates the earpiece and adds more detail to the head. A scaled-down copy of the breastplate serves as a brow and noseguard.

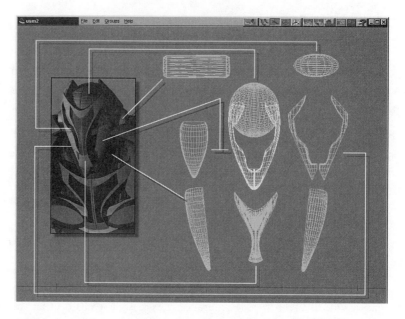

FIGURE 4.30 *An exploded view of the head. The head was created from one cylinder and many spheres stretched and scaled with cookie-cutter objects Boolean subtracted from their surfaces. The breastplate was scaled down and used as the nose and brow for the head.*

All the parts of this character can be found on the CD that accompanies this book. The filename is chapters\chptr04\USCM.scn.

MODELING THE FEMALE FORM FROM A SPHERE PRIMITIVE

The female form has got to be one of the most challenging characters I have ever attempted in trueSpace (see Figure 4.31). Thankfully, because our bodies are symmetrical, you can cheat by modeling one side and copying and mirroring it to add the other half. The type of clothes female characters wear, however, dictates that the underlying geometric shape must have no noticeable seams. The obvious approach would be to model the character as a solid mesh—well, most of it at least. Here is a simple way to accomplish just that.

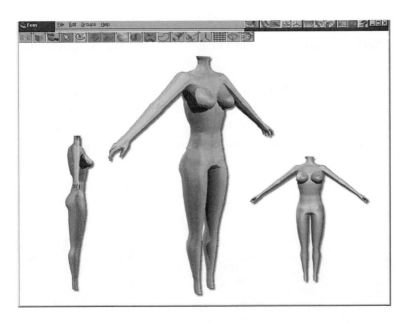

FIGURE 4.31   *The torso and legs of this female form were modeled from a single-sphere primitive.*

SCULPT THE LEGS

As usual, you'll start with the legs.

1. Open a new scene and switch to the Front view.

2. Right-click the Add Cylinder button to open the Cylinder panel. Change the default Latitude setting of 2 to 60. This will create a cylinder with a very dense mesh.

3. Right-click the Object tool to open the Object Info panel. You will notice that the cylinder has a size 2.0 in the x-, y-, and z-axis fields.

4. Disable the X- and Z-Axis buttons in the Coords panel and scale the cylinder along the y-axis until the cylinder reaches 32 in the World Z-Axis field in the Object Info panel.

5. Open the Deform Object panel and enable the Stretch and Deform Perpendicular to Z-Axis buttons. Increase the number of cross sections to equal the same number of segments that make up the 60 latitudes of the cylinder.

6. Reopen the Object Info panel. Select a cross section in the center and scale it along the x-axis from its default size of 2.0 to 4.0. This will be the maximum width of the character's thigh.

7. Working your way down, select the next two cross sections and scale each along the x-axis to around 4.0. Select the next two cross sections and scale each to about 3.8. Continue down the cylinder scaling each group of two cross sections slightly smaller than the previous two until you have deformed about one quarter of the cylinder and have reached 2.0. Remember, you are modeling the thigh. Use Figure 4.32 as your visual guide.

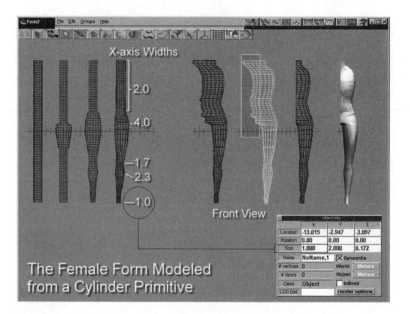

FIGURE 4.32   *Deforming a cylinder into the female form is relatively simple and requires only a few steps and one tool.*

8. To create the character's calf, scale down each subsequent cross section until you reach 1.7. The calf starts to get wider just below the knee, so begin to increase each of the next cross sections a bit until you have reached 2.3 or thereabout. Now that you have reached the maximum width of the calf, decrease the sizes of the next sets of cross sections until you reach 1.3. At that point, you should be just above the ankles. Continue to decrease the size of each cross section by 0.1 until you reach the bottom of the cylinder.

MOLD THE TORSO

Sculpting the torso is easier than sculpting the leg. You need to concern yourself with the curves only on its right side. You will Boolean subtract the left side from the rest of the torso when you are done.

NOTE

Precise measurements aren't needed; just an approximation of the torso's curvature. Keep in mind that the female form has subtle curves so each of the cross sections should have about 0.05 difference from its neighboring cross section.

1. Scale the cross sections remaining from the leg tutorial to 8.0.

2. Enable the Pull/Push button in the Deformation panel and disable the Y- and Z-Axis buttons in the Coords panel.

3. Move each of the cross sections to form the curvature of the torso's right side.

4. Figure 4.33 shows the character from the Left view. As you begin to sculpt the character in the Left view, use the Stretch tool to get the general size of the cross sections along the x-axis. Use the Pull tool to position the cross sections to form the fine curves. Try to take your time; I find that with a little patience and diligence, I was able to model the character in as little as 20 minutes on my first try.

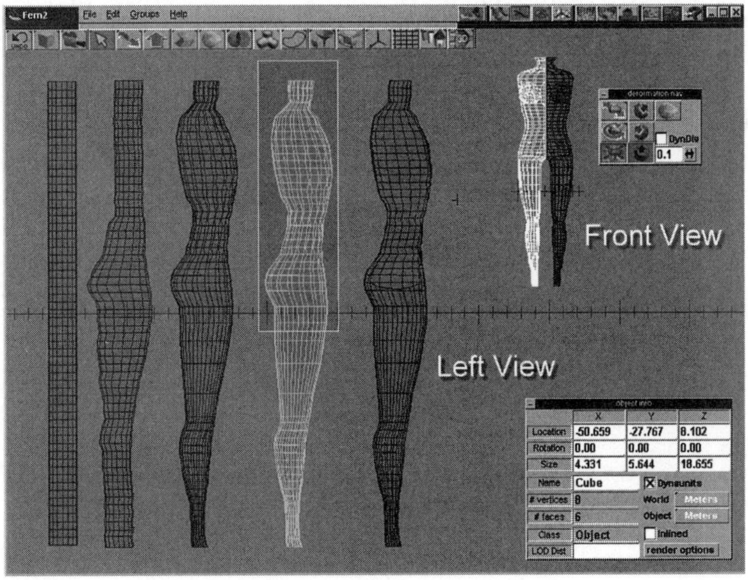

FIGURE 4.33   *Left view of the completed female form.*

5. When satisfied with the overall shape, add a cube primitive and Boolean subtract it from the left side of the torso. Be careful not to include any portion of the character's leg in the Boolean operation.

Arms, hands, feet, and a head can be sculpted by using any combination of the preceding methods and then Booleaned to the object to form the completed right side. To create the left side of the character, copy and mirror the right side and glue the two halves together. This type of mesh is ideal for use with Bones and is easy to animate.

You will find the completed scene on the CD that accompanies this book. The filename is chapters\chptr04\fem.scn.

SUMMARY

The modeling tools in trueSpace have always been powerful. In this chapter, we focused on creating a range of different characters by using different methods. We also managed to create the characters with relatively low-polygon counts without any loss in modeling flexibility. It's now up to you to tap the unlimited potential of these powerful trueSpace assets and create some characters of your own.

One final note: You can be neither too young nor too obsessed to begin your career as a character modeler. Michelangelo was only 13 when he first studied art, and his father never approved of his passion. So, for those of you who hear on a daily basis, "Are you still playing with that (*place appropriate expletive here*) computer?" take comfort in the fact that we all face the same obstacles and criticism regardless of what century we live in.

PART III

SURFACING AND TEXTURING

CHAPTER 5

SURFACING

by Frank Rivera

Good texture mapping is synonymous with good 3D imagery and is considered an art form. A skillfully texture-mapped object can look convincingly real, and in many cases, can be used in place of highly detailed objects that can take hours to model.

In this chapter, we will cover:

- Basic surfacing
- Bump mapping
- Environment maps
- Exploring reflective surfaces
- Understanding UV space
- UV projection per face
- Surfacing groups of faces
- Decaling
- Procedural textures
- Adding fine details to surfaces
- Surface material formulas
- Material libraries
- Selecting images, things to consider

I have taken great care to keep this chapter from turning into an overview of the many panels used to apply textures to surfaces in trueSpace4. I leave that territory to trueSpace4's manual.

Surfacing is one of the two most important skills a 3D artist needs. The other is lighting. What about modeling, you ask? Let's be honest—it comes in dead last. I don't want to offend any 3D modelers out there, but mastering light and texture are the skills we must continually hone if we are to become successful 3D artists. Even the most badly modeled object can look great if textured and lit correctly. Masterful surfacing starts with you, not with a procedural texture or image map. How you see the world eventually ends up in your imagery. So I will be focusing our discussion on visualization and how it applies to surfacing. Before I do, we need to make sure we are all speaking the same lingo.

SURFACING 101

The subject of surfacing can be broad and occasionally confusing because different people use different terms to describe the same operation. In the following discussions, we will define some of the buzzwords associated with surfacing. We will also examine some important surfacing effects and their contribution to an image. When we are finished, you should be able to proceed on your own with solid ground beneath your feet.

NOTE

In many cases the terms "texture mapping," "surfaces," and "decaling" are used interchangeably. Don't confuse texture mapping with decaling. Decaling is a process that allows a texture to be placed on top of another texture, often by means of coplanar geometry. trueSpace4 has such a tool, and we will cover it in this chapter.

The most popular way to think of surfacing (and specifically texture mapping) is that they're like using stickers. You paste a two-dimensional image onto a three-dimensional geometric shape, and that's about it. You can probably get a long way on that analogy. However, there is quite a bit more to know, and once you understand a few concepts, texture mapping starts to get a lot more interesting, and definitely a lot more fun. I will use the term "surfacing" to describe the process of applying and setting material properties of an object.

CONTROL BASICS

The panels you use to apply these properties are the Shader panels. Let's look at some of the changes they have undergone for trueSpace4. The four panels shown in Figure 5.1 appear whenever any of the paint tools—Paint Object, Paint Face, Paint Over Existing Material, Paint Vertices, Paint, or Inspect—is right-clicked on.

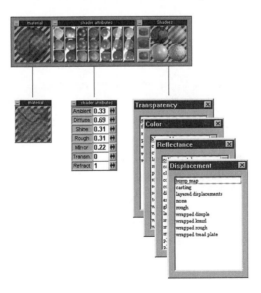

FIGURE 5.1   *A view of the Shader panels.*

- **Material panel:** This panel displays the effects the attributes have on a sample surface in real time. By clicking in the Material panel, you can switch the sample surface from a sphere (the default) to a plane. For surfaces with specular attributes, the sphere is a better choice.

- **Shader Attributes panels:** The main Shader Attributes panel is where the parameters of the selected shader are tweaked. Right-clicking any of the sliders opens a second Shader Attributes panel where you can manually enter the values for each of the sliders. Depending on the shader selected, not all of the sliders or entry fields in the second panel will be visible.

- **Shader panel:** Here the magic begins. This panel has four spheres that represent four general shader types. From left to right and top to bottom, they are Color, Transparency, Reflectance, and Displacement. To assign a shader to one of these shader spheres, left-click the appropriate sphere to bring up a table of shaders. Once you have selected the desired shader, the sphere will be updated to reflect your selection. To further adjust the attributes of the selected shader, right-click the associated sphere to open it.

SURFACE COLOR

We know that in the physical world, the color of an object is the result of the light bouncing off its surface. This depends on both the color of the light before it reaches the object (the sunlight entering a window or the light given off by a desk lamp), and the physical surface of the object itself.

In real life we don't spend much time thinking about these details. To create killer CG, we must think about these fine points very methodically, and, as in most cases, we must bend the rules a bit. This is where some of the confusion begins. You can follow your instincts to a point, but sooner than later you will find yourself branching off into directions that wouldn't make sense in the real world, especially to a traditional artist. You will get my point a little later in our discussion; for now, let's look at the simple white sphere in panel A of Figure 5.2.

The sphere doesn't appear perfectly white, does it? The object shades from white to dark gray, which is exactly what a real white ball would do under the circumstances. If I were to change the overhead light to blue, the white ball would reflect the blue light just as in the real world, and as depicted in panel B of Figure 5.2.

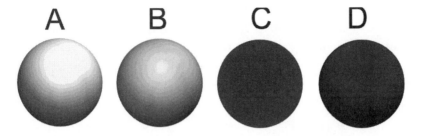

Figure 5.2   *The results of colored lights and ambient glow setting on a simple sphere.*

The color of the sphere in panel B of Figure 5.2 is the result of light (of a given color, in this case blue) interacting with the object's surface color. The color of the object in this example is called *diffuse* color. This will make more sense in a moment. Let's consider some other scenarios.

What if the color of a sphere isn't due to the reflection of light, but rather from light given off by the sphere itself? Panel C of Figure 5.2 depicts the same sphere with a Diffuse setting of 0.0, its Color set to Green, and its Ambient Glow set to 1.0.

Not what you would expect, huh? The *luminosity* of an object can be thought of as the light given off by the object itself, independent of any external light sources. The sphere in panel C is said to be *luminous.* Although the lighting in the scene hasn't changed, the 3D effect is lost. Let's make the sphere's Diffuse setting 0.5 and see what happens.

As you can see in panel D of Figure 5.2, the sphere's surface is now responding to the light; the shadows are visible and once again reveal the 3D shape. If we compare panel D to panel B (Diffuse setting, 1.0, and Ambient setting, 0.0), we learn something new. Without any ambient glow, the shaded area of the sphere is very dark. So an object's Ambient setting can be used to bring color into shaded areas. This is the type of rule bending I was talking about. As you progress as a 3D artist, you will find that in order to model the real world, you have to break the rules. Of course, 3D imagery is nothing more than an illusion anyway, so don't feel guilty.

If the sphere were being photographed, additional lighting would be added to the underlit areas to get the desired result. We could have added light from below, but instead we just increased the Ambient setting of the object. Why turn up the ambient glow of an object when we can add a light to the scene? Good question. Adding or changing the lighting in a scene affects the other objects in the vicinity of the newly added light source. In 3D, it's a lot of work to get the lighting just right; adding another light source not only adds additional render cycles, but it can add unwanted specular highlights to reflective surfaces. So turning up an object's ambient glow setting is a quick, painless solution in this case.

SPECULAR REFLECTION

We know that diffuse light is reflected light. There is another type of reflected light that is integral in creating spectacular 3D imagery. Compare Figure 5.3 with Figure 5.2.

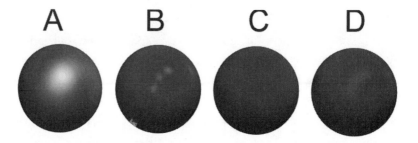

FIGURE 5.3 *The results of applying different surface attributes to a sphere.*

In panels A and B of Figure 5.3, the color blue is determined by the Diffuse setting of the sphere's surface, but the white highlight is caused by reflected light. The color of the highlight is the color of the light itself. This kind of reflection is called *specular reflection*. Specular highlights provide critical visual cues about the shape of the object, its orientation with respect to light sources, and the object's surface attributes.

In trueSpace4, there are three factors that define the overall specularity of an object's surface:

- The intensity of the light source
- The object's Shininess setting
- The object's Roughness setting

Look at each of the panels in Figure 5.3. In panel A, the object's surface has a Shininess setting of 1.0 and a Roughness setting of 0.0. In panel B, the object's Shininess setting is 1.0 and its Roughness is 1.0. In panel C, the object's

Roughness is 1.0, but its Shininess is 0.0. In panel D, Roughness and Shininess are both 0.5. By using an object's Shininess and Roughness settings, you can achieve a very broad range of effects. The smallest specular highlight can make a big difference in interpreting an object's surface, even where barely visible.

TEXTURE MAPPING

With the techniques we've looked at so far, you can surface an object by using a single solid color. For most scenes, however, you need a bit more realism. You need to assign multiple colors to the surfaces of your object. To do so in trueSpace4, you use a process traditionally called *texture mapping*. The colors in the texture map applied to your object's surface are still diffuse colors, but, as you will see, the mapping process gives you more control over how the surface is perceived by the viewer. Applying a texture map to your object can even appear to change the geometry of the object, while leaving the underlying mesh untouched.

There are two methods of altering an object's surface by using texture maps:

- Image mapping
- Procedural mapping

The image mapping approach essentially wraps a specific bitmap image file onto the object. The sphere in Figure 5.4, for example, has a scanned photograph of yellow bathroom tile texture mapped onto it, and the cube is mapped with a bitmap image of a metal storage container.

FIGURE 5.4   *A cube and sphere texture mapped with an image map of a metal storage container and a tiled wall image.*

As you can see, both objects are more convincing in what they portray than solid color versions. Notice how the shadows still affect the surfaces of the objects. These shadows are not part of the image maps, but are caused by the shape of the object's geometry and the location of the lights in the scene. The practical uses of this kind of texture mapping can fill a book. Simple objects become completely convincing when mapped with scanned photographs of realistic surfaces. Throw some good lighting and shadows into the mix and the objects start to look even more interesting.

Unlike the image mapping method, which uses existing bitmaps, procedural mapping uses textures created within trueSpace4. Procedural texture maps are often called *3D textures* because they affect the entire volume of an object. In procedural mapping, the pattern you apply doesn't simply lie on the object's surface like an image map; it "soaks" (for lack of a better word) through the entire object. If you were to cut a block of marble in half, for instance, the veins and feathering would be visible inside, and with every new cut, more veins and feathering would be exposed. The same is true when you procedural map a cube with a marble texture and then cut the cube.

In trueSpace4, you have complete control over the parameters that make up the visible attributes of procedural textures. For example, the marble procedural texture used for Figure 5.5 has seven parameters you can set—Ground Color, Vein Color, Scale, Detail, Vein Contrast, Grain, and Grain Scale. You set the parameters, and trueSpace4 creates the texture map. They are accessed via the Marble panel. To open the Marble panel, right-click the Color sphere in the Shader panel as described previously in Control Basics.

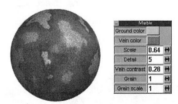

FIGURE 5.5   *A demonstration of a procedural texture applied to a sphere. The Marble Color shader was used to make the sphere more interesting.*

Procedural textures are wonderful and can be animated. You can create some great effects, such as energy columns, lightning strikes, visible haze, and chipped paint, to name a few, but I'm getting ahead of myself. We will cover these types of effects and revisit procedural textures again later in this chapter, and in Chapter 14.

BUMP MAPPING

In life, rarely is anything in our environment perfectly smooth. Think of an orange. Its appearance is almost entirely defined by the bumpy texture of its skin.

Even the seemingly smooth computer monitor in front of you has a small degree of bumps across its surface. As you become accustomed to looking more carefully at the world around you, you will begin to notice the subtle characteristics of the surfaces you want to portray in your imagery.

Our eyes can perceive these subtle differences across a real object's surface in many ways—from the way the object casts and catches shadows, to the way specular highlights become broken up—but how do you mimic these effects in your 3D imagery? In the case of an orange, you could achieve a realistic result by adding a huge amount of detail to a sphere's geometry, subdividing it into hundreds of thousands of polygons, and altering each vertex to get just the right bumpiness. As you can imagine, this is a lot of work and brings even the best SGI workstation to its knees.

The practical approach is to create the *illusion* of an uneven surface on your sphere. You can do this by applying a special kind of texture map—a *bump map*—to your object. Whether you're trying to get a surrealistic, photorealistic, or Play-Doh™ look to your imagery, bump mapping adds the illusion of dimension to the maps you apply to your objects. As Figure 5.6 demonstrates, bump maps can make a big difference.

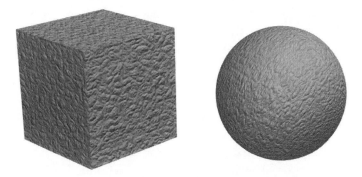

FIGURE 5.6   *Texture and geometry should complement each other. In this image, the same single diffuse color value and bump map were applied to both the cube and sphere. Which is more identifiable as something that exists in the real world?*

A bump map does not assign color or lighting directly to an object or change its underlying mesh, but rather simulates surface relief. When an object is bump mapped, trueSpace makes the lighting calculations for each pixel as if the object's surface were raised or indented. Bump mapping, therefore, simulates the effect of light on an uneven surface without adding a single polygon to the object's geometry.

Like standard texture maps, bump maps can be created with either procedural maps or image maps. The bump map used in Figure 5.6 was created with a procedural bump map: the Wrapped Rough Displacement shader. Notice how the same diffuse color and bump map change the surface of the different objects. For this type of bump map, the curved surface works better. The visual effect of bump mapping (the delicate shadowing patterns generated across the surface) has a lot to do with the shape of the object surfaced, and the location of the light sources.

Scanned photographs of interesting textured surfaces (image maps) can be used to create a realistic surface texture, as well. trueSpace4 uses only the grayscale data of the image map: The lighter parts of the image produce a greater relief effect, while the darker areas produce a lesser relief effect. As you can imagine, image maps with strong contrast between dark and light make the best bump maps. The most important parameter in a bump map is Amplitude (bump height). This factor determines how great the relief effect will be. The greater the amplitude, the higher the peaks and the deeper the valleys. It's important to note that this effect doesn't actually affect the surface height, so the bumps cannot be seen when viewing the object's profile. Another important parameter is the size or scale of the image map.

To help you understand the effects of bump mapping with image maps, consider Figure 5.7 as an example. It uses two separate image maps for both the diffuse color, and as a bump map to create a great-looking surface. In Figure 5.7, a photograph of an asphalt surface (for the diffused color) and a standard kitchen floor tile image (for the bump map) are combined to create a futuristic floor tile. The image map used to add the diffused color to the floor beneath the cyborg's feet is also used for the walls. Interesting how an image of everyday kitchen tile can be used as a bump map to change the surface quality of an object and improve a scene aesthetically. This method of using images as both a texture map and a bump map is very common, and is a great way to add realism to your 3D imagery.

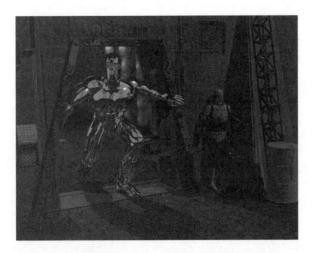

FIGURE 5.7   *In this image (created in trueSpace3), both the wall and floor are texture mapped with an asphalt image map. Applying a tile bitmap image as a bump map to the ground plane separates the two identical surfaces and adds a touch of realism to the floor.*

We now know that the light parts of the image determine the amplitude of the bumps. The lighter the area, the higher the bumps will appear. The darkest areas will seem to sink into the object's surface, producing kind of a dimpling effect. Any image can be used as a bump map, and, in most cases, using the same image for both the texture and bump map on the same surface is all that is needed to add that perfect touch (see Figure 5.8). This is convenient, and the bumps will line up to the texture perfectly. An example can be seen in the opening image of this chapter. The same image was used to texture and bump map the ground.

NOTE

Recognize the large chrome cybernetic character in Figure 5.7? It is the metaball character modeled in Chapter 4.

FIGURE 5.8   *In this image, the same image map was used to texture and bump map the ground.*

Still not convinced of the impact bump maps can make? Take a look at Figure 5.9. The eerie tomb is far more dramatic when a bump map is applied to the wall. It looks as if you can reach out and feel the rough texture of its surface.

FIGURE 5.9   *In this image, the effects of bump mapping are evident in the back wall.*

NOTE

If you're having trouble with surfacing your objects (the textures are not rendering properly), it might be because the object has no UV space assigned. Try reapplying UV space to the object. You will have to reapply the surface materials to the object's surface after doing so. UV is discussed later in this chapter.

So, there you have it. Bump mapping is just another method of varying an object's surface color. So far, we have looked at altering the colors of objects directly; now let's look at altering an object's surface color through the use of environment maps.

ENVIRONMENT MAPPING

Environment mapping is the process of reflecting an image or set of images onto the surfaces of the objects in your scene. The effect is visible on reflective surfaces as if the object were wrapped by the image. trueSpace4 uses a cubic method of projecting an image onto surfaces, by using six sides—four at right angles to each other, and one from below and above. Any of the supported image formats can be used, as well as numbered TGA and AVI files for animated environment maps. Environment maps come in two flavors: Global and Local.

GLOBAL

Global environment mapping affects all the objects in your scene that have reflective surfaces. You can access this option from the Render Options panel by right-clicking any of the render tools: Render Scene to File, Render Current Object, Render Scene, or Render a Portion of the Screen. Global environment mapping is enabled by left-clicking the Foreground Shader button. Once selected, you must right-click the Foreground Shader button which should now read "Environment" to open the Global Environment Map panel. Select the Set Global Environment button to open the Get Environment Map window; from this window, you can select the file you want to use.

LOCAL

Local environment mapping affects only individual objects. You can find the controls in the Shaders panel. To access the Shader panels, right-click any of the Object Paint tools: Object Paint, Paint Over Existing Material, Paint Vertices, Paint Face, or the Inspect tool. Left-click the Reflectance sphere in the Shaders panel to select the Environment Map shader from the Reflectance table. Next, right-click the Reflectance sphere to open the Environment Map panel. Select the button to open the Get Environment Map window, and from this window you can select the file you want to use. Remember that any of the supported file types can be used for this purpose.

An environment map is a handy way to add depth to a scene, as Figure 5.10 shows.

FIGURE 5.10 *The difference an environment map can make with simple scenes and reflective surfaces.*

There is an important lesson to be learned here. In panel A, no environment map is used. The simple scene looks, well, simple. In panel B, an image of a city scene was used as a global environment map. Not only does the scene look more complicated, but the simple sphere is complemented by the environment map, making the scene more interesting. In panel C, the environment map is still present but the background color has been changed from black to white. The environment map is still visible, but only in the areas of the sphere that reflect actual objects in the scene. So, the background color we choose affects how much detail of our environment map is visible, to a degree. It has more to do with the surface attributes of the surface reflecting the environment map rather than the background color. So what are these surface attributes I'm talking about? I wish I could give you a neat numbered list, but there are no simple rules to guarantee great imagery. The best way to tackle this complicated subject is to learn from the finished work of others: Let's carefully examine the scene in Figure 5.11 and discuss some of the complex surfaces and attributes used.

SURFACE ATTRIBUTES: EXPLORING REFLECTIVE SURFACES

Working on an image can be time-consuming. A lot of trial and error is required, and every little detail must be studied, rendered, changed, rendered, and studied again. Why, for example, does the shadow casting light outside the window seem unconvincing? Is it the position of the light source or the placement of one of the objects in the scene? Each possibility needs to be explored, and more visual cues are added with each new render to pull off the illusion. Figure 5.11, for example, is the result of literally 50 or so test renders in which the shadows, lighting, and surfacing effects were changed, tweaked, and changed again to achieve the desired results. (Well, the almost desired results; I don't think I ever finish an image to my satisfaction.)

I have carefully planned the scene to incorporate a wide range of different material surfaces. For the coffee cup, I used a blend of diffuse color, specularity, and ambient glow to get the distinctive glossiness of a glazed clay-like surface. The bread, on the other hand, uses the same image map for both the surface texture and bump map. The silverware has a mirror surface with a gray diffuse color, a good effect to master. The drinking glass is the nucleus that holds everything around it in place. Although it is off center in the image, it is the single-most important object in the scene. The viewer is drawn to it.

FIGURE 5.11 *Experimenting with reflective surfaces.*

It's amazing how a simple object can hold our attention for so long. In our everyday lives, we wouldn't take the time to study how the light moves over a glass's surface, or how the objects behind the glass tend to bend and distort. Place a drinking glass in a 3D image, and our minds work overtime trying to find the flaws (subconsciously at first), as if to prove to ourselves that it isn't real. Getting those little details just right is the secret to bringing your imagery up to the next level. How do you do it? Practice seeing the world through the eyes of a 3D artist—and practice and practice. Let's start by focusing on the little details needed to create convincing glass, a very challenging surface.

> **NOTE**
>
> It's important to note that great imagery isn't achieved solely by texture mapping the surfaces of the objects in a scene. Lights and shadows play an important part as well. For the scoop on lighting your scenes, please see Chapter 12.

GLASS SURFACES

Creating glass isn't as cut-and-dry as reproducing chrome or mirrors. Chrome and mirrors simply reflect the objects around them. Glass, however, has several properties that have to be considered:

- **Texture:** Is it smooth like a bottle? Rough like a piece of beach glass with its smooth surface and frosted appearance? Filled with impurities, such as the bubbles in Mexican blue glass?

- **Color and transparency:** Is it dark like a wine bottle or clear like a milk jar?

- **Shape and thickness:** Is it delicate like a wineglass or hefty like an ashtray?

Each type of glass has unique values, but they all have three things in common: a reflective surface, some measure of refraction, and a transparent appearance.

Look more carefully at Figure 5.11's drinking glass. Can you see how the sense of glass was created? The surface appears perfectly transparent, yet we see… something. What we see is the effect of light refracting through the glass, or rather the effect of the light reflected from surfaces around the glass getting refracted in the glass. Having objects behind and around the glass is critical in pulling off the illusion of glass.

Again, we subconsciously compare the unobscured background with the background as seen through the glass. The distortion caused by the object's material is immediately interpreted in our brain as the effect of refraction through a curved transparent surface. Notice also the difference between the effect as viewed through both the front and back sides of the drinking glass and the effect at the top, where we see drastic distortion through only the back side of the drinking glass. These small differences are the vital cues that sell the illusion of glass.

The more visual cues present, the more realistic your imagery looks. In Figure 5.11, the china pulls off the illusion through its diffuse color, with just the right touch of specularity being a significant factor. The metal spoon relies mostly on reflection. The key to the bread was bump mapping. With the drinking glass, the transparency is the secret, or at least part of it.

It's easy to point to transparency as the key parameter of a glass surface, but there's more to the story. Compare the drinking glass on its own in Figure 5.12 to the one surrounded by objects in Figure 5.11. Hmmm, the glass seemed more convincing when viewed with the rest of the scene. Therefore, our perception of how we see the scene must have something to do with what we consider reality. When the glass was part of a larger scene, the atmosphere created by the light sources and the presence of the other objects distracted us from critically inspecting the drinking glass as much. When the object stands alone, the glass's weaknesses grab our attention.

A technique I use often when I'm having trouble finding that elusive missing detail is to isolate the troubled object after constructing, texture mapping, lighting, and saving the scene. I then remove the surrounding objects from the scene, which usually reveals the flaw that was throwing the scene. I then reload the scene and work on a solution. It's a whole lot easier to fix the problem once you have identified it.

FIGURE 5.12   *In this image, the surrounding objects are removed from the scene to better examine what properties contribute to the illusion of glass.*

Look at Figure 5.12 again. Remember I mentioned that the refraction of the background was influential on our perception of a curved glass surface. For Figure 5.13, I took the refraction parameter out completely and decreased the drinking glass's transparency a bit so that it is still visible.

In this image, the refraction has been removed to better view how refraction contributes to how we perceive glass objects. When refraction is removed, important visual cues, such as the curvature and distortion of the background, disappear, and the glass looks less convincing. Notice how the edges have become sharp—not very realistic, is it? If you didn't know that this object was a drinking glass, would the few visual cues left be enough information for you to interpret what the object is supposed to represent? There's been no change in the lighting, just the removal of the refraction properties. The edges are less visible because they no longer behave as a boundary between two reflected surfaces, the wall and window sill as seen throughout the scene, and the wall and window sill as seen through the glass. Why is this so? Two reasons: First, the wall and window sill display perspective cues that give the viewer a sense of 3D space, a sense of depth. Second, the background being refracted by the glass convinces us that what we are looking at is a drinking glass.

Figure 5.13   *In this image, the refraction parameter has been removed to better view how refraction affects how we perceive glass objects.*

The drinking glass is modeled with inner and outer surfaces, just as a real drinking glass would have; but unlike its real counterpart, the model is just surfaces. With refraction removed, the differences between the two surfaces are now apparent. So, refraction plays two important roles in pulling off the illusion of glass. It distorts the background seen through it, and it distorts the edges of the object's surface. Take a look at a real drinking glass, and you will find that the complex lighting effect at the edges of the object makes you perceive it as made of glass, rather than merely transparent. You can apply this logic to all curved glass surfaces you create.

Look at Figure 5.12 again. Notice the specular highlights along the rim and down the sides of our drinking glass? Glass is a highly specular surface, and the highlights make a big difference in the illusion of reality. When a surface is highly transparent, as the drinking glass started out, the highlights aren't so noticeable.

If we decrease the transparency so that the drinking glass is more translucent (as in Figure 5.13), the specular highlights are much more noticeable.

Let's change our drinking glass from the popular clear type to that of hand-blown Mexican blue glass, without the bubbles and impurities usually associated with it. (My version of blue glass may have less character than the real thing, but it gets my point across.)

The specularity is now a bit more significant, isn't it? In the smaller panel in Figure 5.14, I removed the specularity from the drinking glass. What we are left with is a less-convincing image. This change of color also helps us to understand transparency as a surfacing parameter. If we set the transparency settings to their maximum, the surface, although displaying no color of its own, still reflects specular highlights. If we can generate specular reflections off a transparent surface, we can also generate reflections.

NOTE

Before you experiment, commit these next few lines to memory. Refraction is a computationally intensive process, but render times in trueSpace4 are satisfactory. What you need to watch out for is the use of transparency and glass shaders together. I suggest that you do not use any transparency shaders with objects that have had the Glass Reflectance shader applied. Transparency doesn't contribute to the quality, and in my test it brought my machine to its knees.

FIGURE 5.14   *In this image, the glass is colored to better see what the effect of specularity has on the viewer in interpreting glass objects.*

MIRRORS, CHROME, AND HIGHLY REFLECTIVE SURFACES

Like glass, metal is an extremely important surface to master. For the silverware in Figure 5.11, I wanted a true-to-life look. Creating a metallic surface like the silverware's requires delicately balancing a gray diffuse color, specularity, and reflectivity. As I mentioned before, one surfacing parameter is usually responsible for pulling off the illusion you are trying to portray. For the silverware, it's the reflectivity.

To prove this point, let's experiment on the spoon. Panel A of Figure 5.15 is the original spoon (from Figure 5.11). Panel B is the spoon with the reflectivity and specularity removed. Notice how unrealistically dark it becomes. This is a fundamental quality of metal: Metallic surfaces are dark where they don't reflect their surroundings.

FIGURE 5.15   *The original spoon (at left), and the spoon with various parameter changes.*

For panel C, I brought up the diffuse color to a light gray. The result is a bit closer to what silverware should look like. Note what happens in panel D, however, when I add the specularity and reflectivity back into the mix. The spoon is a bit bright, appearing almost white. Aesthetically speaking, the darker color used in panel A fits the scene better, and the brighter surface in panel D is too washed out. If the underlying diffuse color of an object is very light, highlights and reflections are not visible; remember the same experiment with the drinking glass.

Specularity alone doesn't contribute much to a metallic effect. In panel E, I return the spoon to its original diffuse color and removed the specularity; not much difference from panel A. Unless you're a perfectionist like me, you could probably get away without specularity altogether for Figure 5.11's silverware. It is good practice to eliminate surface attributes that don't contribute to the image.

Before you can apply textures effectively in trueSpace4, you will need to grasp the concept of UV space. There is a lot of material to cover, so let's get started.

UNDERSTANDING UV SPACE

Textures are applied to surfaces in trueSpace4 according to the object's *UV space*. UV space is the mathematical method of describing the horizontal and vertical distance around an object from a given point. UV space, like geometric space, has three coordinates, U, V, and W. The last isn't used in trueSpace.

The U and V coordinates determine which pixel should be used in a texture map, independent of how big the texture map is. I will elaborate. If U and V are 0.25 and 0.5 for a given vertex and the texture map is 512-by-512, the pixel at 128, 256 will be applied to the vertex. The U and V coordinates are also used for procedural shaders, even though there is no texture map. The U and V coordinates are used to compute the shader's value at that specific point.

The difference between texture coordinates and geometry coordinates is what they measure. Geometry coordinates X, Y, and Z reference the placement of geometry in three-dimensional space. An object exists at one set of coordinates. If you move it, it exists at a new set. Texture coordinates only measure texture repetitions. There is always one repetition applied to an object no matter how you scale or stretch the texture. If we use more than one repetition, we start tiling the texture.

Each tile adds 1 to the U and/or the V coordinates. If we were to use the set of texture coordinates U=2, V=2, we would end up with a grid of four tiles resembling a sheet of postage stamps.

UV space is assigned to an object by four methods of projection. They are:

- Planar
- Cylindrical
- Spherical
- Cubic

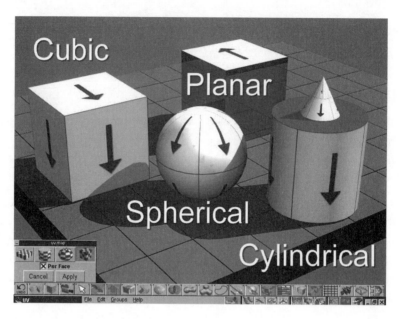

FIGURE 5.16 *The four methods of projecting UV space. The arrows point in the default direction the bottom of the texture map will face.*

PLANAR

Planar projection can be thought of as X-rays passing through an object at the angle and rotation applied. The image being projected will appear on the front and back of the object. Depending on the image being used, streaks may appear on the outer edges of the object. This problem can be worked around by making the pixels along the image's edge a single color. The pixels will still smear, but they will all be the same color, resulting in a uniform fill. Of course, streaking is sometimes a great effect. For example, streaking would look appropriate for an engine piston.

CYLINDRICAL

Cylindrical projection is applied in much the same manner a label is applied to a can. The top and bottom of the can are unaffected by the process, and, depending on the shape of the object, you might get some distortion in these areas. In the case of cylindrical objects, the tops and bottoms will receive the edge color of the image being applied.

SPHERICAL

I think the best way to describe this method of UV projection is that the image will be wrapped around the object. Increasing the horizontal and vertical reps projects the image in an orange slice-like fashion, where each slice can be cut into smaller chunks. This is illustrated in Figure 5.16. Around the equator of the object, the image will appear wider than at the poles. In the case where a small texture and small U rep (horizontal) value are used on a large object, the image might distort around the equator, stretching like an inflating balloon, while a pinching effect may occur at the poles.

CUBIC

The image is projected from six imaginary sides whether the object is six-sided or not. In Figure 5.16, you can see an example of the direction the images will face with each UV projection method.

Now that we have a better understanding of how UV space affects the textures we apply to our object surfaces, let's take a look at some ways to apply texture maps to those surfaces.

UV projections can be moved, rotated, and scaled to fit the object by using the Object Navigation Move, Scale, or Rotate tools. Besides having the ability to move, rotate, or scale UV space, you can also move it outside the object for some interesting effects.

UV PROJECTION PER-FACE

Thanks to UV space, you can apply textures not only to an object as a whole, but also to individual parts of an object. To do so, you use trueSpace4's UV Projection Per-Face feature. UV Projection Per-Face allows any of the four UV projection options to be applied to any one face or group of faces, with each UV projection having its own scale, rotation, and location (see Figure 5.17).

NOTE

It's a good habit to check how your texture looks with the default UV projection assigned to an object. In some cases, the default projection is perfect for what you are trying to accomplish.

NOTE

Keep in mind that light plays an integral part in texture mapping the surfaces of objects in your scenes. Light plays an important part in the textures and bump maps you choose, how you will apply them, and how the light and textures determine the mood of your scene.

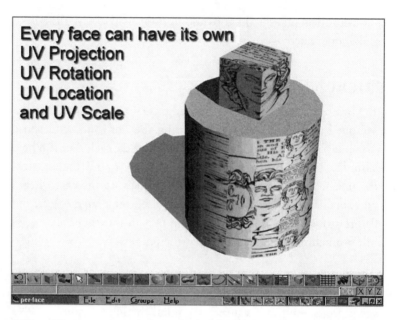

FIGURE 5.17 *UV space can be applied to individual faces with the Per-Face mapping option.*

SELECTING MULTIPLE FACES

The UV Projection Per-Face option is activated via a left click of the UV Projection Per-Face button located in the Render group. Once it's activated, select the UV mapping method in the UV Map panel. To select individual faces, simply click the area of the object. To select multiple faces, you can use one of four methods. You can click individual faces one at a time with your mouse, or you can use the Free-Hand, Lasso, or Rectangle Selection tools. I discussed each of these tools in Chapter 3, but let's recap because in this context the three apply to faces only.

- **Free-Hand:** Use to select multiple faces by dragging your mouse over the desired area; allows selecting faces either by clicking on the surface of an object or by dragging over the surface to select all faces that are crossed by the mouse pointer. The default selection mode adds a new face to the previous selection.

- **Rectangle:** Allows selection of multiple vertices or faces by enclosing the desired faces or vertices in a rectangle.

- **Lasso:** The Lasso selection tool enables you to select vertices and faces within an irregular area by clicking and dragging within the workspace.

You can further define how faces are selected by right-clicking any of these tools to open the Selection panel. The Selection panel has three buttons that enable you to choose whether you want to add faces to, select a subset of, or remove selected faces from the current selection. In addition, the Selection panel offers three other options:

- **Backside:** Allows the inclusion of vertices on the other side of the object's contours.

- **Highlight:** Changes the color of internal vertices or faces as you select them with Lasso or Rectangle.

- **Color button:** A pop-up menu you use to specify the color of the Lasso and the Rectangle tool.

The faces you select for UV Projection Per-Face can be saved as a COB file and reloaded later onto the same object. One of the selection tools must be active and at least one face must be selected on the object when you save to the COB file. When the saved COB is reloaded, the selection is restored to the object. This feature comes in handy in regard to surfacing. For example, different areas of an object can be selected and saved as a COB file. Each of the selected areas could be surfaced differently. If you ever have to go back and change one of the areas, you can load up the COB, and those areas will be reselected. You can now change the selected faces' surface material without affecting the surrounding areas. This is a big time-saver when working with highly detailed painted object surfaces.

You can try out this new feature if you like. I have saved a number of selected faces as a COB on the CD that accompanies this book. The file name is \chapters\05\UV.COB. In a new scene, create a sphere primitive. Load up the UV.COB file. The sphere will have its faces automatically selected. You can add or subtract faces to the selection by using any of the selection tools. Pretty neat, huh?

PER-FACE PROJECTION BASICS

You can change the UV projection, location, scale, and rotation for each face if you like, but each operation must be carried out independently. These are the steps required to apply UV to individual faces:

1. Select the object.

2. Open the UV Map panel via the UV Projection Per-Face button.

3. Select the UV projection method (planar, cylindrical, spherical, or cubic).

4. Select the face or faces you would like the UV projection assigned to.

5. By using the Object Navigation tools, move, scale, or rotate the UV space, if needed. The default navigation mode for UV is Move.

6. Click Apply in the UV Map panel to complete the operation and close the panel.

To assign different UV projections to different faces on the same object, repeat steps 2 through 6 for each face. When you get to step 5, remember that clicking on a new type of projection in step 2 voids any previous move, rotate, or scale operation.

The tool you use to paint the texture map on the object's surface determines the results. If you use Paint Object or Paint Over Existing Material, the entire object will have the texture applied. The mapping on each face is determined by its assigned UV space. If you use Paint Face, only the selected faces will have the texture applied by using the assigned UV space for that face.

PER-FACE UV PROJECTION IN PRACTICE

UV Projection Per-Face is a wonderful tool for surfacing objects with complex shapes and high polygon counts. To illustrate this, we will surface the mushroom we modeled in Chapter 3.

Load up the mushroom.scn located on the CD that accompanies this book. The filename is \chapters\chptr05\mushroom.scn.

1. Switch to the Left view and select the UV Projection Per-Face tool to open the UV Map panel. The last projection method used will still be selected.

2. Right-click the Select Using Lasso tool to open the Selection panel. Disable the Highlight checkbox (this will speed up the selection process) and enable the Add button. Check the Backside option so that the faces not facing you will be included in the selection process.

3. Select the Lasso tool and encircle the mushroom's stem as illustrated in Figure 5.18. If you accidentally select some faces and want to remove them, disable the Add button and enable the Remove button instead. You can now select the faces to remove from the presently selected faces. When done, don't forget to disable the Remove button and re-enable the Add button.

FIGURE 5.18   *In this image, the stem is selected with the Lasso tool.*

4. In the UV Map panel, enable the Cylindrical UV Projection button. You might have to rotate and scale the UV projection to fit the mushroom's stem correctly. If the UV projection needs to be rotated, switch to the Top view to do it and then return to the Left.

5. Click the Apply button in the UV Map panel. If the UV Map panel does not close after you press Apply, don't panic; pressing the Apply button completes the operation. You can press Cancel to close the panel if you want to.

6. The mushroom's stem now has a cylindrical UV space assigned. We will apply a planar UV projection for the cap of the mushroom. Select the Lasso tool and encircle the cap of the mushroom, as illustrated in Figure 5.19.

7. In the UV Map panel, enable the Planar UV Projection button.

8. Click the Apply button in the UV Map panel. Again, if the UV Map panel does not close after pressing the Apply button, you can press the Cancel button to close the panel.

TIP

If you are having trouble selecting faces, you can use the COB files on the CD. Look for mshstem.cob and mshcap.com in the \chapters\chptr05 folder. It's not cheating. Simply select the Object tool to close all the panels and, with the mushroom selected, load the mshstem.cob file from the \chapters\chptr05 folder to select the stem (or mshcap.com to select the cap).

NOTE

You cannot use the Undo option with the Lasso, Rectangle, or Free-Hand selection tools.

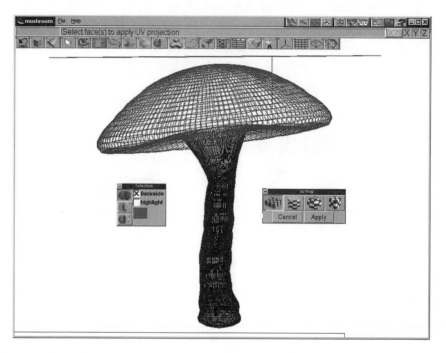

FIGURE 5.19   *In this image, the cap of the mushroom is selected with the Lasso Selection tool.*

Before you apply your final texture to your object, it's a good idea to make sure the UV space is applied correctly. To do so, I like to use a custom image map of a white and blue horizontal stripe so that the UV space assigned to the object is visible. Note that you cannot use trueSpace4's Wrapped U Stripe or Wrapped V Stripe Color shader for this purpose; as their name implies, the stripes will face in the specified direction regardless of the UV space applied to the object. Judging from the test result in Figure 5.20, our mushroom does indeed have separate UV spaces for the stem and for its cap. Now, let's apply an image map more suitable to the object.

1. Right-click the Paint Object tool to open the Material Shader panels.

2. Right-click the Color sphere in the Shaders panel to open the Texture Map panel.

3. Click the Get Texture Map button. I have placed two textures (mshtxt1.jpg and mshtxt2.jpg) in the \chapters\chptr05 folder on the CD. For now, select mshtxt1.jpg. We will be using one repetition each for U and V, so leave the U Repts and V Repts settings at their defaults and close the Texture Map panel for now.

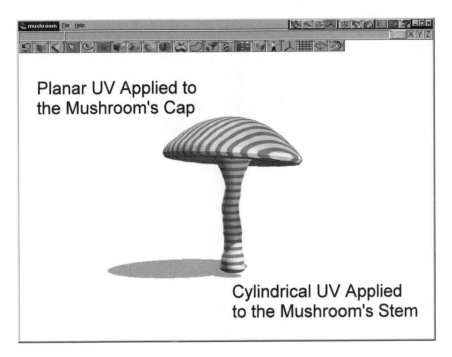

FIGURE 5.20 *The effects of separate UV space applied to a single object.*

4. Select the Reflectance sphere to open the Reflectance table. Choose Matte and right-click any of the Shader Attribute sliders to open a second Shader Attributes panel. Set Diffuse to about 0.8 and Ambient Glow to 0.1.

5. Select the Paint Object tool to paint the texture on your mushroom.

Interesting result: The stem and cap in Figure 5.21 each have the texture applied correctly. In previous versions of trueSpace, I would have modeled the stem and cap separately, but this is no longer necessary in trueSpace4 with its capability to assign multiple UV projection methods to an object's surface.

FIGURE 5.21   *In this image, a marble-like texture is applied to our mushroom.*

SURFACING GROUPS OF FACES

We applied a single image map to the mushroom object as a whole, and, as expected, the texture was applied according to the UV assigned to its surfaces. We can take this a step further. We can select groups of faces and apply a texture to those surfaces as a group. Let's add darker splotches to the cap of the mushroom.

1. Switch to the Front or Left view.

2. If the Shaders panels are not already open, open them now by right-clicking any of the paint tools.

3. In the Shaders panel, left-click the Reflectance sphere and select Phong from the table. The Transparency and Displacement shaders should both be set to None.

4. In the Shaders panel, click the Color Shader sphere. From the list, select Plain Color. Right-click the Color Shader sphere to open the Plain Color panel. Select a dark tan by clicking in the upper-right corner of the Color

Cube just below the yellow area. If you prefer entering RGB values as I do, right-click the Color Cube to open the Plain Color RGB panel. Enter the values 193 in the Red field, 154 in Green, and 113 in Blue.

5. In the Shader Attribute panel, right-click any of the seven sliders. Enter the following: Ambient 0.5, Diffuse 0.6, Shine 0.1, and Rough 0.0.

6. Open the Selection panel by right-clicking either the Lasso, Rectangle, or Free-Hand button. Unselect the Highlight option and enable the Backside option and Add button. Enable the Select Using Lasso tool.

7. By using the Lasso, select the mushroom's stem.

8. Switch to the Top view. You may notice that some of the faces of the mushroom's cap have also been selected. To remedy this, simply disable the Add button in the Selection panel and enable the Remove button. By using the Lasso, select the unwanted faces outside the center of the cap—presto! They are removed from the selected faces of the stem. Switch to the Left view.

9. If you closed the Plain Color panel or the Plain Color RGB panel, reopen them by right-clicking the Color Shader sphere. Right-click the Color Cube, and in the Plain Color RGB panel, enter R193, G183, and B171.

10. Select the Paint Face tool; all the selected faces will be assigned the selected color and reflectance. Your mushroom should look similar to Figure 5.22.

NOTE

The slider on the Plain Color panel does change the RGB values of the color selected from the Color Cube. Many newcomers mistake this slider as an intensity slider. Here is what actually occurs as you move the slider: For each step the slider is moved, the RGB values are stepped up or down depending on the direction. For example, if the RGB values were set to R120, G130, and B140, and the slider were moved up one step, the result would be R121, G131, and B141. If the exact RGB values are important, you can adjust the object's Ambient Glow slider in the Shader Attribute panel or adjust your scene's lighting to compensate for intensity.

You aren't limited to solid colors. You can apply image maps to the selected faces as well, and the applied textures will use whatever UV projection method is assigned to those surfaces. Feel free to experiment with this powerful surfacing feature. Try switching to the Top view and selecting faces in a circular pattern to create splotches on the mushroom's cap.

We looked at applying color and texture maps to surfaces and looked at surfacing individual groups of faces. Next, we will look at applying decals to your objects.

FIGURE 5.22   *In this image, two solid colors are applied to a single object by using the Lasso Selection tool.*

DECALING

Decals are images (usually small) that are applied to an object's surface, like you would apply a sticker to an object in the real world. To accomplish this, we use a tool called the Material Rectangle tool.

The Material Rectangle tool can be used to place individual texture maps onto the surface of an object that may or may not have already been texture mapped. The texture can be freely moved and scaled to fit the surface. This method also supports the layering of images. It is important to note that the bump map of the object's base material is inherited through all the layers. Here are some of the pros and cons of using the Material Rectangle tool.

Pros:

- Up to eight textures can be layered.

- Each of the textures can be moved and scaled independently of one another.

- Textures can be precisely positioned. The material rectangle's scale, position, and texture can each be animated.

Cons:

- Cannot be applied to glued objects as a whole.

- Textures can disappear into the UV seam (see Figure 5.23).

- You can't apply material rectangles onto surfaces that have been painted with the 3D paint or bump maps.

- The texture's rotation and UV scale is totally dependent on the underlying surface's UV space.

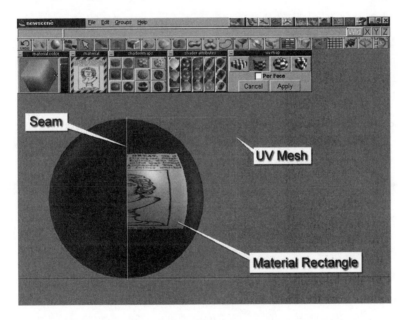

FIGURE 5.23   *In this image, a portion of the decal disappears into the UV seam.*

APPLYING DECALS, THE BASICS

Material rectangles can be deleted, moved, or sent to the front of other material rectangles. The material rectangle moves and scales around the object conforming to the object's UV space. If the object has a planar projection, then the rectangle will be applied to both sides of the object. Selecting the Material Rectangle tool opens its control panel. Both position and scaling of material rectangles can be animated, as well as the material for each rectangle.

Before we get into the practical applications, let's review the Material Rectangle panel.

- **New:** Creates a new material rectangle and displays it on the object's surface. Up to eight material rectangles can be added to an object.

- **Del:** Deletes the current material rectangle.

- **Move:** Lets you move the material rectangle interactively around the object's surface by dragging the left mouse button. Horizontal and vertical mouse movements translate respectively to U and V movement. Right-click on Move to constrain movement either to U or V space.

- **Scale:** Lets you scale the material rectangle interactively by dragging the left mouse button. Horizontal and vertical mouse movements translate respectively to U and V scaling. Right-click on Scale to constrain scaling either to U or V space.

- **</>:** These two buttons cycle through an object's material rectangles, if there are more than one. The Material Preview does not update to show the material on the current rectangle.

- **Paint:** Left-click to paint the material rectangle with the current material.

- **Inspect:** Left-click to see the current material rectangle's material displayed in the Material Preview panel if it is open. Right-click to open all Material property panels.

- **Material Rectangle to Front:** When an object has multiple material rectangles that overlap, select this tool to bring the current material rectangle to the "top of the stack." Normally when rectangles overlap, the topmost is the last created.

To apply a material rectangle, follow these steps:

1. Select the object.

2. Select the Material Rectangle tool and click New. A mesh will appear that you can use to position and scale the decal to the appropriate size.

3. Position and scale the decal by using the Move and Scale buttons.

4. Right-click the Paint Material Rectangle tool to open the shaders panels. Define the surface attributes you want the decal to have.

5. Left-click the Paint Material Rectangle tool.

It's important to note that once you have defined the location and size of the decal, you can change the image map to be used as a decal at any time by right-clicking the Paint Material Rectangle tool in the Material Rectangle panel. Let's look at using the Material Rectangle tool on an object we are familiar with.

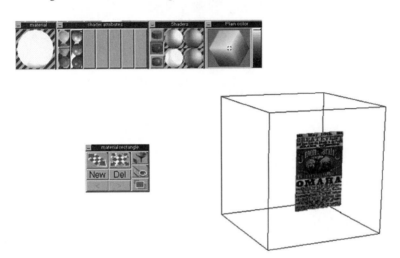

FIGURE 5.24   *The Material Rectangle tool is used to apply decals to objects you create.*

APPLYING DECALS TO FRANKY

In my experience in dealing with other trueSpace users, I have found that many do not use the Material Rectangle tool at all. That's a shame because it's a big time-saver, and is capable of creating some cool effects. Let's look at some examples, starting with the basics.

In Chapter 3, we created Franky and his skateboard, but we didn't add any textures to him. Doing so is a perfect opportunity to explore the Material Rectangle tool. As you can see from Figure 5.25, the results will be impressive.

1. After loading the Franky.scn scene file, set the view in the main window to Front. From this perspective, applying the decals will be a cinch. Select Franky's mesh. (Remember, we glued all the primitives that make up the character together into a single hierarchy.) By using the Move Down Hierarchy tool, select the head. With the head selected, you should be able to open the Material Rectangle panel. If the button is disabled, then the head is still part of a hierarchy. You can't place decals onto objects that are glued together.

FIGURE 5.25   *Franky, the skateboarding terror, after having decals applied to him.*

2. With the Material Rectangle panel open, you are ready to place your first decal: the stitches on his head. For this purpose, I have included a small image called stitches in the images folder on the CD. Franky's head for the most part is cylindrical, and we are going to apply the stitches around the head like a label. Therefore, select the character's head and apply a cylindrical UV space to it.

3. From the Material Rectangle panel, select New to display the Decal Mesh. The Move Material Rectangle button is selected by default. By holding the left mouse button, you can move the mesh anywhere on the head. If for any reason the mesh refuses to move in any direction, check the Navigation Axis buttons, one or more of which may be unselected. We want the stitches to wrap around Franky's head, so we will have to scale the decal to fit.

4. Select the Scale Material Rectangle button. Keeping the left mouse button depressed, drag the Material Rectangle mesh to the desired size as depicted

in Figure 5.26. The Decal Mesh scales from the lower-left corner outward, not from the center as you might expect. You may have to switch back and forth between the Move and Scale Material Rectangle buttons to position and scale the decal mesh just right. Use Figure 5.26 as a guide.

5. Now that we have the Decal Mesh in position, all there is left to do is select the image. Right-click the Paint Material Rectangle button to open the Material and Shader panels. (If you have already selected the stitches as the current texture, you may skip that step.) Left-click the Color Shader sphere in the Shaders panel. This will open a Color Selection table. Select Texture Map, and after the Color Selection window closes, right-click the Color Shader sphere to open the Texture Map panel. Left-click the Get Texture Map button. Select the stitches image located on the CD. The image is tiny and may appear to be stretched out; to get it to wrap around Franky's head without any distortion, we will have to use a U Repts setting of 12 and a V Repts setting of 1. If everything worked out, Franky should have stitches encircling the circumference of his skullcap.

Practice makes perfect, so why don't you give Franky some pupils and eyebrows, and while you're at it, place a "5" on his tee-shirt, as in Figure 5.27. I have placed the images you will need in the images folder on the CD: they are pupil.jpg, brow.jpg, and no_5.jpg, respectively. Remember, when texture mapping your objects, the first step is to make sure the surface you are about to texture map has had a UV space assigned. If you're the type that likes to dismantle things, you can find the finished Franky scene in the scenes folder on the CD.

TIP

Here is a tip for creating textures that scale and fit a mesh perfectly. While Franky is visible in the Front view, load Paint Shop Pro (PSP). You will find this program in the PSP5 folder on the CD that accompanies this book. From the Capture menu, select Setup. Check the Area box, check the Hot Key box, and select F12 as the hot key. Click the Capture Now button. PSP will automatically be minimized, exposing trueSpace's work environment. Render the scene. When it's done, Franky should be looking right at you—well, kind of, he doesn't have any pupils yet. Press the F12 key on your keyboard; the cursor will become a crosshair. Using the crosshairs, select the area around the face by clicking in the upper-left corner just to the left and above Franky's head. Drag your mouse until the marquee (dotted line) encloses the area of the face; left-click. PSP will open with the selected area of Franky's face. You can now paint directly on this image. Save it as a JPG or TGA or whatever file type you prefer and use it as a texture map for Franky's face. This is how I created the stitches, pupils, and eyebrows—a low-budget method, but very effective.

WARNING

You *cannot* apply material rectangles to objects that have been 3D painted.

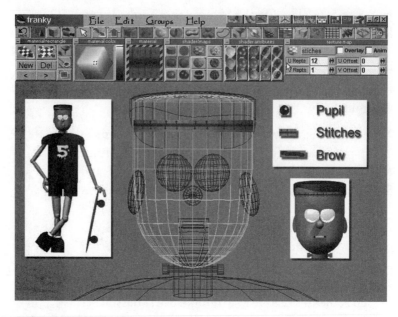

FIGURE 5.26   *Applying the stitches to Franky's head.*

FIGURE 5.27   *Franky with decals for eyebrows, pupils, and a 5 on his tee-shirt. Perfect examples of the basic uses for the Material Rectangle tool.*

DECALS AND TRANSPARENCY

Because up to eight textures can be layered, it is possible to create some great effects with the Material Rectangle tool. In Figure 5.28, the armor of the USCM660 cybernetic Marine was created by using a combination of an image with a transparent center and an image that was solid. Both had a gizmo-like pattern throughout, as depicted in the small window in Figure 5.29.

FIGURE 5.28   *U.S. cybernetic Marine, texture mapped with Material Rectangles.*

By applying both images using the Material Rectangle tool, I was able to achieve a two-tone look to the armor. Figure 5.29 shows the Marine's thigh. A techno bump map and cylindrical UV space were applied to the surface; remember that material rectangles inherit the bump map of the object you are surfacing. The inset window in Figure 5.29 is made up of two panels: one with the solid texture and one with the texture with an alpha channel. The contents of both were applied to the thigh by using the Material Rectangle tool. Notice how the first texture (the lighter-colored one) shows through the second layer? I could have approached this another way. I could have simply applied the solid texture with the Paint Object tool and then used the Material Rectangle with the alpha channel; either method would yield the same result. It's just a matter of preference.

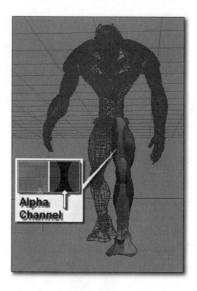

FIGURE 5.29   *In this image, the cyborg's leg is isolated, and the textures applied are displayed.*

When I first built this character, I used a copy of the thigh scaled slightly larger than the original, then subtracted two spheres from each side of the larger thigh. With the smaller version inside the other, its surface was visible, giving me a two-tone effect. All that work just to add more geometry to the scene and increase render time. No, thank you. I settled on using material rectangles to get the same effect.

The material rectangles technique can be useful when dressing your characters in clothing, as well. In Figure 5.30, the Western character's vest and shirt appear to be two separate objects, but they are not—thanks to material rectangles. I modeled the shirt and painted it white, applied the texture of the vest with the Material Rectangle tool, and saved myself the trouble of modeling the character's vest.

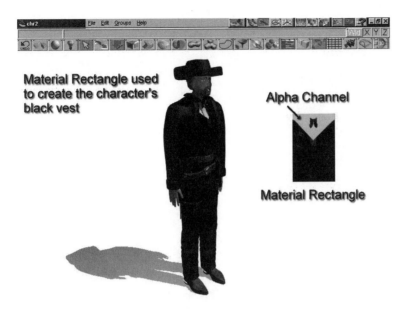

FIGURE 5.30   *A material rectangle was used to create the illusion of a separate shirt and vest. This reduced the need to model the shirt and vest separately.*

PROCEDURAL TEXTURES

We have talked a bit about using image maps and diffuse color to surface our object. Let's look at surfacing objects in trueSpace by using procedural textures.

trueSpace4 offers 16 Procedural shaders. They can be divided into two types: those that do not adhere to an object's UV mesh:

- Blue Marble
- Chrome
- Cubes (checker pattern)
- Marble
- Simple Wood
- Solid Clouds
- Solid Polka

And those that do:

- Wrapped Brick

- Wrapped Checker

- Wrapped Diagonal

- Wrapped Polka

- Wrapped Grid

- Wrapped Texture Brick

- Wrapped U Strip

- Wrapped V Stripe

Some procedural textures have a method of creating random cloud-like blends of assigned colors, while others use just two colors and a grid pattern. One of the obvious advantages of using a procedure as opposed to an image map is you have greater control over the blending of colors and shades of colors with trueSpace4. Another advantage is that identical objects can each have the same procedural applied and not look identical, simply by adding little variations here and there to the procedural texture.

I have never been fond of books that demonstrate how to use control panels; that's what the manual is for. I prefer demonstrations of the tool in action. In that vein, let's use a procedural texture to create a basketball.

1. In a new scene, switch to the Perspective view.

2. Right-click the sphere primitive button to open the Sphere panel. Enter 16 in the Latitude field and 32 in the Longitude field. Add a sphere primitive to the scene.

3. Open the UV Map panel. Enable the Spherical UV projection button and click Apply.

4. Right-click any of the Paint tools or the Inspect tool to open the Material and Shader panels.

5. Left-click the Transparency sphere in the Shader panel and select None from the Transparency table.

6. Left-click the Reflectance sphere in the Shader panel to open the Reflectance table. Select Phong from the Reflectance table.

7. Right-click any of the sliders in the Shader Attributes panel. Enter 0.1 in the Ambient field, 0.9 in the Diffuse field, 0.32 in the Shine field, and 0.1 in the Rough field. This will give our basketball just the right amount of specularity needed to show off its rough texture when we are finished.

8. Left-click the Color sphere in the Shader panel (everyone say it along with me) to open the Color table. Select Wrapped U Stripe from the Color table.

9. Right-click the Color sphere in the Shader panel to open the Wrapped Stripe panel. This panel is comprised of two color selection boxes (Back Color and Stripe Color) and three entry fields (Size, Width, and Fuzz).

10. Click (either left or right) the Back Color button to open the Back Color selection panel. Right-click the Color Selection cube in the Back Color panel to open the Back RGB panel. Enter 255 for Red, 128 for Green, and 60 for Blue.

11. Click (either left or right) the Stripe Color button to open the Stripe Color selection panel. The Back Color and Back RGB panel will close. Right-click the Color Selection cube in the Stripe Color panel to open the Stripe RGB panel. Enter 100 for Red, 45 for Green, and 0 for Blue. Close both the Stripe Color and Stripe RGB panels.

12. In the Wrapped Stripe panel, enter the values 0.11 in the Size field, 0.05 in the Width field, and 0.08 in the Fuzz field.

13. Select the Paint Object tool to apply the procedural texture to the sphere. Select the Close All Panels button.

14. Right-click the Object tool to open the Object Info panel. In the X, Y, and Z Rotation fields enter −120, −45, and −120, respectively. This should give the ball a more natural orientation toward the viewer. Close the Object Info panel.

15. Right-click any of the Paint tools or the Inspect tool to open the Material and Shader panels as you did in Step 4. Left-click the Displacement sphere in the Shader panel and select Rough from the Displacement table.

16. Right-click the Displacement sphere in the Shader panel to open the Rough panel. This panel has four fields: Scale, Amplitude, Detail, and Sharpness. Enter 0.3, 0.05, 1.0, and 1.0, respectively, and close the panel.

17. Select the Paint Object tool to magically transform the sphere into a basketball like the one in Figure 5.31.

FIGURE 5.31   *The basketball was created from a sphere and the Wrapped U Stripe procedural texture.*

As you can see, procedurals do far more than create marble textures. They can be used to create some stunning visual effects, as well. We will explore using procedurals to create effects in Chapters 13 and 14. The Material Rectangle tool was used to place a small NBA logo on the basketball.

Getting procedural texture settings just right generally takes a lot of trial and error. Don't let this time go to waste; treat your surfacing experiments as a chance to discover new ways to simulate surfaces for other projects. You now have 16 procedurals in trueSpace4 to experiment with, and the word from Caligari is that in the next release you will be able to create your very own custom shaders.

ADDING FINE DETAILS TO SURFACES

You worked on the scene for hours, and you just finished your first test render. It looks great, but it's missing a small detail. Maybe a chip, scratch, dent, or faded area. You could go back and alter a texture map or two to achieve the desired result, but that would require that the image map be altered in the perfect position. If it's not, you will have to go back and alter the image map again. If the texture has many U or V Repts settings, this can cause the texture to become unrepeatable. If you could only add a blemish or nick quickly—paint it on the object in the exact spot—you wouldn't have to spend so much time outside the trueSpace environment in some paint package. Well, my friend, you can.

trueSpace4 has the capability to paint directly on an object's surface. You can also add nicks and cracks to surfaces without ever leaving the trueSpace environment.

3D BUMP

You can paint bumps onto an object in real time from within the trueSpace environment. As with the standard bump mapping tool, the bumps you create with the 3D Bump tool are not part of the object's geometry.

The 3D Bump tool has three brush shapes: a cube, a sphere, and a cylinder. You can adjust the bump height by using the first slider in the tool's panel. The slider is split into two parts: The top half causes the selected brush to create indentations, while the bottom section causes bumps. The Amplitude setting can be adjusted on a per-face basis. Acceptable values range from −50 to 50. The second slider is used to adjust the selected brush's size. The amplitude of the bumps created with the 3D Bump tool is global to an individual face. In other words, if you apply a ding or dent with a specified amplitude and then apply a dent or ding with a different amplitude to the same face, the previous bumps will be assigned this new amplitude. To close the 3D Bump panel, select the Object tool. In Figure 5.32, the detail of the pilot's helmet was created with the 3D Bump tool.

FIGURE 5.32   *In this image, the fine dings and dents of the pilot's helmet were created with the 3D paint tools.*

3D PAINT

The 3D Paint tool applies circular patterns regardless whether you use the Fill Brush, which creates solid lines, or the Airbrush, which produces a feathered edge. The density of the Airbrush can be adjusted by using the first slider in the 3D Paint panel. The second slider on this panel is Brush size, and it controls the shape of the Erase Brush tool, as well. The third and final slider is the color's transparency. 3D paintstrokes can also be erased by using the Erase Brush tool located in the 3D Paint panel's lower-left corner. You can even erase strokes after loading the object from disk. It's important to note that the Erase Brush tool does not erase any 3D bump mapping applied to an object.

You cannot use the 3D Paint tool on surfaces that have had texture maps applied, nor can you 3D Paint with textures. For best results, you should subdivide large surface areas before applying 3D paint. Any noncoplanar face that has had the 3D Paint tool applied automatically gets triangulated. Faces with more than four sides will also become triangulated.

WARNING

If the QuadDivide, Smooth QuadDivide, or Triangulation tools are used on objects that have been painted with the 3D Paint tool, you cannot apply any additional 3D paintstrokes.

To use the 3D Paint tool, select an object and then select the 3D Paint tool. The object is then rendered. On complex objects, this will take a few moments. When everything is a go, the mouse cursor will change to a paintbrush.

PAINT AND BUMP COMMONALITIES

The 3D Paint and 3D Bump tools work by creating a separate texture for each of the faces you paint on. These textures are stored in individual files and placed in a subdirectory of the present directory. The filename is used with a TGA extension. For example, if the name of the object is sphere1 and you save the scene in \trueSpace\scenes, the textures will be stored in \trueSpace\scenes\sphere1tex\.

Right-clicking either the 3D Paint or 3D Bump tool opens the Paint Draw Type panel. This panel contains two radio buttons, Free Draw and Line Draw. When Free Draw mode is selected, dragging the mouse in any direction will draw on the surface. In Line Draw mode, you must click to where you want the end points of the line to appear on the object's surface. trueSpace4 draws a straight line connecting the two endpoints selected.

The Connect option in the Paint Draw Type panel applies to the Free Draw mode only. Why it resides at the bottom of the panel I will never know. When it is selected, smooth brushstrokes are created no matter how fast you move the brush. When it is unchecked, moving the brush quickly across the object's surface will cause a skipping effect.

This panel also has a display field that shows the unique prefix that the 3D Paint tool assigns to the textures it creates. You cannot edit the name, but you can click in the box and use the arrow keys to scroll through the entire name field.

Both the 3D Paint and 3D Bump tools make a powerful combo that can be used to add fine details to surfaces that would otherwise have to be created in a paint package.

To get the most out of these tools, you will have to perform a little bit of a balancing act. You can't paint on a group of objects. You will have to move down the object hierarchy until you isolate the object you want to add detail to. You also cannot use the 3D Paint and 3D Bump tools on objects that have had textures applied, but the number one thing you will need to do is be patient. Once you have isolated your object and have set up your brushes, you will need to control your desire to paint in long, continuous strokes. Doing so will slow the process to a crawl.

A method I found that works well is to apply strokes with short clicks of the mouse. You will find that with a little patience, the 3D Paint and 3D Bump tools are great for adding the little details that count.

MATERIAL LIBRARIES

When you create a material you're especially pleased with, you can save it in a trueSpace's material library file to reuse later. Everything about the material is saved, including the image maps, shaders assigned, and UV repetitions. If you can't quite remember a material's name, a section of the Material Library panel lets you view your choices.

To open the Material Library panel, click the Material Library button located in the Navigation group. If it isn't visible, left-click and hold the Object tool to open the popup where the panel resides.

To open a material library, left-click the Load/Save Material Library button to reveal the four options available: New, Load, Save, and Save As.

The Material Library panel displays eight materials at a time on either spheres or planes, as in the Material panel (found by right-clicking the Paint tools). The state the Material panel is in (displaying as a sphere or plane) when the material is saved determines whether the Material Library panel uses spheres or planes.

To choose a material from the displayed library, simply left-click on the appropriate sphere/plane in the Material Library panel. The name of the selected material appears in the lower-right corner of the Material Library panel. The currently selected material is easily identified by the red line drawn beneath it. Once a material is selected, the Shader panels will reflect its properties. You can immediately assign this texture to an object via the Paint tools.

Materials can be added to the open library with a click of a button. If you have a material you would like to save in the open material library, click the Add Material to Library button. To remove a material from the open library, click the Remove Material from Library button.

CREATING CUSTOM MATERIAL LIBRARIES

The best feature of Material Libraries is the capability to create and save your very own custom materials for later use. To create your own material library, left-click the Load/Save Material Library button. Select New from the popup. At this point, you can reopen the popup and choose Save As and give the library a name. Or you can add materials to the library as described previously and save the material library when done.

It's a good idea to place your textures into groups of individual material library files, for example, metals, glass, ceramics, and so on. A good place to start your own collection is with the formulas I provide later in this chapter. Open a new scene and place a sphere, cylinder, cone, and cube in the scene. Place them so that each is visible in the Perspective view window. Place them so that they do not intersect one another. Assign each of the formulas in this chapter to each of the objects in the scene to help you visualize how the material appears on objects of different shapes. Season the materials to taste and save them into your own library, as already described. As you add each material, give it a unique name that best describes its properties by entering it in the Material Name entry field located in the lower-right corner of the Material Library panel. For example, you may have two materials that use the same image map, but one may be highly reflective, and the other might not be, or one might be assigned a bump map where the other has not. This will help you quickly identify the attributes from the name displayed in the lower-right corner without the need to view its attributes in the Shader panels.

It's never too late to start your custom material collection. You can load objects or scenes you have created in the past and save their assigned surface material to your custom library.

SELECTING IMAGES, THINGS TO CONSIDER

No discussion of texture mapping would be complete without talking about the images' files themselves.

In 3D, there's a constant pressure between the highest possible quality and the lowest possible render times. Beautifully simple geometry is fast, but lacks the detail a complex mesh can give. Likewise, perfect textures on a million-polygon object are going to break the render cycle bank. The factors that affect this decision most (as far as textures and geometry are concerned) are image format, image size, and mesh complexity.

When building your image collection, careful image selection can reduce the total render time and improve the overall appearance of your imagery so you can use your render cycle coupons elsewhere. Experimentation is a good way to determine the resolutions that work best for you and your modeling style, but it is a time-consuming process. Here are some things to consider when selecting textures for your project.

IMAGE FORMATS

Image format might not seem like an issue but it can be. trueSpace4 supports eight popular raster image formats:

- JPG
- TGA
- BMP
- DIB
- AVI
- PNG
- DDS
- TIF

Let's consider a few of the more popular formats. The JPG (Joint Photographic Experts Group) format, for example, is great for textures with its support for 16 million colors (truecolor) and relatively small size, but it doesn't support alpha channels (transparency). This brings us to the TGA (Truevision) format and its alpha channel support. trueSpace4 will play back a series of numbered TGA files just like an AVI file and with the added support of transparency. TGA is great for such effects as explosions and fireballs (discussed in Chapter 14). trueSpace4 supports two TGA flavors, 24-bit and 32-bit. The 24-bit version has no advantages over the JPG format, but the 32-bit version supports alpha channels. The BMP (Microsoft Windows) format supports truecolor but at a cost in file size and really has no advantage over the 32-bit TGA or JPG formats.

So, where do we stand on the image format issue? Simply, if you require truecolor support and alpha channels, the 32-bit TGA format is the answer. For your general textures, JPG offers support for 16 million colors and reasonable file size.

REPEATABLE PATTERNS

Seamless doesn't always mean the image has a repeatable pattern.

You have just built a model of the great wall of China. Everything is perfect, right down to its snake-like shape disappearing into the distance. You search through your collection for the perfect stone wall texture. You find a seamless image; edge to edge, the texture has no noticeable seam, or does it?

For large areas that will require a texture to be repeated, seamless textures work only if the overall pattern is uniform. Take the case of the dirt road texture in the opening image to this chapter. This kind of pattern will work as a seamless texture because our brains won't focus on the small details; the repeating patterns sneak by unnoticed. However, place a large stone in the middle of the texture and the repeat pattern will stick out like a sore thumb. Another example is a burlap texture evenly lit. We can set the U and V repetitions to any number we choose without any noticeable pattern. But place a tear somewhere in the texture, and the texture can't be repeated no matter how seamless it is. One discolored stone in that seamless texture can ruin the Great Wall of China.

SIZE

A quick answer to the question "how big should my images be?" is "the highest resolution possible," not "as small as possible." When collecting images or scans for your material collection, always try to have the highest resolution on hand. The reason for this strategy is if you need a smaller texture for a project, you can scale the image down in a paint program to the desired size without fear of fuzzy distortion. On the other hand, if you have a small 64×64 image and try scaling it up to 320×320, the texture will appear pixelated, and the image will lose its crisp, sharp look when applied to the object's surface. Furthermore, to hide this effect, you will have to turn up the U and V repetitions. This often causes the detail of the textures to get lost, and those details are what we're after in the first place.

Let's face it: All the textures in your collection are not going to be the same size, and they are not all seamless with repeatable patterns. Here is a trick you can use to get the best out of those seamless and nonseamless textures, and how to determine the correct scale of your scenes when using them.

We know that when modeling, we can use one object as a scale for the rest of the objects we add or build to our scene. This is fine for determining the scale of all the objects in relation to one another; however, nowhere is it written in stone that this is the scale at which you should apply your textures.

Each texture has its own volume. That's right—I said *volume*. Wrapping the texture from end to end without any visible distortion is the texture's natural volume. When applied to an object with the same volume as the object, the texture will look its best. So, naturally, we want our object with a volume as close to the texture's natural volume as possible.

We are not after an exact number but an approximation. A simple technique I use is to place a simple primitive in a new scene. I try on all the textures I will be using in the scene and scale the object until the texture fits and looks great. I repeat this process until I have a general idea of the best scale that fits the textures. I then load the scene and scale the entire scene to this scale or the volume of the textures I will be using.

SUMMARY

Well, we have finally come to the end of another chapter. We managed to cover a lot of ground, but as I said at the beginning, surfacing is a broad subject, and, therefore, we have only scratched the surface (no pun intended).

We started by focusing on developing our surfacing skills through visualization. We examined two of the most important and sometimes difficult surfaces to master. We also experimented with the new tools, and managed to walk away unscathed, hopefully with a newfound respect for surfacing.

CHAPTER 6

TEXTURE CREATION AND MANAGEMENT

by Tom Marlin

High-quality textures can make a great difference in your scenes, bringing life to your art and enabling you to reduce the polygon count of your geometry (meshes). The difference between good 3D artists and award-winning 3D artists can be measured by the caliber of textures used in their art.

The release of trueSpace4 added a new dimension to surfacing, by adding material shaders. To fully take advantage of these new shaders, you'll want some high-quality, photorealistic texture maps and bump maps, and the knowledge to create them. Although there are many advantages in purchasing an off-the-shelf texture collection, you might not find the right texture to make your finished image a classic. Knowing how to create these professional-level textures is a valuable asset.

This chapter examines the use of photorealistic texture maps only. The subject of creating textures in 2D-paint and texture creation programs is so vast, it could be the subject of an entire book. There are several graphics programs designed specifically for creating 2D textures, which can be found on the Internet or through software resellers. Also, this chapter deals with the creation of textures for digital art displayed on a monitor, not necessarily for the print media, where higher resolution textures are usually required.

In the pages that follow, you'll learn how to

- Shoot photographs for use as textures, using digital or film cameras

- Digitize images from film

- Recognize the legal limitations of using other people's photos and textures

- Post-process photos into texture maps

- Create seamless textures from texture maps

- Modify texture maps for use as bump maps

- Create alpha channel textures containing transparent areas

- Incorporate all of the preceding techniques into a sophisticated trueSpace scene

Through a series of tutorials, you'll get first-hand experience with these concepts and create your own scene. The resource CD-ROM includes a trueSpace SCN file complete with accompanying textures. Preferably, you'll be able to create your own textures for this scene with the knowledge you gain.

Experience with 2D-paint programs is assumed, and access to a digital or a film camera and digital scanner is preferred. For those without these photographic resources, sample source images are supplied on the accompanying resource CD. While there are many good 2D-paint programs on the market, Adobe Photoshop is used here to demonstrate texture creation techniques because of its widespread use.

ACQUIRING IMAGES

The purpose of photorealistic textures is to bring the look of real-world objects into your trueSpace art. To accomplish this, you have to capture these textures through photography. Although the best photographic equipment available is always preferred, you can still grab some remarkable textures with the least expensive cameras.

DIGITAL PHOTOGRAPHY

In recent years, the rapid technological improvements, extreme price reductions, and mass marketing of digital cameras has made them available and affordable to most 3D artists. Just a few years ago, a high-quality digital camera cost upwards to $10,000. Now you can buy one suitable for a variety of purposes—including the capture of digital images for photorealistic textures—for under $500 (see Figure 6.1).

Maximum resolution usually determines the cost of the camera. In most cases, a 640×480 pixel resolution digital camera will suffice for capturing images to be used as average textures. For capturing texture images to be used in close-ups, backgrounds, and alpha channel textures, a 1,024×768 pixel resolution or higher would be more suitable.

There are several advantages to digital photography:

- **No media change:** The photographic image is captured in the media for which it is intended: output on a digital monitor. There is no "middle man" involved—no processing from film negative to print or from print to digital scanner. Both these methods can cause variances in colors from the original image seen through the lens.

- **Processing speed**: You have the opportunity to view your images immediately after you upload them into your computer, rather than waiting for film processing time.

- **Costs:** Once you buy the camera, you'll never pay for film or processing. There is a drawback here: You'll find yourself using lots of batteries!

FIGURE 6.1   *A good digital camera can serve as a great source for capturing photorealistic textures.*

FILM PHOTOGRAPHY

If you don't have access to a digital camera, a good film camera will do fine, but you'll need access to a scanner to digitize the film print or negative. A quality 35mm camera is preferred, but sometimes even a small disposable camera will do the trick. Like digital cameras, digital scanners have also improved in quality and become affordable in recent years.

Film processing is a strong consideration when converting textures captured on film to digital images. Standard machine prints from the local drugstore are fine for the family photo album, but there may be cases where these prints don't provide the color quality or resolution required for some texture applications. An example is a texture that would occupy most of a 1,600×1,200-pixel screen image; here, you would probably require an 8×10-inch custom color print to ensure a quality image under close scrutiny. An option is 5×7-inch or larger matte prints from a custom color studio, where professional processors can create custom prints that best represent the original images seen through your lens. These studios can also, in many cases, create digital images directly from your film.

Film cameras, like their digital counterparts, have their own advantages:

- **Resolution**: You can create much higher resolution textures with a good film image than you can with the average digital camera. Most affordable digital cameras come with a maximum resolution of 1,024×768 pixels, while a film negative can, in most cases, be printed and digitized at a much higher resolution.

- **Features**: Because digital photography is in its relative infancy, digital cameras rarely possess the features provided by film cameras. These features include interchangeable lenses, aperture adjustments, and the many other refinements that have been made to film cameras since their inception almost 150 years ago.

- **Detail Quality**: Because digital photography is still a relatively new technology, some degree of "artifacting" occurs when photographing images in digital form. These artifacts are usually visible only at the detail level when the resulting textures are used at or above their maximum intended resolution. Some of the cheaper digital cameras are more prone to produce inferior images, so reading some reviews and viewing sample images on the Internet is worthwhile.

Clearly, the decision to use digital or film cameras for texture creation is dependent on many factors. But for average use in trueSpace scenes, either technology is acceptable.

PHOTOGRAPHIC TECHNIQUES

Shooting photographs for textures is an art in itself. You must possess the ability to visualize the end product as you are shooting a photo. The title "I am a Camera" really applies here, as you capture the beauty and drama of everyday life for use in your trueSpace scenes. Here are some basic guidelines to follow that will help you refine this art.

- **First of all, *visualize*.** As you line up your subject through the lens, try to *visualize* what you're going to do with this photo. Visualize what the mesh will look like and how the texture will be applied. Will the texture be wrapped around a cylinder or perhaps mapped on a flat plane? Will it be tiled multiple times without showing seams? Will the mesh require a texture that is more vertical than horizontal? Visualize the resulting texture and its place in a trueSpace scene. Think about whether you can *really use* the texture. While shooting texture photos, you can sometimes become so wrapped up in the magnificent scene through your lens that you forget the purpose of the photograph. Just because a subject appears attractive as a photograph, it's not necessarily going to result in a good texture. Texture photography is entirely different than photographing petunias on a sunny day (unless you're hunting for petunia textures!).

- **Shoot exterior photos on a cloudy day.** Because trueSpace, like other 3D programs, allows you to define your own light sources and the shadows they cast, you need textures that don't bring unwanted shadows into your scenes (see Figure 6.2). For example, if you photograph a tree on a sunny day, you might end up with a texture that indicates the sun source was up and to the right. When you import that texture into your trueSpace scene, this won't look correct if your sun source is above and to the left. If you happen to be outdoors with a camera on a sunny day and find a texture you can't live without, go ahead and try to capture it. You can always attempt post-production work to remove the shadows.

FIGURE 6.2   *Shooting texture photos on a sunny day can produce undesirable shading effects.*

- **Shoot interior photos with some extra lights**. You'll be surprised how dark your home really is when you go around shooting photos of paneling, wall textures, or other household objects. Your camera's light meter will frequently give you a "no-go" and want to use its built-in flash. Photos taken with a flash frequently leave hot spots in the image that are almost impossible to remove with post-production. If you don't have some good studio lights, try using lamps without their shades, correctly positioned to light up the subject you're photographing. A good book on photographic lighting will help you learn more about these techniques.

- **Use a tripod when possible**. Using a tripod can help ensure a quality texture photograph. If you haven't priced one, you'll be surprised to find them relatively inexpensive. Tripods are helpful for outdoor scenes, allowing you to frame your subject more accurately, and to allow your camera's lens (diaphragm) to stay open longer if that's what the ambient lighting dictates. Indoor tripod work is helpful for the same reasons and is especially important when photographing small objects in macro mode.

- **Take aim at the proper angle**. Be aware of the parallax distortions that lenses produce. If you look through your lens and see a brick wall that curves at the top and bottom (radial distortion), your resulting photo will show it even more. Make sure your lens is parallel to the subject, move closer, move farther away, or change lenses if you have that luxury. If you need a certain texture that appears distorted through your lens, go ahead and shoot your photo. You might be able to correct the distortion when you create the texture.

- **Look for the seams**. If you're planning on making seamless textures, carefully examine the subject you're photographing. Notice how the top matches the bottom, and how the sides match each other. By zooming in or out, or moving closer or farther away, you can adjust your photo's potential for becoming a seamless texture. Don't tell yourself, "I'll just fix this later when I open up Photoshop." If you do, you may end up kicking yourself when you encounter the difficulty of making the image seamless.

- **Don't ignore the ugly stuff**. Sometimes you'll find very usable textures in places where you wouldn't ordinarily look. The rust on the side of a trash dumpster, for example, can result in a great texture for adding realism to an aging spacecraft modeled and rendered in trueSpace (see Figure 6.3).

FIGURE 6.3   *The texture from a dumpster photo can make a great texture to age a spacecraft and give it character.*

- **Don't forget the small stuff**. Some of the finer textures you'll find sometimes are hidden by their size. Macro lenses are available with some cameras and enable you to shoot extreme close-up photos. These lenses afford you the opportunity to discover tiny new worlds with exciting textures of their own. For example, the small facets on the side of a rock can end up as the texture for an entire mountain in your trueSpace scene.

DIGITAL SCANNING

As mentioned previously, digital scanners have improved in quality and have become more affordable in recent years. If you're using a film camera to capture your texture images, you'll need to digitize them with a scanner. The four common types of scanners are:

- **Affordable flatbed scanners**: There are many flatbed scanners on the market that range from under $100 to over $1,000. Prices vary according to resolution and color depth. These are excellent sources for scanning prints of your texture photographs and usually include "twain" software for linking with your favorite 2D-paint program. The advantage of owning a flatbed scanner over a film scanner is its capability to scan from any media, not just film. A flatbed scanner can also be useful for the business side of a graphics business.

- **Handheld scanners**: Like flatbed scanners, handheld scanners can convert your texture photographs to digital input. These scanners are generally low-priced (sometimes below $100), but usually require extensive practice in perfecting their use. The only real advantage to handheld scanners, other than price, is their capability to scan images that are difficult to load into a flatbed scanner.

- **Film scanners**: Film scanners are capable of directly digitizing your 35mm film, precluding the step of having prints made (see Figure 6.4). This is an advantage because you don't have to depend on the quality of color print processing to digitize your photographs. These scanners are usually in the same price range as flatbed scanners. Some of the newer, inexpensive film scanners are designed more for the amateur photographer who wants to scan family photos from film. The better film scanners are capable of high resolutions and color depths.

- **Drum Scanners**: Sophisticated drum scanners are capable of digitizing ultra high-resolution photos in the range of 1,200×1,200 pixels to 9,600×9,600 pixels and can cost as much as $15,000. Rarely would you need images scanned at these resolutions, unless you are creating textures for extreme close-ups or ultra high-resolution work where the textures would occupy most of the screen. Most drum-scanned textures are intended for use in print work.

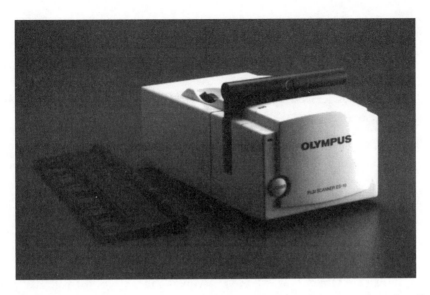

FIGURE 6.4   *A film scanner can be a good source for digitizing photorealistic texture photos from film.*

CAPTURE AND DIGITIZE A TEXTURE PHOTO

Now that you've learned all about digital and film cameras, digital scanners, and photographic techniques, you're ready to go out in the world and shoot a texture photo. A simple tree bark is a good subject to begin with because photographing it demonstrates many of the techniques used in shooting other texture photos. Also, the tree bark will be used in subsequent exercises. If you don't have a handy tree nearby, go to a local park or forest preserve—you need to get out in the fresh air anyway! And if you're "tree impaired" because you live in a geographical area that's completely devoid of trees, we've provided a sample tree bark source photo (BARK10.JPG) on the accompanying CD. Once your image is captured and digitized, you'll learn some post-production techniques for modifying it.

1. Find a good tree in a shady spot or on a gray, cloudy day and you won't have to worry about shadows. Because your texture will be tiled mostly in a vertical direction, pick a wide tree. This will give you plenty of vertical area to photograph, as you'll be rotating your camera 90 degrees.

2. Pick an area of consistent bark that doesn't contain notable features, such as knobs, darkened areas, and so on. Because the texture will be tiled, you don't want these features to show repeatedly and give away your tile effect.

3. With the camera rotated and the tree framed in the vertical position, zoom in or out (or move closer or farther away if you don't have a zoom feature) until the sides of the tree fill the viewing area. Make sure your camera's vertical axis is parallel to the vertical axis of the tree. This will give you a consistent focus across the photo and prevent blurring at the top or bottom (see Figure 6.5).

4. Take several photos from various angles. When you get back to your computer, it will be nice to have a wide variety of photos from which to choose. If you've got another tree handy, it wouldn't hurt to repeat this process so you'll have even more photos at your disposal.

5. If you're using a digital camera, upload your digitized photographs into your computer. If you're using a film camera, process your film and digitize the prints with a scanner. If possible, save your original image as a 24-bit Targa (TGA) file. This will serve as your source image that you may want to use again later.

Figure 6.5   *When shooting texture subjects like bark, rotate the camera 90 degrees to allow for plenty of vertical area.*

OTHER PEOPLE'S STUFF

Some artists collect textures like philatelists collect stamps. Many of these are *OPS textures* (Other People's Stuff). The mass availability of textures on the Internet, as samples on resource CDs, and a variety of other places can provide you with enough textures to map the Sistine Chapel inside and out.

In the legal world, the act of creating art—or, more specifically, textures—gives you the right of intellectual property to that creation. As a 3D artist, you must be careful with the textures you download from the Internet, borrow from a fellow artist, or copy from a CD. Even if the source of these textures claims they are "royalty free," you must still exercise discretion and consider the source.

Most established companies that sell texture collections have gone to the pains of creating their own textures. Generally, you're safe if you purchase one of these collections, especially if the company includes a legal statement enabling you to use these textures in your work.

This doesn't necessarily apply to textures you download on the Internet, which is a free, unpoliced medium. Anyone can copy a collection of textures from a hard drive and kindly make them available for download on a Web site. Even if the distributor of these textures claims they're royalty-free, remember what your mother said, "You don't know where that's been!" You have no way of knowing whether those textures are someone else's intellectual property.

Some 3D artists make the mistake of thinking if they modify a texture, it becomes their intellectual property. For example, if you pick up a texture from a royalty-free CD and decide to make it seamless, that doesn't mean you own the intellectual property rights. The subsequent texture is called a *derivative work*, and the original artist still holds the rights. Derivative works result from any form of modification, including changing size, color, or proportion.

The legalities of derivative works also apply to creating textures from existing photographs. Unless you own the rights to a photograph or you're absolutely certain the photograph is in public domain, you can't legally modify it into a texture.

"Why should I be concerned with all this?" you ask. "I'm just using this texture for an image I'm doing for my grandmother!" Well, that scene may turn out better than you think. You might, at a later time, decide to enter it in a competition. You just might win, and a magazine might pick up the scene for national distribution. Then you'll start to worry about the legality of your work. Never underestimate your own abilities or where your art may end up someday. To be safe, always use textures from a reputable source or use those you create. Using some-one else's intellectual property can subject you to costly civil liabilities or even criminal action.

POST-PRODUCTION MODIFICATIONS

The most important phase of creating texture photos, other than shooting the photo, is post-production. It would be great if you could shoot a photo, load it into your computer, and then wrap it around your favorite mesh. In a few cases, you'll be able to achieve this with just the right photograph. But most of the time, it's necessary to do some pixel manipulation in your favorite 2D-paint program. I'll use Adobe Photoshop to demonstrate these principles.

1. Load your tree bark TGA image into Photoshop. (If you were unable to shoot your own texture photograph, use BARK10.JPG on the accompany-ing resource CD.)

2. From the Toolbar, select the Marquee tool. Use the Marquee to select the area of the bark image you want to use. For example, if bark on the sides of the image seems smaller due to tree curvature, omit it from the selected area. Next, from the Image menu, choose Crop (Image>Crop). At this point, you can use Save As and another filename so your original source image will be preserved.

3. If some of the bark runs askew from other areas of the image due to pho-tographic distortion, use the Marquee or Lasso tools to select these areas. Try copying the selections, rotating them to the proper angle, and pasting them back onto the image.

4. Select Image>Adjust>Brightness/Contrast. Use the sliders on this tool to achieve a brightness/contrast level that appears correct to you. If the bark contains areas that are much darker than other parts of the image, use the Lasso tool from the Toolbar to highlight that area, and then use the Brightness/Contrast tool again.

5. If your image isn't quite the color you desire or contains undesirable colors (like unwanted green moss in certain areas), select Image>Adjust> Hue/Saturation. Use the sliders in this tool to adjust the saturation, or pos-sibly hue, to achieve a desired result. There are several other tools on the Image>Adjust menu that can improve the look of your image, such as Auto Levels and Color Balance, just to name a few. It would be worth your while to become familiar with these tools.

6. Once you have the proper crop, intensity levels, and colors adjusted, try using the Sharpen filter, available from the Filter menu.

7. Resize the image with Image>Image Size to a size below 640×480 pixels (you can use a much larger texture resolution if you like, depending on your hardware capabilities). Save the image as BARK10.JPG. A Quality setting of about "6" is fine for the purposes of this tutorial.

8. From trueSpace, open the trueSpace scene file, TEXTURE_TUTORIAL. SCN, on the accompanying resource CD. Apply your texture to the tree mesh in the foreground. Use the surfacing principles covered in Chapter 5. You'll notice how the bark texture repeats itself, and you can see the texture's seams. Next, you'll learn how to make seamless textures.

Creating Seamless Textures

Seamless textures are those that can be repeated multiple times across a mesh without showing where the repetitions meet. These are sometimes referred to as *tilable* textures because they're like floor tiles that repeat themselves across a floor.

It's no small trick to make a texture seamless, although there are several programs that claim to do this. Most of these programs merely take the four edges of the image and, through some sort of blending algorithm, make the top and bottom, and the left and right sides more compatible.

Basic Steps for Producing Seamless Textures

Creating seamless textures is an art in itself and best left to humans, not algorithms. The art of creating these textures can be divided into the following steps:

1. Find a way to bring together, for comparison, the top, bottom, left, and right edges of an image. This is called *rolling* in most 2D-paint programs (see Figure 6.6).

2. Use smudging, cloning, and other pixel manipulation techniques to match the edges of the image.

3. Bring the edges back together.

4. Test the seamless texture for effective tiling on a 3D mesh.

5. Repeat steps 2 through 4, if necessary.

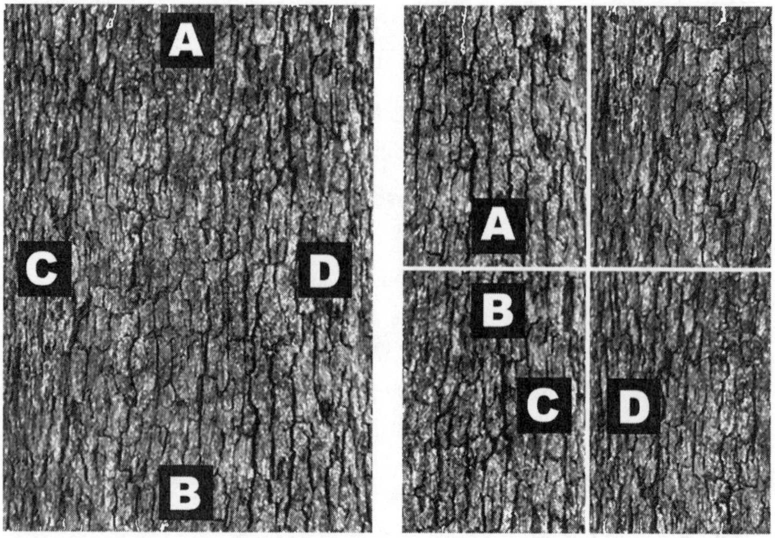

FIGURE 6.6 *The image on the right is "rolled" to bring together the top and bottom, and left and right sides of the original image (left), to allow for seamless pixel editing.*

CREATE A SEAMLESS TEXTURE

Rather than reading a long-winded narrative on creating a seamless texture, you can learn much faster through hands-on work. Because you already created a tree bark texture in the previous exercise, it will serve as a good texture to make seamless. Again, Adobe Photoshop is used here to create the seamless effect.

1. Load the "Fantastic Machine Tile Tools" demo located on the Resource CD in your Photoshop directory, as specified in the program's installation instructions.

2. Open Photoshop and load the image you created in the previous example (BARK10X.JPG).

3. Choose File>FM Tile Tools>Roll Image.

4. Move the x-axis and y-axis sliders all the way to the right. Click on Apply.

5. Notice how the edges of the image are now all aligned in the center of the image. Unless you're a world-class photographer or very lucky, you'll probably see that some edges are darker than others are. You'll need an image with a consistent tonality to give it the seamless effect. To achieve this, use the selection tools (Lasso or Marquee) to select areas that are darker. Choose

Image>Adjust>Brightness/Contrast. Gradually try to match the tones of the darkened areas with their surrounding areas.

6. Now that you have a consistent tone across your image, you can begin to match the edges. Start with the top and bottom edges, which are currently separated by an obvious seam that runs horizontally across the image. Select the Clone tool from the Toolbar. Hold down the Alt key and pick an area above or below the seam. Carefully clone that area in the middle of the seam so areas above and below the seam flow into one another. Follow the pattern of the bark and its small details so the seam line begins to disappear.

7. Pick the Smudge tool from the Toolbar and carefully drag small areas below the seam to areas above the seam. Both the clone and smudge techniques require some practice, so be patient.

8. Repeat steps 6 and 7 for the left and right sides of the image, which are separated by the obvious seam that runs vertically across the image.

9. Experiment with any of the Photoshop or FM Tile Tools filters to make the image more consistent and eliminate the seams.

10. When you're pleased with the absence of seams, click again on Filter>FM Tile Tools>Roll Image.

11. Move the X and Y sliders all the way to the left, and the original orientation of your image is restored.

12. Save this image as BARK10S.JPG.

13. From trueSpace, open the trueSpace scene file, TEXTURE_TUTORIAL. SCN, on the accompanying resource CD. Apply your new seamless texture to the tree mesh in the foreground. You should now have a consistent image up and down the tree trunk and across the limbs. If you're not satisfied with the UV settings, modify them.

CREATING BUMP MAPS

Bump maps (sometimes called *elevation maps*) take the fine qualities of your textures and give them the added look of depth. They are used to simulate high spots and low spots, as if the surface of the mesh being textured actually has those properties. Mapping a texture and matching bump map onto a flat plane can give it the look of a highly detailed 3D mesh. Using "bumped" texture maps can significantly reduce the number of polygons in your trueSpace scenes.

HOW BUMP MAPS WORK

Bump maps are interpreted in trueSpace in accordance with their grayscale tones. Simply, a dark area is interpreted as a low area and a bright area is interpreted as a high area. Black (though rarely used) is the ultimate low, white is the ultimate high, and gray areas in between are proportionately higher. The bump map may be a grayscale image or a desaturated RGB image with gray tones only.

Creating a bump map from a texture, then, sounds simple. You might assume that all you have to do is create a grayscale image of your texture and *voilà!* You have a bump map. In some cases, this may be true, especially with simple textures. But most textures have many colored facets that, when turned to grayscale, interpret as gray areas that don't necessarily indicate the heights or depths of those facets.

Consider a texture of an artist's palette board with many different colors of paint daubs. You could map such a texture and its matching bump map onto a mesh shaped like a palette and end up with a beautiful rendering. The different colored paints would range from bright to dark shades when converted to grayscale, but those shades don't necessarily indicate the height or depth of the paint daubs. A yellow paint daub would convert to light gray, but that doesn't mean it's a paint daub at a higher elevation than a navy blue, which would interpret to dark gray. Here's where you must use your 2D-paint program skills to eliminate the dark areas of your bump map that don't represent depth or the bright areas that don't represent height.

Also consider an example where you might want shadows in your texture. The shadows would be interpreted as dark gray areas on your bump map, which don't necessarily indicate depth. You would again have to modify your grayscale image to select the proper areas, which indicate height and depth. Bright "hot spots" in an image follow the same criteria as shadows, with the opposite effect (this is one of the many reasons it is easier to work with consistently lit textures).

BASIC STEPS TO PRODUCE A BUMP MAP

As with creating textures, making bump maps is an art, or at least a skill you must learn. Here are the basic steps:

1. Load your texture into a 2D-paint program and convert it to a grayscale image or desaturated RGB image.

2. For trueSpace bump maps, add plenty of brightness and contrast, and then modify the image as appropriate, eliminating dark or light areas that don't represent height and depth.

3. Test the image in trueSpace by mapping the bump map and its matching texture onto an appropriate mesh.

4. Repeat steps 2 and 3 until you're pleased with the results.

CREATE A BUMP MAP

Because you've already captured and digitized a tree bark texture and made it seamless, it's only fitting that you now make a bump map for that texture. As with the previous two exercises, Adobe Photoshop is used for the example.

1. Open Photoshop and load BARK10S.JPG, the seamless texture you created earlier.

2. Click on Image>Adjust>Desaturate. You should see a black and white representation of your image.

3. Click on Image>Adjust>Brightness/Contrast. Move the Brightness slider bar all the way to the right (+100 setting).

4. Move the Contrast slider slowly to the left until you have a low-contrast image (approximately −80 setting).

5. Click on OK. If the image is not satisfactory at this point, repeat steps 3 and 4 until you're pleased with a low-contrast combination.

6. Save this image as BARK10B.JPG with a Medium Quality setting of about 5.

7. Without closing your new bump map image, reopen BARK10S.JPG and align it next to the bump map for an on-screen comparison (see Figure 6.7).

8. Look for dark and light areas in the new bump map which are not really representations of high and low areas, such as any bark discoloration.

9. You can remove these areas in one of two ways: Increase the brightness settings or use the Eyedropper and Paint tools to manually lighten or darken these areas (the Clone and Smudge tools can also be used here).

10. Save the bump map image again.

11. From trueSpace, open the trueSpace scene file, TEXTURE_TUTORIAL. SCN, on the accompanying resource CD. Apply your new bump map with the seamless texture to the tree mesh. Ensure that the bump map UV settings are identical to those of the texture. Adjust the Amplitude setting to give the bark the desired height.

12. Inspect the image closely and alter the Amplitude setting again if necessary. Make sure the bump map lines up perfectly with the texture.

13. If you're not pleased with the alignment or effect of your bump map, you might need to adjust your Brightness/Contrast settings or remove more unwanted areas.

 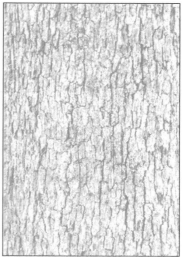

FIGURE 6.7 *Aligning the bump map (right) with its original image is a good way to compare the two when editing the bump map for areas that don't reflect depth or height.*

CREATING ALPHA CHANNEL TEXTURES

Alpha channel textures contain areas that display as transparent. The alpha channel itself is an 8-bit sector added to a 24-bit image and is used to store various pieces of information about the image, including transparency. This is why alpha channel textures are commonly stored as 32-bit Targa images. An alpha-channel–textured plane in a trueSpace scene is analogous to a sign pasted across a roadside billboard, whereby the texture is the sign, which is mapped onto a plane, which is the billboard. Examples include a window frame texture with transparent panes so you can see through the glass, and a tree with the background dropped out and made transparent, both examples of which are mapped onto flat planes.

USES FOR ALPHA CHANNEL TEXTURES

Alpha channel textures are an effective way to create low-polygon trueSpace scenes (see Figure 6.8). When applying them to planes and substituting them for high-polygon–count meshes, you can save thousands of polygons in your scenes. For example, a typical automobile mesh can range anywhere from 5,000 polygons to well over 100,000 for more detailed meshes. If an automobile is used in your scene in the background, you'll hardly notice a difference with an alpha channel texture mapped on a single plane. Substituting strategically placed alpha channel textures can make your scenes render faster by minimizing the polygon count.

FIGURE 6.8 *An alpha channel texture, shown with its corresponding alpha channel map (right).*

While alpha channel textures are great for low-polygon work, they're also quite useful on higher-polygon meshes. Most extra-high polygon work done for the film industry makes extensive use of alpha channel textures, not to mention seamless textures and bump maps. Alpha channel textures are used not only as backdrop planes or as stand-ins, but also for adding seamless detail to surfaces. Instead of making a single, extremely complicated texture, you can use an alpha channel texture to add a scar to a character or a dent to a car. Alpha channel textures can be applied by using material rectangles or layers, where the superimposed texture has feathered edges in the alpha channel to provide a smooth, seamless transition to the base texture.

You can also use alpha channel textures to cast shadows upon other meshes or even other alpha-channel–textured planes, enhancing the realistic look of a detailed mesh. An alpha-channel–textured plane placed out of the viewing area in a scene to cast shadows on other objects is called a *gobo* (see Figure 6.8). You might have seen examples of these in images where the shadows from leaves are cast upon the ground or an object, giving the impression of a nearby tree.

FIGURE 6.9   *An alpha channel map can be used as a gobo, which casts shadows on an object but is not seen in the picture.*

ELIMINATING THE HALO EFFECT

Alpha channel textures generally should be created in a higher resolution than most texture maps. This is to eliminate the "halo" effect that can occur due to alpha blending (see Figure 6.10). The halo is caused when the texture attempts to blend in with the background behind it. If this occurs in your trueSpace scene, you can do one of several things:

- Make sure the super-sampling antialiasing (2X, 3X, 4X) is turned on.

- Increase the distance between the alpha-textured object and the camera.

- Use a higher-resolution version of the alpha channel texture.

- Change the color of the background on which the alpha channel is displayed (only if all other methods fail).

FIGURE 6.10   *The white outline around the tree is called a halo effect and is caused by improper alpha channel map creation, too small a texture, or the object being too close to the camera.*

Careful planning of your alpha channel textures can avoid any of the preceding results. A critical factor in eliminating the halo effect is the size of the alpha channel mask relative to the size of the image. The mask is the transparency information stored with an image and is usually a black-and-white representation of the image, with black defining the transparent area and white defining the area to be displayed. This is the "fourth channel" in a 32-bit image. By slightly downsizing this white silhouette along its borders, the blending (halo) occurs under the texture image and not around it. The potential for the halo effect is minimized.

When creating alpha channel images, you must consider the minimum size of the mask (the white area) that will be downsized. For example, if you have a tree image containing limbs within the image, and transparency between the limbs, keep in mind that your downsized mask will reduce not only the exterior borders of the tree, but also the exterior borders of the limbs. For example, if you downsize the overall size of the mask by one pixel on its borders, you'll also be reducing the border size of your tree limbs. Therefore, the minimum size of any limb in the image must be three pixels, or it will disappear when a pixel is removed from each of its two borders.

In Hollywood blue-screen work and other sophisticated applications, expensive software packages have been developed to eliminate the halo effect and ensure seamless blending. There are other less expensive ways to reduce the alpha channel halo in trueSpace, which will be demonstrated in the next exercise.

BASIC STEPS TO CREATE AN ALPHA CHANNEL TEXTURE

The following steps are required to create an alpha channel texture. An expansion of these concepts is provided in the exercise that follows, which will provide a more in-depth understanding.

1. Open Photoshop and load the texture to which you want to add an alpha channel map.

2. Define the transparency area by defining a mask (dropping out the background).

3. Select the area masking the image as a fourth channel, which will be a black-and-white representation of the image.

4. Edit the black-and-white representation for artifacts and slightly reduce its overall size in relation to the image.

5. Save the entire image as a 32-bit Targa.

6. Test the image in trueSpace.

7. If necessary, repeat the procedure.

PRODUCE AN ALPHA CHANNEL TEXTURE

In previous exercises, you've captured and digitized tree bark, made it seamless, and created a bump map for it. Because most bark isn't transparent, it's time to switch to another subject, which will require you to go out in the woods or a park again. As with the other exercises, if you don't have some handy nearby trees, a photograph is provided for you (FOREST05.JPG). What you'll be creating is an alpha channel texture of a treeline, which is useful for background display against the sky or clouds of your choice.

1. Photograph, digitize, and do post production on a treeline, as detailed in previous exercises. For your subject, select a line of trees with a clear path for you to photograph at a distance of about 100 yards. Alternatives could

be a row of buildings or homes, a city skyline, a mountain range, and so on. However you capture the photo, save the digitized image in as high resolution as possible, preferably 1,024×768 pixels. Lower resolutions will work, but not as well.

2. Save the image as FOREST05.JPG.

3. Open Photoshop and load the image.

4. From the Toolbar, select the Magic Wand tool. Double-click on the Tool icon to bring up the Options box.

NOTE

Included on the resource CD is a demo of Extensis MaskPro, a Photoshop extension, which gives you some extended features for creating alpha channel masks. Please feel free to use this program to substitute for steps 4 through 9. Refer to that program's documentation for detailed instructions.

5. Select a Tolerance setting in the range of 35–50 to begin.

6. Click on the sky area of your image. If the marquee selection doesn't select all your sky, try clicking on Select>None. Increase the Tolerance setting on your Magic Wand and repeat the process until your sky is mostly selected.

7. When you have the entire sky selected (or most of it if you have varying cloud shades), choose Edit>Fill. In the box displayed, select White from the Contents, Use box. Your sky should fill with white.

8. Deselect the sky, click on the area below your trees, and repeat the process in step 6.

9. You may need to clean up the image somewhat by manually using the Paintbrush or Pencil tools, using a large-sized brush. Make sure the color you select is the same pure white as that used in the fill in step 7.

10. When you have removed everything from the scene except the treeline, click on the Marquee tool from the Toolbar and drag a box around the image to crop out most of the white area. Leave about 75 pixels of white on the top and bottom. Then choose Image>Crop.

11. Choose Select>Color Range. On the box that displays, select a Fuzziness value of about 40 and select Sampled Colors from the Select list. Next, use the Eyedropper tool to select the white color from your image.

12. Click on Select>Save As. On the dialog box that appears, make sure Channel New is selected under Channel, and New Channel is checked under Operation. Leave the title next to Document unchanged—it should be FOREST05.JPG. Click on OK.

13. Select Window>Show Channels. The Channels dialog box should appear.

14. On the Channels dialog box, move down below the Blue Channel to #4 Channel. Click on the "#4" and the black-and-white alpha channel mask will appear. If you see any white artifacts in the black area or vice versa, deselect the image and use the Paintbrush or Pencil tools to remove them. Click on Select>Color Range. Pick the white color with the Eyedropper.

15. Select Filters>Other>Minimum. Set the Radius setting all the way to the left to 1 pixel. Your alpha channel mask is now one pixel smaller on the radius.

16. Deselect the image, then click on the RGB channel on the Channels dialog box.

17. Save the image as FOREST05A.TGA.

USING TEXTURES IN trueSPACE SCENES

The best way to learn to use textures in trueSpace is hands-on experience. So far, you've created a bark texture, made it seamless, and created a bump map for it. You've also learned to make an alpha channel map and create a treeline texture. This final exercise incorporates those textures and adds a few more. Included on the resource CD are the scene file (texture_tutorial.scn) and all texture files necessary to create the scene. Try using all your own textures, as shown in Figure 6.11, to create a scene with your own look. You may be surprised at the final output of your own scene. You may even want to add some of your own objects, change the lighting, or use some of the effects offered in trueSpace and detailed in other chapters.

FIGURE 6.11 *Create this scene by using your own textures or use the textures included on the resource CD.*

SUMMARY

By now, you've learned how to shoot texture photos, digitize and post-process them, create bump maps, create alpha channel textures, and incorporate them into your trueSpace scenes. Hopefully, you've been able to try out these techniques with the included exercises. If you apply this knowledge to your trueSpace scenes and use textures in places you've never thought of before, you'll be surprised at the dramatic improvement in the quality of your art.

LOGICBit

PART IV

ANIMATING

CHAPTER 7

ANIMATION

by Frank Rivera

Because of its relatively low-cost and virtually limitless capabilities, computer animation has become a standard part of our lives. Feature films, TV commercials, corporate videos—almost every kind of production is touched by computer animation. trueSpace has always been capable of creating great animation, but with the release of version 4, it is now easier than ever to create stunning 3D computer-generated animations. This chapter looks at some of the tools available to us in trueSpace4.

Specifically, we will cover

- Creating a simple animation
- Animating with a standalone deformation object
- Animating with the Deform Object tools
- Bones basics
- Animating a fish with bones
- Spline paths and reusing spline paths

CREATING YOUR FIRST ANIMATION

Animating in trueSpace is very simple. Basically, you tell trueSpace

- What you want to animate
- Where you want to start
- The number of frames the action should last
- Where the action should end

It really is that simple.

For the next few exercises, you will need the Animation Controls group open. Click File>Groups>Animation Controls to display these basic animation controls.

The tool bar consists of seven buttons, which resemble those on a VCR. From the left, they are

- Return to Start
- Reverse to Previous Key Frame
- Play
- Advance to Next Key Frame
- Record
- Start Simulation
- Rewind Simulation

These basic controls can be used to create an animation, but they are not the only ones. trueSpace has a complete set of tools for managing keyframes and viewing function curves. E.W. will give you a tour of these in Chapter 8. For now, we are just warming up.

For the first exercise, we will create a simple animation of an object moving from point A to point B. Hvymetal.avi in the Chapter 7 folder on the resource CD shows you the final result. Play the animation back a couple of times. When you're ready, close the animation and load the scene hvymetal.scn located in the same folder.

The scene is pretty basic: It consists of a few cubes—one resembles a steel door and one's a simple cube for the floor—and a couple of lights. All it will take to create our animation is a few mouse clicks; trueSpace will do the rest. Let's see how it is done. Switch to the Front view. The large door should be facing you.

1. Select the door if it isn't already. In the Current Frame Number field, enter 30. This will make our animation 31 frames long. Frame 0 counts as a frame in all your animations, so if you want only 30 frames, you have to enter 29 for Current Frame Number.

2. Left-click and then right-click the Object Move tool to open the Coords panel. Click the Toggle Navigation Using Y Axis button. With the Y button disabled in the Coords panel, you can move objects along the x-axis without fear of moving an object out of position vertically.

3. Move the door to your right until the two circular objects on the door meet with the door jamb on the right.

4. Click the Record Key button to record the door's new position at frame 30.

That's it; you're finished. Press the Play button in the Animation Control group and watch the door slide open. When we started, the door was closed. We entered 30 as our current frame number. We didn't press the Record Key button at this time because we didn't change anything yet. We moved the door to the open position and then clicked Record Key, which recorded the door at that position for frame 30 of our animation.

It's important to note that you could have recorded this animation without ever pressing the Record Key. If you right-click the Record button, the Set KeyFrame panel will appear. This panel has only one option, AutoRecord, which is on by default. With the AutoRecord feature enabled, keyframes are recorded automatically for each action you perform. For example, suppose you wanted to rotate and scale a sphere. With AutoRecord on, each of those actions would create a keyframe simultaneously—one for the rotation and one for the scale. If the AutoRecord feature were off, then for each tool you use you would have to click the Record Key button—once to record the rotation and once for the scale operation.

So why did I have you press the Record Key if you didn't have to? Because the AutoRecord feature can become a crutch to a newcomer. Understanding how to manually record a keyframe and when a keyframe will be recorded is mandatory if you want to progress quickly as a trueSpace animator. We will discuss when and when not to use the AutoRecord feature in Chapter 10, "Character Animation," but for now let's look at changing our animation.

1. Enter 30 in the Current Frame Number field.

2. With the door object selected, select the Move Down Hierarchy button.

3. Select the two circular objects and place them on the right side of the door.

4. Select the Move Up Hierarchy button and click Play.

Notice the two tumbler covers of the door go off on their own path. This would be okay if this were our intention, which, in this case, it was. I just wanted to make a point a bit more clear. If at any time you need to adjust an animated object or an element of an animated object, you must perform the adjustment at frame 0. The circular objects went off on their own because we moved them at frame 30, not 0. Let's try the adjustment again, but this time set the Current Key Frame to 0.

1. Select Undo.

2. Enter 0 in the Current Frame Number field.

3. With the door object selected, select the Move Down Hierarchy button.

4. Select the two circular objects and place them on the right side of the door.

5. Select the Move Up Hierarchy button and click Play.

As you can see, the adjustment worked out fine. The circular objects stay with the door in the position they were placed.

Pretty basic stuff, but it's good to know. Now on to a bigger and better way of animating in trueSpace.

ANIMATING WITH DEFORM PRIMITIVES

There are two ways of animating an object using object deformation. The first is by using deform primitives. (We'll look at the second—deforming the object itself—shortly.)

WHAT ARE DEFORM PRIMITIVES

There are three deform primitives, each accessible from its own button: a plane, a pipe, and a cube.

NOTE
Caligari calls the cube an object in the Help bar, but it is a cube nevertheless.

Deform primitives are in every respect identical to any other primitive in trueSpace, except one—they do not render. Selecting one of these tools opens the Deformation Nav panel and adds a standalone deform object that you can use to change the shape of other objects dynamically. The standalone deform primitive is displayed as a semitransparent object in Solid mode and as an orange object in Wireframe mode.

A deform primitive follows the Volume Deform rules. That is, it is subdivided by moving the mouse pointer away from the object, pressing and holding either or both mouse buttons, and dragging up or down. The only difference is that by subdividing the number of cross sections, the deform primitive is also subdivided. This allows the deform primitives to remain flexible.

A deform primitive's shape can be changed by choosing any of the Volume Deform tools from the Deformation panel. Its position, orientation, and overall size can be modified with the Object Navigation tools.

When a deform primitive is attached to an object with the Start Deforming by Stand Alone Deform Object tool, the object is forced to conform to the deform primitive's shape. It is important to note that deforming a deform primitive can be keyframed.

NOTE
Dynamic division is not possible with a deform primitive.

START DEFORMING BY STAND ALONE DEFORMATION OBJECT

The Start Deforming by Stand Alone Deformation Object tool creates a connection between an object and a standalone deform primitive. To create the connection, select the object, select the Start Deforming by Stand Alone Object tool, and finally select the deform primitive (or you could select the primitive first and the object second). When any part of the object comes in contact with the deform primitive, the object will be deformed by the deform primitive. Deform primitives can themselves be animated.

STOP DEFORMATION BY STAND ALONE DEFORMATION OBJECT

The Stop Deformation by Stand Alone Deformation Object tool breaks the connection between the deform primitive and the object. To break the connection, select the object, select the Stop Deformation by Stand Alone Deformation Object tool, and then select the deform primitive (or you could select the primitive first and the object second).

That's really all there is to the tool set for deform primitives. Don't let its simplicity fool you into thinking that deforming objects via primitives is not a powerful feature, though, because it can be a big timesaver. Let's look at one example.

WAVE THE FLAG

On the resource CD, you will find the file flag.scn located in the Chapter 7 folder. You will notice that I placed a simple plane primitive in the center of the scene. The plane is texture mapped with an image of a flag. Select the plane and click the Render Current Object button to view the object.

If you wanted to make the flag wave in the wind, how would you approach it? An AVI could be used as a texture map, but that would work only when the flag (plane) is viewed head on. A good solution would be to use a deform primitive to animate the plane. Take a look.

1. Select the plane and click the Quad Divide tool five times. This will increase the plane's face count from 2 to 2,048.

2. Click the Add Stand Alone Plane tool. Switch to the Top view and scale the standalone plane larger than the plane that represents the flag. Try to keep it roughly the same rectangular shape. Figure 7.1 illustrates the deform primitive's size in the Perspective view.

3. Click the Object tool and then the flag plane. Reselect the standalone plane. The reason for this short routine is to exit the Deform Stand Alone tool momentarily so we can increase its mesh's density.

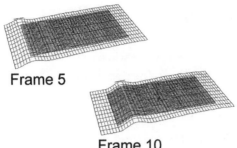

Frame 5

Frame 10

FIGURE 7.1   *An example of the procedure to animate a flag.*

4. The Deform Nav panel should be open. Select the Deformation Along a Plane Perpendicular to X-axis button. Click anywhere in the workspace not occupied by a mesh and drag your mouse right to add six cross sections to the mesh, counting the two cross sections on each end of the deform primitive, for a total of nine cross sections.

5. Switch to the Perspective view and select the second cross section from the left.

6. Enter 5 in the Current Frame Number field and press Enter.

7. Right-click and drag your mouse up vertically to raise the selected cross section. Click the Record Key button. This step is depicted in Figure 7.1.

8. Enter 10 in the Current Frame Number field.

9. Reposition the selected cross section to its original position. Select the third cross section from the left.

10. Right-click and drag your mouse up vertically to raise the selected cross section as you did before and click Record Key. Repeat steps 8 and 9 for each of the cross sections, increasing the value in the Current Frame Number field by five each time.

11. Once you have completed the preceding operation, you should be at frame 35; click the Return to Start button in the Animation Control group. Click the Start Deforming by Stand Alone Deformation Object. Your cursor will change to a glue bottle. Select the flag plane.

THE ANIMATION PARAMETERS PANEL

Before you play back an animation, you need to tell trueSpace that you would like to view all the motion in the scene when the animation is played. You do this by right-clicking Play in the Animation Control Group panel to open the Animation Parameters panel. Let's go over each of the options in this panel. In the order of appearance, they are

- **Draw Object/Scene:** Determines whether the current object or all the objects in the scene are animated when the animation is played. It is important to note that with the Object option selected and two or more windows open (including the main view window), the currently selected object will animate in all open view windows. With the Scene option selected, the animation takes place only in the active view window.

- **Base Rate:** The rate that the animation plays, expressed in frames per second (fps). The choices are 30 fps for NTSC, 25 fps for PAL, and 24 fps for film.

- **Loop:** Loops the animation during screen playback. To interrupt playback, press the Esc key or double-right-click in the workspace. This option can be combined with Toggle.

- **Toggle:** Plays the animation forward, then backward.

- **Start** and **End:** These values show the current start and end frames for animation preview. By default, Start is set to the first frame (0), and End is set to the last frame of the currently selected object. If you were to change Start to 15 in a 30-frame animation, it would start from frame 15 and play to frame 30 when the animation is played back. Note that specifying a lower value for End than for Start does nothing.

- **Reset to Zero:** Resets the value in the Current Frame Number field in the Animation Control group to 0 after animation playback. This option was undocumented at the time of this writing. It would be great if Caligari would add an option to return to the frame of the animation where the playback started.

Now that you're familiar with the Animation Parameters panel, let's play back our flag animation. In the Animation Parameters panel, select Draw Scene. Close the panel and play back the animation.

You will find the finished animation titled flag.avi on the resource CD located in the Chapter 7 folder.

ANIMATING WITH THE DEFORM OBJECT TOOLS

Earlier I mentioned that there are two ways to animate an object using deformation. In addition to using deform primitives, you can animate an object by deforming it directly with the Deform Object tool. (Yes, this is the same tool we used to model objects in Chapter 3. Pretty versatile, eh?) To illustrate this method, we will animate the tail fin of the fish from Chapter 3 using three keyframes. This is a little tedious, but the results are pretty cool.

1. Load the ani_fish scene from the resource CD's Chapter 7 folder. The fish will be displayed on the right side of the screen in the Perspective view along with a small view window set to Top. The tail should take up most of the smaller view window.

2. In Chapter 3, we used the Deform Object tool to model objects. You have probably guessed by now that I love the deformation tools. All those actions we performed with the Deform Object tool are keyframable. Let's put this tidbit of information to some use. Select the object and enable the Deform Object tool. This will open the Deformation Nav panel.

3. In the large window, switch to the Left view. This will give you a better view of what we are about to do.

4. In the Deformation Nav panel, click the Deform Along a Plane Perpendicular to the Z-axis button.

5. Place your cursor in the lower-right corner of the small view window anywhere not occupied by the fish's mesh. Drag your mouse upward until six cross sections (starting at the base of the fish's tail) appear in the large window, as depicted in Figure 7.2.

6. If the Animation Control Group panel isn't already open, open it now. Click Return to Start, then right-click the Record button to open the Set Keyframe panel and check the AutoRecord radio button. The AutoRecord option sets a key frame for every animated parameter that is recordable, for the current object, for the current frame. This option is checked by default, but it's better to be safe than sorry. It's an awful feeling when after performing some tedious work you realize you have to start all over again.

NOTE

In the previous exercises, I had you manually click the Record Key button in the Animation Control Group panel even though there was no need because the AutoRecord option was enabled. This was so that you would develop the habit of knowing when a keyframe is being recorded. In the upcoming exercises, you can refrain from clicking Record Key. We will be using the AutoRecord option throughout the remainder of this chapter.

NOTE

If AutoRecord is off, keyframes are recorded for the currently active tool only when the Record Key button is clicked.

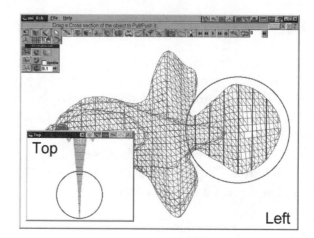

FIGURE 7.2 *A view of the six cross sections added to the fish's tail.*

7. Enable the Pull/Push button in the Deformation Nav panel. Right-click the Pull/Push tool to open the Coords panel. Disable the Y-axis button. This will enable you to work with greater precision along the x-axis.

8. In the small window, click the tip of the tail and drag the cross section to the left side of the small window. Working your way up to the base of the tail, select each of the cross sections of the tail and move them to the left to create a smooth curve. Panel A of Figure 7.3 illustrates the desired shape. Once the cross sections are in position, enable the Twist button in the Deformation Nav panel. Use your right mouse button to rotate the cross sections for a smoother curve.

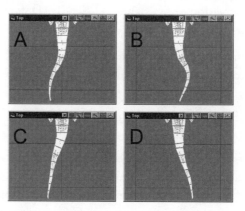

FIGURE 7.3 *The four positions of the fish's tail.*

9. You have just created the start of the animation loop that will be the tail action. Let's move on to the next phase. Enter 10 in the Current Frame Number field of the Animation Group panel.

10. Re-enable the Pull/Push button in the Deformation Nav panel.

11. In the small window, click the tip of the tail. Drag the cross section to the right of the window's center as you did before. Working your way up to the base of the tail, select each of the cross sections of the tail and move them to the right to create a curve similar to the one you created before, only reversed. Panel B of Figure 7.3 illustrates the desired shape. Once the cross sections are in position, enable the Twist button once more in the Deformation Nav panel. Use your right mouse button to rotate the cross sections to further smooth out the shape.

12. Enter 20 in the Current Frame Number field of the Animation Group panel. Re-enable the Pull/Push button in the Deformation Nav panel.

13. In the small window, click the tip of the tail once more. Drag the cross section left of the window's center. Working your way up to the base of the tail, select each of the cross sections and move them to the left to create a curve similar to the one you created in the previous steps. Panel C of Figure 7.3 depicts the desired shape. Once the cross sections are in position, enable the Twist button again in the Deformation Nav panel. Use your right mouse button to rotate the cross sections to further smooth out the shape.

14. Now that we have 20 frames, we need to backtrack a bit to tweak the power stroke of the tail. Enter 15 in the Current Frame Number field of the Animation Group panel and re-enable the Pull/Push button in the Deformation Nav panel.

15. In the small window, click the tip of the tail once more. Drag the cross section to the right of the window's center. Working your way up to the base of the tail, select each of the cross sections and move them to the left to straighten out the tail. Panel D of Figure 7.3 illustrates the desired shape. When the cross sections are in position, enable the Twist button again in the Deformation Nav panel. Use your right mouse button to rotate the cross sections to further straighten the tail. During the power stroke, the fish's tail momentarily stiffens. This will give the fish a more natural look.

In step 15, I went back and recorded keyframe 15 after recording keyframe 20. It might seem strange at first, but there is a reason for this approach. It's easier to obtain fluid movement if the major actions are recorded first. Objects tend to get a jittering effect when lots of keyframes are recorded close together, and working out the jitters sometimes takes longer than recording the actual animation itself. This is especially true when animating characters.

To play the animation, click the Play button in the Animation group. I have provided a preview animation for your review and critique on the resource CD. You will find it in the Chapter 7 folder. The filename is fishtail.avi. Use this animation as a guide to tweaking fluid movement out of your fish animation. When you're satisfied with your results, use the Deform Object tool to further animate the fish. In case you haven't noticed, the fish is a little stiff from the base of the tail to the head, and the other fins are motionless. Try to add a little wiggle to the rest of the body as the fish propels itself forward.

If you are happy with your fish, you can save it as a COB file. The animation will be saved with the fish. The next time you load the object, the keyframes will be intact. The same can be done with the characters you created in the character modeling chapter, a subject we will discuss shortly. First, let's look at another great tool for animating objects in trueSpace.

BONES

If you haven't experimented with trueSpace bones, you're missing out on a lot of fun. The Bones feature in trueSpace4 is easy to use and a powerful tool for modeling and animating objects, enabling you to easily animate complex organic structures intuitively. Before we experiment a bit, let's go over some terms you will come across in this chapter and Chapter 9, "Advanced Bones."

- **Skin:** The mesh that is deformed by an attached skeleton.

- **Bone:** A primary component of the skeleton that deforms the surrounding mesh (skin).

- **Joint:** An object that connects two objects and specifies the degree of rotational and slide freedom of this connection.

- **Skeleton:** An IK object made up of bones arranged in a hierarchy and connected by joints.

- **Branch:** A bone with three or more joints.

- **Muscle:** The faces of a mesh (skin) that surround a bone, contracting and expanding as the bones are flexed.

- **Tendon:** The faces of a mesh (skin) that surround and bend around a joint.

- **Contractor:** A muscle (group of faces) that contracts as the joint bends.

I know you can't wait to get started, so let's get started.

Modeling with Bones

A big misconception is that bones are solely used for animating characters. This isn't so. In Chapter 3, for example, I discussed how to create bent pipes and tubes by using the Sweep and Point Edit tools. This task could have been done effortlessly and faster with bones. Why am I mentioning it here in an animation chapter? Because the basic use of bones would have to be reiterated here anyway, and because most people think bones are for animation only—what better way to get your attention? Let's take a quick look at using bones.

1. In a new scene, add a cylinder to the scene with a Latitude of 9, a Longitude of 16, and a Top Radius of 1. If you are unfamiliar with how to do this simply, right-click the Add Cylinder tool to open the Cylinder panel. Enter the values and left-click the Add Cylinder button.

2. Switch to the Left view. Scale the cylinder along the y-axis. Reposition the cylinder by using the Eye move tool if necessary.

3. Select the Build Skeleton tool. The button looks like a green stick figure. If you can find the button with the little man holding his arms out, then you're close. The Build Skeleton button is just above this button in the Animate group. This will activate the tool and open the Build Skeleton panel. (I will discuss this panel in Chapter 9.)

4. Using your left mouse button, click the top center of the cylinder. This will add a single bone to the scene; ignore it for now.

5. Moving your mouse down the center of the cylinder vertically, divide the cylinder into thirds by left-clicking the third, sixth, and bottom latitude lines of the cylinder. You should end up with three bones and two joints. Where the bones meet, a diamond-shaped object appears, representing the joints.

6. You have just created a simple skeleton. What we need to do next is attach the skin of the cylinder to the bone structure. Remember that button I described with the little man on it? That is the Attach Skin to Skeleton tool. Click on it to activate it. Your cursor will change to a glue bottle. Select the cylinder.

7. Select the Object tool to disable the Attach Skin to Skeleton tool. You will notice that the cylinder and bone structure are one.

8. Click on any of the two bones at the bottom of the cylinder. With your left mouse button depressed, drag your mouse from left to right. Notice how easily the cylinder is deformed. Pretty cool, huh? Can you see a use for modeling with bones? Bent pipes are child's play. See Figure 7.4.

9. When you're finished playing, select the Undo button to restore the cylinder to its original shape.

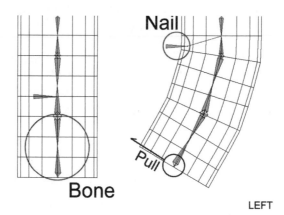

FIGURE 7.4   *Deforming a cylinder with trueSpace bones.*

You may have noticed that there is a triangle attached to the center bone. This is the *nail* or *anchor*. trueSpace creates this entity automatically when you complete the build skeleton operation. The nail remains permanently attached to the object.

The nail can be manipulated at any time by clicking and dragging it onto a different component of the object. To grab the nail, click near its tip or apex. Let's move the nail and see what happens.

1. Click and drag the nail to the second bone.

2. Select the bottom bone and drag it from left to right as you did before.

Notice anything different about the way the cylinder becomes deformed? The nail has in effect isolated the movement of the bottom bone from the rest of the bone structure by anchoring the second bone. The same would hold true if you moved the top bone. Let's move the nail one more time.

NOTE

You don't have to position the nail directly on the bone, just near it. The nail always identifies the bone it is assigned to by a leader that runs from the nail's tip to the bone to which it is attached.

1. Select Undo to restore the cylinder to its original position.

2. Move the nail to the bottom bone.

3. Select the top bone and move it from left to right.

The bottom bone remained anchored, didn't it? If you move the anchored bone, the entire object moves.

As you can see, there is nothing to using trueSpace Bones tools, especially if you are familiar with trueSpace's IK features. This simple exercise demonstrated that bones are a great tool that can be used to deform an object's mesh. Can you think of other uses for bones modeling? Let's look at animating something with bones.

ANIMATING WITH BONES

Now let's breathe some life into our boned cylinder. A plain old cylinder isn't very interesting, so let's dress it up a bit, say as a soda pop can. Take a look.

NOTE

We will be revisiting animating with bones in Chapter 10, "Character Animation."

1. Load up the canOcoke scene located on the resource CD. The file is located in the Chapter 7 folder.

2. The scene will open with the soda pop can in the Left view.

3. Click the Build Skeleton button.

4. Starting from the top, left-click the center of the can, working your way down to the bottom. Use the five lateral lines in the can's center to space your mouse clicks evenly for a total of seven clicks. Figure 7.5 depicts the seven areas where you should click your mouse and the finished bone structure.

5. Select the Attach Skin to Skeleton button and select the soda pop can. If the Animation Control Group panel isn't already open, open it now.

6. Select the nail and place it at the bottom bone.

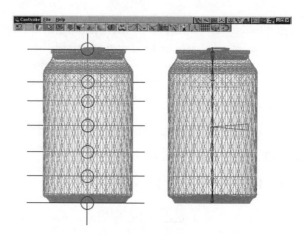

FIGURE 7.5 *Use the can's lateral lines to position the joints of the bone structure.*

7. Enter 10 in the Current Frame Number field of the Animation Control Group panel.

8. Using your left mouse button, click and drag the top of the can to your left as depicted in frame 10 of Figure 7.6. Click the Record key in the Animation Control Group panel.

9. Enter 30 in the Current Frame Number field of the Animation Control Group panel.

10. Using your left mouse button, click and drag the top of the can back to your left as depicted in frame 30 of Figure 7.6. Click the Record Key button in the Animation Control Group panel.

11. Enter 40 in the Current Frame Number field of the Animation Control Group panel.

12. This time around, straighten the soda pop can as depicted in frame 40 of Figure 7.6. Click the Record Key button in the Animation Control Group panel. Do not close the scene when you are finished; we will be using it for the next exercise.

Switch to the Perspective view and play the animation. I have included a short sequence for you to view on the resource CD—the filename is canOcoke.avi located in the Chapter 7 folder.

The Bones feature doesn't make much sense applied to an inanimate object, so let's take what we now know about bones and apply it to a suitable object.

FIGURE 7.6 *Animating a dancing soda pop can with Bones.*

ANIMATING A FISH WITH BONES

A wonderful thing about bones and IK in trueSpace is that both IK and bones (bone structures) are totally reusable. You just created a reusable action when you animated the soda pop can. We can save the bone structure as a COB with the animation intact and apply it to another object. Here is how it is done.

1. Switch to the Left view and select the soda pop can.

2. Select the Move Down Hierarchy tool.

3. Select the Unglue tool to remove the can from the bone structure.

4. Select the Move Up Hierarchy tool. The bone structure should be selected at this point. Click the Play button. See how the bones still have the animation intact? There is an important lesson to be learned here: The skeleton (bone structure) is what is animated. trueSpace bones actually deform the object they are assigned to, similar to the way the deform primitives were used at the beginning of this chapter.

5. Save the bone structure as a COB by clicking the Save Object As option in the File menu. Call the file fishbone.cob.

6. Load up the scene fishbone.scn from the resource CD. You will find the file in the Chapter 7 folder.

7. Load fishbone.cob by using the Load Object option in the File menu. The bone structure might appear offscreen so switch to the Top view.

8. Right-click the Object tool to open the Object Info panel. In the X Rotation and Z Rotation fields, enter 90. Close the Object Info panel.

9. If the bone structure isn't in the same position as the fish, select the Object Move tool and place the fish so that the bone structure is centered with the fish. The bottom tip of the fish's tail should be aligned with the bottom tip of the bone structure or close to it. Switch to the Left view to better place the bone structure vertically. Use Figure 7.7 as a guide.

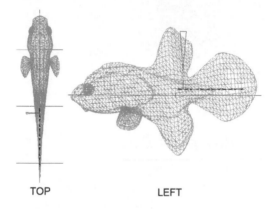

TOP   LEFT

FIGURE 7.7   *From the Top view, place the bone structure you created and saved as a COB centered on the fish's tail.*

10. From the Left view, select the bone structure then select the Attach Skin to Skeleton tool.

11. Select the fish. Give trueSpace a few moments to do its thing. After the hourglass goes away, select the Object tool to change your mouse cursor back into a pointer.

Click the Play button and watch your fish use the animated bone structure created for the soda pop can. For a better view of the action, switch to either the Top or Perspective views.

Reusing elements is nothing new to trueSpace; it was supported as far back as version 2. Animated deform primitives could be saved and reloaded to be used with different objects. Version 3 also supported this feature with IK structures.

ANIMATING WITH SPLINE PATHS

You can also use a path to animate an object. You have seen how an object can be made to follow a specified path by using the keyframing method at the beginning of this chapter. This is usually all that is needed if you want an object to move from point A to point B. What if you want an object to follow a complex path? If you're thinking you can also do it by using the keyframe method, you're right. It might take a little longer to get the path just right, but you can do it with little effort.

What if you want to see the path as you mapped it out? What happens a month from now when you return to the animation? Will you remember all the paths your objects take? How difficult would it be to change the path later altogether or to start the path from another location? You will be happy to know that all these points are moot. trueSpace enables you to define complex paths that are visible, easy to create, and easy to maintain.

Having an object follow a path in trueSpace is child's play; seriously, it takes only a few mouse clicks. An animation path is created in much the same way that a spline polygon is. You assign an object a path by selecting the object to be animated. You then define the path by selecting the Path tool and clicking in the workspace to lay out the path. Before we use this important tool, however, we should look at the two panels involved. Figure 7.8 illustrates them.

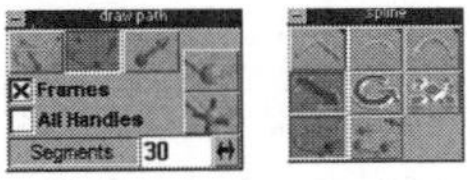

FIGURE 7.8   *The Draw Path and Spline Property panels.*

THE DRAW PATH PANEL

The Draw Path panel is where you add nodes and define the number of frames between each node. The available options are:

- **Point Move:** Enables you to edit the location of the path nodes (control points). Simply enable this option, click on the control point, and drag it to a new location.

- **Draw New Spline Point:** Lets you place the path control points. As you place the control points that define the path, trueSpace uses the number entered in the Segments field to add the number of frames that will be used between each set of control points. For example, if you were to draw a path by clicking in the center of the workspace and then clicking in the upper-right corner of the workspace, this would be the path the object would take, point A to point B. The amount of frames it would take to get there when the animation is played back would depend on the value in the Segment field. If Segments were 30, the object would travel from point A to point B in 30 frames. At 30 frames a second, the move would take 1 second. If you later added a control point C by clicking in the lower-right corner, another 30 frames would be added to the animation, making it a total of 60 frames and 2 seconds.

- **Start New Spline:** Enables you to discard an existing path and create a new one. If you want to delete a path, open the Draw Path panel click the Start New Path button, and close the panel.

- **Add New Spline Point:** Enables you to add a new control point to an existing path. Remember that adding a control point (node) adds frames to the animation. The number of frames that are added is determined by the value entered in the Segments field in the Draw Path panel.

- **Delete Spline Point:** Removes a control point. If Draw New Spline Point is active, then the last control point will be deleted. On the other hand, if the Point Move tool is active, then the currently selected control point is deleted. It is important to note that if you delete a control point, you also delete the number of frames associated with that control point. For example, if you set the number of Segments to 5 and create a path from point A to point B, that would be 5 frames. If you increase the value in the Segment field to 10 and add 2 more control points, C and D, you would end up with 25 frames. If you were to select and delete point C with the Move Point tool active, the 10 frames that were added with control point C would also be deleted. It wouldn't matter what value is in the Segments field at the time.

- **Segments field:** Lets you specify the number of frames used between control points, as discussed previously. (I think this field should be renamed Frames.) You can change this value as you define your path. Larger values add more frames; more frames slow down the action. A path consisting of two nodes, point A and B, with Segments set to 30 would cause the object to move from point A to point B in about a second (at 30 frames a second). Increase the Segments value to 60 and it will take the object 2 seconds to move from point A to point B.

- **Frames:** Displays the frames (segments) visually, when enabled. The frames appear as light blue dots in your scene. (Notice how Caligari now refers to what it called Segments as frames in this context. Personally, the Segments field should be changed to Frames and the Frames check box should be changed to View Frames, but that's just me.)

- **All Handles:** Displays each control point's handle, when enabled. When All Handles is selected, dragging your mouse outward or inward toward the control point increases or decreases the distance between the selected control point, its frame, and the previous and subsequent frame. Also, by dragging one of the ends of the handle, you can rotate the previous and subsequent frames around the control point, creating a curve in the path.

THE SPLINE PROPERTY PANEL

The Spline Property panel is opened by right-clicking either of the Spline Polygon or Path tools.

- **Sharp, Smooth,** and **Very Smooth Corner**: Select one of these three options to determine how the path intersects with the control points.

- **Change Move, Rotate** and **Scale Spline Parameters**: These options control how the Spline Path control point's location is interpolated.

- **Change Spline Parameters for Selected Point Only:** The default setting; causes only the currently selected control point to be affected by your corner type selection—Sharp, Smooth, or Very Smooth Corner.

- **Change Spline Parameters for All Points:** Causes all the control points to be affected.

CREATING A SIMPLE PATH

With a firm understanding of the control panels involved, it's time to reload our trusty fish and animate it with a path. The end result should be interesting. On

NOTE

In Chapter 17, "Creating a Short Film," I discuss cameras, camera targets, and complex paths.

the resource CD, you will find the file anifish2.scn located in the Chapter 7 folder. Load the scene and switch to the Top view. The fish will appear in the lower-left corner of the screen.

The object being assigned a path could already be animated—it doesn't matter, but it can have only one path. The fish in the scene has an animated tail. Press the Play button in the Animation Control Group panel to view it. When done, click the Return to Start button in the Animation Control Group panel. The fish isn't going anywhere, so let's give him a path.

1. Select the fish and then select the Path tool. This will open the Draw Path panel.

2. Enter 30 in the Segments field in the Draw Path panel and left-click in the center of the fish's head.

3. Create a path by clicking in the center of the workspace and once again in the upper-left corner.

4. Click the Play button.

TIP

If you want to move an object and its animation path, make the object's path visible before you move it. Do this by clicking on the Path tool. If you move an object without the path being visible, you will move only the current keyframe, but if you move it while it is visible, you will move the whole path. The same is true for rotating objects and their paths.

The fish follows the path, but not like you would expect. You could rotate the fish and keyframe him in the correct position, but what if the path were very complex? Rotating and setting all those keyframes would be too much work. What we need is an easy way to have the fish follow the path more naturally; that is, the fish should follow the path head first. You're in luck. trueSpace has a tool that makes performing this task a breeze.

LOOK AHEAD

The Look Ahead tool is used to make an object point its z-axis along its path during animation, re-aiming on each frame. The fish's z-axis runs from the fish's tail to its head. This is the ideal setup for our fish because the fish should point in the direction it is traveling. Let's get our fish to look ahead.

Select the fish and select the Look Ahead tool (see Figure 7.9). That wasn't tough. The fish is now pointing its head in the direction of the path. Click Play and watch the fish swim along the path. I have included a short sequence for you to view in fish.avi on the resource CD. It is located in the Chapter 7 folder.

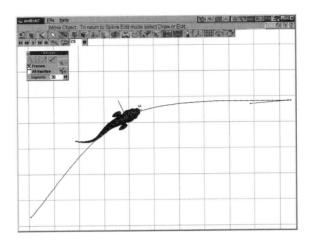

FIGURE 7.9   *A fish COB set on the correct path with the Look Ahead tool. The fish's tail is also animated, making the fish appear as if it is propelling itself forward.*

When an object is under the influence of the Look Ahead tool, it is constrained and cannot be rotated manually, unless the Look Ahead option is disabled for the object. Text, cameras, and Spotlights automatically look ahead without your having to worry about their axes.

The Look Ahead option is keyframable. You can turn it on or off during the course of the animation, and the object will respond accordingly. The Look Ahead tool has three parameters you can adjust:

- **Bias:** Controls how much curve will be added to the selected node. A high Bias setting will cause the spline on each end of the selected node to bow like a fishing rod.

- **Tension:** Controls the pinch at the node. A high Tension setting will cause the spline on each end of the selected node to form a sharp angle to each other, forming a point at the node.

- **Bank:** When the setting is enabled, the animated object "leans" into curves in its motion path. The bank amount can be specified numerically by degrees.

We have been lucky so far. Just about every tool we have used can be saved, reloaded, and used on different objects. Paths are no exception.

NOTE

After you have animated an object, you can't adjust its axis. You must first delete the animation before adjusting the object's axis.

REUSING PATHS

When I animate, I think *reusability*, and you should, too. trueSpace enables you to create libraries of actions that can be used on different characters and objects. Learning to exploit this feature will save you the hassle of performing repetitive tasks over and over.

Earlier, we animated a soda pop can with a bone structure. We then saved the bone structure as a COB and later used the same bone structure on a fish. The same can be done with paths. You can copy and paste animation paths from one object to another by using a little feature called the Path Library. This is how it is done.

1. Select the object that has had a path assigned to it.

2. Open the Draw Path panel to display the path and click on the path.

3. Open the Path Library panel and click the Add Path to Library tool.

The path name will appear as ANIM; click on it. You can now change the name in the upper-left corner of the Path Library panel.

To reuse a saved path on another object:

1. Select the object. Remember an object can have only one path, so select an object that has not had a path assigned.

2. Open the Draw Path panel.

3. Open the Path Library panel and select the path name from the list.

The same animation path will be applied to the new object starting from its current location.

If you load a previously saved path with the Draw Spline panel closed, the loaded path will become a spline polygon. This is great if you want an object of the same shape as the previously saved path. For example, you can create a fancy path for the fish used in the previous exercise and save the path to a path library. You can then load up the path and sweep it with the Sweep tool. Scale it down just a bit, and when you play back the animation, the fish will appear to swim around the object's perimeter perfectly.

SUMMARY

Contrary to popular belief, trueSpace is a full-fledged animation package. As you have seen, many tools have been made available to us for animating. With the addition of the Bones feature in version 4, you can create some cool animated characters, a subject we will cover in Chapter 10.

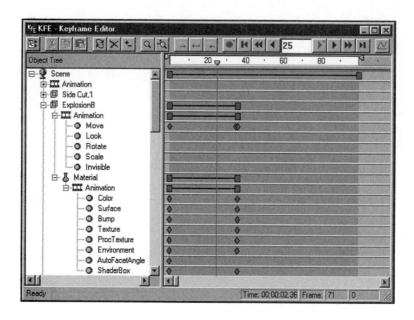

CHAPTER 8

SECRETS OF
THE KEYFRAME EDITOR

by Frank Rivera

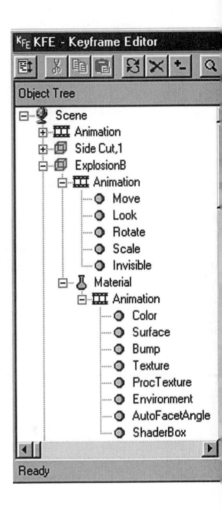

In 4.0, the KeyFrame Editor (KFE) has been revamped to help make the task of animating objects in trueSpace manageable. With the new KeyFrame Editor, you can edit keyframes by using function curves, drag and drop keyframes between objects, and visually manage object hierarchies, just to name a few of the new features. KFE use goes beyond the task of managing animated objects. As you will see, you can even manage object hierarchies, as well as glue and unglue objects to each other.

In this chapter, we will cover

- The KFE Toolbar
- The Object Tree pane
- The Animation Track pane
- Creating and editing keyframes
- Function curves

KeyFrame Editor Basics

The KeyFrame Editor gives you complete control over all aspects of your animation. As shown in the opening image, the KFE has four major components:

- **Toolbar**: A collection of icons for editing, managing, and previewing your scene's animation.
- **Object Tree pane** (on the left): A hierarchical display of the objects in the scene.
- **Animation Track pane** (on the right): Contains the timelines and keyframes of all the objects in the scene.
- **Status Bar** (across the bottom): Displays important information, such as the current frame number, running time, and total number of frames. The Status Bar also provides you with a short description of the tools in the Toolbar. Moving your cursor over an icon in the Toolbar displays the name of the tool in the left half of the Status Bar.

The KFE window can be resized by clicking and dragging any of its four corners. The KFE window also has the standard minimize, maximize, and close buttons located in the upper-right corner of the window's title bar. When you minimize the KFE, an icon will appear in trueSpace4's title bar. You can restore the KFE to its previous state either by clicking on the Restore button or the KFE tool. The Object Tree and Animation Track panes can also be resized by clicking and dragging on the divider that separates the panes. You can rename, copy, delete, or render an object by right-clicking an object in the Object Tree.

THE TOOLBAR

The Toolbar is the home for all the tools necessary for editing, copying, pasting, and deleting keyframes. You will also find controls to manage the contents of the Animation Track pane. Let's take a look at them in order of appearance.

OBJECT FILTER

The Object Filter is the first icon in the Toolbar. Left-clicking the Object Filter tool opens the Filter panel (see Figure 8.1). Here, you determine which objects appear in the Object Tree and Animation Track panes. Here are options available in the Object Filter panel:

- **Object Tree:** Used to disable the visibility of an object by left-clicking the object.

- **Display group:** This block contains two radio button options: All Objects and Animated Objects Only. Selecting All Objects displays every object that is not a light or camera in the Object Tree and Animation Track panes. (More on viewing lights and cameras later.) A word of caution: If you have a scene that has many, many objects—for example, particles—do not choose this option because it will clutter up the KFE panes. Use the Animated Objects Only option. Selecting Animated Objects Only displays only those objects that have keyframes.

- **Animation Tracks group:** The options in this field let you select which animation properties are displayed in the Animation Track pane. You can choose Show All, Do Not Show Empty Tracks, or Show None.

  Show All displays the complete range of animatable properties for all the objects in your scene, including those that do not have keyframes.

  Do Not Show Empty Tracks restricts the KFE from displaying those properties that do not have keyframes. For example, an object may have move keyframes but may not have texture keyframes. In this case, only the movement keyframes will be displayed.

  Show None displays only the objects in your scene. Each object that has keyframes will have all their actions associated with that object combined into one action bar in the Animation Track pane.

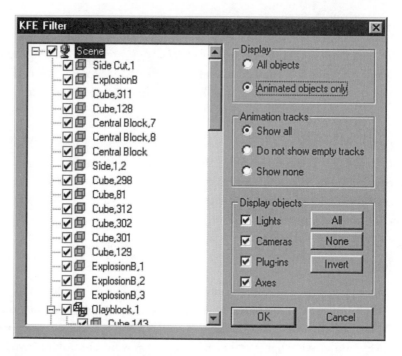

Figure 8.1 *The KeyFrame Editor Filter panel enables you to limit what is visible in the KeyFrame Editor's Object Tree and Animation Track panes. Lights and cameras are unselected by default.*

- **Display Objects group:** Enables you to select the visibility of lights, cameras, plug-ins, and axes. The *All* button selects all four, the *None* button deselects all four, and the *Invert* button reverses the current selections. For example, if you have Lights, Cameras, and Plug-ins checked off, pressing Invert would uncheck Lights, Cameras, Plug-ins and would check Axes. If your scene contains animated lights or cameras, you should enable these two options in the Display Objects group.

CUT

The Cut button removes the currently selected keyframe from the Animation Track pane and places it into the KFE clipboard. You can then paste the keyframes in the KFE clipboard into another area of the same animation track. We will cover cutting and pasting from the Animation Track pane later in this chapter.

COPY

The Copy button copies the selected keyframes and places them into the KFE clipboard. Copied keyframes can be pasted into another area of the same animation track later. You can also use this button to copy an entire object. Selecting an object instead of a keyframe prior to depressing the Copy button will copy the entire object.

PASTE

The Paste button pastes keyframes from the KFE clipboard into the selected animation track. You can paste keyframes of the same type into the animation track of another object. For example, you can paste a texture keyframe from one object into the texture animation track of a second. The pasted keyframes will be pasted at the current frame. The current frame is identified by the Current Frame marker at the top of the Animation Track pane.

REFRESH

Refresh updates the Object Tree and Animation Track panes. When Refresh is selected, the Object Tree collapses. You must use the Expand/Collapse button to view the objects in the Object Tree after using the Refresh tool.

DELETE

The Delete button is used to delete objects, animation parameters, and individual keyframes. If you have selected an object in the Object Tree, clicking the Delete button deletes the object completely. On the other hand, if you select an animation parameter in the Object Tree, the Delete button deletes all the keyframes of the selected animation track. If you have selected keyframes in the Animation Track pane, clicking the Delete button will delete the selected keyframes. To remove all the movements associated with an object, for example, select the object's Move parameter in the Object Tree, click the Delete button, and the object's move track will be cleared.

EXPAND/COLLAPSE TREE

This button toggles the Object Tree and Animation Track pane from fully expanded (all objects and animation parameters are visible) to a single-scene object.

ZOOM TRACK

The Zoom Track tool is used to expand or shrink the contents of the Animation Track pane. To use this tool, select it, and then click and drag left or right within the Animation Track pane. Dragging left collapses the timeline, displaying more frames within the Animation Track pane. Dragging right expands the contents of the animation tracks, displaying less detail so that you can focus on a specific segment. The tool remains active, so you will have to deactivate it when you are done. The button remains depressed when activated. To deactivate it, simply click the button again.

FIT ZOOM

The Fit Zoom function expands or collapses the Animation Track pane to fully contain the selected object's animation track. To use it, first select an object from the Object Tree pane, and then click the Fit Zoom tool. The items in the Animation Track pane are immediately resized to fit within the Animation Track pane.

REPEAT

The Repeat button repeats the "action" of the currently selected keyframes, starting at the frame number of the last keyframe. To use the tool, select the desired action—Move, Scale, and so on—or the entire object in the Object Tree. If only an action is selected, then the action is repeated, but if the object is selected, then all the actions—Move, Scale, Rotate, and so on—will be repeated.

REVERSE

The Reverse button reciprocates the keyframes of the selected action or, in the case when an object is selected, all the keyframes of all the actions for that object will be reversed.

REVERSE REPEAT

The Reverse Repeat button "ping-pongs" the selected action. For example, if you have a ball bounce away from the camera, using this tool will make it bounce back toward you. It produces an effect similar to playing a videotape forward and then backward.

THE KFE ANIMATION CONTROLS

Found at the right side of the Toolbar, the KFE Animation Controls are a set of VCR-style controls used for viewing and browsing keyframes. For example, by clicking on an object's Kinematic animation parameter in the Object Tree, the Toolbar's Advance to Next Keyframe and Reverse to Previous Keyframe buttons can be used to cycle through the Kinematic keyframes. You can define whether trueSpace updates only the selected object or the whole scene by right-clicking the Play button. This opens the Animation Parameters panel. Once the panel is open, you can choose to update the object or scene with every click of the Advance or Previous Keyframe buttons. If the Object option is selected, the Advance, Reverse, and Play buttons will affect the selected object only. On the other hand, if the Scene option is selected, the entire scene is updated as you advance or backtrack through the frames. This comes in handy when all you would like to view is an object's motion or path.

NOTE

You can enable the Autorecord option by right-clicking the Record button. On every keyframe number other than 0, the Autorecord feature records keyframes automatically for the current frame number every-time you make a change to your scene, whether it is a texture, the scale of an object, or its location.

RECORD

The Record button records a keyframe at the current frame. If the object is selected in the Object Tree, then Move, Scale, and the Rotate parameters are recorded for that frame. On the other hand, if you selected only one parameter of an object in the Object Tree (for example, Move), then a keyframe is recorded for that parameter only.

RETURN TO START AND ADVANCE TO END

The Return to Start button sets the current frame number to 0. Advance to End sets the current frame number to the last set keyframe in your scene.

REVERSE TO PREVIOUS KEYFRAME

Depending on whether you have Draw Object or Draw Scene set in the Animation Parameters panel (reached by left-clicking Play), the current frame number will be set to the next (previously set) keyframe for the selected object or scene. You can also use this with an object's animation parameter to jump to the next keyframe for that parameter only.

ADVANCE AND REVERSE TO PREVIOUS FRAME

Advance increases the Current Frame number by one. Reverse to Previous Frame decrements the Current Frame number by one.

CURRENT FRAME ENTRY FIELD

The value displayed in the Current Frame field is the number of the currently active frame. You can change the frame number by typing a new value in the field and hitting the Enter key. You can also change the number by clicking and dragging the Frame Marker at the top of the Animation Track pane.

PLAY

The Play button is used to preview an animated object or the entire scene. If you right-click the Play button to open the Animation Parameters panel, you can restrict playback to a specific range of frames. You can also do this by clicking and dragging the Start and End Frame markers at the top of the Animation Track pane.

ADVANCE TO NEXT KEYFRAME

The Advance to Next Keyframe button shifts the Current Frame number ahead to the next keyframe of the selected object or action. The selected keyframe changes color in the Animation Track pane.

THE OBJECT TREE

The Object Tree is a hierarchical representation of all the objects in your scene (see Figure 8.2). The Object Tree makes it easy to view object hierarchies and their animation parameters.

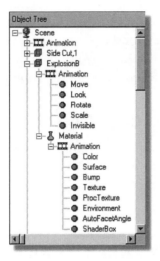

FIGURE 8.2   *The KFE's Object Tree pane.*

EXPANDING AND COLLAPSING BRANCHES

Clicking on the small box with the plus sign expands the tree. Clicking the Scene object in the Object tree expands the tree so you can see all the objects in the scene (taking into account any KFE filters applied, of course). If any object's box contains a minus sign, clicking it hides the underlying branch.

The tree itself is made up of objects and animation information. You can easily identify the objects of the tree by the icon displayed to the left of the object name. You can select any object by clicking on the object or its name.

WORKING WITH ANIMATION BRANCHES

All animated objects contain an animation branch identified in the Object Tree by the small filmstrip icon. In the Animation Track pane (to the right of the Object Tree's animation branch) is an Action bar that represents one or more keyframed properties. Manipulating this bar affects all keyframes under this branch. You can view more detailed keyframe information by clicking on the plus/minus sign next to the animation branch.

To select an action, click the name of the action in the Object Tree. It's important to note that with an action selected, the Advance to Next Keyframe and Reverse to Previous Keyframe tools will cycle through the keyframes of the

NOTE

The Copy command from the pop-up menu will make a copy of the currently selected object but will not copy the selected action.

selected action only. Right-clicking on any object or action in the Object Tree opens a pop-up menu that enables you to perform functions such as copying, deleting, renaming, rendering, and applying the Repeat/Reverse functions.

GLUE/UNGLUE OBJECTS

The Object Tree can be used in place of the Glue As Sibling and Glue As Child tools. To glue two objects together, drag and drop the first object over the second object. To unglue an object from a hierarchy, drag and drop the object onto the scene icon.

THE ANIMATION TRACK PANE

The Animation Track pane gives you an overview of all the animated objects, their keyframes, and their timelines (see Figure 8.3). The Animation Track pane allows you to view and manage actions, individual keyframes, and groups of keyframes.

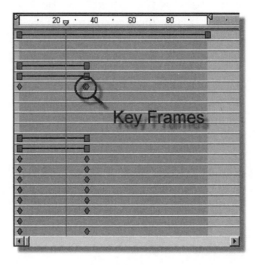

FIGURE 8.3   *The KFE's Animation Track pane. The vertical line is the Current Frame marker.*

TIMELINE

The timeline at the top of the Animation Track pane is used to measure your scene's time in frame units. To view more frames, click the Zoom Track View tool in the KFE Toolbar, and then click and drag your mouse left in the Animation Track pane. To focus in on a specific area of the timeline, click and drag your mouse left in the Animation Track pane.

THE CURRENT FRAME MARKER

The purple vertical line in the Animation Track pane is the Current Frame Marker. You can move the Current Frame Marker by clicking and dragging the arrow at its top.

START/END FRAME MARKERS

The Start and End Frame markers can be used to set animation preview start and end limits. This is the same as setting these limits numerically in the Animation Parameters panel.

ACTION BARS

The Action Bars are bookended by two blocks indicating the start and end time of a particular action. You can also shorten, lengthen, or delay the timing of an action by clicking and dragging on these blocks. By dragging the bar, you can shift an entire action to occur sooner or later in your animation. This is also true of the Action Bar for the scene. In this case, all the animated objects in the scene will have their timing adjusted or shifted.

KEYFRAMES

The diamond-shaped markers represent individual keyframes. You can easily shift the position of keyframes on the timeline by clicking and dragging left and right. You can also cut, copy, and paste keyframes by using the tools in the KFE Toolbar. To select a keyframe, click on a keyframe marker. To select groups of keyframes, click and drag around the area where the keyframes reside. Selected keyframes change color.

EDITING KEYFRAMES AND ACTIONS

The KFE has an enhanced set of tools for editing keyframes. Let's look at a few ways to animate your objects and edit those actions within the KFE.

RECORDING KEYFRAMES

NOTE

To animate an object's surface material, you must use the Paint Over tool to apply the new surface texture.

To animate an object, set the Current Frame number to the frame where you would like the animated sequence to start, either by typing the number in the Current Frame field and pressing Enter, or by dragging the Current Frame marker at the top of the Animation Track pane to the desired frame on the timeline. Move, rotate, scale, or deform your object. If the AutoRecord option is disabled, you must click the Record key to set the keyframe manually.

SELECTING KEYFRAMES

To select an individual keyframe, you must first expand the animation branch (filmstrip icon in the Object Tree) of your object if it isn't expanded already. This will expand the keyframe timelines to expose the individual keyframes.

To select an individual keyframe, click on one of the diamond-shaped markers in the Animation Track pane. It changes color when selected. To deselect a keyframe, click anywhere in the Animation Track pane not occupied by another keyframe.

Selecting multiple keyframes is easy: Hold down the Ctrl key and click on the desired keyframes. This method enables you to pick individual keyframes one at a time. Alternatively, you can click and drag around a group of keyframes to select them all in one clean sweep of the mouse. It's important to note that before you select a group of keyframes, you must start the click-and-drag process in an area not occupied by a keyframe. The selected keyframes may now be deleted, shifted, or copied.

MOVING KEYFRAMES

Simply click and drag on any individually selected keyframe or group of keyframes to move them.

CUTTING AND COPYING KEYFRAMES

After you have selected keyframes, you can move them from the animation track to the clipboard by clicking the Cut button in the Toolbar. You can also right-click in the Animation Track pane to select the Copy tool from a pop-up menu.

PASTING KEYFRAMES

The Toolbar's Paste button is used to insert keyframes into an animation track. You can paste keyframes into the same type of action only—for example, Move, Color, Scale, and so on. Here is a method you can use to ensure that pasted keyframes end up in the correct location:

> **NOTE**
>
> When pasting Inverse Kinematic keyframes from one object to another, you must make sure that your objects are constructed identically. Otherwise, the results might be unpredictable.

1. Select the object.

2. Click and drag the Current Frame marker to the frame number you want to paste the keyframe into.

3. Click the Paste button to place the keyframes into the selected track. If you are pasting a group of keyframes, the position of the Current Frame marker is where the first keyframe of the group will be pasted.

ERASING KEYFRAMES

Selected keyframes can be deleted by pressing the Del key on your keyboard.

RETIMING ACTIONS

An *action* is a collection of keyframed parameters and is represented by a solid bar in the Animation Track pane. Manipulating the action bar controls all the actions (sets of keyframes) as a group.

To make an action occur sooner or later, click and drag anywhere on the bar and drag it left or right. You can use this action bar to quickly adjust the timing of animated objects in your scene.

To stretch out the time it takes for an action to be played back, or to compress the action into a smaller number of frames, click and drag on either of the blocks that bookend the action bar.

SCENE KEYFRAMES

Scene keyframes are keyframes of plug-ins, fog, ray tracing, backgrounds, and global environments. To enable the scene keys, Draw Scene must be enabled in the Animation Parameters panel (right-click Play).

You can keyframe trueSpace4's Fog Color, fog extents, maximum percentage, and the Fog's on and off state. Background images and color changes can be keyframed, as well as an environment's bitmap or color. Ray tracing can be keyframed on and off, as well as the reflect value.

FUNCTION CURVES

The Function Curves tool located at the far right of the KFE Toolbar toggles between the Animation Track pane and the Function Curve Editor panel. You can also use the Ctrl+Tab key combination to toggle between the KFE's Animation Track pane and the Function Curves tool (FCT). The FCT enables you to fine-tune the movement, scaling, and rotation keyframes of your animated objects (see Figure 8.4).

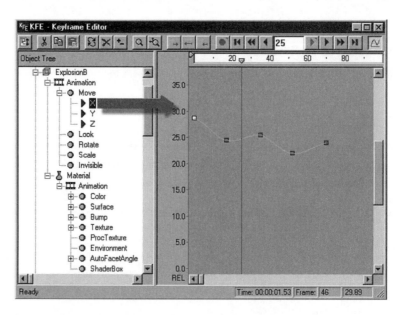

FIGURE 8.4   *The KeyFrame Editor's Function Curves tool (FCT).*

While the FCT is open, additional x, y, and z values are displayed in the Object Tree. The x, y, and z values are used for tweaking movement, scale, and rotation keyframes. To view the x, y, and z values, you must expand the action's tree by clicking the plus sign to the left of the object's icon in the Object Tree. The spline curve displayed in the Animation Track pane represents the rate at which the object approaches the keyframes over time.

EDITING KEYFRAMES

You have several options for editing function curves. You can click and drag the keyframe to change its vertical position. You can hold the Ctrl key while you click and drag your mouse to move the keyframe horizontally, adjusting the frame number of the selected keyframe. You can double-click on the keyframe to bring up control handles to adjust the tension, bias, and continuity of the spline curve at the selected keyframe.

ADJUSTING KEYFRAMES

The value of an individual keyframe or group of keyframes can be changed by clicking and dragging up or down within the Function Curve editor.

After you have selected the keyframe, you can smooth out the function curve by dragging your mouse. If no keyframes exist at points you would like to smooth in the curve, you can add additional keyframes by right-clicking at the desired frame position to open a menu. Select New from this menu, and the keyframe will be added at that point on the spline curve.

ADJUSTING KEYFRAME TIME

In some cases, it is necessary to create a smooth function curve by shifting the frame number of an existing keyframe. To do this, simply hold down the Control key while dragging on a selected keyframe. Drag the mouse right to advance the keyframe to its new position, and left to move it back. This also affects the position of the keyframe in the other two axes.

KEYFRAME PROPERTIES

You can access an individual keyframe's properties by right-clicking on a keyframe to open the KF Properties panel (see Figure 8.5). The KF Properties panel is where you can enter keyframe values manually, as well as set the spline corner settings.

FIGURE 8.5   *The KF Properties panel.*

- **KF:** The frame number of the selected keyframe.

- **KF Value:** Displays the movement, scaling, or rotational value of the keyframe at the frame number displayed in the KF field.

- **Tension, Continuity,** and **Bias:** Determine how smoothly or sharply the function curve spline eases into or out of the specified keyframe. The Tension, Continuity, and Bias settings affect the movement, translation, or scaling along all axes.

ADJUSTING TENSION, BIAS, AND CONTINUITY (TBC)

NOTE

Because only one axis is shown at a time, take care when adjusting Tension, Bias, or Continuity. I suggest checking the other two axes often to ensure things don't get out of hand.

Double-click on a keyframe to bring up control handles that work similarly to those found in the Spline tools. By using these handles, you can change the shape of the curve as it enters and exits the selected keyframe. The bright gold handle controls the shape of the spline curve as it exits the keyframe, and the dark gold handle directs the shape of the curve as it enters the keyframe. To adjust the Continuity, it is best to right-click the node you want to alter and select Properties from the menu. There you can change the Continuity setting manually.

Changing the orientation of a handle adjusts the Bias value for the selected ani-mation parameter. Changing the length of the handle by dragging the handle's bar closer to, or farther away from, the keyframe controls the Tension. Lengthening the handles causes movement, scaling, or rotation to occur at a faster rate around the keyframe, whereas shortening the handles slows it down.

SUMMARY

The new KFE makes the task of managing animated objects and their keyframes as simple as click and drag. In a later chapter, we will use the KFE to adjust the timing of one of our animations.

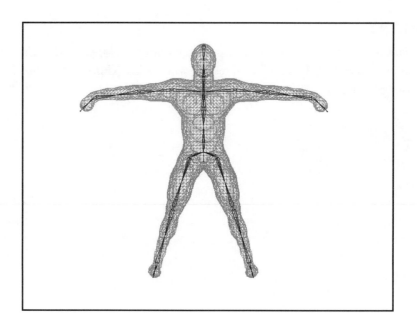

CHAPTER 9

ADVANCED BONES

by Frank Rivera

trueSpace4's Bones features (skeletons and deformable skin) enable you to create and animate characters like never before. By now, you have heard of bones and what they do. We know that they can be used to bring inanimate objects to life; unfortunately, at the time of this writing, a lot of trueSpace users find them a little intimidating. Believe it or not, trueSpace bones are easier to use than you might think.

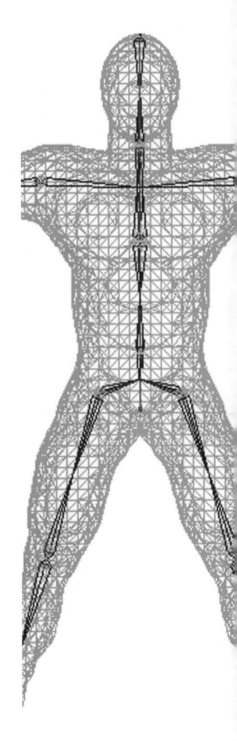

In this chapter, we will be looking at the mechanics involved in creating a skeleton for your bipedal humanoid characters. We will cover the following:

- Building a skeleton
- The Build Skeleton panels
- Creating a bone structure for bipedal humanoids
- Editing joints
- Attaching a skeleton to an object
- Flexing muscles
- Editing muscles and tendons
- Adding and removing vertices from muscle groups

BONES AND HUMANOID CHARACTERS

In Chapter 7, I skimmed over the Bones panels because all the functionality built into the Bones features wasn't needed for animating simple objects with bones. Here, we will be creating more complex skeletal structures, and, therefore, a review of the panels and tools involved is in order. As soon as we get the panels out of the way, we will look at the practical applications of trueSpace bones.

To animate a character with bones, you first must link several bones together with joints. This creates a hierarchy called a *skeleton*. Bones (a skeletal deformation tool) perform the same basic tasks as other deformation tools in trueSpace; they deform a mesh's vertices, except in a controlled manner so the vertices move and flex like skin. Joints are just a method of linking two objects together (in this case, bones) with the capability to adjust the amount of rotational freedom of the link itself. Like everything else in life, when using bones you have to have a good structure to build upon, so let's look at what's involved in building a bones structure.

BUILDING A SKELETON

There are three ways to build a skeleton in trueSpace4. You can

- Extract a skeleton from an existing IK object
- Manually create each bone and create each joint to construct the skeleton
- Build the skeleton by clicking your mouse where the joints should appear

The Extract Skeleton from IK Object tool enables you to create a skeleton from an existing object with an IK structure by replacing the IK-linked polyhedra with bones. An extracted skeleton retains the animation information of the original object. The original IK object remains unchanged, but the new skeleton can then be applied to another polyhedron by selecting the Attach Skin to Skeleton tool. When you load any object with an IK structure, trueSpace converts the IK structure to a bones structure for you automatically. There is something interesting about this tool. Let's try a short experiment.

1. Load up the CaliBot.scn file located on the resource CD.

2. Click the Extract Skeleton from IK Object tool.

3. Select the Caligari robot and drag him to your left.

This should reveal a second bone structure—an identical copy of the robot's skeleton. As you can see, Extract Skeleton from IK Object is a nifty skeleton copy tool.

With the Add New Bone tool, you can create individual bones and use them to build a skeleton. You can then attach the bones to one another by using the Add Custom Joint tool by clicking each of the bones.

The third choice, the Build Skeleton tool, is the one you will most likely use to construct your bone structures for your characters. The Build Skeleton tool makes it possible to construct a skeleton directly in 3D space or inside an object.

You can use the Build Skeleton tool to create a whole new skeleton from scratch, edit an existing skeleton, or make changes to a skeleton that has been skinned. Once in Build Skeleton mode, you can manipulate or delete existing joints, or add more joints and bones to the skeleton. To exit the Build Skeleton mode, click the Build Skeleton tool again.

You can construct your skeleton in an orthogonal or perspective view window. In the Perspective view, if there is no object under the cursor while placing bones and joints, the skeleton will be built in the xy plane parallel to the grid. In an orthogonal view, it is built in a plane perpendicular to the selected view—Front, Left, or Top. If there is an object under the cursor, however, the skeleton is built inside of that object.

Let's take a closer look at the Build Skeleton tool and the panels associated with it.

WARNING

If an object that has had a skeleton attached is selected, clicking the Build Skeleton tool reverts the skeletal structure to its original state when it was attached to the skin. All the keyframes associated with the bone structure (skeleton) will be deleted.

THE SKELETON PANELS

The skeleton panels are vital in the creation of a workable skeleton that can be applied to a character. There are two panels involved, the Build Skeleton panel and the Build Skeleton Properties panel, as shown in Figure 9.1.

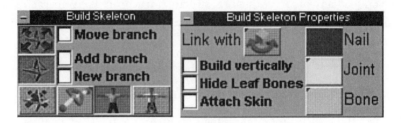

FIGURE 9.1 *The Build Skeleton and Build Skeleton Properties panels.*

THE BUILD SKELETON PANEL

You will spend a lot of time in the Build Skeleton panel when constructing skeletons or what I like to call bone structures. The Build Skeleton panel consists of six buttons and three check boxes. Here is a rundown of each.

MOVE JOINT

Clicking and dragging on a joint moves the individual joint. If the Add Joint tool is active (button depressed), the newly created joint can be immediately moved as long as you don't release the mouse button. When the Move Joint button is activated, holding down the Ctrl key while dragging a joint moves the branch that makes up the joint and the two bones connected to it. This has the same effect as enabling the Move Branch option in this same panel. You will grasp this better with a short exercise.

1. Open a new scene and Switch to the Front view. Click the Build Skeleton tool to open the Build Skeleton panel.

2. Click in the lower-left corner of the workspace. Working your way up to the upper-right corner, left-click five times.

3. Deselect the Add Joint button in the Build Skeleton panel. If for some reason the Move Joint button isn't depressed, click it now.

4. Select the center joint and drag it up and down. Notice the rubber band effect as you move the joint. Release the joint and press the Undo button.

5. While pressing the Ctrl key, reselect the center joint and move it as you did before. Notice anything different about the Bones movement? The entire branch moves instead of just the joint and two bones attached to it.

Move Joint is extremely handy when you want to resize a bone that is part of a branch without affecting any of the other bones. This has the same effect on an attached Bone and its size as enabling the Move Branch option. I find that using the Ctrl key is easier to work with, and it's nice not having to remember to disable it when you're done. Just release the Ctrl key.

ADD JOINT AND ADD BRANCH

Add Joint creates a new joint and adds a bone connected to the most recently added branch of the skeleton (bone structure). Here is the neat part: By clicking on an existing bone with the Add Joint tool active, a new joint is created dividing the existing bone in two.

When Add Branch is checked, a left-click with the Add Joint tool active adds an extra joint to the bone nearest the cursor. If the nearest bone is a leaf bone, the new joint will become attached to the leaf bone's end. The new joint becomes the active branch. That means if the Add Joint tool is enabled as well, joints and bones will be added from this new branch. This is interesting; let's try it out.

> **NOTE**
>
> The Add Joint and Move Joint functions can be used together (enabled/disabled) to prevent moving a joint when you want to add a joint, or from adding a joint when you want to move one.

1. Open a new scene and switch to the Front view. Click the Build Skeleton tool.

2. The Add Joint button should be depressed, as well as the Move Joint button. Click in the lower-left corner of the workspace. Working your way up to the upper-right corner, left-click three times.

3. Click the area between the middle joint and the first joint. A new joint should appear splitting the bone in half. Let's try adding a branch.

4. Select the Add Branch option in the Build Skeleton panel.

5. Click anywhere above the bone structure in between two joints. Be sure not to click on any of the bones. A new branch should appear attached to the center of the closest bone where you clicked.

Normally, if the Add Branch option was disabled and you clicked outside the bone structure, a new joint would have been added in that spot with a bone leading back to the last joint that was selected.

MOVE BRANCH

When Move Branch is enabled, clicking and dragging on one joint in a branch moves all joints from the selected joint away from the nail in tandem. Remember, while the Move Joint tool is active, holding the Ctrl key while dragging a joint does the same thing as the Move Branch Option without having to remember to disable it.

DELETE JOINT

In the last exercise, we added new joints to a skeleton. Let's assume that we didn't want one of the joints in our new bone structure. This is where the Delete Joint tool comes in. When Delete Joint is active, clicking on a target joint deletes it. trueSpace4 then reverts to Add Joint mode. If the joint you want to delete was created as the last operation, selecting Undo will accomplish the same thing.

EDIT JOINTS DIRECTLY

The Edit Joints Directly button enables you to edit the joint rotation and constraints directly. Clicking this tool will display the joint's control handles. They appear as a circular object resembling the Pac-Man video game character in the center of the joint called the joint's *radial indicator,* which is used to adjust a joint's pitch, roll, and yaw (see Figure 9.2). In plain English, it's a wonderful device for adjusting the resistance to rotation and the amount of free movement (swing) the attached bones will have.

Let's take this opportunity to discuss rotating joints and controlling the swing of the bones attached to the joint.

1. Open a new scene and switch to the Front view. Click the Build Skeleton tool.

2. The Move Joint and Add Joint buttons should be depressed. Click in the lower-left corner of the workspace. Working your way up to the upper-right corner, left-click three times.

3. Click the second joint. This makes it the active joint.

4. Click the Edit Joints Directly button. The joint's radial indicator should appear as depicted in Figure 9.2.

5. Select the outer edge of the radial indicator. Drag your mouse out and away from the joint. This controls the resistance to rotation. The larger the value, the more resistance, making it harder to move the bones attached to this joint.

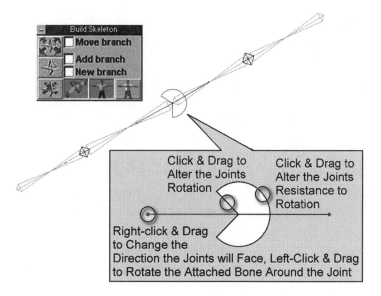

FIGURE 9.2   *You can interactively change the pitch, roll, and yaw of a joint via the joint's control handles.*

6. Select either of the two handles that run from the outer edge of the radial indicator to its center (where a piece of pie looks like it has been cut from it). If you drag your mouse, you can define the degree of rotational freedom the attached bones will have.

7. Right-clicking the far end of either of the two control handles running through the center of the radial indicator and dragging your mouse will rotate the joint. If you left-click and drag this area, the bone attached can be moved.

As you can see, working with trueSpace allows a lot of freedom. Now on to two very interesting buttons.

BUILD SKELETON INSIDE SKIN AND LINK IK OBJECT

Build Skeleton Inside Skin is a toggle button. When it is depressed, the Link IK Object button is disabled. The Build Skeleton Inside Skin tool is the default mode of building a skeleton. It enables you to build the skeleton freely by adding joints anywhere in the workspace, a different approach to what Link IK Object does.

When enabled, Link IK Object disables the Build Skeleton Inside Skin button. It allows the creation of a skeleton from an object with hierarchies. To use this tool, select the object made up of glued parts and enable the tool. Click one of the sub-objects belonging to the hierarchical object. The tool finds the two closest objects and links them with a joint.

If it seems as though this is a lot to absorb at first, don't worry; you will have a chance to use many of the Build Skeleton panel's tools in the upcoming exercises. Now, let's look at the second panel.

THE BUILD SKELETON PROPERTIES PANEL

Right-clicking the Build Skeleton tool opens the Build Skeleton Properties panel (as well as the Build Skeleton panel). This panel (in my opinion) is where you separate the well-built skeletons from the weak, hard-to-work-with kind. The first item on the panel is the Link With button. This is where you choose which kind of joint to use when constructing your skeletons. The Caligari documentation states:

> "Link with: Use this pop-up menu to determine the type of joint to be used by the Build Skeleton tool. The default type is 1D Hinge. You can adjust the properties of a joint at any time by using the Edit Joints Directly tool in the Build Skeleton panel."

That is a generic statement that doesn't tell us much. It doesn't mention that this is the secret to good skeletal motion, that it is the most important button in the whole mix of Bones tools. Here is my take on this panel. Follow along with me in Figure 9.3.

When constructing your skeletons, keep the Build Skeleton Properties panel open. As you construct your skeletons, you will want to switch to different types of joints at different points of the construction process. For example, take the human arm: Starting at the wrist, a 2D Spherical Joint would be used because our wrists rotate in two directions. At the elbow, a 1D Hinge Joint should be used because our elbows swing in one direction (with a limited amount of movement). Our arms swing at the shoulder basically in two directions, so a 2D spherical Joint should be used at the shoulder. If you were to use the default 1D Hinge Joint throughout the skeletal build process, you would find that your character would become difficult to pose naturally.

A rule of thumb should be to keep the Build Skeleton Properties panel open during the skeletal build process. We will discuss selecting the right joint a little later in this chapter. For now, let's continue to look at the other items in the Build Skeleton Properties panel.

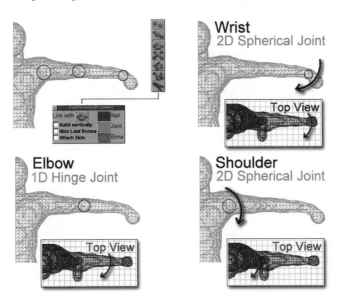

FIGURE 9.3   *Two types of joints should be used when creating a skeleton for a humanoid character.*

- **Build Vertically:** This option pertains only to the Perspective view. Use this option to build the skeleton from the ground up (or vice versa). With this item unchecked, the bones will be placed parallel to the ground.

- **Hide Leaf Bones:** A joint links two bones. One or both of these bones can act as a leaf bone. A leaf bone isn't connected to other bones. The direction the leaf bone will face is extrapolated from the direction of the previous bone. You can hide leaf bones during the skeletal build process by clicking Hide Leaf Bones in the Build Skeleton Properties panel. If the leaf bones are visible, you can alter their direction by clicking and dragging the unattached end. If you hide the leaf bones, they will appear after exiting the Build Skeleton mode.

- **Nail, Joint,** and **Bone Color:** These three buttons enable you to choose a color for the three visible elements of a skeleton: the nail, joints, and bones. Click and hold the color buttons to view a pop-up menu with a selection of colors to choose from.

That just about covers the panels. As I promised, now that the panels are out of the way, we can construct a skeleton for a bipedal humanoid character.

CREATE A BONE STRUCTURE FOR BIPEDAL HUMANOIDS

Let's put the skeleton panels to work. For this next exercise, we will construct a skeleton for the superhero character we built in Chapter 4. Before you tackle this exercise, please review Figure 9.4. Get familiar with the names of these basic components of a skeleton because I will refer to them throughout this chapter.

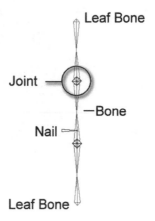

FIGURE 9.4 *The anatomy of a simple skeleton (bone structure).*

1. Load AniHero.scn from the resource CD. You might remember this guy from the character-modeling chapter. He was created by using trueSpace metaballs. I converted him into a solid polyhedron for this exercise.

2. Right-click the Build Skeleton tool to open the Build Skeleton panel and Build Skeleton Properties panels.

3. We are going to start with the head of the character and work our way down, creating the character's spine. Can you guess what kind of joints should be used for the character's spine? If you said 2D Spherical joints, you are correct. In the Build Skeleton Properties panel, set the Link With option to a 2D Spherical Joint. In the Build Skeleton panel, make sure the Move Joint and Add Joint options are enabled (depressed), as well as the Build Skeleton Inside Skin button. I like a clean workspace free of unnecessary clutter, so click the Hide Leaf Bones option in the Build Skeleton Properties panel.

4. Starting with the character's head, click the top of the skull and click at the neck. This will create one bone that extends from the top of the skull to the neck. Try to keep the joints lined up vertically.

5. To complete the character's spine, click the center of the chest, the center of the abdomen, and the crotch area where the legs meet. Figure 9.5 illustrates the locations.

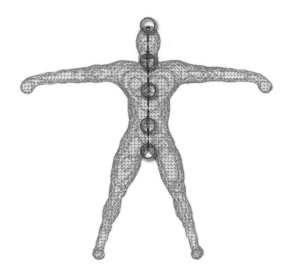

FIGURE 9.5   *The locations of the 2D Spherical joints that make up the character's spine.*

6. For the arms, we will have to create two branches to create the shoulders. In the Build Skeleton panel, click the Add Branch option. Click on the left side of the second bone (from the top) near its center. This should add a branch to the second bone to form the left shoulder. Click on the right side as you did before to form the right shoulder. Click the Add Branch option in the Build Skeleton panel to disable it.

7. The joints that make up the shoulder need to be moved into place. To do this without adding unnecessary joints, disable the Add Joint button in the Build Skeleton panel. Click the left shoulder joint and drag it near the top of the shoulder where the arms connect to the torso. Do the same for the right shoulder. Enable the Add Joint button in the Build Skeleton panel.

8. Up to this point, we have used 2D Spherical joints for the spine and shoulders. For the character's elbow, we need to change the type of joint from a 2D Spherical joint to a 1D Hinge joint because elbows swing 90 degrees in

one direction; any other type of rotation would be painful. In the Build Skeleton Properties panel, set Link With to 1D Hinge Joint.

9. Starting with the arm on your left (character's right arm), click where the elbow should be. A guess is okay. You can move the joint later if you need to. To construct the character's left elbow (on your right), click the center of the joint that makes up the character's left shoulder. This won't do anything at this point. All you have done is made that joint the active joint. Unfortunately, there is no way to tell whether a joint is the active joint. Click where the character's left elbow should be.

10. For the remainder of the character's arms, we will need to change the type of joint from a 1D Hinge joint to a 2D Spherical joint because our wrist rotates along more than one axis. In the Build Skeleton Properties panel, set Link With to 2D Spherical Joint.

11. Click the wrist area of the character's left arm (your right). Remember that the left elbow was the last joint we added; therefore, it should be the active joint. To finish the character's left arm, click the end of the character's fist. For the character's right arm, click the right elbow to make this joint the active joint. Click the right wrist and the tip of the right fist. Use Figure 9.6 as a guide.

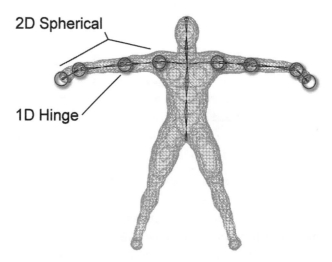

FIGURE 9.6 *The location of the joints that make up the character's arms. The character's shoulder and wrist are 2D Spherical joints, and the character's elbow is a 1D Hinge joint.*

12. Creating the hips of the character will require a branch at the last bone of the spine. In the Build Skeleton panel, click Add Branch. Click the left side of the last bone of the character's spine near its center. This will create the branch where the thigh bone and waist will meet. Disable the Add Joint button and Add Branch option in the Build Skeleton panel. Click the newly created joint and drag it where the thigh and torso meet. Click and drag the last joint in the spine and place it where the character's left thigh and torso meet.

13. To create the character's knees and ankles, we will need to change from the present 2D Spherical joint to a 1D Hinge joint. In the Build Skeleton Properties panel, set Link With to a 1D Hinge Joint. In the Build Skeleton panel, enable the Add Joint button.

14. Click the knee, the ankle, and the bottom of the character's foot to complete the character's left leg. Click the joint in the character's right hip to make it the active joint. Repeat the previous steps by clicking the knee, the ankle, and the bottom of the character's right foot to complete the character's skeleton (bone structure). Take a look at Figure 9.7 to see the finished character's skeleton.

15. Click the Object tool to close the Build Skeleton panel.

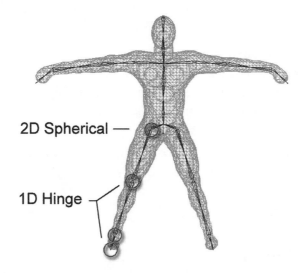

FIGURE 9.7   *The complete skeleton. The character's legs consist of a 2D Spherical joint at the hips and three 1D Hinge joints for the knees and ankles.*

ALWAYS TEST YOUR WORK

That covers creating the basic skeleton, but it isn't ready to be attached to an object just yet. We have to test our bone structure before attaching it to a character. Save the scene locally on your drive and call it HeroBones.scn. If anything flakes out on you during the next few steps, simply reload the scene and start over. In the next discussion, I will refer to parts of the skeleton as belonging to the character. What I am referring to is the area of the character mesh where a joint or bone is located. Because we haven't attached the skeleton to the character yet, the two are still separate individual objects.

In Chapter 7, we briefly discussed bones, and we practiced using the nail. If you are familiar with using the nail, skip this paragraph. For those of you who may have skipped ahead, let me recap. The nail is used to anchor a bone so you can manipulate the other portions of the bone structure. You can move the nail by dragging it onto a different bone.

NOTE

When creating characters that will later be animated with bones, it is best to model the character in the "neutral pose" prior to building and attaching bone structures to your character's. This makes the attaching of skin to bones easier and eliminates vertices from different parts of body becoming attached to a limb. The neutral pose is depicted in Figure 9.7.

What I would like you to do now is drag the nail to the character's waist. With the skeleton's center of gravity anchored, click the left or right fist and manipulate the skeleton. Bones uses inverse kinematics, so moving the character's fist should move the forearm, which moves the bicep, which pulls at the character's shoulders, making him bend at the waist. When you're done fooling around, click Undo to restore the skeleton to its original pose.

The reason I had you do this is to get a feel for how the joints are orientated. By manipulating the skeleton before attaching it to an object, we can check the orientation of the joints and make any adjustments necessary. This is good practice and can save you some headaches later.

Reset the skeleton to its original position (pose) by clicking Undo. Let's take a look at the joints of our bone structure and how we can manage their placement, orientation, resistance to rotation, and the freedom of movement of the bones attached.

EDITING JOINTS

You can use the Build Skeleton tool to edit a joint's degree of rotational freedom by double-clicking on any joint to display its control handles. You can use the

THE MARLIN STUDIOS' GET FAMOUS CONTEST WINNERS

**GRAND PRIZE ALL
AROUND WINNER**

Image created by Andrew Moffitt. Drew@netins.net

**FIRST PRIZE ALL
AROUND WINNER**

Image created by Gene R. Gunderson. Geneg@earthlink.net

SECOND PRIZE ALL AROUND WINNER

Image created by Karl Stocker. Karlcs@earthlink.net

RUNNERS UP

Image created by Andrew Moffitt. Drew@netins.net

Image created by Robert Rak. Rakr@sysoff.ctstateu.edu

Image created by Tito A. Belgrave. Bajanlub@globalserve.net

Color Images from Chapter 12, "Lighting in trueSpace"

Figure 12.10 Using a Projector light to cast light patterns.

Figure 12.11 Some interesting effects using Projector lights and volumetrics.

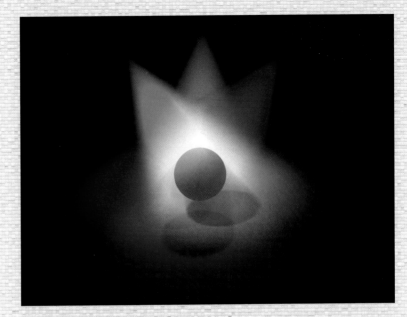

FIGURE 12.27 The additive nature of light.

FIGURE 12.28 The full color spectrum of light.

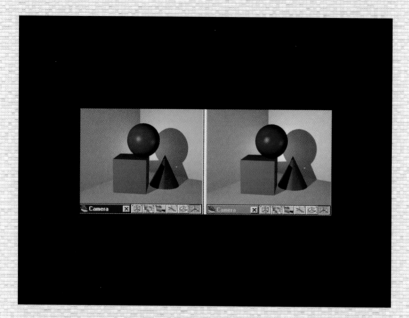

FIGURE 12.29   Color can convey temperature.

FIGURE 12.30   Color can convey the time of day.

trueSpace Image Gallery

Image created by Christopher Myatt. shezam@home.com

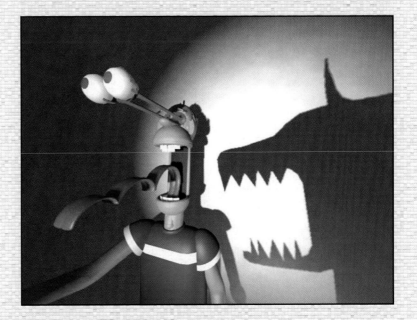

Image created by Joseph Brewer. jbrewer@tsenvy.com

Image created by Geoff Holman. zargon@powerlink.com

Image created by Terry Halladay. thallad@pcnet.com

"End of an Era" created by Tom Marlin. (c)1998 Tom Marlin.
www.marlinstudios.com

Image created by Jarrett Heather. jheather@inreach.com

"Broken Memories" created by Tom Marlin. (c)1998 Tom Marlin. www.marlinstu-dios.com

Image created by Garry Davis.

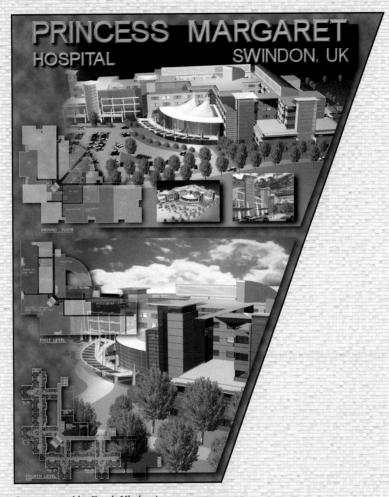

Image created by Frank Kholousi.

Image created by Arie Sztajnworc.

Image created by Jarrett Heather. jheather@inreach.com

"Blues Alley" created by Tom Marlin. (c)1998 Tom Marlin. www.marlinstudios.com

Image created by Terry Halladay. thallad@pcnet.com

Image created by Geoff Holman. zargon@powerlink.com

"Gull Harbor" created by Tom Marlin. (c)1998 Tom Marlin. www.marlinstudios.com

Image created by Geoff Holman. zargon@wkpowerlink.com

Image created by Chris Lerma. sorenl@lightspeed.net

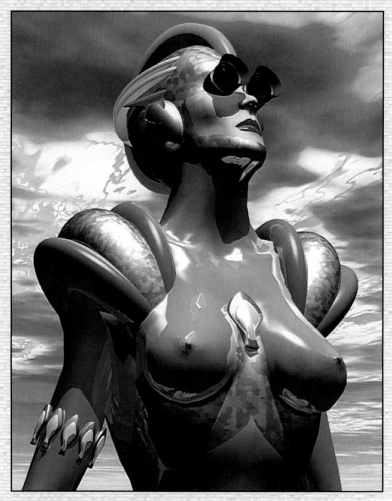

Image created by Michael A. Marunchak. marunchak@earthlink.net

Pitch, Roll, and Yaw indicators to change the degree of freedom for the selected joint. To adjust the Min/Max values for the selected joint, click directly on the radial indicator and swing the joint around to set Min/Max to the new values. When you release the mouse button, the branch will return to its previous position. You can display the properties of any other joint simply by clicking on the desired joint. A second double-click will exit Joint Edit mode.

It should be noted that using the double-click method of editing the joints directly can sometimes become difficult with bone structures of medium complexity. There is always more than one way to skin a cat in trueSpace. You can edit the joints directly via the Edit Joints Directly button located in the Build Skeleton panel. We briefly looked at the radial indicator earlier in this chapter; let's examine it a little more closely and with the skeleton we created.

1. Switch to the Top view and zoom in on the character's right arm, keeping the shoulder to the fist within the view window.

2. Right-click the Build Skeleton tool to open the Skeleton panels. In the Build Skeleton panel, click the Edit Joints Directly button. Click the elbow joint to reveal the joint's control handles. You might notice that the elbow joint doesn't seem to have a radial indicator to adjust the joint's pitch, roll, and yaw. It's there, but it's facing the wrong way. To correct this problem, right-click the tip of the red control handle and drag your mouse until the joint rotates 90 degrees, revealing the radial indicator.

3. Select the Object tool to complete the operation. Now for the test, if we positioned the elbow joint correctly, the forearm should swing vertically in the Top view. Open a smaller window and set it to the Front view. Position the view so that the whole character is visible. Click and drag the nail from its current position to the bone that runs through the character's right bicep. If you attempt to do this and the eye of the camera moves, select the Object Move tool and try it again. Close the smaller view window when done.

4. In the large view window, select the bone in the character's right fist and drag your mouse down toward the bottom of the screen. The bones that make up the forearm should move freely. Click Undo and drag the fist toward the top of the screen. Ouch! That isn't natural, is it? Our arms do not bend in that direction. Let's fix it, and while we are at it, let's adjust the amount of resistance to movement the forearm has.

5. Click Undo to reset the forearm to its original position. Right-click the Build Skeleton button to open the Skeleton panels if they aren't already open. In the Build Skeleton panel, click the Edit Joints Directly button. Click the elbow joint to reveal the joint's control handles and radial indicator.

6. The radial indicator at the center of the joint has two functions. The first is it can be used to adjust the amount of resistance to rotation the attached bones will have. You change its value by clicking and dragging on its outer surface. The radial indicator control handles will change color when under your cursor control. A larger value (larger size) creates more resistance, and, therefore, it would take more force to rotate the forearm. Go ahead and increase its size, but not too much. You want to be able to swing the character's arms. The second function the radial indicator provides is it can be used to limit the degree of movement. In our case, we want to limit the forearm from bending backward. To adjust the amount of freedom the forearm has to swing, click and drag either of the two control handles that connect the outer surface of the radial indicator and its center. In our case, we are concerned with the top one. Click and drag it; you will notice that the forearm follows the control handle. This is what's so wonderful about trueSpace—its feedback is above par. Drag the control handle until the forearm is parallel to the character's arm.

7. Select the Object tool to close all the panels. Click and drag the character's right fist up toward the top of the screen. It won't budge, and, unlike what you can with the human elbow, you can't force it. Click and drag the fist down toward the bottom of the screen. The arm bends, but with a little more resistance than before. If you are having a hard time bending the arm at the elbow, you probably set the elbow joint's resistance a bit too high in the previous step. You will have to go back and edit the joint directly and decrease the joint's resistance to rotation.

Not all the joints will be out of whack, but you should check each to ensure that the bones will react as expected. If it helps, delete or move the character mesh out of the way so you can see the joints better. Remember to use the nail to limit movement to specific areas while testing your joints.

When you have the skeleton to your liking, select the skeleton and click the Attach Skin to Skeleton tool. Your mouse cursor will change to a glue bottle. Select the character's mesh. After a few seconds, the character can be posed by using trueSpace bones. Select the Object tool to end the process.

As you can see, there are a few details involved in setting up a workable skeleton in trueSpace. After you have built a few, you should be able to create a skeleton in just a few minutes.

You can adjust any of the joints of a skeleton after it has been attached to an object in the same manner as performed previously by right-clicking the Build Skeleton tool.

We have created a bone structure and edited the joints of the bone structure; now let's look at what's involved with attaching an object's skin to a skeleton. When we are finished, we will get into trueSpace's tendon and muscles features.

ATTACHING SKIN TO SKELETON

The Attach Skin to Skeleton tool makes it possible to attach an object (skin) to a skeleton to aid in animating your characters. trueSpace automatically assigns parts of the skin surface to the skeleton to form muscles and tendons. You can later edit the degree of influence a muscle or tendon has on a particular bone if needed. You can attach a skeleton to a single object or to a group of objects that are glued together. You can also attach a skeleton to several objects at once, which can overlap one another. Portions of the skin that extend beyond a leaf bone are deformed along with the surface that is attached to this bone.

The skin surrounding a bone between two joints forms one muscle. This muscle can be the contractor with respect to either of the two joints, but it cannot be the contractor for both joints simultaneously. We will discuss the contractor muscle further shortly.

On a branch bone (a bone that has more than two joints linked to it), the portion of the skin that encloses the bone is divided into as many muscles as there are joints. Each of these muscles can be a contractor for a corresponding joint.

The Attach Skin to Skeleton tool also enables you to separate the skin from the skeleton so that you may change the position, rotation, or size of the skeleton within the skin. When the Attach Skin to Object tool is active, you can click and drag the selected object to move it into position. If the skeleton is dragged completely away from the skin, the skeleton will become detached, allowing you to

NOTE

You do not have to use a combination of 1D Hinge and 2D Spherical joints when constructing skeletons for your characters. You can use 2D Spherical joints for every joint in your character, but you will have to set each of the joints' degree of freedom accordingly via its radial indicator. The orientation of the joints is totally dependent on the type of character you are working with.

NOTE

The skeleton does not have to be completely contained within an object. Bones can extend outside the object they are attached to.

NOTE

It may be a little confusing at first, but the muscle performing the bulge is considered the *contractor* muscle. It is being contracted to shrink by drawing together.

edit the skin (object) without interference from the bone structure. Here's a step-by-step look at some common Attach Skin to Skeleton procedures.

To attach a skeleton to an object:

1. Select the skeleton.

2. Click the Attach Skin to Skeleton tool. The cursor will turn into a glue bottle.

3. Click the target object (skin).

4. Click the Attach Skin to Skeleton tool again, or click the Object tool to exit the Attach Skin to Skeleton tool.

To detach a skeleton from its skin:

1. Select the object that has been assigned a bone structure.

2. Click the Attach Skin to Skeleton tool.

3. Hold down the Ctrl key and click, or you can hold the Ctrl key and drag the skin outside the skeleton.

4. Click the Attach Skin to Skeleton tool, or click the Object tool to exit the tool.

To reorient or resize the skin:

1. Select the object that has been assigned a bone structure.

2. Click the Attach Skin to Skeleton tool and select Object Scale, Object Move, or Object Rotate. You can now move, rotate, or scale the skin as you would any other object.

3. Click the Attach Skin to Skeleton tool, or click the Object tool to exit the tool.

Once the skin has been attached to the skeleton, you can begin to deform the object's mesh (skin) by clicking and dragging on any part of the skin surface. You can also place the nail anywhere on the skin to anchor that portion of the object.

We will revisit bones again in the next chapter when we animate Franky, our little skateboarding terror, but first we must learn how tendons and muscles are used.

FLEXING SOME MUSCLE

Once you have created a bone structure for your character, you can edit the degree of muscular contraction of your character's limbs. trueSpace4 has a full complement of tools that allow you to visually edit the muscles and tendons of your characters (see Figure 9.8).

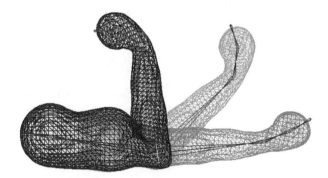

FIGURE 9.8   *You can add impressive muscle bulges to your characters with the Muscle and Tendon tools.*

EDITING TENDONS

The Edit Tendons tool enables you to change the Tendon Rate of the selected joint. When clicked, the bones structure will revert (temporarily) to its original position (pose) when the skin was first attached. You will also see two planes that define the selected limits of influence of the selected tendon. Click on the control handle below the selected tendon and drag right to increase the Tendon Rate; dragging left adjusts the proportions between the tendon and the muscle. To select a different tendon, click on a different joint.

THE SKINNING PANEL

Right-clicking on the Attach Skin to Skeleton tool or the Edit Tendons tool opens the Skinning panel, which is used to control how muscles and tendons are assigned to the skin. Let's review this panel and each of its options.

- **Tendon Rate:** Adjusts the proportions between the tendon and the muscle. Higher values increase the influence of the tendon, the area between the two planes depicted in Figure 9.9. The arm at the top of Figure 9.9 has a Tendon Rate of 0.07; the one below it has a Tendon Rate of 0.20. Notice how the planes visually define the area of the tendon. The Tendon Rate can also be adjusted by clicking on the control handles that appear just below the selected tendon. The acceptable range is from 0.01 to 0.99. The default value is 0.20.

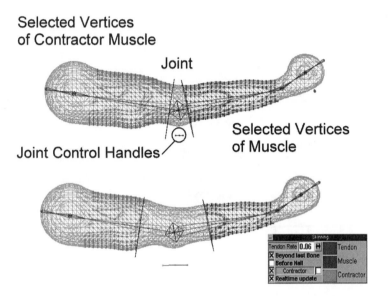

FIGURE 9.9 *A model of a character's left arm. Once the bone structure is assigned to the object, clicking the Edit Tendons tool opens the Skinning panel. Clicking the elbow joint displays the muscle, the contractor muscle, and their influence on the character's mesh.*

- **Beyond Last Bone:** When checked, any area of the skin that is beyond a leaf bone is attached to the selected bone. Otherwise, that portion of the skin will remain immobile. This is selected by default.

- **Before Nail:** When enabled, any area of the skin that does not enclose any bone is attached to the bone that has the nail attached. This is selected by default.

- **Contractor:** Switches which muscle will act as the contractor. On each side of the word Contractor are two check boxes; if you want to swap the muscle and contractor muscle, click the opposite check box.

- **Realtime Update:** This option is primarily used to disable the visual feedback of Tendon Rate. With this option disabled, only the planes representing the tendon's edges will be updated onscreen. The update to the skin, tendon, and neighboring muscles will be performed after the mouse button is released. This is checked by default.

- **Tendon**, **Muscle**, and **Contractor Color**: Provides a choice of six colors for identifying the vertices of the tendon. The default color is red.

Now that we have looked at trueSpace tendons, let's look at trueSpace muscles.

EDITING MUSCLES

To edit the muscles of your object, left-click the Edit Muscles tool. This will place trueSpace4 in Muscle Edit mode and open the Muscle Properties panel. When you first use the Edit Muscles tool, the first muscle from the nail will be selected; otherwise, the vertices of the last bone you edited will become highlighted. You can select another muscle by clicking near the desired bone.

The vertices of the muscle contractor will become highlighted, and a small control handle will appear above the muscle. This control handle might be visible, depending on the object you are working with. So, in the upcoming exercise, we will use the Muscle Properties panel to make any adjustments; but for the sake of clarity, let's go over the Muscle Properties panel, the control handle, and its hot spots.

THE MUSCLE PROPERTIES CONTROL HANDLE AND PANEL

Left-clicking the Edit Muscle tool opens the Muscle Properties panel and places trueSpace in Edit Muscle mode. A control handle will appear above or below the selected area, either a tendon, muscle, or muscle contractor.

- **The center point:** Adjusts the volume of the muscle bulge (strength). A numeric value can be manually entered in the Strength field located in the Muscle Properties panel. To use the control handle, click and drag your mouse left to extend the bulge; drag right to decrease the bulge.

> **NOTE**
> When adjusting muscle settings, you should have the muscle you will be working with contracted. This way, you can see some visual feedback as you make your adjustments.

- **The handles parallel to the bone:** Adjusts the strength along the bone. (I prefer to call this the muscle tone setting, and I will show you what I mean in a second.) You can enter a numeric value in the Length field located in the Muscle Properties panel. To use the control handle, click and drag your mouse right to widen the muscle bulge from the muscle's center outward along the bone; drag left to reduce this value. Let's look at an example of this effect.

In Figure 9.10, the arm on the left has a better tone than the one on the right. By using a larger Length value, the muscle bulge is spread over a wider distance; therefore, the muscle bulge has less tone or at least it appears that way. If you look closely, you can see what is really going on at the center of the muscle. Compare the two arms and their muscles' center. You can see increased separation of the muscle vertices.

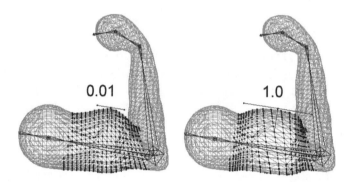

FIGURE 9.10 *Adjusting the muscle's length along the bone separates the muscle's vertices around its center. I like to refer to this setting as the muscle tone setting. Notice how the muscle flattens out with a higher setting.*

- **Handle perpendicular to the bone:** Adjusts the width of the muscle bulge. You can enter a numeric value in the Width field located in the Muscle Properties panel. Click and drag your mouse to the right to increase the muscle's bulk perpendicular to the bone, and drag left to make the muscle less bulky. The difference can be seen in Figure 9.11.

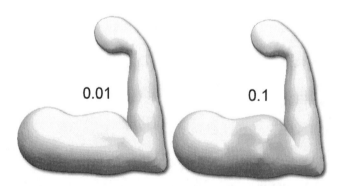

FIGURE 9.11 *Increasing the width of the muscle makes the muscle look more bulky and more impressive.*

- **The handle extending toward the bone:** Adjusts the falloff of the muscle's bulge. A low falloff value causes wider muscle bulging. A large value creates a sharper bulge. Right-clicking on the control handle turns the muscle into a bidirectional flexor/extensor type. A blue and red line indicating the direction of the contraction will appear running through the muscle. Dragging the line on either the red or blue side will change the direction of muscle flex.

While in this mode, the flexor and extensor get their own separate set of the parameters described previously, enabling you to specify independent values for each. Only one of them can be contracted at a time, and the flexor/extensor line will adjust the parameters of the contracted part of the muscle. To reset the muscle to be omnidirectional, right-click on the control handle again. You can also set this with a check box in the Muscle Properties panel. The Flexor/Extensor check box allows switching between all-directional and bidirectional contraction of the muscle. Figure 9.12 illustrates this setting.

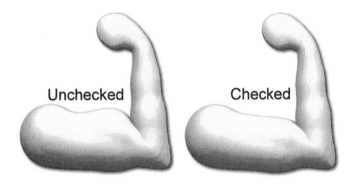

Unchecked   Checked

Flexor/Extensor

FIGURE 9.12   *In this image, the results of setting the Flexor/Extensor option are visible. As you can see, the muscle bulges when this option is unchecked.*

- **Sharpness:** This is related to the joining tendon. Clicking on or near a joint will select a tendon. A small control handle appears above or below the tendon. Use this setting to adjust the sharpening of the tendon when bent. Figure 9.13 illustrates this.

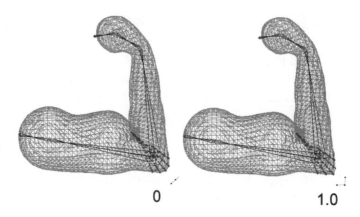

0   1.0

FIGURE 9.13 *In this image, the tendon sharpness setting is visible around the character's elbow.*

MUSCLE EXERCISE

To get your character's muscles to bulge realistically, you must learn how the relationships between muscles, tendons, and muscle contractors affect the objects attached to a skeleton. In the previous discussion, we covered a lot of ground and saw through illustrations how the muscle and tendon settings affect the muscle bulge. It's now time to put this information to some practical use. For our next exercise, we will add a bone structure to a character's arm and adjust the tendon and muscle settings. When we are done, you will be able to flex the character's arm and see its muscles bulge. Let's get started.

1. Open the file HeroArm.scn located on the resource CD. The arm used in the previous illustrations will appear in the Front view window.

2. Click the Build Skeleton tool; this will open the Skeleton panels.

3. For this exercise, we will use only 1D Hinge joints for the arm. Click once near the edge of the fist. Continuing down the arm to the shoulder, click the center of the fist, the wrist, near the elbow area, and the center of the shoulder area. This will create the basic skeleton we will need to flex the arm realistically. Use Figure 9.14 as a guide.

4. Click the Attach Skin to Skeleton tool. Your cursor will change to a glue bottle; click the arm mesh. A dialog box will appear warning you that you are about to delete a metaball structure. Click yes to convert the arm (created with metaballs) to a polyhedron.

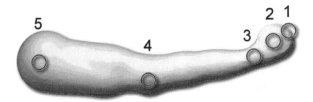

FIGURE 9.14   *The five areas of the arm you should click to create the arm's bone structure.*

5. Click the Object tool to exit the Attach Skin to Skeleton tool. The skeleton and mesh should both appear to be selected.

6. Click the nail and drag it to the bone in the bicep. Select the tip of the leaf bone sticking out of the fist and drag it to the shoulder in an arch over the arm. The arm doesn't bend realistically, and the bicep muscle doesn't bulge like I illustrated earlier because only the bone structure and joints have been defined so far. We need to tell trueSpace what the joints' limitations are, as well as how we want the muscle and tendons to be defined.

7. Click the Build Skeleton tool to open the Build Skeleton panel. Make sure the Add Joint button is disabled. Double-click the elbow joint to enter Joint Edit mode. The joint's radial indicator will appear.

8. Select the top control handle that runs from the center of the radial indicator to the radial indicator's outer surface and drag it until the forearm points straight up. Release your mouse. The forearm will revert to its original position. Click and drag the lower control handle until the forearm is horizontal, similar to its present position. These two actions will limit the forearm's swing as we manipulate it later during this exercise.

9. Click the wrist joint and perform the same operations as you did for the elbow joint. Set the wrist joint's rotational limits close to your own. Make a fist and study how far it bends; do the same for the character's arm. When you're satisfied with the wrist joint, click the Object tool to exit Edit Joints mode. Click and drag the tip of the leaf bone exiting the fist as you did before. It should bend more realistically now that you have defined the joint's rotational limits. When you're done, click Undo to reset the arm to its original pose.

10. Click the Edit Tendons tool. The vertices that define the contractor muscle and the muscle will change color. You can change the color of each by right-clicking the Edit Joint tool. Click and drag the control handle below the elbow joint to your left until the two planes move in close to the elbow joint, as depicted in the top half of Figure 9.15.

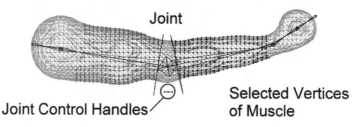

FIGURE 9.15 *Using the Edit Tendons tool, make the arm bend at the elbow more naturally.*

11. Click the wrist joint and draw the two planes in toward the joint as you did with the elbow joint. Click the Object tool. Click and drag the leaf bone exiting the fist left until the forearm won't move anymore.

12. Click the Edit Tendons tool (don't panic; the arm will be temporarily straightened during this operation) and then right-click it to open the Skinning panel. Enter 0.06 in the Tendon Rate field. Close the Skinning panel.

13. Left-click the Edit Muscle button to open the Muscle Properties panel. Click on the center of the bone running through the bicep. Drag the center of the bone up to the shoulder near the shoulder joint. This will provide us with only one set of vertices to worry about.

14. In the Muscle Properties panel, enter 0.1 in the Strength field, 0.1 in the Length field, 0.2 in the Width field. Use these settings as a starting point when working with muscles. Click the Object tool to close all the panels.

15. Click and drag the tip of the leaf bone that exits the fist left and right. The character's bicep muscle should flex impressively.

For those of you who like to see how things work for yourselves, you will find the finished character's arm on the resource CD, complete with bone structure, tendon settings, and muscular bulges. The filename is LeftArm.scn.

REMOVING AND ADDING VERTICES TO A MUSCLE

You now know that the Attach Skin to Skeleton tool automatically assigns vertices to bones to make the muscles of your characters. However, there is no guarantee that the vertices assigned will work with your character.

You can use the Muscle Properties panel to add or remove vertices by using either the Point, Lasso, or Rectangle selection tools. These work identically as the standard Lasso and Rectangle selection tools. To add vertices to the selected muscle, use either of the Point, Lasso, or Rectangle selection tools, click the sphere with the plus sign, and highlight the desired vertices. To remove vertices from a selected muscle, use either the Point, Lasso, or Rectangle selection tools and click the sphere with the minus sign. The vertices removed from the group will be automatically reassigned to the nearest adjoining tendon.

When you're finished selecting vertices or want to select another bone, disable the selection tool.

ATTACHING AN OBJECT TO A BONE

The Attach Object to Bone tool enables you to link a polyhedron to a bone. This is a great tool to use if you want your character to hold an object.

NOTE

You cannot attach an object with its own bone structure to another bone with the Attach Object to Bone tool.

To attach an object to a bone, position the object of choice near the bone you want it attached to. Click the Attach Object to Bone tool and then click the bone. The bone will be highlighted to indicate your selection.

Once you have selected the bone, click the glue bottle on the target object. trueSpace4 will group this object with the selected bone. When you move this bone, the attached object will move with it. I think you will get a better idea of how this works if we perform a short exercise.

1. Load the scene LftArm.scn and the Barbell.cob file from the resource CD. The barbell will be placed around the character's fist.

2. Select the arm and click the Attach Object to Bone tool.

3. Click the bone between the leaf bone and wrist joint. The bone will become highlighted.

4. Click the barbell and then the Object tool.

5. Click and drag the forearm from left to right. The barbell will stay attached to the assigned bone.

Removing an attached object is easy. Click the Attach Object to Bone tool and hold down the Ctrl key while clicking on the attached object. Pretty simple, but this can be an easy process to forget. A button for this task would really be more intuitive.

Summary

Well, we created a skeleton, edited its joints, muscles, and tendons, and managed to flex a little muscle. In the next chapter, we will look at what's involved in animating a character with bones, the things you should consider before getting started, and how to use saved skeletal animations on other characters you create.

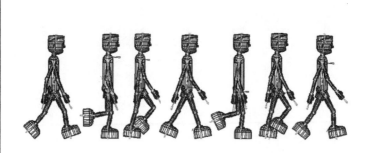

CHAPTER 10

CHARACTER ANIMATION

by Frank Rivera

The illusion of motion is a wonderful thing. We create a series of images and play them back in sequential order, and our brains are fooled into seeing motion. Until recently, traditional cel animators had to create 24 separate images for one second of film. In trueSpace, we can get away with creating as little as seven frames to create a complete walk cycle, and trueSpace will do the rest for us.

Character animation in trueSpace starts with proper character design and construction. After the character has been modeled, a skeleton is created, and the main poses of the character's actions are recorded. We have already looked at creating a skeleton and animating with trueSpace bones; now we will combine these skills with good character design and skeletal animation to bring your characters to life.

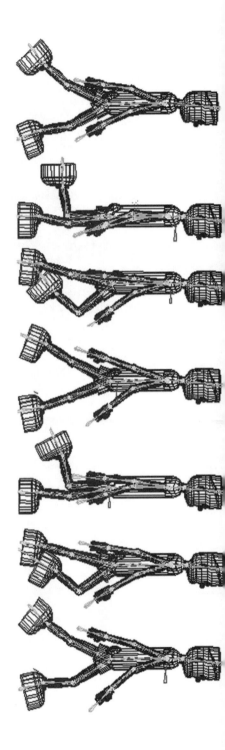

NOTE

This chapter isn't so much about character animation "the art form" as it is about the mechanics of animating characters with trueSpace bones. I was tempted to discuss the art of character animation, but why reiterate what has already been written and written well? If you are interested in the art of character animation, I suggest you pick up a copy of *Digital Character Animation* by George Maestri. He does a wonderful job of explaining the concepts involved, and I personally think the book is a work of art. No digital animator's bookshelf is complete without it.

I have waited until this chapter to discuss character design because it must be taken into account if you want to animate characters in trueSpace successfully. With a little planning, you will get great results from trueSpace's animation tool set.

In this chapter, we will cover the following:

- Modeling concerns and character animation
- Segmented versus solid mesh characters
- Avoiding character design flaws
- Posing your characters
- Creating a walk cycle
- Skeletal animation and reusability

Before we animate a character, we must cover some ground in the area of character engineering. In the world of CG character animation, a lot comes before the actual act of animating a character. I have three laws I follow before I animate anything.

Frank's three laws of character animation:

1. **Know your character before you design him.** This involves thinking through things such as the character's body type, persona, and storyline. For example, will the character be a lumbering giant, a cute bug-like creature, or a realistic humanoid cybernetic bad guy who gives chase to another character?

2. **Know your character before you construct him.** Will your character have to run, jump, or swim? What will your character be wearing? Will your character interact with other characters or the audience through the use of dialog? Will the character have to manipulate objects in the scene? Will the character's hands be visible up close?

3. **Know your character before you animate him.** Does your character have a funny gait when it walks? Does your character wear clothing that can conceal seams, aid in the animation process, or eliminate the need to animate certain parts? For example, a wizard wearing a large cloaked robe that reaches the floor probably doesn't need his legs animated.

Here is the road most often followed by new animators: A spark ignites an idea; the beginner becomes enthusiastic and begins to construct a character. The character is constructed using the latest tools available in their software package. The character is finished, and the task of animating it begins. Frustration soon sets in because the character can't be animated as expected. What causes a character to become unanimatable? Bad planning.

PLAN, PLAN, PLAN YOUR CHARACTER FIRST

I can't say it enough: Plan your character first. Successful character animation starts with a well-thought-out, well-built model. Often the method used to build the character will dictate how well you can animate the character and what actions the character will be able to perform. Before we actually animate a character, we should look at the different methods used to construct characters and how each of these methods can affect how well a character can be animated.

The first question you might ask yourself is whether your character should be constructed using segments—separate objects linked together to form a hierarchy—or constructed from a single mesh that can be deformed with a bone structure, or perhaps a combination of the two. The decision you make can have a big effect on how the character looks and moves, and how easy it is to animate.

SEGMENTED CHARACTERS

A segmented character is made up of separate objects linked together in a hierarchy to form the character. The character on the left in Figure 10.1 is an example. Such characters are animated by moving or rotating each individual section. Let's review the pros and cons of segmented characters.

Pros:

- They are less taxing on your hardware. Animating only portions of a segmented character uses less processing power.

- They are easy to set up. After you've set the axes for the pivot points and have created the hierarchy, you can begin to animate the character. You don't have to spend any time constructing a skeleton to deform the character's mesh. An example of this type of character animation can be found on the resource CD located in the Chapter 10 folder. The filename is Far_run4.flc. You will have to use the free animation player provided on the resource CD in the Player folder.

Cons:

● Visible seams and broken joints. While you can try to hide the seams of the segments, there will always be poses where the seam is noticeable. Visible seams make your character look unsophisticated.

● Lack of flexibility. The segments of the character can't be bent. You are essentially tied to the jointed areas for posing your character. The build process has to be carefully planned out.

FIGURE 10.1   *This is an example of a character created from segments and a character created as a solid mesh. The one on the left is made up of individual objects glued together in a hierarchy. Which of the two looks more organic?*

SOLID MESH CHARACTERS

These types of characters are made from a single mesh. For example, the character's arm is modeled as one mesh that is then deformed by placing a bone structure inside it. This bone structure is then manipulated, deforming the mesh and causing the arm to bend at the elbow.

Pros:

● A smoother, more professional look. I hate to say it, but segmented models look less professional. Of course, this depends on the context they are placed in. For example, if the entire animation is to look puppet-like or screwed together, then the character fits, and the fact that it is segmented will be overlooked. Characters made from a single or combination of single parts look more organic.

● Flexibility. The position of each vertex can be changed with each pose. Bending is limited only by the resolution of the character's mesh. The areas that bend are smooth and more natural-looking.

Cons:

- Resource-intensive. The more vertices involved, the more resources your processor has to consume.

- Time-consuming setup times. Some sort of deformation method has to be setup for the character. In the case with bones, a skeleton has to be constructed that will define the joints, their position, and freedom of movement. The more complex the method, the more time you will have to spend setting up the character to be animated.

SOLID MESH AND SEGMENTED CHARACTERS

In many cases, the best answer is to use a combination of the two methods. Figure 10.2 illustrates a character modeled in this fashion.

FIGURE 10.2   *The character in this image sporting my face was constructed by using a combination of solid geometry with its own bone structure for bending the character at the knees, and so on, glued to other segments with their own bone structure, to form a hierarchy.*

Areas of a character can be one solid mesh that can be deformed with a skeleton and attached to other segments that have their own skeletons, which can be deformed. This method has the most flexibility in terms of character design freedom.

Okay, you know that you have options and you know some of the pros and cons of each, but what decides your approach? How do you avoid possible design flaws? Every animator takes their own path on this one, so I can't give you a definitive answer on how everyone else solves this problem. I can tell you, however, what method I use to make my decision.

Avoiding Character Design Flaws

How easy it will be for a character to be animated and the type of actions the character can perform are directly related to how the character was constructed.

What is usually overlooked is the step that comes before all of this, character design. Character design is where the decisions are made. You have to know what type of movement your character will need to perform before you can construct and animate him, and you need to know how the character's design affects its construction.

Will your character have to leap, jump, run, or dance?

If your character will have to dance, he will need a complete set of joints. If the character is seen standing behind a counter and can be seen only from the waist up, the legs and joints that accompany them do not have to be constructed. If the character isn't required to manipulate other objects in its environment, then the hands don't need to be articulated.

How does the action play a role? If all your character will do is sit in a rocking chair, then there's no reason to animate a walk or run cycle. It's obvious that those types of motions don't need to be animated, but should the character be built to include such actions just in case? That question can be answered only by you and is usually based on the amount of modeling time you can devote to a single character, whether or not you would like to reuse the character in another project, and, of course, your modeling proficiency and the limitation of your tools.

How does the character's design affect the construction decisions? Take the case of a character wearing a short sleeve shirt and one wearing a long sleeve shirt. In the case of the short sleeve shirt, the character's hands have to be attached to the arm. If the character is cartoony, then a seam at the wrist is no big deal. Therefore, the character's arm can be segmented, but if the character is to be realistic, then the arm and hand should be modeled as one mesh to avoid the seams. If the character's hand is to be articulated, then this makes things a little more complicated and will require additional work when the time comes to add a bone structure or IK chain to the arm. In this case, I prefer to isolate the hands from the rest of the object if at all possible. I usually use some sort of clothing, like a jacket or long sleeve shirt, to hide the fact that the hands and arm are not the same mesh. With the hand isolated from the rest of the body (with its own bone structure), I have greater control over its movement; the hand's skeletal animation will show up in the KFE separately; I can reuse the bone structure on other models that require such movement; and my setup times are shorter.

Let's look at an actual character and how its design dictated how it was constructed.

I use a character sheet before I model and animate a character. The character sheet contains a list of actions the character will have to perform and any project guidelines that must be followed. For example, look at Figure 10.3.

FIGURE 10.3   *A character sheet used at LOGICBit Studio for the short film* Tin Badge. *A character's actions and role in a project are carefully studied before the character is modeled or animated. The first rule to character animation is know your character.*

Looking at the character sheet, I know that I need to create a character that will need a walk and run cycle. That is, I can create a short sequence that can be repeated to create any length shot. I will also need to take into account the single actions of jump, kick, crouch, and draw.

The use of cycles sometimes can make motion seem mechanical and a bit too linear. For example, animating a robotic welding arm using a cycle to illustrate the arm swinging down, welding, swinging up, welding, and swinging down again works and looks great. Using the same technique to animate a character bending down to grab a box, place it on the counter, and bend down again to pick up another looks synthetic. For these types of short shots, I prefer to animate the character by using a frame-forward technique, a method we will discuss in the next section.

I know that I can use segmented parts to create the character (to a limited degree). The hands must be articulated, and because they are gloved, they can be modeled separately and attached to the wrist. The gloves will help hide the fact that the hands aren't attached to the arm. This will also give the hands freedom of movement at the wrist. This works out great; the complexity of the character's hands will be isolated from the rest of the model, making the posing of the character with bones less of a hassle. The head and neck can be modeled separately, with the neck disappearing into the shoulders of the character. The torso and arms will have to be one object because the torso will be covered by a jacket or duster. The legs can be modeled together or separately, and glued together because the seam can be hidden by the zipper flap. Where the legs attach to the torso will be hidden by the character's belt. The boots will have to bend at the toes and ankle. They can be modeled separately like the gloved hands and tucked beneath chaps or jeans.

As you can see, the character's dress dictates how the character would have to be constructed. It is easier to spend a little time designing your character first than it is to struggle with a character that just can't be posed and won't perform as you expected.

CHOOSE AN ANIMATION METHOD

You should also give some thought up front to which animation method you want to use to make your character perform. When animating characters in a 3D package, you're essentially posing your character. There are two basic methods of animating characters in trueSpace: *pose-to-pose* animation and *frame-forward* animation (also called *straight-ahead*). Each of these methods uses poses in different ways and has its advantages. The frame-forward approach begins by drawing the character at the first frame of the sequence and every frame thereafter is created in a linear fashion from one pose to another. This is how traditional cel animators were forced to work prior to the introduction of software. With the pose-to-pose method, the action a character is to perform is broken down into specific poses. These poses are then keyframed (recorded). These are the points in the animation where the character's action changes direction. After all the major poses have been recorded, the computer is left to create the frames between the keys, a process called *tweening*. With computers, we don't have to worry about the time-consuming task of producing the frames between each pose, a luxury traditional cel animators don't have.

The pose-to-pose method can make the job of animating a character easy, but it can also make the character's motions look synthetic. Take the case of a shot where a character is sitting at a table, reaching for a glass of water to drink. Keyframing the action from the point where the character lifts the glass to the frame where the character places its edge to his lips will look too mechanical. In this case, I prefer to use a combination of pose-to-pose and frame-forward techniques. For example, I would first create the two main poses—the first when the character lifts the glass and the second when the character drinks from it. I then move frame to frame, tweaking the wrist's rotation and the forearm's position and rotation, keyframing each frame as I go. When the animation is played back, the shot looks more spontaneous and complex.

POSING YOUR CHARACTERS

No matter which animation method you choose, make sure your character's poses convey three key elements:

- Balance
- Asymmetry
- Mass

So where do you start? The best place to start is to physically pose your character first; pose him taking a step, for example. It doesn't matter which parts of the character you start to pose as long as you get the pose you want. After you have your character's limbs in their appropriate locations, the character's center of balance should be worked out. For example, a bipedal character's balance starts at the hips. This is the character's center of gravity. The character's spine rests on the hips, and the shoulders rest on the spine. The hips themselves rest on the character's legs.

WARNING

In the modeling chapter, I reiterated how to use symmetry to your advantage when modeling your characters. When physically posing your characters for still shots or for your animated short films, symmetry should be avoided. Symmetry in a character's pose looks unnatural.

While posing the character, try to make the pose as asymmetrical as possible. Contrary to popular belief, bipedal creatures don't rest all their body weight on both feet. We don't do it when we walk or run, and we don't do it when we stand still. Take a look at Figure 10.4. Which of the two characters appears to look more natural; which of the two appears to have actual mass? Bipedal humanoids rest their weight on one leg, shifting their weight from foot to foot as they stand.

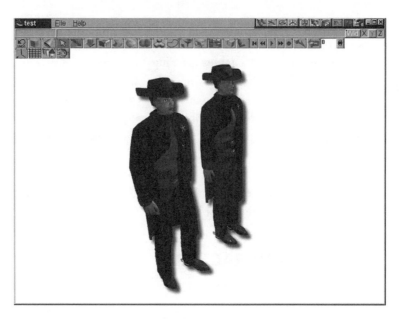

FIGURE 10.4   *The character on the left seems to be standing more naturally while the character on the right looks stiff and unnatural and doesn't appear to have any weight or mass. The use of balance and asymmetrical poses look more natural and cause your characters to appear to have mass.*

By placing the character's weight on the right foot and bending the arms slightly, the symmetrical look of the character on the right is made to look more natural in the character on the left.

Having your character appear to have mass is a complex subject and many, many things play a role in pulling off the illusion. I can't cover every scenario, but here are a few simple rules that work well with bipedal characters in most cases. Any limb that your character is not using to exert force on any surface should be slightly bent at the joint. For example, a character standing at a bus stop places his weight on one foot, exerting force on the ground. The other foot should be slightly bent at the knee. Where there is one there is the other—balance, that is. If your character looks balanced, then it will appear to have mass. Where the right hip is, the right shoulder is opposite and vice versa. For example, take the case of the character standing at the bus stop. The leg not exerting any force is slightly bent at the knee, which tends to add a slight tilt downward to the character's hip on that side; this in turn causes the character's shoulder on the same side to tilt upward in the other direction to compensate. This balancing act is subtle and subconsciously imprinted on our brains. If it isn't there, we notice it. Without it, characters seem to float and don't seem as though they are part of the environment. Use a strong shadow beneath your character. This has the effect of anchoring your character's feet to the ground. If you consider each of these points when posing your characters, they will look more natural. Always try to obtain balance in your shots. If you can get your character to look balanced, it will appear to have mass, and it's that simple.

After the pose was made asymmetrical, I checked the character from all views to ensure that the character was still in balance. That is, the character's center of gravity was at the hips, the hips rested on the legs, and the spine and shoulders were aligned correctly. Next time you visit a mall, grab a seat for a few moments and watch how folks stand.

If your character doesn't appear to have mass or weight, then your animated sequence won't look right. Having your character appear to have mass is often a by-product of getting the other two elements correct when posing your characters. If your character's pose is balanced and asymmetrical, your character will often appear to have weight.

In the next exercise, we will create a walk cycle for a character by using the pose-to-pose method. As you pose the character, keep in mind balance, asymmetry, and mass (BAM).

TIP

When posing your characters, you should use the technique of *silhouetting*. This is a technique used by actors and animators alike. Pose your character and paint your character flat black, and render the scene with a white background as depicted in Figure 10.5. If the silhouette is easy to read, then your audience will interpret the character's actions easily. Use a silhouette to check your character's pose and its orientation to the camera whenever you need to convey body language. A silhouette is effective and easy to create in trueSpace. I will revisit the subject of silhouettes in Chapter 17, "Creating a Short Film."

FIGURE 10.5 *Using a silhouette of your character's pose is an ideal method of ensuring that your character's body language will be interpreted by your audience correctly.*

ANIMATING FRANKY

In an earlier chapter, we modeled and texture mapped Franky the skateboarding terror, and in Chapter 9, we learned how to construct a skeleton for a humanoid character. Now it's time to add a little skeletal animation into the mix.

The character we will be animating in this chapter has been reconstructed and glued together for your convenience and to make the exercises more enjoyable (see Figure 10.6). Let's get started.

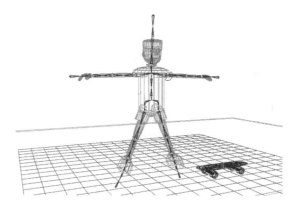

FIGURE 10.6   *Franky and his skeleton.*

GETTING FRANKY OUT OF "NEUTRAL"

Before we can animate Franky, we must make the transition from the bone construction pose (neutral pose) to a normal stance that can be used as a starting point for run and walk cycles, leaps, and so on.

1. Load the scene file Franky.scn located in the resource CD directory for Chapter 10. You will notice that I have already constructed the bone structure for you. Go ahead and investigate the joints to see how they are orientated. When you're done experimenting, simply reload the scene and continue with the exercise from the Front view.

2. Select the skeleton and select the Attach Skin to Skeleton tool. Click Franky's mesh to assign the skeleton to Franky. Click the Object tool to exit the Attach Skin to Skeleton tool.

3. The nail should be positioned in the center of the character's chest. Having the nail in this location makes the next step easy because the chest is anchored in its present position. Click and drag the bone just above the character's elbow until the character's arm is by its side. It doesn't matter which arm you start with. Repeat the same process with the other arm.

4. Now that the arms are in their natural position, we can work with the character's legs. Click and drag the nail from the character's chest to one of the

bones that make up the character's hips. You will have to place it close to the bottom of the joint for it to take hold of the hip bone. Figure 10.7 illustrates the location.

NOTE

If you are eager to get started, load the scene Franky2.scn from the resource CD for Chapter 10. The Franky2.scn file has Franky posed and ready to go.

5. Click and drag each of the character's thigh bones just above the knee inward toward each other until the character appears to be standing upright, as depicted in Figure 10.7.

That about covers getting Franky ready to animate. From this pose, you can have Franky sit, bend down, walk, or run. When you attach bone structures to your characters, it is a good idea to save the scene with the bone structure and character in the "neutral pose" and save the scene again with the character in a natural standing pose. This way, you can load the scene whenever a new pose or animated sequence is needed without changing a scene that may already have the character performing some other task.

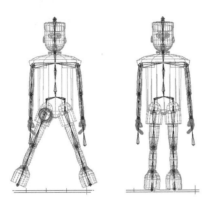

FIGURE 10.7   *The character on the left illustrates where you should drag and release the nail to anchor the character's hips. After the hips are anchored, you can pose the character's legs. The character on the right illustrates how the legs should be moved into place.*

In the next exercise, we will create a walk cycle for our Franky character that can be saved with the character. The character can then be loaded in any scene, ready to strut its stuff. Let's get started.

IT'S ALIVE! CREATING A WALK CYCLE FOR FRANKY

Creating a walk cycle is a fundamental skill every animator should practice. The proper place to start is with a basic walk, concentrating on the mechanics. It is important to note when creating a walk or run cycle for your character that you don't really have your character walk across the screen. The character is actually animated walking or running in place, kind of like walking on a treadmill. Your body is going through the motions, but you aren't going anywhere. The reason I will have you do it in this manner will be made clear a little later in this exercise; for now, let's examine the poses necessary to animate Franky walking.

SET UP THE FIRST POSE

If you loaded Franky2.scn, then a small Perspective view has been opened for you. If you have not opened Franky2.scn, do so now.

1. Switch the large view window to the Perspective view. If the Animation Control Group isn't open, open it now.

2. A walk cycle usually starts with the character's feet extended with the character's weight on the heel of the leading foot. If the character's hips aren't anchored, anchor the character's hips by placing the nail on any of the vertical bones that make up the hips. Switch the large view window back to the Left view.

3. In the Left view, click and drag the leaf bone protruding from the character's foot. It doesn't matter which foot as long as you move only one. Swing the foot out slowly until it is about one quarter of the way up, as depicted in panel B of Figure 10.8. Without releasing your mouse, drag the leaf bone back down toward the ground until the character's heel meets the ground. The character's knee should have a slight bend. Use Figure 10.8 as a guide.

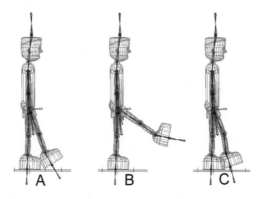

FIGURE 10.8   *Swinging the leg out and back down adds a natural-looking bend at the knee.*

4. Click and drag the leaf bone of the other foot to your left until the toe of the foot is level with the heel of the other foot. The pose we are trying to

achieve is illustrated in Figure 10.9. I didn't mention using the ground because the hips are anchored and the knees of the character are bent, so the character's feet won't touch the ground. This is perfectly all right at this stage. We will return and use this to our advantage in a later step.

5. In the small Perspective view, click and drag the nail from the character's hips to its shoulders.

6. Click and drag the leaf bone of the character's left arm out in front of the character until the character's fingertips are about waist high.

NOTE

For this exercise, you can choose to animate the feet first and then return after they have been keyframed to pose the arms. This technique eliminates having to move the nail from the torso to the waist throughout the process. Any method you choose is fine; it is the end result we are after.

7. Click and drag the elbow joint of the character's right arm behind the character until it won't go any farther. The arm will appear a little stiff in this position so click and drag the nail to the bone just above the elbow joint in the right arm. Click and drag the leaf bone of the right arm forward a bit to add a slight bend to the character's right arm. Figure 10.9 illustrates the finished pose.

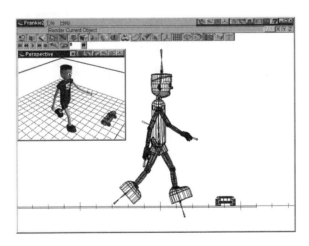

FIGURE 10.9 *The first pose of the walk cycle. When creating the walk cycle poses, try not to have the feet and arms exactly the same distance apart. Our arms and legs don't swing the same distance precisely. Remember BAM: balance, asymmetry, and mass.*

After the first pose has been worked out, we can start to think about the character's gait (length of the character's walk cycle). At a normal walk, a full cycle usually lasts around a second. This is just a starting point; the size and attitude of the character has a lot to do with the number of frames used to create the appropriate walk cycle. For example, a small character has a faster gait than a large, fat character. The female characters tend to walk a little faster than male characters, and sad characters walk more slowly than happy characters. A character's stride is usually directly related to the character's mood.

I know it's a lot to think about, and you would probably like me to list formulas for a walk, run, jog, and so on, but that would mislead you into thinking that there are rules etched in stone. The fact is, every character you build should have a slightly different gait, especially if the characters are interacting in the same scene. If all your characters walk the same, your animation will look mechanical. In trueSpace, this is easily avoidable since the KeyFrame Editor (KFE) can be used to tweak a walk cycle to fit a character's mood individually. We will look at using the KFE to change a character's mood by altering the character's gait later in this chapter. For now, let's start with a basic walk cycle.

Our character Franky is a small guy, so a one-second walk cycle should be fine (that is 30 frames at 30 fps). If the speed doesn't look right, we can fix it later. All we are concerned with at this point is getting the mechanics of the walk cycle keyframed. Figure 10.10 illustrates the seven poses and keyframe numbers that we will be creating.

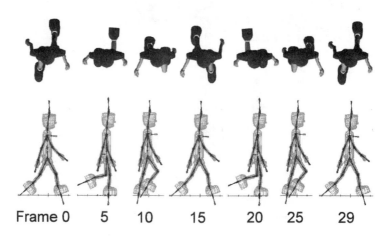

Frame 0   5   10   15   20   25   29

FIGURE 10.10   *The seven poses and keyframes used to create Franky's 30-frame walk cycle.*

Creating a walk cycle for our character is just a matter of knowing where to place the nail to successfully pose the character at each of the keyframes. Let's create the remaining six poses needed to animate Franky.

CREATE A SMOOTH TRANSITION FROM BEGINNING TO END

To begin a walk cycle, you must start with the end. The walk cycle needs to loop smoothly when played back; that is, frames 25 through 29 should make a smooth transition back to the pose in frame 0. To accomplish this, we will add a frame 30 that is identical to frame 0. When we are done, we will discard frame 30 (which is actually frame 31 since frames start at 0).

NOTE

If you would like to dive right in to animating the character, you can open the Walk.scn file located in Chapter 10 on the resource CD. The scene consists of Franky in the first keyframe pose and a ground plane viewed from the Left and Perspective views via a small window as illustrated in Figure 10.9.

1. If the Animation Control Group panel isn't open, open it.

2. Enter 30 in the Current Frame Number field in the Animation Control Group panel, press Enter, and click Record.

This will accomplish two things. First, we now have one less pose and keyframe to worry about. And secondly, trueSpace will tween the frames from 25 to 29 for us. Because frame 0 and 30 are identical, a smooth transition from frame 29 back to frame 0 is complete.

CREATE THE POSE FOR FRAME 5

This is where we begin the actual animation process. We posed Franky taking his first step. Now it is time to create the pose that will start to form a transition between the first step and the second.

1. Enter 5 in the Current Frame Number field in the Animation Control Group panel, press Enter, and click Record. Click and drag the nail to one of the hip bones. Click and drag the leaf bone exiting the right foot to your left until the bottom of the foot is level with the ground, as illustrated in frame 5 of Figure 10.10.

2. Click and drag the left knee to your right, just behind the right knee. Anchor the left thigh with the nail. Click and drag the ankle of the left foot up and to your right until the left calf is almost level with the ground plane. Use frame 5 of Figure 10.10 as a reference.

3. Move the nail to any of the bones that make up the shoulders. Click and drag the leaf bone of the left arm down until the arm is by the character's side but still slightly in front of the character. Do the same with the character's right arm, but it should be slightly behind the character.

4. Click the Record button in the Animation Control Group panel.

CREATE THE POSE FOR FRAME 10

Frame 10 is the point where Franky leans forward and starts to place one foot in front of the other.

1. Enter 10 in the Current Frame Number field in the Animation Control Group panel, press Enter, and click Record. Click and drag the nail to one of the hip bones. Click and drag the right knee to your left until the right knee is just behind the left knee as viewed from the Left view window. Anchor the character's right thigh and drag the character's right ankle until the right leg is straightened.

NOTE

Don't worry if your character's feet don't make contact with the ground during these exercises. The character's feet are made to touch the ground only after the mechanics of the walk have been keyframed.

2. Click and drag the left knee to your right until the knee is well in front of the character. Anchor the left thigh and click and drag the ankle of the left foot up and to your left until the heel of the left foot appears to make contact with the right knee. Use frame 10 of Figure 10.10 as a reference.

3. Anchor the character's shoulders with the nail. Click and drag the leaf bone of the left arm to your left until the arm is just behind the character. Do the same with the character's right arm, but it should be slightly in front of the character.

4. Click the Record button in the Animation Control Group panel.

CREATE THE POSE FOR FRAME 15

Frame 15 is a mirror of frame 0 where the character's left leg is extended in front of the character and the right leg is behind.

1. Enter 15 in the Current Frame Number field in the Animation Control Group panel, press Enter, and click Record. Anchor the character's left

thigh. Click and drag the left ankle to your right until the right leg is straight. This is where the left heel will make contact with the ground.

2. Anchor the character's hips. Click and drag the right knee until the right leg is far behind the character and the toe of the right foot is level with the heel of the left foot. Use frame 15 of Figure 10.10 as a reference.

3. Anchor the character's shoulders and click and drag the leaf bone of the left arm to your left until the arm is well behind the character. Do the same with the character's right arm, but it should be well in front of the character. Remember that as seen from the Left view, the character's left arm moves backward and vice versa as the character's left leg moves forward. The same goes for the other side of the character.

4. Click the Record button in the Animation Control Group panel.

CREATE THE POSE FOR FRAME 20

Frame 20 is a mirror pose of frame 5, just as frame 15 was a mirror pose of frame 0.

1. Enter 20 in the Current Frame Number field in the Animation Control Group panel, press Enter, and click Record. Click and drag the nail to one of the hip bones. Click and drag the leaf bone exiting the left foot to your left until the bottom of the foot is level with the ground, as illustrated in frame 20 of Figure 10.10. Remember always to keep a slight bend in the knees in all your poses.

2. Click and drag the right knee to your right just behind the left knee. Anchor the right thigh with the nail. Click and drag the ankle of the right foot up and to your right until the right calf is almost level with the ground plane. Use frame 20 of Figure 10.10 as a reference.

3. Anchor the shoulders and click and drag the leaf bone of the right arm down until the arm is by the character's side but still slightly in front of the character. Do the same with the character's left arm, but it should be slightly behind the character.

4. Click the Record button in the Animation Control Group panel.

CREATE THE POSE FOR FRAME 25

We're at the last pose—actually the second to last. We started this exercise by defining the last pose, which will give us a smooth transition from the last pose back to the first.

1. Enter 25 in the Current Frame Number field in the Animation Control Group panel, press Enter, and click Record. Anchor the character's hips. Click and drag the left knee to your left until the left knee is just behind the character as viewed from the Left view window. Anchor the character's left thigh and drag the character's left ankle until the left leg is straightened.

2. Click and drag the right knee to your right until the knee is well in front of the character. Anchor the right thigh and click and drag the ankle of the right foot up and to your left until the heel of the left foot appears to make contact with the left knee. Use frame 25 of Figure 10.10 as a reference.

3. Anchor the character's shoulders. Click and drag the leaf bone of the right arm to your left until the arm is just behind the character. Do the same with the character's left arm, but it should be slightly in front of the character.

4. Click the Record button in the Animation Control Group panel.

TIP

I often preview just the keyframes of the walk cycle so I can see whether the movement from keyframe to keyframe looks right. To do this, right-click Preview Scene to File in the Perspective view window to open the Preview Setting panel.

Set Step to 5; because our keyframes occur every 5 frames, only the keyframes will be rendered to the file. Close the panel and render the scene to a file. This is a quick way to see whether you are on the right track. You can see an example of previewing keyframes to a file by playing prvw.avi, located on the resource CD in the Chapter 10 folder.

DISCARD FRAME 30

Now that we have recorded all of the poses, we can discard frame 30 but first we must make frame 29 the last keyframe. Enter 29 in the Current Frame Number field in the Animation Control Group panel, press Enter, and click Record.

To discard frame 30, open the KFE. Click the Expand/Collapse button in the KFE window. The Object Tree on the left side of the KFE window will expand, revealing all the objects that make up the character's skeleton. On the right side are diamond-shaped markers that indicate the keyframes for Rotate, Move, Scale, and Kinematics. Right-click each of the oval markers under frame 30 and select Delete. Close the KFE.

CHECK AND POLISH YOUR WORK

Preview the scene to a file in Wireframe mode. This won't take very long, and you will see how well Franky walks.

If at any point during playback the animation doesn't look right, it is a good idea to restart from the beginning—that's right, from the first pose. Having to tweak the basic movements often causes a jittering effect that is hard to get rid of later. Your goal when first setting up the walk cycle is to achieve smooth, fluid movement. As for everything in life, a good foundation is critical for a walk cycle.

If you are satisfied with the walk cycle, it's time to add the little details that make the walk cycle more interesting. For example, you may have noticed that although Franky's walk looks smooth, he seems a little stiff. Especially around the upper torso, there is no bobbing effect. The bobbing effect is caused when the character reaches the recoil position in the walk cycle. The recoil position is the lowest point in the walk cycle and occurs when the weight of the character's body is transferred to the leading foot, causing the knee to bend to absorb the energy and the weight of the character.

Before we fix the problem, review the animation I have provided on the resource CD under Chapter 10. The filename is wc1.avi. I suggest you use the free animation player provided on the CD. It will automatically loop the animation so you can study the walk cycle. The animation player can be found on the resource CD in the Player folder. When you play the animation, notice how the character's walk appears stiff. Now load wc2.avi to view the tweaked version. The walk cycle looks a lot better, doesn't it?

TIP

You can preview your character's skeletal animation to a file by following these steps:

1. Open the Display Option panel.

2. Set Detail to Always Boxes; close the Display Options panel.

3. Add a plane primitive to the scene.

4. Select Preview Scene to File.

Because the plane is the selected object, your character will be rendered as a box wireframe, revealing the bone structure underneath. What you will end up with is an animation of the character's skeletal motion. In the Chapter 10 folder on the resource CD, you will find a short animation that illustrates the result. The filename is wcs3.avi.

The fix is simple: Cycle through each keyframe, 0, 5, 10, 15, and so on. At each keyframe move, move the character along the y-axis in the Left view window until the foot supporting the character's weight touches the ground plane placed underneath the character.

TWEAKING A WALK CYCLE TO CHANGE A CHARACTER'S MOOD

I said earlier in this chapter that the size and attitude of the character has a lot to do with the number of frames used to create an appropriate walk cycle. I also said that a smaller character has a faster gait than a large, fat character, and sad characters walk more slowly than happy characters. Let's look at how easy it is to change a character's mood with a few simple changes.

You will find two short animations of Franky walking, Walk1.avi and Walk2.avi, on the resource CD. The latter is identical to the first, except for the number of frames the walk cycle takes to complete. Franky is looking at the ground and he is dragging his feet. Let's make the transition from a happy character to a sad character.

Load up scene Walk1.scn from the resource CD. For our next exercise, we will try to make Franky look sad by increasing the number of frames of his walk cycle, but first let's have him drag his feet as he walks.

1. Click the Advance to Next Keyframe button in the Animation Control Group panel. Anchor the character's left thigh. Click and drag the character's left ankle down until the toe of the left foot meets the ground. Click the record button in the Animation Control group.

2. Enter 20 in the Current Frame Number field in the Animation Control Group panel and press Enter. Anchor the character's right thigh. Click and drag the character's right ankle down until the toe of the right foot meets the ground. Click the record button in the Animation Control group. Click the Return to Start button in the Animation Control Group panel.

Now Franky will drag his feet as the animation is played back. We want Franky to look really sad, so let's have him look at the ground as he walks. For each keyframe, anchor the character's neck and tilt Franky's head down. Press the Record button and move on to the next keyframe.

The walk cycle in this scene is 30 frames long and is about right for a happy Franky, but it is much too fast for a sad character. Having Franky drag his feet isn't enough, so we will lengthen the walk cycle from 30 frames to 60 frames in two easy steps.

1. Open the KFE and expand the Object Tree.

2. Click and drag the top Action Bar to frame 59 and close the KFE.

That's it. Play back the animation and see what you think.

Reset the animation to 30 frames and have Franky strut. For a strut, the character's back is arched and his arms swing and pump.

Throughout this chapter, I have mentioned that it is possible to create a skeletal animation that can be saved and reused on other characters. We will look at doing just that in our next exercise.

SKELETAL ANIMATION AND REUSABILITY

In the last few exercises, you managed to create a walk cycle for a character. The walk cycle can be looped so that a minimum of keyframes will be needed for any shot and can be made to follow a path. Once a walk cycle has been created, the skeletal animation can be saved with the animated sequence intact. In this exercise, we will save the skeleton as a COB and reuse it on another character.

1. Load up Walk1.scn, located on the resource CD in the Chapter 10 folder. This is the same 30-frame walk cycle we created earlier.

2. Select the Move Down Hierarchy button. The character will become isolated from its skeleton. Press the Delete key on your keyboard. This will leave the character's skeleton behind. Click the Move Up Hierarchy button.

3. The skeleton can now be saved as a COB with its skeletal animation intact. Go ahead and play back the animation to see what I mean. After you are done, save the skeleton as a COB file.

4. Load My_Hero.scn located in the Chapter 10 folder of the resource CD. The character should look familiar to you because we constructed him from metaballs in an earlier chapter.

Load up the walk cycle COB I just had you save in step 3. Remember that I mentioned that characters that will be animated should be constructed in the neutral position. We do this because adding a skeleton to the character's mesh is a lot easier and less prone to vertex hassles. Well, our skeleton isn't in the neutral position, so how do we attach a skeletal animation to it? We cheat.

1. Open the KFE and expand the Object Tree. Click and drag the topmost Action Bar one frame to the right.

2. Click the Record button in the Animation Control group panel and close the KFE.

Now what we have is a walk cycle that is 31 frames long with an identical frame 0 and frame 1. From frames 1 to 31, we have our saved walk cycle. At frame 0, we have an extra frame that we will use to pose the skeleton into the neutral position so we can attach the skeleton to our character. When we are done, we can remove frame 0, and our character will use our saved walk cycle. Let's take a look.

1. Click the Return to Start button in the Animation Control panel.

2. Pose the skeleton in the neutral position by using the character as a guide and the nail to anchor different parts of the skeleton. Switch between all your views to get a good look at where each bone is placed. Use Figure 10.11 as a guide.

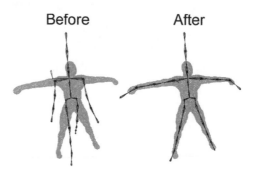

Perspective View

FIGURE 10.11   *In this before-and-after image, you can see that the character's mesh is in the neutral position, but the skeleton is not. By adding a temporary frame 0, we can manipulate the skeleton without ruining the skeletal animation we want to apply to the character.*

3. When you are satisfied that the skeleton matches the neutral pose of the character, select the Attach Skin to Skeleton tool and click on the character's mesh. Click the Object tool to complete the operation and to exit the Attach Skin to Skeleton tool.

4. Open the KFE and expand the Object Tree. Right-click each of the oval keyframe markers under frame 0 and select Delete.

5. Click and drag the top Action Bar to the left, release your mouse, and close the KFE.

WARNING

Editing the skeleton's joints or resizing bones will remove any keyframes associated with the skeletal animation of the skeleton.

Switch to a Perspective view and render the scene to a file. It's important to note that this works best when the character and skeleton are the same scale. You can scale either of the two prior to attaching the skin to the skeleton.

SUMMARY

Your character's walk tells a lot about your character. The next time you're in a public place, observe people walking, talking, gesturing, standing, and eating. When creating short films that involve characters interacting, body language is very important. Like most creatures, we communicate visually, not just audibly. Sometimes a gesture or a character's posture is all that is needed to communicate a point to the audience. Public places make a wonderful research tool—exploit them.

Although bipedal humanoid characters are usually the most common characters used in today's short films, they are not the only types of creatures you may want to create and animate in trueSpace. Rest assured that the mechanics are the same, and you can apply techniques in this chapter to all your characters.

Frank Rivera, LOGICBit

Part V

Lighting and Camera

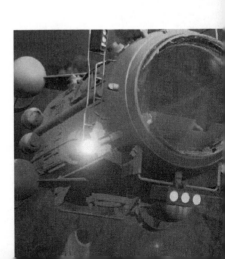

CHAPTER 11

RENDERING PRECURSOR, WHAT ARE YOUR OPTIONS

by Frank Rivera

Before you jump into the myriad of choices trueSpace4 has to offer the 3D illustrator/animator, you need to understand a few concepts and all the bells and whistles that complement the final rendering process. If some of this subject matter is covered in your manual, I apologize, but for the sake of clarity and completeness, I must touch on these areas.

3D imagery is all about light. Any way you want to look at it, we always return to the topic, so let's cover the subject in depth (in relation to how it is used in trueSpace4) and put this baby to rest.

In this chapter, we will cover

- Understanding 3D light
- The render options panel
- The radiosity panel
- Hybrid radiosity
- Previewing a scene to file

UNDERSTANDING 3D LIGHT

The color of any point on the surface of an object in a scene is a function of the material properties of that surface and the light illuminating it. Two methods are used to describe how the surfaces in a scene reflect and transmit light, *local illumination* and *global illumination*.

LOCAL ILLUMINATION

This set of algorithms describes only how individual surfaces reflect or transmit light. These mathematical algorithms predict the intensity, color, and distribution of the light bouncing off that surface. The next step would be to determine from where it originates.

GLOBAL ILLUMINATION

To create truly accurate images, the rendering engine must take into account not only the light sources, but also how all the surfaces of the objects in the scene interact with the light. For example, some surfaces obscure light, thus casting shadows on other surfaces; some surfaces reflect light onto others; and some surfaces are transparent. Global illumination takes into account the way light energy is transferred among all these surfaces.

trueSpace uses two global illumination methods, *ray tracing* and *radiosity*. We'll get to the differences between the two in a bit; first you need a basic understanding of how light is distributed in the physical world.

Think of light in terms of single particles (photons) that travel out from the light source until they encounter a surface in the scene. Depending on the material of the surface, some particles are absorbed, and others are scattered back out into the scene. The fact that one group of particles gets absorbed while another does not is what determines the surface color we see (the name for this phenomenon is *spectral reflectance*).

The way a surface reflects these particles (photons) depends primarily on the smoothness of its surface. Every surface reflects light. If it didn't, we wouldn't see the objects.

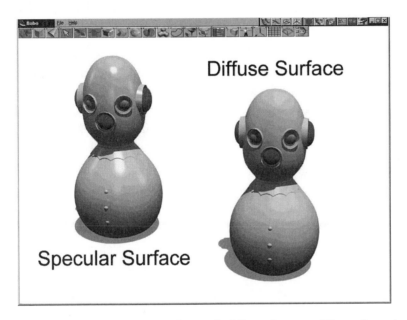

FIGURE 11.1   *The two toys in this image illustrate the difference between a diffuse surface and a specular surface.*

Very smooth surfaces reflect light uniformly with most of the rays bouncing off in the same direction. These surfaces are known as *specular* surfaces. A mirror is an example of a perfect specular surface. The shiny toy in Figure 11.1 also has a specular surface. Surfaces that reflect light in all directions are known as *diffuse* surfaces. These rays bounce off the surface at varying angles.

So we know that the illumination of a scene is determined by the interaction of the billions of photon particles streaming through the environment (scene), striking the surfaces of the objects, and either being absorbed partially or in whole, or being reflected back out into space by the objects they encounter. Not only do these photons arrive at a surface directly from the light source (*direct illumination*), they also arrive at an object's surface indirectly, from other surfaces (*indirect illumination*).

RAY TRACING

In the real world, billions of photons stream all around us. It would be impractical to calculate each and every photon and its interaction with the surfaces in the environment. Luckily, we don't have to worry about light at the subatomic level of photons and wavelengths. If we looked at the light in our scene as rays leaving a light source and bouncing off the objects in our scene, eventually entering our eyes, it becomes an efficient process. We can further simplify the task by taking into account only those rays that will reach our eyes—well, kind of.

Commonly, when I come across a problem that is difficult to solve, I start with the solution and work backward. This isn't a new technique; mathematicians use this method often. In fact, it is exactly how a ray-tracing engine works. By starting at the end and tracing the path of the ray backward from your eyes (your computer screen) outward toward the objects in your scene, and eventually tracing back to the light source, we end up with a mathematical model that is backward from the way light works in the real world.

The scene description provides the reflectivity of all the surfaces in the scene but not the amount of light reaching the surface. The total illumination is determined by tracing the ray back from the point of intersection to each light source in the scene. If the ray to the light source is not blocked by an object, that light is contributed to that ray's source to calculate the color of the surface.

We're not done tracing that ray. An intersected surface can be shiny or transparent, which means the algorithm must also determine what is seen through the surface. The first few steps are repeated in the reflected or, in the case of transparency, transmitted (specular reflection passing through an object and coming out the other end) direction until another surface is intersected. The color at the new intersection is calculated and factored into the original ray. The ray-tracing process repeats until no more surfaces are intersected (the ray has reached the light source) or the user-specified maximum number of iterations for the algorithm has been reached.

Ray tracing accounts for the light arriving directly from the light source. But light also arrives from other surfaces (indirect illumination). This is often referred to as *ambient light*. It's usually accounted for by adding an arbitrary value to the indirect illumination as a constant throughout the scene. This causes ray-traced images to appear flat.

Another disadvantage of ray tracing is that it does not account for the characteristics of diffuse interreflections—in other words, the reflection of diffused light between two or more surfaces.

On the other hand, ray tracing can accurately portray the characteristics of direct illumination, shadows, specular reflections, and refraction.

RADIOSITY

In 1984, researchers at Cornell University and two Universities of Japan (Fukuyama and Hiroshima) were searching for a method superior to that of ray tracing for simulating light propagation. They chose a technology nearly 25 years old at the time, a technology developed in the late 1950s for computing the radiation exchanged between surfaces. That technology and its use in CG today is called *radiosity*.

So what's radiosity? Well, in techno-babble, radiosity is defined as the radiation leaving a surface per unit time per unit area. Simply, radiosity is a method of computing the radiation transferred between surfaces. With respect to imagery and trueSpace4, this radiation is in the form of light energy.

The surfaces in a scene are illuminated not only by direct illumination, but also by the light bouncing off the other objects in the scene (indirect illumination). The whole radiosity process evolves around a single goal, to find the point of equilibrium of all the radiation (light energy) in the scene. Radiosity is based on the fundamental Law of Conservation of Energy for a closed area. This closed area should not have any radiation leaks; otherwise, finding the scene's point of equilibrium will be hampered.

Early uses of radiosity assumed that all of the surface's reflected diffuse lighting went in all directions equally. This yielded great results but lacked the type of realism achievable in today's rendering engines. These advanced rendering engines can handle nondiffuse surfaces, such as mirrors, as well as nonuniform specular surfaces, creating exceptionally realistic images.

Radiosity differs from ray tracing in one major respect: Rather than determining the color for each pixel displayed on screen, radiosity calculates the illumination at selected sample points in the scene. This is accomplished by first dividing the original surfaces into a mesh of smaller surfaces (elements). It is the vertices of these elements where the illumination values are stored. The amount of illumination is calculated from each element to every other element and so on. It then stores the final radiosity value for each element of the object's mesh, what I will refer to from now on as the object's *energy mesh.*

Once these values have been found for all the elements in the scene, any view of the environment can be displayed. This is referred to as *view independence* because the light distribution has been calculated for the whole environment in advance and does not have to be recalculated for each specific view. Ray tracing, on the other hand, is known as *view dependent* because the lighting must be recalculated for every view.

Radiosity Versus Ray Tracing

Although the ray tracing and radiosity are very different in their approaches, they can be complementary to each other. Each has its own unique advantages and disadvantages (see Figure 11.2). One of the advantages of ray tracing is it

- Accurately portrays direct illumination, shadows, specular reflections, transparency, and refraction

Some of its disadvantages are

- Resource hog—the time required to render an image is affected by the number of lights in the scene
- View dependent
- Does not take into account diffuse interreflections

Radiosity has two advantages:

- Calculates the diffuse interreflections between surfaces
- View independent

Radiosity's disadvantages are

- 3D energy mesh requires more memory than the original surfaces
- Surface sampling is more susceptible to image artifacts
- Does not take into account specular reflectivity or transparency

FIGURE 11.2   *Ray tracing versus hybrid radiosity.*

As you can see, neither radiosity nor ray tracing offers a complete solution. Radiosity is best for situations that require diffuse interreflections, and ray tracing is best for specular reflections.

Why not use both? By using both radiosity and ray tracing, you can have the best of both worlds. In trueSpace4, you can combine ray tracing with a radiosity solution to add specular reflection and transparency, leading to a more realistic image. The combination is referred to as *hybrid radiosity*. An advantage of this hybrid rendering method is that direct lighting is calculated as part of the radiosity solution so the ray tracer only has to concentrate its efforts on the reflected and transmitted rays. This reduces the time it takes to ray trace an image. We will revisit the subject of hybrid radiosity in Chapter 15.

Creating stunning, high-quality imagery is now possible with trueSpace4, and Caligari also built in the added special effects, such as volumetric lighting, lens flares, and glows, eliminating the need to purchase third-party products. You also have a choice between scanline and raycast rendering. One thing is for sure; you have a lot of rendering choices in trueSpace4.

ILLUMINATION IN ACTION

All this theory is good background, but it doesn't show you how to better illuminate your scenes. In the sections that follow, I'll go over the two main control panels—Render Options and Radiosity—you need to get the job done. Keep in mind, however, the discussions are simply introductions. In later chapters, you will have a chance to actually implement these tools in your scenes. For example, in Chapter 15, "Radiosity," I will cover how to get good results with trueSpace's render engine and radiosity. Oliver Zeller will demonstrate how to create atmospheric effects in Chapter 13, and Jeff Wall will discuss lighting techniques in Chapter 12. I know it's tempting to skip ahead and start playing with the tools, but you should first have a firm grasp of what your options are.

THE RENDER OPTIONS PANEL

At any point during the construction of your scenes, you may choose one of several render-quality options for a faster preview of your work in process (WIP). These options can be found in the Render Options panel. To open the Render Options panel, right-click on any of the Render tools—Render Current Object, Render Scene, Render Scene to File, or Render Portion of Screen (see Figure 11.3). The available options are organized into seven sections:

- Quality
- Visibility
- Antialias
- Ray trace
- Foreground
- Background
- Color

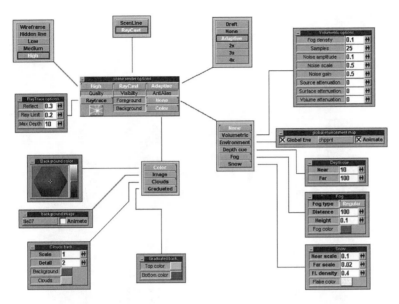

FIGURE 11.3   *An exploded look at the Scene Render Options panel, buttons, pop-up menus, and dialog boxes. The Glows and Lens Flares button is discussed in Chapter 13.*

QUALITY

Depending on what stage of scene construction you are on, you can use any of the following settings to specify the quality of rendered output. The five Quality options (see Figure 11.4) come in handy when all that is needed is a general idea of how objects are positioned or how the lighting interacts with the objects in your scenes. Using a low-quality setting gives the fastest feedback but does not display textures. A medium setting, on the other hand, displays textures while still maintaining relatively fast render feedback. Here are your choices:

NOTE

Base transparency is visible if Raycast Visibility is used (see the "Visibility" section that follows).

- **Wireframe:** Objects are rendered as wireframe meshes. I especially like this option when performing character animation. I use this setting to quickly visualize the action and movement of my characters. You can equate this option to that of the onionskin pencil previews traditional cartoonists use before creating their cells on acetate.

- **Hidden Line:** The same as Wireframe with all hidden surfaces not visible.

- **Low:** Displays only the base surface color and shading of the objects in your scenes.

- **Medium:** Displays shading and texturing, except alpha channels.
- **High:** Best quality; includes ray-traced shadows, reflections, transparency, alpha channels, the whole ball of wax.

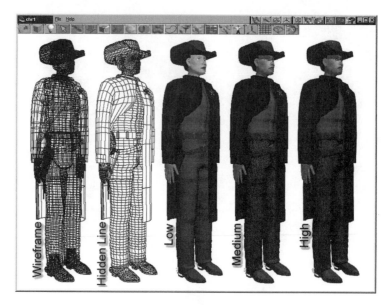

FIGURE 11.4   *The five rendering-quality settings available in trueSpace4.*

VISIBILITY

Use either of the Visibility options to complement the render-quality settings.

- **ScanLine:** Objects within the camera's view are ScanLine-rendered.
- **RayCast:** Objects within the camera's view are determined by casting a ray from the camera to the objects in the scene (hence the name RayCast). This option gives crisp, sharp edges.

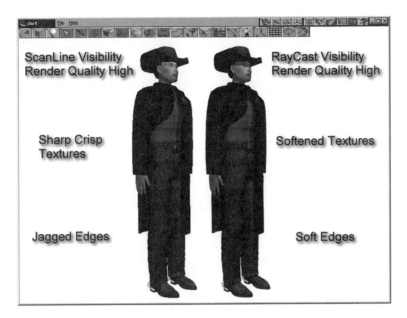

FIGURE 11.5   *A comparison of visibility settings.*

I prefer to use a Visibility setting of RayCast and a Quality setting of Low during the build process until I'm ready to perform a full render. At that point, I use the highest settings possible for the best-quality image. Ray-traced shadows, Quality set to High, Visibility set to RayCast, Raytrace set to On and 2X for Antialias. I use the same setting for hybrid radiosity as well. Complex scenes and models benefit from raycasting, so use the ScanLine Visibility option for quick previews only.

ANTIALIAS

Use the Antialias settings to sample the pixels of your rendered image and eliminate the jagged, stairstep effect. This smoothing of the jaggies is done by sampling the surrounding colors and blending them along their edges.

NOTE

When ScanLine rendering is enabled, transparency is not visible when Quality is set to medium.

- **Draft:** This is really just a preview option. The output is rendered at half-resolution.

- **None:** When the scene is rendered, no antialiasing will be used.

- **2X, 3X, 4X:** Use caution when making your choice; the more samples you select, the longer it will take to render your scenes.

- **Adaptive:** This option is available only when High Quality is used and performs antialiasing when and where required. In previous versions of trueSpace, you had to enable ray tracing to get this functionality.

RAYTRACE

Click the Raytrace button to toggle ray tracing on and off.

By default, trueSpace renders all scenes in ScanLine mode, which takes into account only the relative placement of your objects and light sources when rendering your scene. True reflections, transparency, refraction, or accurate shadows aren't calculated, making this render mode fast and perfect for general-purpose use when constructing your scenes.

The imagery you create in trueSpac4 can have accurate reflections, transparency, and shadows for a photorealistic look. trueSpace4, like its predecessor, has the capability to ray trace your scenes. Ray tracing is the process of calculating the paths of rays of light (as described previously) in your scenes. Be forewarned that there is a price to pay for having realistic shadows, accurate reflections, and the like: the time required to complete a render of an image. Take a look at the Raytrace Options panel and a few tips for decreasing the render times of your ray-traced scenes.

RAYTRACE OPTIONS PANEL

Right-click the Raytrace button in the Scene Render Options panel to open the Raytrace Options panel and access its three settings.

- **Reflect:** The Reflect value determines which objects, based on their reflectivity, are rendered with surface reflections. Valid values are from .01 to 1. Set a higher Reflect value in the Raytrace Options panel. By setting a higher value, only the objects whose reflectivity is higher than this value will reflect their surroundings. This will save you some time.

- **Max Depth:** Essentially determines the complexity of ray-traced reflections. The values range from 1 to 15. Picture two mirrors facing each other. The higher the value, the more reflections within reflections within reflections you will see. Personally, I wouldn't adjust this setting. The default setting is perfect.

- **Ray Limit:** This can come in handy if you want to limit the ray-tracing process to the important reflections in your scene. The range of values is 0 to 1, and the default value is 0.2. If you want to speed up the ray-tracing process, increase this value. Raising this value any higher than 0.85 will cause reflective surfaces to appear whitewashed, diffused, and void of any specular highlights.

FOREGROUND

Choices, choices, choices. Left-click the Foreground button to select one of six Foreground shaders: None, Volumetric, Environment, Depth Cue, Fog, and Snow. Any of these effects can be incorporated into your scene without post processing. Right-click the selected Foregound shader to adjust its options. To disable the use of a Foreground shader, select None.

VOLUMETRIC

Simulating the scattering of light as it passes through the atmosphere, the Volumetric shader uses volume sampling to generate accurate and consistent results, including volumetric shadows. This effect is animation-friendly in that it is possible to move light sources, as you would need to in a lighthouse scene. You can even move objects or the camera. Volumetric lights also work in conjunction with projector lights for some sophisticated effects.

You can enable volumetric lighting through the Volumetric setting on the Foreground shader. Once you have selected Volumetric as your Foreground shader, right-click on the Volumetric setting to open the Volumetric Options panel.

Volumetric lights may seem a little intimidating at first, but rest assured you will have a firm grasp of how to get the most from them in Chapter 10. For now, let's look at all the parameters of the Volumetric Options panel.

- **Fog Density:** Increasing this value results in a more visible atmosphere, while decreasing it creates an atmosphere perfect for visible light. The default value is 1. As for the Fog Foreground shader, Volumetrics

TIP

If speed is an issue, you can decrease the overall render times of your scenes by decreasing the number of shadow-casting lights. If your scene calls for lots of shadows, you can reduce the number of ray-traced shadows in your scene by mixing shadow maps with accurate ray-traced shadows and still achieve great results. By eliminating half or so of the ray-traced shadows from your scenes, the rendering process can be shortened. I prefer ray-traced shadows because the blocky look of shadow maps tends to ruin a good image. Use shadow maps for your test renders. Use ray-traced shadows for the finished products—the extra oohs and ahhs you will get are worth the extra render times. In Chapter 12, the subjects of raycast shadows and lights are covered in more depth.

NOTE

It is not possible to mix different types of Foreground shaders. However, you can switch between different types of Foreground shaders at any time while constructing your scene.

NOTE

For a light source to be visible in a scene with volumetrics turned on, you must select the light source and check the Volumetric setting on the Light Options panel.

NOTE

Volumetric light can also cast shadows. Simply set the light you want to be visible to cast ray-traced shadows.

NOTE

Remember, visible lights are directly related to the size of your scenes. The key word here is *volume*. When using volumetrics, think of filling a room with fog. The larger the scene, the more fog required to achieve the desired effect.

should be used in enclosed areas for the best results. The fog density is consistent throughout this enclosed area and is directly related to its size. In other words, the larger the area, the greater you will have to set the Fog Density value to see any visible effects.

- **Samples:** This value represents the number of calculations performed per ray per light source. A higher Sample value results in more accurate shadows, but increases the render time accordingly. If you are doing a quick test render, lower this value to 4.

- **Source Attenuation:** This has got to be the most undescriptive item on the panel. Source Attenuation is the falloff of the light over distance. The larger this value, the quicker the visible beam will fade. If the light sources are overwhelming your scene, try increasing this value to tone down the volumetric scattering. Lower this value to increase the scattering of the light.

- **Surface Attenuation**: Surface Attenuation can be thought of as "visibility falloff." Objects farther away from the eye appear darker. Beware, though, because a very high Surface Attenuation value causes the objects in the scene to lose their visible detail, which makes them appear as shadows. The default value is 0, no attenuation.

- **Volume Attenuation:** The falloff of scattered light over distance. Adjusting this value controls the visibility of the light scattering. A higher value progressively dims the scattered light with distance; the farther away from the eye, the more the scattering will blend into the distance. The default value is 0, no attenuation.

- **Noise Amplitude:** Use Noise Amplitude to add fractal noise to the light-scattering effect caused by volumetrics. This is an effective way to vary the volume of the fog in certain areas of your imagery. This option also increases the render time, so use it sparingly.

- **Noise Scale:** Used in conjunction with Noise Amplitude, Noise Scale controls the size of the fractal noise. Smaller values create smaller granular noise, and larger values create a puff-like effect.

- **Noise Gain:** High values result in a sharper definition between the brighter and dimmer areas of the fractal noise. Low values create a gradual fading. Acceptable values range from 0 to 1. The default value is 0.5, which bypasses noise gain altogether.

GLOBAL ENVIRONMENT

Use environment maps to simulate reflections and to prevent those empty areas of your scene from being reflected in specular surfaces. To set up these maps, right-click the Global Environment button to open the Global Environment panel. Click on the File button to choose a file to use as the global environment map.

- **Global Env:** Toggles global environment mapping on and off.

- **File:** Enables you to choose the global environment map image file. You can use any file format supported by trueSpace4.

- **Animate:** If the selected environment map is an animation file or sequence of numbered images, clicking the Animate box will cycle through each frame.

DEPTH CUE

Depth cue shading is not fog, although the concept is similar. Surfaces that are farther along the z-axis will gradually fade into the background. Right-click on the Depth Cue button to open the Depth Cue panel.

- **Near:** The starting point in units where depth cue shading begins (from your point of view, camera location). A low value causes objects to become depth cue shaded sooner.

- **Far:** The maximum distance before all objects are completely obscured by the background color. Objects outside this range are not visible.

FOG

Whether you call it fog or haze, with this shader, the farther away a surface is from your point of view or camera, the more it will fade into the distance. This works great when creating a smoke-filled environment.

NOTE

The fog color does not affect background shading, only surfaces in the foreground.

Two types of fog are available to you in trueSpace4. *Regular* fog, which is consistent throughout the entire scene, and *ground* fog, which fades with height. To adjust the fog parameters, right-click on the Fog button.

- **Fog Type:** Choose between Regular or Ground. Ground fog appears thickest at ground level, but gradually fades with altitude.

- **Distance:** Determines how far from the camera the fog reaches 100% opacity.

- **Height:** The ceiling of the ground fog. Use a lower value for misty fog that clings to the ground.

- **Fog Color:** The overall color of the fog.

SNOW

The Snow shader enables you to simulate falling snow.

- **Near Scale:** Adjusts the size of the flakes closest to the camera. Increase the value for larger flakes.

- **Far Scale:** Adjusts the scale of the flakes in the distance. As with the Near Scale, larger values result in larger flakes.

- **Fl Density:** Flake Density determines the number of flakes in the scene. Use smaller values to simulate a light snowfall.

- **Flake Color:** Selects the flakes' color and brightness.

BACKGROUND

The Background option enables you to fill in those pixels in the background that are not visibly occupied by polygons. You have four main choices for background filler:

- Color

- Image

- Clouds

- Graduated

COLOR

This setting is pretty basic. It enables you to choose a solid color as your backdrop. Right-click on the Color option to bring up the Color panel. Select the background color by clicking the appropriate area of the colored cube. You can use the slider on the panel to adjust the brightness of the color.

IMAGE

Use this setting to choose any supported bitmap image as your background. Right-clicking on the Image button opens the Background Image panel. To select a file as a background image, simply click on the button to open the Get Texture Map dialog box. If the background image is an animation file or a series of sequentially numbered stills, check the Animation box to enable the Animate Background option. If the animation is shorter than the frames in your scene, the frames of the background animation will loop.

CLOUDS

This option lets you create a fractal cloud scheme as your backdrop with a maximum of two colors. The following settings can be used to adjust the fractal cloud formations:

- **Scale:** Enter any number in the range of 0 to 10 to control the size the individual clouds. The larger the value, the larger the clouds appear, filling up the sky. Smaller settings create concentrated cloud formations.

- **Detail:** Controls the definition around the edges of the cloud formations. A lower value creates smooth round clouds, while a higher value creates wisps and curls around the cloud borders. You can enter any number in the range of 0 to 10.

- **Background:** Sets the sky color.

- **Clouds:** Sets the cloud color.

GRADUATED

Use the gradient shader to choose two colors that blend together from top to bottom as your background. Right-click the Graduated button to open the Graduated Back panel to select the two colors.

THE RADIOSITY PANEL

trueSpace4 incorporates support for radiosity by using the global illumination method discussed earlier. TrueSpace4's radiosity takes into account all of the diffuse interreflections in your scenes and is independent of any particular viewpoint. Once the light distribution has been generated (a solution has been shot), images can be rendered by using any of trueSpace4's standard shading facilities.

To use radiosity in your scene, simply enable the Radiosity button.

Don't touch that button yet! We need to cover a few important options first to ensure your scenes render successfully. I also will be referring to them later on in the Radiosity chapter, so let's get familiar with the Radiosity panel (see Figure 11.6).

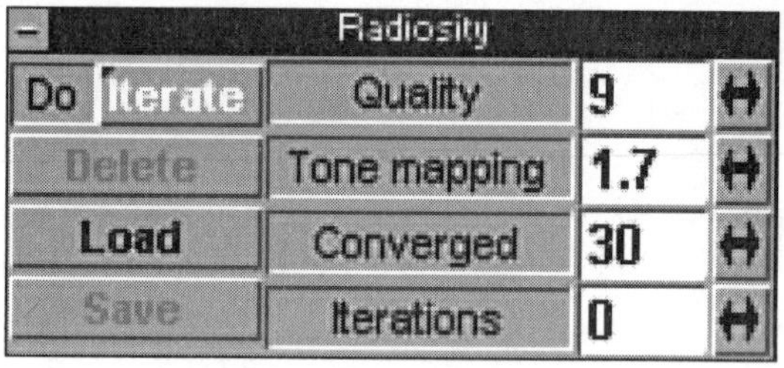

FIGURE 11.6   *The Radiosity panel in all its glory.*

- **Quality:** During my tests with the beta version of trueSpace4, I was unable to see any difference in render speed or quality when setting this parameter to its maximum. I did get the test scenes to respond to the adjustment, but when I used this value with full environments, the Quality doesn't do much. You're not out of the game, though; in Chapter 15, I will discuss other methods you can use to increase the quality of your radiosity imagery and how to fix artifacts. In any case, the acceptable values are from 1 to 9. I suggest setting Quality to its maximum of 9 and forget about it until Chapter 15.

- **Tone mapping:** Radiosity depends on real-world units and is defined as the radiation leaving a surface per unit time per unit area. In trueSpace4, the unit of measure used is *Watts per square meter.* These units are stored at the vertices of the energy mesh generated during the solution stage. In some cases, these radiosity values may exceed the range of values that your display device can accommodate. Tone Mapping enables you to linearly map the resulting radiosity solution to a range displayable on your output device. If the scene is dark or seems underlit, use higher values to make the scene brighter (see Figure 11.7).

Tone Mapping can be thought of as a manual illumination tool. If you were to enter a dark room, you wouldn't be able to see any of the details at first, but after a short period, your eyes would adjust to the illumination of the room. Use Tone Mapping to make this sort of adjustment.

FIGURE 11.7   *An example of using the Tone Mapping setting in the Radiosity Options panel to adjust the lighting to best fit your output device for the best results.*

- **Iterations:** Specifies how many iterations to perform between each rendering of the scene during the radiosity solution phase. A value of 0 performs no screen update during the radiosity solution phase. This is the setting I prefer because it's faster and allows me to shoot a solution, render, and shoot another solution in a relatively short period of time.

  Selecting Lights Only implicitly sets the Iterations to 1, which in turn visually displays the effect of each of the lights in the scene while the solution is being shot.

- **Converged**: Specifies the convergence criterion for the radiosity solution. Don't let the phrase "convergence criterion" scare you—it means this value is what the convergence will be based on (convergence criteria). A big misconception is that it is necessary to wait until 100% of the energy in the scene has been accounted for. This is not true because the visual impact of the last bit of energy isn't visibly significant.

WARNING

A radiosity solution is tied to the original scene geometry; only the energy mesh is stored in the LWR file. In other words, save your scene because the radiosity solution is totally useless without it. If you attempt to load a radiosity solution into an unrelated scene, you will bring your PC to a screeching halt. Don't say I didn't warn you.

NOTE

You can stop the radiosity solution stage at any time by pressing the Esc key on your keyboard.

WARNING

Once a radiosity solution has been started, altering the quality settings, adding objects, moving objects, or changing an object's material will cause the present solution to become moot. You will have to delete the solution and reshoot from square one.

You can save and load radiosity solutions in trueSpace4 via the Radiosity Options panel. Once a radiosity solution has been started, it can be saved as a LightWorks LWR file.

The progress of the radiosity solution is visible in the Help bar. When Do Lights is selected, the energy of the light sources is shot one by one and the number of completed and remaining light sources is displayed in the Help bar. But in the case where Do Iterate is selected, the number of completed iterations is displayed (a single iteration [step] means an energy transfer from a single light source or patch to the rest of the scene).

ANIMATED OBJECTS AND RADIOSITY

Animated objects cannot be included in the radiosity solution. The radiosity solution should include only the static objects in your scenes.

You can exclude an object from the radiosity solution via the Object Render Options panel. This essentially causes the object to be ignored during the radiosity solution, but trueSpace4 will render it by using either the ScanLine or ray tracing method after the radiosity solution has been shot.

HYBRID RADIOSITY

You now know that radiosity is an accurate method for reproducing diffuse interreflections in your scenes. That's great, but what if you want specular reflections or specular highlights?

Not to worry—you can have the best of both worlds. Simply shoot the radiosity solution first. Turn on ray tracing and ray trace the scene. TrueSpace re-evaluates the effects of the primary light sources and adds the specular effects, including reflections.

PREVIEW SCENE TO FILE PANEL

If you ever have a need for previewing an animation in Wireframe mode, you can render it to a file from the Preview Scene to File. You're probably thinking that you can simply set the render quality to Wireframe and render it to a file. Sorry, but you can't do that. Preview Scene to File is the only option available to you for the task. To access this panel, right-click the Preview Scene to File button in the Render pull-down menu located in the main window's title bar.

The options are self explanatory:

NOTE

Once a radiosity solution has been started, the standard rendering tools (Render Object, Render Scene, Render Area) will use the radiosity database until you remove the radiosity solution via the Radiosity Options panel. The reason for this (as explained earlier) is that radiosity is view independent.

- **Change Name:** Name your file here. If you don't, the default of preview.avi will be used.

- **Change Player:** You can name your AVI viewer here, but don't expect it to automatically start the player when the animation is done.

- **Grid:** Check this box to include the grid in the preview.

- **D3D in Wireframe:** If you have the capability to use D3D, you can check this box to use colored wireframe in your preview.

From the Preview Scene to Render panel, you can also specify the start and end frames to save to the file.

SUMMARY

In this chapter, we briefly looked at all the rendering options available to us in trueSpace4. This is only a precursor to what's to come, so hang tight. We will return to the subject of radiosity, volumetric lighting, and special effects in just a bit. Next, let's look at effectively lighting your scenes in trueSpace4.

CHAPTER 12

LIGHTING IN TRUESPACE

by Jeffrey W. Wall, M.D.

The three main aspects of scene design are modeling, texturing, and lighting, yet lighting seems to get left behind and neglected in the rush to finish a project. This is unfortunate because lighting can play the most important role in your scene. Indeed, lighting can sometimes make or break your scene. It sets the mood and atmosphere for the scene and provides contrast, depth, and harmony. It can clarify or confuse. Lighting should never be automatic. It is not good enough to just throw in a few lights and call it finished. Lighting needs and deserves to be thought about, considered carefully, and planned accordingly. Subtle changes in color, shadows, intensity, and angles can have profound effects on the overall outcome of the finished scene.

trueSpace4 adds many new features in the area of lighting—new light models, a new rendering engine and modes, and new lighting special effects. This chapter highlights and explain the different types of lights and how to use them effectively in your scene. Specifically, it covers

- The Light Control panel
- The different types of lights
- The default light setups
- The ins and outs of shadows
- Color and mood
- Putting it all together

THE LIGHT CONTROL PANEL

When a light is selected or created in trueSpace, the Light Control panel automatically pops up (see Figure 12.1). Here, you can set each of the different properties of the light.

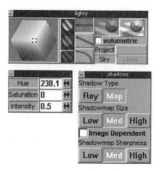

FIGURE 12.1 *The Light Control panel.*

The color wheel enables you to interactively choose the color of the light, while the slider bar next to it sets the intensity of the light. Right-clicking on either the slider or the color wheel brings up a dialog box where the color and intensity values of the light can be set manually with numeric values.

Unlike the color wheels in the texture shaders that use the RGB color system, the lights color wheel uses the HSL system. *Hue* sets the basic color of the light, *Saturation* sets how light or dark the shade is, and *Intensity* sets the brightness (or *luminance*) of the light. A good way to think of how these work is: What color do I want, how much of that color do I want (or "how blue is the blue"), and how bright do I want the light to be?

The numeric values for Hue start with red at 1 and proceed counterclockwise around the perimeter of the color wheel up to 360, which puts you back at red again. Saturation values go from 0 to 1. A value of 0 is white, whereas a value of 1 would be a fully saturated color.

If you move the Intensity slider up, you will notice that it increases up to a maximum value of 2.0 only; however, the actual value can be set to much higher levels, creating far brighter lights. Alternatively, it can be set to negative values, creating *negative lights* that remove light from the scene.

Next to the color wheel is a column of three buttons for setting the light's falloff. *Falloff* describes how the energy of the light is dispersed over distance or how dim the light gets the farther it is from its source. A light with no falloff (the top button) retains its intensity for an infinite distance from the light source, never becoming dimmer. Lights set with linear falloff (the middle button) dim in direct proportion to how far away the light is from its source. With squared falloff (the bottom button), the light dims in proportion to the square of the distance from the light source. With squared falloff, light two units away from the source will be only one fourth as bright as it is at the source. Squared falloff is the most realistic setting and more accurately reflects the true behavior of light.

Lights can be made shadow casting or nonshadow casting by clicking the appropriate button on the right side of the panel. Right-clicking on the Shadow Casting button brings up the Shadows dialog box, where you set the type of shadow, either ray traced (the Ray button) or shadowmapped (the Map button). We'll explore the other options later in the "Ins and Outs of Shadows" section.

Back in the Light Control panel, clicking the Volumetric check box toggles volumetric effects on and off for the current light. It should be noted that simply checking this box is not sufficient to enable volumetric effects; Volumetric must also be turned on as the Foreground shader in the Render Options dialog box.

The image to be used in a projector light can be chosen by clicking the gray Project box. Although this option appears to be active at all times with all lights, only projector lights can be made to project an image. The final option on the Light Control panel is a toggle to set the type of Sky light you would like to use: Overcast, Clear, or Intermediate.

LIGHT TYPES IN TRUESPACE4

TrueSpace has six types of lights:

- Local lights
- Spotlights
- Infinite lights
- Projector lights
- Area lights
- Sky lights

The first three provide the main illumination sources for the scene, and the final three are specialty lights used for special lighting situations or when a specific effect is needed. Each light has its own special representation within the scene, depending on whether you're running in Solid or Wireframe mode. The Solid versions have active surfaces, showing the current light color and allowing for interactive manipulation of the light. It should be noted that you need to double-click on the light's surface in order to manipulate it.

LOCAL LIGHTS

Local lights (see Figure 12.2) cast an even light uniformly in all directions and function much like a light bulb. They can be set with no falloff, linear falloff, or squared falloff. They do not render any volumetric effect, but they will generate a lens flare.

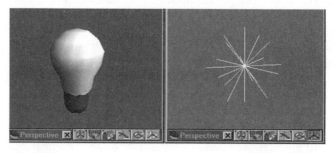

FIGURE 12.2   *Local lights.*

The Local light representation in Solid mode, a light bulb, mimics its function. Clicking on the screw portion of the light allows it to be dragged to a new location, while clicking with both mouse buttons anywhere on the light scales it to make the light more visible (but has no effect on its properties or how it lights up the scene). The color of the light is reflected in the bulb portion. In Wireframe mode, a star represents the local light.

Local lights function well as the main illumination source or as accent lights in the scene. Because they radiate light in all directions, they will light up the whole scene and, as such, may not be appropriate in all lighting situations. When used as the main light source in the scene, they are best with linear or no falloff. When used as practical lights (like a lamp or a candle), they should be set to squared falloff.

SPOTLIGHTS

Spotlights (see Figure 12.3) focus a cone-shaped beam of light radiating from a single point in space and can be set to no falloff, linear falloff, or squared falloff. The size and intensity of the cone can be varied to give differing effects.

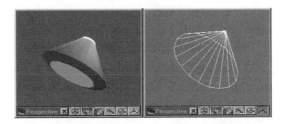

FIGURE 12.3   *Spotlights.*

In Solid mode, there are several ways of manipulating the spotlight. You can move the light by clicking on the white tip, whereas clicking on the body of the light rotates it. The blue ring on the face scales the size of the light in your scene. Clicking and dragging on the face of the light interactively varies the aperture and the falloff of the cone of light. The face itself shows the current color of the light. In Wireframe mode, the green focus ring on the face represents the size of the aperture.

Aiming spotlights by hand can be difficult; fortunately, there is an easier way of doing it. Identify the object you would like the light to shine on, and then attach it to the light with the Look At function. Alternatively, if you would like it to focus on a general area rather than a single object, you can create a small sphere, place it where you want the light to shine, attach it using Look At, and then delete the aiming object. You can also make the aiming object temporarily invisible so that you can adjust the lighting later. To check its placement, use the View from Object (camera view) function to make sure it is shining where you want it.

The effect of changing the size of the aperture is illustrated in Figures 12.4, 12.5, and 12.6.

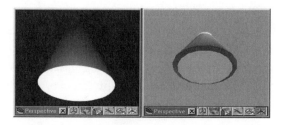

FIGURE 12.4 *When a fully opened aperture is used, the edges of the light are sharp and distinct.*

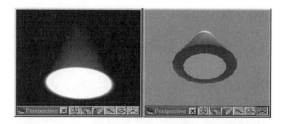

FIGURE 12.5 *Closing the aperture down a little bit begins to soften the edges of the hotspot.*

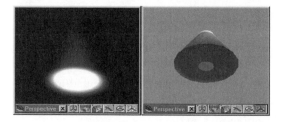

FIGURE 12.6 *An almost completely closed aperture gives very soft edges to the light's hotspot.*

Spotlights function very well as a scene's key light, as well as to provide focused fill lighting as needed. Combined with volumetrics, they can yield fantastic atmospheric effects. Spotlights will generate a lens flare, but only when they are almost completely facing the camera. Key lights are the main light sources in your scene. Fill lights provide extra lighting as needed (more on these later).

INFINITE LIGHTS

Infinite lights (see Figure 12.7) cast a uniform light through the scene in one direction. The source is infinitely distant and all rays of light are parallel. Another way of thinking of these is that they cast a "sheet" of light across the whole scene. Infinite lights have direction only and thus can be placed anywhere in the scene. They can cast shadows, but they have no falloff. This is important to note because the falloff buttons on the Light Control panel appear to be active for this light even though they aren't.

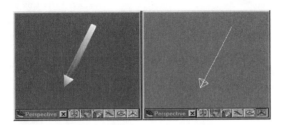

FIGURE 12.7 *Infinite lights.*

In both Solid and Wireframe modes, the pointer at the end of the light indicates the direction of the light rays. Clicking on the shaft in Solid mode rotates the light. Scaling the size of an infinite light makes it more visible in your scene, but has no effects on the properties.

Infinite lights work well for simulating the sun in outdoor scenes. They can also function well as a low-level fill light, where an even level of lighting is needed throughout the scene.

PROJECTOR LIGHTS

Projector lights (see Figure 12.8) are specialty lights that project an image as a light source, like a slide projector does. Any supported image type can be chosen (JPG, TGA, BMP, and so on), even AVI files. They can have no falloff, linear falloff, or squared falloff.

The Solid mode representation of Projector lights is a little bit more complicated than some of the others. The color of the light is shown on the knob on the top of the light; clicking on this knob also allows for movement of the light. The light can be rotated by clicking on the body, and scaling is accomplished by clicking on the face and handles. The currently selected image is shown on the face of the light. Scaling with the left mouse button changes the size of the projected image only. Scaling uniformly with both mouse buttons pressed changes the size of the light (for better visibility in the scene) but will not affect how the image is projected. Projector lights can be aimed by using the Look At function, just like Spotlights.

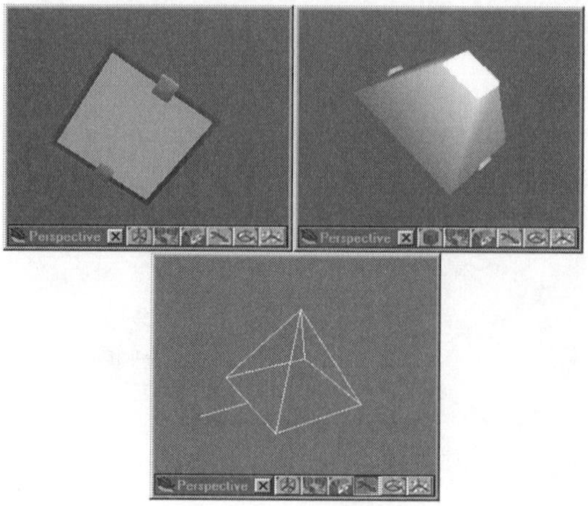

FIGURE 12.8 *Projector lights.*

Figures 12.9 and 12.10 illustrate how Projector lights can be used to shine a pattern of light or shadows in your scene; the actual image projected is shown in the lower-right corner of each image. Used in conjunction with volumetrics, any number of interesting special effects can be achieved, as Figure 12.11 shows.

FIGURE 12.9 *Using a Projector light to cast shadows.*

FIGURE 12.10   *Using a Projector light to cast light patterns.*

FIGURE 12.11   *Some interesting effects using Projector lights and volumetrics.*

SKY LIGHTS

Sky lights (see Figure 12.12) simulate the diffuse light radiating from the sky itself. Perhaps a simpler way of thinking of them is that Sky lights are the trapped light bouncing around in the dome of the atmosphere. Their light is coming from the sky but not from the sun directly. If necessary, a separate Infinite or Local light can be used for the sun along with the Sky light. A Sky light renders in trueSpace as if it were an infinitely large sphere centered over the scene with the sun's position represented by the direction of the light.

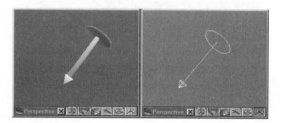

FIGURE 12.12 *Sky lights.*

In Solid mode, the light can be rotated by clicking anywhere on its surface. Scaling the size of a Sky light makes it more visible in your scene, but has no effects on the light's properties. The current color is represented on the shaft, which points in the direction the light is traveling. Sky lights have direction only and thus can be placed anywhere in the scene without affecting how the light shines. They have no falloff and are exclusive to radiosity.

NOTE

Sky lights will work only when you render with Radiosity. This is an important point to remember. When rendering with ScanLine or RayCast only (with or without Raytracing enabled), Sky lights will cast no light or shadows in the scene and will have no effect at all.

There are three settings for Sky lights, each accessible from the Light Control panel. The Clear setting results in the brightest part of the sky (and thus the position of the sun) following the direction of the light. When using the Overcast setting, the brightest part of the sky is always overhead regardless of the light's direction (because the sun is not visible on an overcast day, and shadows are minimal). Intermediate is somewhere between these two (think of it as partly cloudy). When using the Clear or Intermediate settings, it may be necessary also to use an Infinite light to account for direct sunlight.

Sky lights can be difficult to set up correctly. Often they require high light levels, and at times the results can be very subtle. Much experimentation is needed to get the right effect.

AREA LIGHTS

Area lights (see Figure 12.13) are specialized light sources that radiate light from a sizable rectangular area as opposed to a single point in space. They work like a big diffusing lens placed in front of the light, giving off a diffuse light with soft shadows. In fact, the strength of Area lights is their capability to cast soft shadows. In prior versions of trueSpace, you had to create a large array of 30 or more lights to achieve soft shadows (more about light arrays later in the chapter); now, you can get the same effect by using Area lights. Area lights have no falloff and do not exhibit volumetric or lens flare effects.

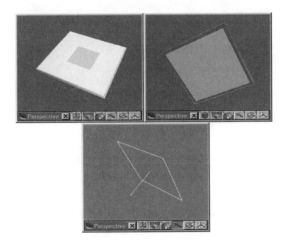

FIGURE 12.13   *Area lights.*

In Solid mode, the light can be moved by double-clicking on the small square in the center. The blue surface on the top and the orange rim on the bottom are for rotating. Clicking the edge of the light or the light panel on the underside scales the light's size. The light's color is shown on the undersurface.

Area lights serve two main functions: lighting up a large area and casting soft shadows. Scaling up the size of the light will give a more diffuse light pattern with softer shadows. Conversely, scaling down will give a sharper shadow and a brighter light. Figure 12.14 illustrates how the shadows become softer with larger lights.

An important characteristic of Area lights to note is that they are visible when viewed from below the level of the light or when the light faces the camera. When viewed from above, they cannot be seen (see Figure 12.15).

FIGURE 12.14   *Scaling an Area light affects its shadow pattern.*

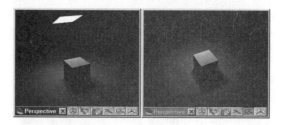

FIGURE 12.15   *The same scene viewed from both below and above the same Area light. Notice that the light is not visible in the right view.*

Area lights work most effectively with radiosity renderings. In fact, trueSpace uses different algorithms for calculating the soft shadows, depending on the method of rendering used. With radiosity, the shadows are very soft with a real penumbra (the soft part of the shadow) calculated. When rendered without radiosity, however, the shadows appear overlapped, as if from a number of different sources. This is the same effect you would get by using a small array of lights. Figure 12.16 illustrates this.

FIGURE 12.16   *Soft shadows look different depending on the render method.*

THE DEFAULT LIGHT SETUPS

trueSpace4 has four default light setups to choose from:

- Colored
- Textured
- White
- VRML

They can be accessed from the Display Options panel and are provided as an aid to the modeling and texturing process. Although you could use them as the final light setup for your scene, you are better off doing your final lighting "by hand."

The Colored setup places three Local lights in a triangular pattern around the scene's origin. One light is white, one is blue, and the other is orange. Each has the same intensity. The three different colors coming from different sides enhance contrast and highlight the faces of your model. This is a good light setup to use when modeling.

The Textured setup has two white Infinite light sources at the origin. One is parallel to the ground plane, and one is at a 45-degree angle to it. Two Local lights with linear falloff are placed at a distance from the origin. One of the Local lights has a faint orange tint to it, and the other is white. The Textured light setup is so named because it combines two different light sources, providing a layered or *textured* lighting effect.

The White setup has four Infinite lights clustered and pointed at the origin. They provide an even white light coming from all directions. This setup is ideal for texturing your objects. The even light allows you to observe how the textures apply without color distortion or extra shadows.

The VRML setup presents two white Infinite lights converging at the origin. As the name implies, the setup is designed for use in VRML worlds.

THE INS AND OUTS OF SHADOWS

Shadows play an important role in lighting. They add depth to the image and enhance the 3D illusion. The position, angle, and length of the shadows can impart mood and atmosphere, as well as enhance mystery and drama. They can accentuate your modeling and hide your mistakes. Without shadows, your scene will appear flat and lifeless.

In trueSpace, shadows can be created either with *shadowmaps* or the *ray-tracing/RayCast* method. Which type you choose depends on several factors, including accuracy of the shadows, render times, and personal preference. Right-clicking on the Shadow Casting button in the Light Control panel brings up the Shadows dialog box (see Figure 12.1). Here, you can decide between ray-traced/RayCast shadows (the Ray button) and *shadowmaps* (the Map button), as well as set your shadowmap options.

Ray-traced and RayCast shadows are the most accurate; the shadows are cast in the scene as they would be in real life. They accurately follow the contours of the object and respond correctly to transparency. All this comes at a cost, though. Ray-traced/RayCast shadows are computationally expensive, and thus will take longer to render. In prior versions of trueSpace, the only render options were ScanLine and ray tracing. trueSpace4 adds a new render option called RayCast. Somewhere between ScanLine rendering and ray tracing, RayCast accurately calculates shadows (but not reflections) and, as such, leads to a faster render time. The advantage here is obvious if you need accurate shadows without the overhead of ray tracing. The major drawback besides long render times (which isn't so much of a drawback with the RayCast option) is that all shadows created by this method are *hard*—that is, all the edges are sharp. The problem is that not all shadows in the real world have sharp edges. Depending on lighting conditions, some shadows have soft, fuzzy borders. There are workarounds to this problem, but it is something to be considered when setting up your lights. We'll revisit hard and soft shadows later in this section.

SHADOWMAPS

Shadowmaps are a different story, though. Instead of accurately computing the shadows, trueSpace kind of "fakes" them by making a guess at the shadow's boundaries and then generating a low-quality "shadow" image that trueSpace applies behind the objects in the scene. Shadowmaps will never be quite as sharp as (which is either good or bad, depending on what you need) and will never follow the contours quite as accurately as ray-traced/RayCast shadows will. Their render time, however, is significantly quicker. At their worst, they are terrible, and at their best, they can actually look quite good. Shadowmaps are a good choice when rendering animations because they are quick, and whatever inconsistencies there are in the shadows will most likely not be noticed.

There are three settings for Shadowmaps in the Shadows dialog box. They are Shadowmap Size, Shadowmap Sharpness, and Image Dependent.

- **Shadowmap Size:** The actual amount of memory retained by the map. It is not a setting for the physical size of the map. An easier way of thinking of this is how "finely" generated the map is. The Low setting leads to a fairly crude shadow, and the High setting leads to a more finely rendered one.

- **Shadowmap Sharpness:** How sharply the edges of the shadow are rendered. The Low setting gives soft edges, while the High setting gives you sharper (but still a little fuzzy) edges.

- **Image Dependent:** Sets the size of the generated shadowmaps based on the size of the final rendered output. When Image Dependent is checked on and Shadowmap Size is set to Low, the maps are 1/16 the size of the final render, with a Medium setting, they are 1/4, and with High they match the final rendered image resolution. Figures 12.17, 12.18, and 12.19 illustrate some of the different combinations of settings for shadowmaps with and without image dependency. It should be noted here that shadowmaps render differently in trueSpace4 than they do in previous versions of trueSpace.

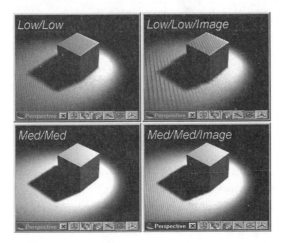

FIGURE 12.17   *Different shadowmap settings yield different results. Here we are comparing Low and Medium settings with and without Image Dependency. In each image, the first setting is Shadowmap Sharpness and the second is Shadowmap Size.*

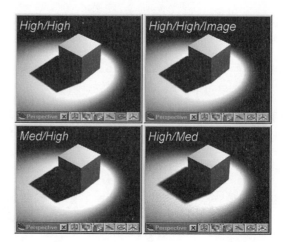

FIGURE 12.18 *This image compares High settings as well as both combinations of Medium and High settings. In each image, the first setting is Shadowmap Sharpness and the second is Shadowmap Size.*

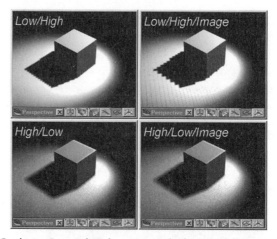

FIGURE 12.19 *Combining Low and High settings can lead to very different results. In each image, the first setting is Shadowmap Sharpness and the second is Shadowmap Size.*

As you can see, the results of different settings can lead to disparate results and some stunning artifacts, especially when adding image dependency and combining High and Low settings. High and Medium settings yield the best results. The advantage of making the shadows image dependent is debatable. For comparison, Figure 12.20 illustrates ray-traced/RayCast shadows as well as the soft shadows of Area lights when used with radiosity.

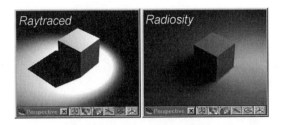

FIGURE 12.20 *The difference between hard and soft shadows.*

SOFT VERSUS HARD SHADOWS

All this leads to a discussion of soft shadows and hard shadows. A little bit of this is personal preference. Some people prefer one to the other, but as far as realism goes, there are situations where one will be preferable to the other. In situations of high-contrast lighting, hard shadows will be appropriate. You will see this in brightly lit outdoor scenes and indoor scenes with stark lighting, such as a darkened room with light streaming in from a window. Long, hard shadows give a heightened sense of mystery and suspense to a scene.

Soft shadows are encountered more often in the real world. With all the ambient light bouncing around us, it is rare to see many shadows that aren't softened somewhat. Most indoor scenes, as well as some outdoor scenes (overcast weather, for instance), will benefit from soft shadows.

Area lights probably represent the best source of soft shadows in trueSpace4, especially when rendered with radiosity. Radiosity, however, is not an option for all renders. What, then? Well, you can still use Area lights, but the output will not be as good as with radiosity (see Figure 12.16). Shadowmaps work well in certain conditions, especially if you need to render an animation, and avoiding long render times is a consideration.

If you are not using radiosity, don't like shadowmaps, and render time is not a factor, but you would still like soft shadows, then a *light array* might be the right answer. If you group enough lights together and make them all shadow casting, their overlapped shadows will coalesce into a soft shadow with a nice penumbral effect. The downside to this is that you need upward of 40 lights (although smaller numbers of lights might work just as well), and this can dramatically increase your time to render. You can build one of these yourself, but an automated plug-in will make your life a lot easier. Figure 12.21 shows an array of 60 local lights generated by the Coolpowers2 plug-in suite for trueSpace from Windmill-Fraser Multimedia.

Figure 12.21   *Light arrays can be an effective way of making soft shadows.*

Lights and Shadows

The angle at which you place your lights will affect how they illuminate the scene and cast shadows. A light positioned directly in front of the subject or back by the camera will give an even illumination with shadows falling behind the subject. A light placed directly overhead casts few shadows. As the light is brought down the side, the shadows lengthen, and the mood deepens. A light directly alongside the subject casts very long shadows. Figure 12.22 illustrates the effect of the angle of light and shadows.

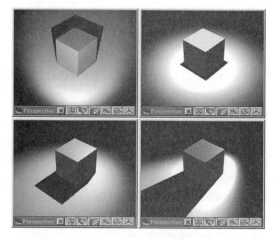

Figure 12.22   *The angle of the light affects how the shadows are cast.*

In some instances, you may need to enhance the effect of shadows and shadowed areas in your scene. An effective way of doing this is with *negative lights*. You can manually set the light value to a negative number; by doing this, you create an "anti-light" that removes light from your scene. Figure 12.23 illustrates this. The image on the left is before and the image on the right is after a negative Spotlight has been shined into the corner. You can use this to pull the light out of certain parts of the scene, thus enhancing the shadows to great effect.

FIGURE 12.23   *Before and after a negative light has been added to a scene.*

EFFECTIVE LIGHTING

Lighting in trueSpace is similar to lighting in stage and film, only different. How is that for being vague? The basic principles that govern good lighting in a movie also work in trueSpace. The difference is that in the real world, light is subject to the laws of physics. In 3D, the lights are modeled on the real world but can do things normally not possible. An example of this is the simple capability of making a light cast shadows or not cast shadows. Try that with a flashlight! These same capabilities bring in limitations, too. There is no real ambient light in 3D; we have to make our own, faking light sources, adding lights and shadows, anything to make our scenes look real. Nonetheless, we can easily apply the time-tested principles of film lighting to trueSpace.

THREE-POINT LIGHTING

The classic lighting scheme consists of three lights:

- Key light
- Fill light
- Backlight

This combination is called *three-point lighting* and is usually the most effective way of lighting things up. Sometimes additional lights need to be brought into the scene, and sometimes lights need to be deleted from the scene, but the three-point system is the best place to start.

You do not need a lot of lights to properly light your scene. A common mistake is that someone thinks the more lights, the better. A good thing to remember is that the more lights you have in your scene, the harder your machine has to work, and the longer it will take to render. This is especially important when doing animations that could take days to render. It behooves you to figure out the most effective lighting with the least amount of lights.

THE KEY LIGHT

The first thing you should do is delete all lights from your scene. Do a test render; it should be all black. Then start adding your lights. The first one added should be your key light, and it will be the primary light source in your scene. It radiates the majority of the light and is responsible for casting shadows. The position of the key light will go far in helping establish the mood of your scene. It is usually placed in front of or just off to the side of your main subject (at about 10 to 45 degrees from the camera). When placed frontally by the camera, the objects will cast a minimum of shadow. When moved off to the side, shadows will begin to develop. The farther it is placed to the side, the longer the shadows and the more dramatic the lighting will be. If there is a window in the scene, the key light should be placed so that its shadows coincide with any shadows cast by the window. In most instances, the key light is the only shadow-casting light in the scene. Too many lights casting different shadows are confusing to the eye and decrease the sense of realism.

Local lights and Spotlights work best as the key light in scene, although Area lights will do if a broad diffuse light with soft shadows is needed. In outdoor scenes, the key should be an infinite light.

THE FILL LIGHT

The next light to add is the *fill light*. In the real world, there is a certain amount of ambient light bouncing around us and giving most things a degree of illumination. In 3D, however, the world is completely black. You have to add "extra" light yourself. This is where the fill light comes in. It is used to lighten up the dark areas in the scene and to bring out the details within shadows. The fill light is usually 25–50 percent the strength of the key light and is positioned opposite it. The light cast by the key light alone often tends to be hard; the fill light softens it up by reducing the amount of contrast between light and shadow (more about hard and soft light in Chapter 16, "trueSpace Cinematography"). The more intense your fill light is, the brighter your scene will be. In night scenes, usually only a small amount of (if any) fill light is needed.

Any type of light can function as a fill light. Use an Infinite light if you need an even level of ambient light across the scene. Spotlights work well providing localized fill to highlight certain areas of the scene, whereas Area lights can provide a nice soft fill light without falloff. In outdoor scenes rendered with radiosity, Sky lights provide a good fill, lightening up the shadows. Fill lights are very flexible; some scenes may not need any, some just one, and some scenes may need several. They are there to accent your key light by removing unwanted darkness and shadows. Be careful not to let them overpower your key light.

THE BACKLIGHT

The third light in three-point lighting is the *backlight*. It is often difficult to separate the objects from the background. By placing a backlight, you heighten the sense of depth within the scene. It separates the objects from the background, giving them definition and form. The backlight should be 50–100 percent the intensity of the key and can be placed above or below the level of the objects, but always behind them.

One thing to remember is that even though a backlight is used to add depth to the scene, when overdone it will have the opposite effect. If set too bright, it will shorten the foreground and flatten your scene. Of course, under the right conditions, this can be used to great effect and can be very dramatic.

LIGHTS IN ACTION

Now that we have the basics down, let's look at some examples.

Figure 12.24 illustrates a simple scene with just a key light (a Local light set at camera level and 45 degrees to the left) and just a backlight (a Local light set at the level of the sphere and half the intensity as the key). Notice the difference between the key and backlights. The key light adds color, shadows, and light, and the backlight outlines the shape of the objects.

FIGURE 12.24   *The difference between key lights and backlights.*

Figure 12.25 illustrates the same scene with just the key light and a fill light (a Local light set 45 degrees left of the camera and half the intensity of the key), and then with just the key and backlight. Compare these examples with Figure 12.24. Notice how the addition of a fill light softens the overall lighting while subtly increasing the illumination. The addition of the backlight adds depth by accentuating the outlines of the objects against the background.

FIGURE 12.25   *Adding fill lights and backlights.*

Figure 12.26A shows the same three lights combined together in the finished scene. Notice that this scene is brightly lit. Figure 12.26B shows the same scene with the lights altered. Whereas all the lights in A were Local lights, the key light in B has been replaced with a Spotlight, and the fill light has been replaced with an Infinite light. The key has been moved to the same side as the fill light but has been positioned higher than the camera. The three-point light scheme has been retained but the results are very different. While scene A is bright and cheerful, scene B is dark and full of mystery.

Additional lights, sometimes called *kicker* lights, can be added as needed to enhance the illumination within the scene. Actual lighting fixtures (such as lamps or headlights) are known as *practical* lights and can be used as sources of illumination or merely for effect.

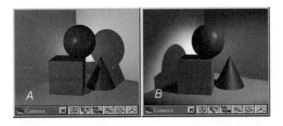

FIGURE 12.26 *Three-point lighting in action.*

The actual lights you use and how you use them will depend entirely on how you picture the final scene. Rigid adherence to three-point lighting doesn't necessarily give the best results. Sometimes you have to throw out the three-point scheme and go for more dramatic lighting. The bottom line is that ultimately the lightning plan will need to be individualized to your scene. Which lights you use and how you place them can have a profound effect on the mood and feeling of your scene. We'll cover lighting for different occasions later in the chapter. You also might want to check out Chapter 16.

COLOR AND MOOD

Lighting isn't just all about shadow and angles, though; it is also about color. Light in trueSpace is *additive*—that is, when the three primary colors of light (red, blue, and green) are combined, they add up to white. The overlap of these individual colors leads to the secondary colors of light: cyan, magenta, and yellow. You therefore need to be cognizant of the interplay of lights in your scene. Two markedly different colors may add up to an unexpected result.

Figure 12.27 illustrates the additive nature of light. Notice how the primary colors combine to form white above the sphere. The secondary colors are most clear in the shadows beneath the sphere.

Normally, the light we see around us is a combination of wavelengths *tinted* the color we perceive. Objects in the real world appear their *real* color because of this admixture of light. Light in trueSpace is different, though. It is all of one wavelength. The color of the light is *pure*—that is, blue light is pure blue light and red light is pure red light. This is important to remember because the colors you choose for your lights will not only affect the mood and atmosphere of your image, but will also affect the color of the textures on your objects. Shine a blue light on a yellow object, and it will look green. Once your lighting is set up, you will need to study how it affects the surfaces in your image. If textures and colors are not what you expected, you may find it necessary to adjust the color of the light or even change the texture to fix its representation within the render.

FIGURE 12.27 *The additive nature of light. You can see a corresponding full-color version of this image in the color section.*

The color of light plays an integral role in establishing the mood and feel of a scene. Humans are emotional creatures, and the colors we perceive around us can markedly affect our mood. From feelings of sadness to feelings of passion, color is often our emotional compass.

FIGURE 12.28 *The full-color spectrum of light. You can see a corresponding full-color version of this image in the color section.*

Colors on the left side of the spectrum (see Figure 12.28)—the reds, oranges, and yellows—we associate with passion and anger. As we continue on to the greens, we encounter feelings of peacefulness and contentment, but progressing on to the blues leads to sadness and depression. Now, this may be oversimplifying the range of human emotion and its response to color, but it is simply to highlight that we are visual creatures, and we respond to visual stimuli on a subconscious level.

Beyond emotion, though, we also use color as a visual indicator of temperature. Reds, yellows, and oranges we associate with heat and warmth, while the blue hues we find cold and icy. Figure 12.29 illustrates this.

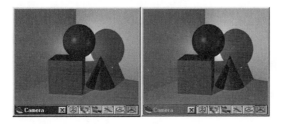

FIGURE 12.29 *Colors as visual indicators of temperature.*

Color can convey temperature. You can see a corresponding full color version of this image in the color section. Notice the difference in light color between the two images. The yellowish tint on the left feels much warmer than the bluish tint of the image on the right.

You can use these perceptions of temperature and emotion to your advantage when setting up your lights. By carefully choosing your colors, you can impose certain emotions on the viewer without them ever knowing it.

Color can also tell us a lot about the time of day. We associate certain colors of light with certain times during the day. We can use these associations to help set a time reference for the scene. We tend to think of mornings as pinkish and noon as white, while the evening hours tend toward yellows and then blues as we fade to dusk.

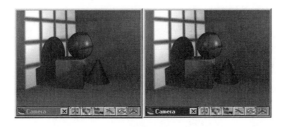

FIGURE 12.30 *Color can the convey the time of day. You can see a corresponding full-color version of this image in the color section.*

Look at Figure 12.30. The pinkish tint to the Projector light in the image to the left makes us think of morning, while the yellowish tint in the image to the right suggests late afternoon.

Like any other facet of lighting, color needs to be thought about and planned. From an emotional to a practical level, the colors chosen for your scene can have a profound effect, not only on the image itself but also on how the image is perceived.

PUTTING IT ALL TOGETHER

None of the principles set forth in this chapter are set in stone. The lighting plan you ultimately develop for your scene will be individualized and *must be* individualized to ensure that everything is properly lit and conveys the right emotion. A scene with bad lighting is obvious. Overlit or underlit, everything from the texturing to the modeling will look wrong. It will be flat and emotionless, with no "feeling" or mood. A scene with good lighting is just the opposite. The lighting will tell the story and convey the mood and atmosphere of the scene. It will "look right." You will know it when you see it. After you have put all that effort into modeling and texturing the objects in your scene, don't go and ruin it by ignoring lighting. Spend some time on it. Think about how you want the viewers to feel when they look at your work. What kind of mood do you want them to have? What do you want them to take away from the experience? Lighting is the "touchy-feely" part of 3D, and it pays to spend some time ruminating on it.

THE LIGHTING PLAN

Before starting out, write down how you want your final scene to look. Develop a lighting plan. An example would be: "A darkened room, moonlight streaming in through the window, long shadows with an ominous feel to them, a sense of anticipation edged with fear, objects fading into shadows in the corners." Sounds silly, but it is always a good idea to have it clear in your head how you want the scene to look before starting.

A good thing to keep in mind when finally setting up lighting for your scene is that the more lights you add, the longer it will take to render. If you have a powerful machine with a lot of RAM or are only creating a still image, then this might not matter. However, if your machine is underpowered or you are creating an animation, then the number of lights in the scene is very important. Creating the best lighting with the fewest lights is something to strive for.

WORK METHODICALLY

Once you have your lighting plan, you can start adding your lights. This is the long part because most likely you will be doing many test renders. Add lights one at a time, do a test render, and add another light. The same goes for changing the light's parameters; do it one at a time and then do a test render. It can be very difficult to isolate the effect of a change if you have changed three or four different things at once. Incrementally fixing your lights will allow you to fine-tune their effects. *Area renders* are especially useful in this phase. Also try rendering with low poly or "dummy" objects in your scene instead of the actual objects. This way, you can quickly check lighting angles and effects without having to render out the full scene.

Try to make the upper part of the image lighter than the lower and try to keep the main subject of the scene within the key light's parameters. The human eye is naturally drawn to the highest and lightest part of the image, so that is where most of the lighting action should be. A foreground that is darker than the rest of the scene will enhance the depth and interest of the scene.

MATCH THE TIME AND THE LIGHT

Keep in mind the time of day you are lighting for and adjust your lights appropriately. Set color and angle to reflect the sun's position. Sky lights and Infinite lights work best for outdoor scenes. For mornings, use a cool color and set the light low and angled up to represent the sun coming over the horizon. Conversely, for late afternoon and dusk, use warmer colors and angle the light down. The lower the light, the longer the shadows and the later in the day it will seem. Morning light should be softer than afternoon light, but midafternoon light is fairly sharp and hard. Because there is no direct sunlight on overcast days, there should be no (or just faint) shadows.

Moonlight can usually be created with one Infinite light set to a low intensity and a bluish tone. The angle should be mid to low and the shadows should be hard. In areas that are brightly lit at night, the shadows may be softened somewhat by many conflicting light sources. Remember, we lose color vision in low light and thus most night scenes should be fairly black and white. If you can see a lot of color in your night scene, then your light may be too bright, or the ambient level on your textures is set too high. If the moon is visible in the scene, be sure to set up the light so that shadows don't conflict with the moon's position.

INDOOR LIGHTING TIPS

Lighting indoors is harder to set up and takes more work. Using practical lights as the main light sources in the scene is usually not practical. A lamp in your own bedroom may cast enough light, but it probably won't work so well in trueSpace. The lighting you choose does not necessarily have to be ultrarealistic; that is, it does not have to correspond exactly to the light sources evident in the scene. In fact, it usually never does. The lights in trueSpace are modeled after the real world but don't behave like real-world lights and thus a certain amount of faking of light sources is needed.

Most indoor scenes require a degree of soft light and shadows. This depends on the overall brightness of the scene and the number of light sources. The more lights there are interacting in the real world (and thus the more ambient light there is), the softer the shadows and light are. This same principle should apply when setting up your lights in the 3D world. Low-light and night scenes will usually have harder shadows. The same scene during daylight or brightly lit should be softer and the shadows less harsh. You might find that you have to depart from three-point lighting to achieve the desired effect. Not every scene will need to be backlit or require a filler light. Conversely, you may require extra fill lights or even two key lights to get the right effect. There are no hard and fast rules.

IN THE MOOD

It should be clear in your mind what the intended mood of the scene is, and the lighting should reflect this. Brightly lit scenes reflect a happy or lighthearted attitude. Darker scenes tend to be more depressing or sinister. Long shadows suggest mystery and suspense. Odd color combinations seem surreal and dreamlike. More traditional color combinations will add to the realism of your scene. High contrast between the tones in the image will make the viewer "edgy," whereas soft contrast is calming. Use negative lights and Spotlights to increase the effect.

DON'T OVERDO IT

After you have spent so much time modeling your objects and getting their textures just right, you might be tempted to overlight your scene—don't. Just because you put extra effort into that object doesn't mean that it necessarily needs to be lit up. Try to remember what you want the visual impact of the scene to be and light appropriately. Placing lights all over to highlight this and that is distracting and detracts from the whole scene. Conversely, if there is some particular detail that needs to be seen, then highlight it. Just try to remember what the central focus of the scene is.

SUMMARY

Lighting can easily be the most tedious and trying part of scene creation. It can also take the longest. When the lighting is just right, it will be obvious. When it is all wrong, it will be just as obvious. Getting it right takes patience and a lot of test renders. Spend time thinking about lighting. Observe the interplay of light, color, and form in the real world and apply it to your scene. Experiment with different lights, colors, and setups. Dig deep into your scene and pull every last emotion out of it. Put the extra effort into lighting, and you won't regret it. Your scene will look great.

CHAPTER 13

ATMOSPHERIC EFFECTS AND ADVANCED LIGHTING

by Oliver Zeller

Lightning strikes in the distance, a low rumble echoing through the neon-lit city streets. A lone, shivering figure obscured by steam rising from a manhole, slowly crosses a street. The figure pauses, captured in a stream of visible light, and disappears into a back alley.

Imagine this scene lacking atmospheric effects such as the lightning, neon and visible light, and steam. The use of atmospheric effects and advanced lighting can greatly infuse an image or animation with mood, atmosphere, and emotion. Furthermore, they aid in developing a story and adding symbolic elements, a lightning strike for example, highlighting a sense of impending doom. Perhaps the most common use of atmospheric effects and advanced lighting is to add dynamic flair and realism to images and animations, such as sparks from broken, dangling wires to water ripples from raindrops.

Lighting often serves the same purpose as atmospheric effects. For the purposes of this chapter, "advanced lighting" encompasses those lights that feature a vast array of options and are aftereffects of standard lighting. For example, mist, fog, and dust can make light appear visible. Lens flares, which occur in reality when light shines directly into a camera lens, can be used to create simple effects, such as warp effects, in your animations.

This chapter examines a small corner of the diverse realm of atmospheric effects. I'll focus on the techniques that can be used to implement atmospheric effects and advanced lighting in your scene, and each method is illustrated with tutorials or examples. From there, the only limit is your imagination.

Specifically, this chapter will cover

- The power of particle systems
- The magic Photoshop filters produce
- The world of compositing effects
- Generating lightning and liquid geometry
- How to use shaders and alpha channels for atmospheric effects
- Fog
- Volumetric lighting and how to fake volumetric lights
- Lens flares and glows

CREATING PARTICLE EFFECTS

Particle systems enable you to control the behavior of a vast number of tiny objects. This makes particles ideal for creating a great range of atmospheric effects, such as steam, smoke, bubbles, debris, twisters, and more.

Particles are a popular method of creating atmospheric and special effects in Hollywood films. Digital Domain used particles for the smoke coming from Titanic's smokestacks in James Cameron's film. The breathtaking Oort Cloud and other astronomical features in the opening sequence of *Contact* come to life with particle animation. Weekly television series, such as *Star Trek: Voyager* (the opening solar flare and gas cloud were done by Santa Barbara Studio), *Buffy: The Vampire Slayer*, *Millennium*, and *Earth: Final Conflict* also use particle effects.

While trueSpace does not natively feature particles, several particle plug-ins are available. The most feature-rich of these plug-ins is Primitive Itch's brilliant Primal Particles 1.5, which we'll be using in this section. You'll find the demo in the plug-ins directory on the accompanying CD. To set it up, install Primal Particles, click on the trueSpace eXtensions icon, select an open space in the eXtensions panel, navigate to the directory where you installed Primal Particles, and double-click.

Luckily, the vast amount of options in Primal Particles is supplemented with a well-organized and compact interface (see Figure 13.1), which we'll unveil as we progress through the next tutorials.

FIGURE 13.1 *The Primal Particles Interface.*

SMOKE TRAILS

Particles can be used effectively to simulate realistic smoke trails from aircraft, car exhaust, missiles, and rockets. A key element to a smoke trail is a particle leader, a small animated object where the particles are generated from and follow.

1. Start a new scene and with Primal Particles open, click on all the control groups, such as Particles, Flow, Effects, and so on, to bring up the various options.

TIP

Altering the color of the particles allows you to simulate a variety of atmospheric effects. White semitransparent particles can be used to simulate steam, for example. Particles with orange, red, white, and yellow shades can create fire effects.

2. In the Scene Render Options panel, change the background color to 100% white. The white color will be used for transparency during the compositing process later. Using white separates the background from the particles that will be black to more closely resemble thick smoke.

3. Create a circle by right-clicking on the Regular Polygon tool and set the regular polygon number of sides to 12. Draw a small circle in the Perspective view, approximately 0.35 meter in length. This circle will become the particle type.

4. Open a small Front view and rotate the circle on the x-axis to 90 degrees.

5. Copy the circle and move the copy to the left in the Left view. This new object will be the particle leader. You can use other objects as the particle leader, such as an entire rocket, or use the circle as a more specific particle leader on an object by attaching it to a larger object, such as the rocket. See Figure 13.2.

6. Pick the copied circle, the particle leader, and set the frame number to 60 in trueSpace's Animation Controls group. Verify that Auto Record is on by right-clicking on the Record key. Then move the circle a fair distance—10 meters should be sufficient—and click on the Return to Start icon.

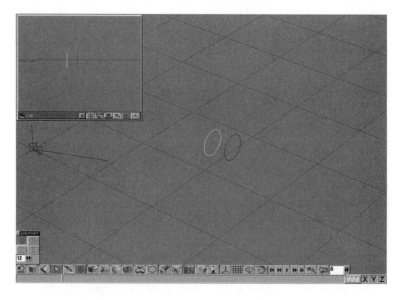

FIGURE 13.2 *Our particle leader is all set and ready to go.*

7. With the original circle selected, click the Selected Object button in the Kind subgroup of the Particles control group in Primal Particles.

8. Also in the Particles control group, keep Count at 100, and set the size of the particles to 0.2. Because we want the particles to stay the same size in this tutorial, keep the Jitter at 0%.

9. The highest density of smoke should be at the beginning of the smoke trail. The smoke trail should be long, but not too long, with a clearly visible falloff. We can control this falloff by setting the rate of particle generation. Set the Rate option under the Flow control group to Stream.

10. Keep the defaults of 100 frames for Lifespan and Lives. For the smoke trail, the Lifespan of a particle needs to stay above the animation frame count, which will be 60 frames.

11. Verify that the Power feature, which handles the speed and strength of the particles' motion, is at 100%. No randomness is required, so Power Jitter should equal 0%.

12. At the end of the Flow control group, three rows of knobs are present. The top row handles the angle of the particles spraying from the generation point, the particle leader in this case. Set all the knobs on the first row to Average.

13. The second row determines the density of particles along each axis. The x-axis should have Average density. Set the density knobs for the y- and z-axes to Mist.

14. The last row of knobs controls the direction of the particle spray. Set the x-axis to +, the y- and z-axes to +/− (see Figure 13.3).

15. Now onto the Effects control group: Set the first function, Rotation, to Spin. Any higher degree of rotation and the smoke might look too fake.

16. Under the Gravitation/Wind submenu, turn the X, Y, and Z Gravitation knobs off. In the Expansion submenu, toggle off the Expand/Contract box.

TIP

The circle is ideal for many particle effects including steam, smoke, and flames because its polygon count isn't as large as a primitive's. With the amount of particles being generated, keeping track of the polygon count is important to maintain efficient particle generation and rendering; otherwise, a scene with several thousand particles can become extremely difficult to manage.

A circle also has an organic shape, necessary for convincing atmospheric effects. Using polygons with fewer than ten sides may affect the quality of the atmospheric effect, depending on the distance the effect is from the camera.

Don't discount the use of planes or triangles for the particles. If the atmospheric effect is in the background, for example, higher detailed particles may unnecessarily slow scene interaction and rendering. Other objects, such as cylinders, are great for weapons' tracers, and spheres make good bubbles.

FIGURE 13.3   *These are the settings you should have under the Particles and Flow control groups.*

17. Pick the copied circle if it isn't already selected. In the Leader submenu, which is part of the Interactors control group, click the Selected button to make your animated circle the particle leader. Retain the default settings of all other options in the Interactors control group.

18. Type 60 in the Frames field, located within the Recording control group.

19. To finish it off, click the Create Particles button (the top icon on the left side of the Primal Particles interface) to create the particles.

20. To see the results, hit the Show Preview Animation button and there you go (see Figure 13.4). Click on the Build TS Animation icon to generate the particles permanently into the scene if you own the full version of Primal Particles.

TIP

You can save your particle setup and load it later by using the last two icons to the left of the Primal Particles interface.

The particle smoke trail can also be found on the CD under /scenes/particles/psmoke.scn. Unfortunately, trueSpace4 and Primal Particles don't automatically handle post-processing of particles to make them appear vaporous. However, we can replicate the vaporous appearance of smoke you'll need by applying a Gaussian

Blur filter. We'll cover this later in the "Enhancing Effects with Photoshop Filters" section of the chapter.

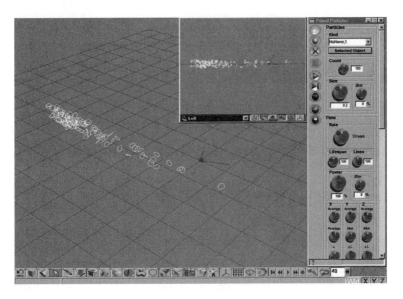

FIGURE 13.4   *The generated particle smoke trail without a vaporous appearance.*

Whenever animating particle effects, take time to study the realistic source of the atmospheric effect and take into consideration external effects such as wind. Observing the objects and browsing through photographs and footage are all good ways to aid you in creating convincing smoke and other atmospheric effects.

BUBBLES

No underwater scene would be complete without bubbles. Or perhaps you have a scene containing a glass filled to the brim with alcohol or some carbonated soft drink.

The next tutorial covers random bubbles floating from bottom to top and provides a glimpse of the power particle emitters possess. By using a particle emitter, particles will be generated from an object's vertices, often a large surface area, rather than the position of the first particle. In addition, we will investigate the useful Ceiling option where particles can interact with an invisible ceiling, rebounding off it, sticking to it, and more.

1. Create a new scene and open Primal Particles.

TIP

A common problem is to have the particles generating in the same spot without moving outward, while everything looks fine in Primal Particles. If this happens to you, check the measurement units of the particle object and the particle emitter or leader. Check that the object's measurement units are equal to or greater than the world measurement units in the Object Info panel, accessible by right-clicking on the Object tool. Generally, it's best to keep the world and object measurement units set to meters.

2. First off, we need to create a particle emitter. Make a new plane and scale it larger into a rectangular shape around 8×5 meters.

3. Quad divide the plane two times. Quad division is often necessary when using a particle emitter because particles are generated from the vertices of an object (see Figure 13.5).

4. With the plane still selected, in Primal Particles, click on the Selected button in the Emitter section of the Interactors control group.

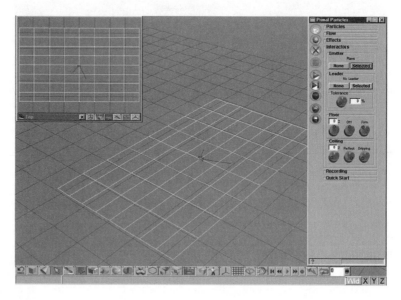

FIGURE 13.5 *Our particle emitter, quad divided to allow more bubbles to generate from its surface.*

5. Time to make those bubbles. In the Particles control group, select Sphere from the Kind drop-down list.

6. Because we want a fair amount of bubbles, increase the Particle Count to 500. Beware this many particles can bog down your system, though it shouldn't be a problem on most Pentium systems.

7. The bubbles should be fairly small—lower Size to 0.02.

8. The bubbles should be generated slowly. Change Rate to Dribble in the Flow control group.

9. Because we don't want the particles to return to the start position, keep the Lifespan and Lives at the default of 100. If you increase the animation time

to more than a 100 frames when experimenting later, remember to raise Lifespan so it's greater than Primal Particles Frame Count.

10. Set the power of the particle flow to 80% with no jitter.

11. We want the bubbles to rise to the "surface" at a fair speed without spraying out at an angle. To accomplish this, the X, Y, and Z Spray Angle knobs (top row in the Flow control group) should be set at Off, Off, and Weak, respectively.

12. Let's make the density of the bubbles random by turning the second row of knobs to Mist on all three axes.

13. To make the bubbles multidirectional on the x- and y-axes, turn the last row of knobs to +/−. We only want the particles rising, so rotate the Z knob to + so the particles move to the top.

14. Tiny bubbles don't appear to rotate to the human eye; turn Rotation off in the Effects group.

15. Add some buoyancy by turning the Gravitation/Wind to Weak and + on the z-axis. The x- and y-axes should be off.

16. Toggle the Expand/Contract box off to ensure the particle size stays constant.

17. Eventually, the bubbles have to rise to the surface. You can combine this with foam that could even be created with particle bubbles, but a very large amount would be required. For the bubbles to stop at the surface, we need a *ceiling* (see Figure 13.6). In the Interactors group, change the Ceiling Height to 6. The ceiling's action should be Reflect. Set it by turning the first knob under the Ceiling subgroup. The third knob controls the elasticity; set it to Gripping so the bubbles stay at the top of the liquid's surface.

18. We'll keep this bubble animation short. Type 60 in Frames located in Primal Particle's Recording group.

19. Create the particles and preview the animation, and there you have it, bubbles galore.

NOTE

In a final scene of decent scope, due to the small size of bubbles, at least several thousand bubbles may be necessary. In one of the 12 shots ILM handled for *Titanic*, millions of bubbles were generated to surround the sinking ship.

Bubbles look best when painted with a semitransparent, refractive shader; however, beware of the slowdown this may cause if you have several thousand particles. You can also change the background to blue to help bring out the bubbles more.

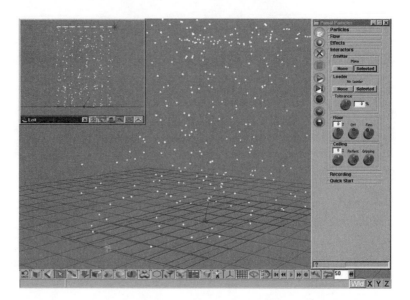

FIGURE 13.6   *Note the bubbles clumped together at the top; this is due to the ceiling option we set.*

FIGURE 13.7   *A rendered frame from the bubble sequence.*

You'll find the complete scene in scenes/particles/bubbles.scn, on the book's CD (see Figure 13.7). Unlike smoke, steam, toxic gases, and other vaporous effects, a Gaussian Blur isn't as necessary. Still, applied with subtlety, it can help to heighten the bubbles' realism.

EXPLODING DEBRIS

One of the great features of Primal Particles is its Decompose Object tool, which enables you to shatter and explode objects. The Decompose Object tool is perfect for creating the small debris that is a byproduct of many atmospheric effects. For example, small debris flies off an object hit by lightning or gets formed by an object that is torn apart and thrown into the air by a tornado. To demonstrate, we'll try the tool on a sphere in the next tutorial.

1. Start a new scene and create a sphere that is 2×2×2 meters. See Figure 13.8.

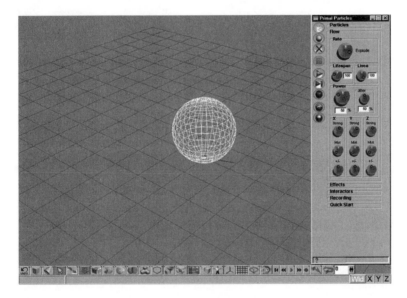

FIGURE 13.8   *The sphere all set to be blown up with the Flow settings in the Primal Particles interface.*

2. With Primal Particles open, click the Selected Object button to pick the sphere as the particle kind.

3. Change the Flow Rate to Explode.

4. Give some variance to the particle explosion by shifting the Power knob to 50% and the Power Jitter value to 50%.

5. To better represent an explosion, change the X, Y, and Z Angle knobs to Strong.

6. The particles need to explode evenly without any distinct shape. To accomplish this, set X, Y, and Z Density to Mist.

7. Change the X, Y, and Z Direction knobs to +/–.

8. The particle pieces should rotate a bit. In the Effects group, move the Rotation knob to Twirl.

9. Verify that the remaining options are off, including Gravitation/Wind, Expansion, and Interactors.

10. Limit the animation to two seconds by setting Frames to 60 in the Recording group.

11. Instead of clicking on the Create Particles button, click on the icon below it, the Decompose Object button (see Figure 13.9).

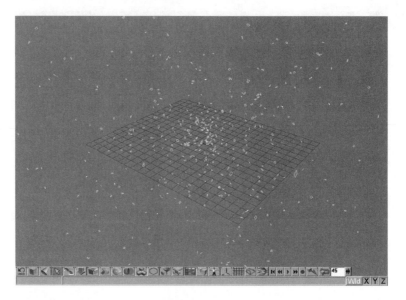

FIGURE 13.9   *After everything's set, hit Decompose Object, and the sphere will explode.*

TIP

The Decompose Object tool works by separating the faces of an object. Knowing this allows you to specifically control how an object breaks up. For example, you could use trueSpace4's point editing tools, such as Add Vertex or Polygon Draw, to create the shape of the broken pieces.

Check out the preview: You have small exploding debris. You may want to make the sphere smaller so the primitive shape isn't as noticeable.

Primal Particles decompose object tool can be very powerful. Constraining the XY flow angle and tweaking some other settings can get you a layer of streaming particles, which with some post-processing using Photoshop filters, can be made to appear like a layer of fire around a meteorite.

ENHANCING EFFECTS WITH PHOTOSHOP FILTERS

Some effects are best achieved in the post-production phase after a still image or frame of an animation has been rendered. Adobe Photoshop-compatible filters are popular and highly effective for adding post-production effects. Filters enable you to do everything from adding glowing highlights to applying "film clutter" to give your animation an aged, film appearance.

Photoshop-compatible filters can be applied to your rendered trueSpace image in several image-editing programs apart from Photoshop, including Corel Photopaint and JASC Paint Shop Pro (the latter is on the CD). Some of these filters also work in video and animation-editing programs, such as Adobe Premiere and IMSI Software's Lumiere. Unfortunately, unlike versions 2 and 3, trueSpace4 cannot directly use Photoshop filters (.8bf files), although direct filter support may appear in a later upgrade.

Free filters and demo versions of filters that are useful for applying over rendered trueSpace scenes can be found in the filters directory of the CD that comes with the book. To use them, copy these filters into a directory on your hard drive—for example, C:\tS\2dplugins. Next, open Photoshop and go to the File> Preferences>Plug-Ins & Scratch Disks. Click on the Choose button, navigate to the directory where you installed the filters, and click OK. Click OK again, exit Photoshop, and reload. The filters will now be available from the Filters menu when you open a new or existing image.

The number of Photoshop-compatible filters available is truly staggering. For the filter enthusiast, you can even create filters with Filter Factory, which comes with the Photoshop 4 and 5 CD. Commercial filter collections that I highly recommend for creating atmospheric effects are Kai's Power Tools (KPT) 3.0 from Metacreations and Positron's Genesis VFX. Genesis VFX is geared entirely to creating custom effects, such as smoke, liquids, glows, lens flares, fire, clouds, and more. There is also a possibility that a native trueSpace4 version of Genesis VFX will be released in the near future.

Photoshop filters can be a valuable tool to create atmospheric effects that simply aren't possible in trueSpace without them. We will explore the use of three popular filters:

- Gaussian Blur (native to most image-editing programs)
- Glow 'n Sparkle (Axion)
- Flare Effects and tSX (Axion)

GAUSSIAN BLUR

A Blur filter averages the pixels between defined lines in an image and shaded areas, creating a smooth transition. A Gaussian Blur filter handles this more specifically and visually produces a hazy effect, sometimes with a subtle glow. In simpler terms, it produces a defocusing effect. Use this filter on particles and other objects to give them a vaporous appearance.

NOTE

If you don't already own Adobe Photoshop, there's a demo version of Photoshop 4 in the /photoshp directory on the CD. Double-click on the ps4try.exe file. Then read the readme.wri file for further installation instructions. You can also follow the rest of the tutorials in this chapter by using Corel Photopaint, JASC's Paint Shop Pro, and other image-editing programs aside from Photoshop. It may be a little more difficult with those programs, though, because they possibly lack some of the tools presented or the tools are located in different areas of the program.

Because Primal Particles does not automatically apply a vaporous appearance to particles, we must use the Gaussian Blur filter to turn particles into realistic steam, smoke, flames, and other vaporous effects. The process takes two basic steps: Blur the rendered particles in Photoshop or another image-editing program and composite the particle layer with a rendered image. We'll get to compositing later in the chapter.

Even if filter support returns in trueSpace4.x, applying the Gaussian Blur filter over particles in trueSpace has its disadvantages, despite the application taking less time. Compositing allows a higher degree of control when adding a Gaussian Blur. Furthermore, except for one filter, getting the desired gaseous look will affect an entire scene, rather than the specific group of particles. The one filter that works on specific particle groups and objects is the cool Blur 'n Feather from Brendan Hack. You'll find this free filter in the book's CD in the filter directory.

ADDING REALISM TO PARTICLE SMOKE

In this tutorial, we'll blur the particles you made in the smoke trails tutorial. We'll apply the Gaussian Blur filter in Photoshop 4.

1. Open Photoshop 4.

2. Load the rendered image, smoke.jpg, in the /smoke directory on the CD or render a frame from the smoke trails tutorial.

3. From Filter menu, select Blur and Gaussian Blur (Filter>Blur>Gaussian Blur).

4. In the Gaussian Blur dialog box, set Radius to 6.0 pixels.

5. With the Preview option, you can see the results before you apply the filter and tweak if necessary. Don't worry about transparency in the atmospheric effect; this will be added when compositing.

6. Hit the OK button or press Enter to apply the filter on the particle image. There's your smoke trail! See Figure 13.10.

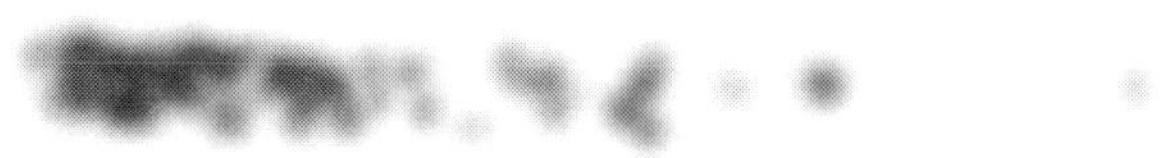

> **TIP**
>
> When you apply a Gaussian Blur filter, the particle's original circular shape shouldn't be visible. However, if you raise the intensity or radius of the Gaussian Blur too high, the particles will become a blurry glob. Spaces between particles, gradation, and falloff of the color density should still be apparent.

FIGURE 13.10   *The particle smoke trail now resembles smoke after you apply the Gaussian Blur filter.*

The Gaussian Blur filter is simple to use, yet very powerful. Use it often to enhance the realism of your atmospheric effects.

AXION'S GLOW 'N SPARKLE FILTER

Briefly take a look at a real light bulb and chances are you'll see a glow. This is especially the case with high transparency bulbs where the filament is visible. Lights in trueSpace, as in most 3D graphics packages, do not automatically glow. There are a variety of methods for creating glow effects.

One is to duplicate a light bulb over the existing one, slightly increase the duplicate's size, and use a semitransparent, high-ambient shader. The results, however, are only mediocre. To achieve a higher-quality glow, we can use a glow filter, such as Steve Yeager's excellent Glow 'n Sparkle filter. As you'll see in the following tutorial, Glow 'n Sparkle truly shines!

NEON LIGHTING

Neon lighting is great for adding atmosphere to a modernistic or futuristic scene, especially dark and seedy locales. The glow exhibited by neon lighting also makes it an excellent candidate for glow filter application.

TIP

Because neon lettering or symbols are tubular, continually sweeping a cylinder is the best way to model neon lighting in trueSpace. The Sweep tool has already been covered in the modeling chapter, but let's do a quick review. To model the letter "u" in tubular form, we can begin by creating a cylinder. Then select the bottom face, sweep, rotate the selected face, sweep again and repeat until the face is at a vertical, 90-degree angle. Continue sweeping and replicate the other side or mirror the object and combine it.

TIP

The secret to the glow filter is in the shader you use. High ambience, the illumination of an object that isn't influenced by light, and a bright color in shader attributes are needed for the glow filter to work at its peak.

1. With a new scene started, load the bar.cob file located in the CD's /filter directory.

2. Bring up the shaders panel. Choose the Plain Color shader and the colors R0, G190, B255.

3. Select Caligari Metal as the Reflectance shader. This shader works well for neon lighting and includes Ambient Glow, Reflectance and Refractive shader attributes, important for neon lights.

4. For the Transparency Shader, pick Plain Transparency and change the Opacity to 0.7. While not necessary for this tutorial, the transparency will be useful for animation purposes if the light is switched off or the neon light is added to a scene.

5. Pick the Smooth option to help add a smooth look to the neon light in case any slightly sharp corners or low polygon count is being used.

Set the Shader Attributes to the following values:

Ambient	=	1
Shine	=	0.4
Rough	=	0.4
Mirror	=	0
Transm.	=	0
Refract	=	1.6

The critical aspect is that the ambient glow has been cranked up to the maximum setting. The other numerical values are rough estimates that will work fine.

7. Paint the object and render an image. It should look like Figure 13.11. (If you're short on time, load barsgn01.jpg in the CD's filters/glow directory instead of rendering the image.)

FIGURE 13.11   *The Neon Bar Sign without the glow filter applied.*

8. Open Photoshop and load the image.

9. Choose Filters>Axion>Glow 'n Sparkle to open the Glow 'n Sparkle filter (see Figure 13.12).

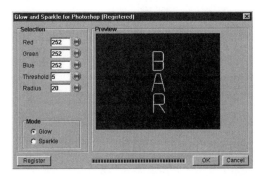

FIGURE 13.12   *The Glow 'n Sparkle interface.*

10. This latest version of the filter now offers direct interactivity. Click on a central piece of the blue neon lettering in the filter's Preview window.

11. Raise the Threshold to 100 and lower the Radius to 8.

12. Check that Glow is toggled on, not Sparkle, although the latter is a feature definitely worth looking into.

13. After you click on OK, your neon sign is complete (see Figure 13.13)! To get rid of the blue bars that appear over the image after applying the glow, you'll need to register the filter.

FIGURE 13.13 *The power of Axion's Glow 'n Sparkle is shown with the complete neon bar sign.*

To bring out the neon lights, dark shadows or a dark background behind them can help greatly. Neon lights are often backed with signs featuring painted lettering matched to the neon lettering or symbols, which can also help bring out the neon element. The physical creation of neon lights and their designs is an art within itself worth looking at.

SPECULAR BLOOM EFFECTS

A *specular bloom effect* is where a specular highlight on an object glows. We sometimes see such an effect when the sunlight brightly hits an area of a car or building, often enhanced by reflective windows or polished metal. The sunlight in that area of the car or building can appear as a hot spot with a visible glow.

This effect can be simulated by using the Glow 'n Sparkle filter and using the same techniques as you did in the neon lighting tutorial. Shading an object with a bright, specular highlight and clicking on that part of the object in Glow 'n Sparkle's preview window will produce a specular bloom.

FLARE EFFECTS FILTER AND tSX

Pointing a camera lens toward a bright light produces lens flares, due to refraction through the lens. Cinematographers often attempt to avoid this effect. Ironically, lens flares have become a popular special effect in 3D CGI. The trend arguably began with Foundation Imaging's use of LightWave's lens flares for visual effects in the television series *Babylon 5*.

Although trueSpace4 has a new lens flare feature, I prefer Steve Yeager's Flare Effects Filter and tSX. Every aspect of a lens flare, even specifying the distance between the flare, rays, and rings, is possible. Options are far more abundant with Flare Effects than in trueSpace4's flares. Unlike trueSpace4, the lens flares in Flare Effects also do not affect every light in the scene. After creating a lens flare in Flare Effects tSX, simply pick a small object in the scene to which to key your lens flare. Flare Effects churns out a lens flare filter, which you can apply in trueSpace2, 3, or an image-editing program, such as Photoshop. However, Axion has released a version of Flare Effects specifically for Photoshop, similar to the Flare Effects trueSpace eXtension. We can now apply a lens flare in Photoshop over any rendered image.

EXPLOSION FLASH

Flare Effects has greater capabilities than merely producing basic lens flares. Warp signatures, the sun, distant explosions, and more are all possible. For example, imagine a massive space battle as viewed from a planet or moon and the gun flash when a weapon is fired. Such a distant flash explosion is fairly easy to implement.

1. Open Photoshop and create a new image with a black background.

2. Activate the Flare Effects filter in the (Filter>Axion>Flare Effects).

3. Click on the Edit button at the bottom left of Flare Effects interface to bring up the Flare Effects Editor (see Figure 13.14).

4. With the Flare Effects Editor, you have complete control over every aspect of your lens flare. Click on the New button to start a new lens flare.

5. In the Element List, you'll see a flare listed. In the large window up top, position the flare around the thick white circle and expand it so it's fairly large but doesn't go beyond the left side of the flare positioning window.

6. This flare is the key of the explosion, so let's change the color to white by clicking on the Color box.

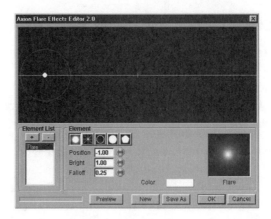

FIGURE 13.14 *The heart of Axion's Flare Effects filter, the Flare Effects Editor. Position the first flare element around the white dot as indicated in this figure.*

7. The flare element should also stand out, so set the Brightness to 1.00 and the Falloff to 0.25.

8. Let's add some yellow color: In the Element List click on the + button to insert another flare element.

9. I centered the flare element closely around the white-filled circle in Flare Effects Editor's interactive window. Choose a yellow color such as R240, G240, B3.

10. Set the second flare element's Brightness to 1.00 and the Falloff to 0.15 to put a yellow rim around the white, helping to create a more believable representation of fire.

11. Insert another element into the Element List box and change the flare element to the rays element by depressing the small button with a rays symbol.

12. Change the color to white to match the first flare element. This ray element will add some visible chaos to better simulate an explosion.

13. Change the element attributes for the Ray to

Brightness = 0.20
Count   = 8
Sharp   = 0.00
Rotation = 180
RNoise   = 0.00
SNoise   = 0.15

RNoise controls radial noise, and SNoise controls the sharp noise.

14. Position this rays element between the smallest and the large flare element, closer to the larger flare element, though.

15. Now for the final element, add a rays element with the following settings:

    Brightness   =   0.10
    Count   =   8
    Sharp   =   0.00
    Rotation   =   360
    RNoise   =   0.00
    SNoise   =   0.10
    Color   =   RGB: 255, 35, 35

    This last element should be slightly bigger than the original flare (see Figure 13.15).

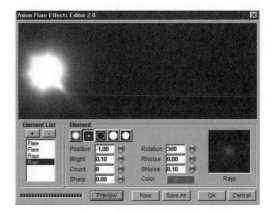

FIGURE 13.15   *Two flare and ray elements each create a convincing explosion flash.*

16. Check out the Preview and tweak if you'd like and save the filter for future use. Hit OK to get back to the main Flare Effects for Photoshop window.

17. Position the lens flare in the preview window, change the size, and so on. Hit OK to process it to your image, and that's all there is to it. The flare file, explos.lns, and the image, flare.jpg, with the flare applied is in the /flare directory on the CD.

While animation for the explosion flash is possible in Flare Effects for Photoshop by changing the settings for each frame, it is somewhat tedious. Luckily, animation capabilities are also included in Flare Effects for trueSpace.

FIGURE 13.16 *The final explosion flash.*

TRUESPACE4'S LENS FLARES AND GLOW

Although trueSpace4's new Lens Flare and Glow tools don't quite have the feature set as Axion's Flare Effects filter, they have their uses. With the first release of trueSpace4, the Lens Flare and Glow tools work on a global level only. If you use them, they're applied to all local lights in the scene. This makes the Lens Flare feature less useful, though Glow can be used effectively in several instances, like a city street at night, for example.

The glow of a car's headlights and the light from street lights on a lonely road is another example where trueSpace's Glow function can come in handy. Considering this scenario, you'd begin to implement this effect by using the circle as the lens shape. Next, get rid of any lens flare type aftereffect that would include the Ghosts and Rays options by setting them to 0. Rays can be turned off quickly by selecting None for Rays Type. Cut the halo down to minimal amounts and toss around some variables in the Intensity and various glow options until you're pleased with the effect. The light color and intensity also affects the glow effect's outcome. As the film *Blade Runner* vividly displayed, clever use of lens flares and glows, along with other atmospheric effects, can enhance any visuals where these effects are fitting.

EFFECTS COMPOSITING

Atmospheric effects, rendered images, live footage, and other elements can be combined by the process known as *compositing*. The majority of computer-generated visual effects shots in films are composited over live-action footage. A classic example of composited atmospheric effects can be seen in *Titanic*. The abundant cold breath from the actors in the final hour of the film was not real because filming took place in large tanks with a relatively warm temperature. Instead, it was computer generated and composited over the footage by VIFX.

For the next tutorial, we'll use Photoshop to layer separately rendered images of particles from trueSpace over rendered scenes. Photoshop is great for compositing various elements over still images with its powerful layering system. Although Photoshop is capable of handling animation composites to some extent, it is ideal for handling still images because it lacks adequate animation support. Programs such as Adobe's After Effects and Discreet Logic's Effect are better suited for this and are worth looking into. These are compositing programs with powerful layering and transparency tools with complete animation capability. These programs also offer animated special effects that can be applied for animation or footage clips. For example, Flat Earth Productions uses After Effects to composite their 3D visual effects over live action footage in the television series, *Hercules* and *Xena*. Many animation editing packages including Premiere and Lumiere also offer basic compositing tools; however, their tools are geared toward cutting and organizing 3D-rendered or live-action shots.

APPLYING A PARTICLE SMOKE TRAIL TO A RENDERED IMAGE

For this example, we'll combine a test rendering of the zeppelin model I've been working on and a frame from a particle smoke trail, similar to the one we made earlier. This will create the illusion of the control car's propeller engine straining and sputtering smoke. You'll find two images (zeptest.jpg and engsmoke.jpg) rendered in the CD's /composite directory. Compositing is necessary because the Gaussian Blur filter would also affect the entire scene. Try to apply it to the smoke, and it would also blur the zeppelin.

While you're creating a scene, it's often best to have the particles in the scene for setting up the effect in relation to the rest of the scene. Render the main image without the particles, though. To render the particle frames, hide all the other objects present in the scene. This can be accomplished quickly with the useful showmehideu plug-in, in Windmill Fraser Multimedia's plug-in suite, CoolPowers 2. This plug-in will hide all objects in the scene, except for the currently selected object. Once this is done, change the background color to a color suitable for the type of compositing you'll be handling. In the case of the smoke, white will work the best.

1. Time to composite. Open Photoshop 4 and load both images. See Figures 13.17 and 13.18.

FIGURE 13.17   *The image of a WWI zeppelin.*

FIGURE 13.18   *The particle smoke for compositing over the zeppelin image.*

2. Pick engsmoke.jpg and Select All (Ctrl+A). Now copy the selection (Ctrl+C) and select the zeppelin image.

3. Paste (Ctrl+V) the copied selection over the zeppelin image.

4. Choose Windows>Show Layers.

5. Highlight layer 1, which contains the smoke trail. Click on the drop-down box next to the Opacity slider and pick the Multiply option. The Multiply mode multiplies the color in the two layers. Multiplying black with any color produces black, ideal for the thick smoke. Multiplying white, the background color of the smoke layer, with any color leaves that color unchanged, meaning white becomes transparent.

That's it, the smoke now appears to be puffing out the back of the control car hanging under the zeppelin, as shown in Figure 13.19.

Compositing effects is a rewarding area worth adventuring into on your own. Inserting atmospheric effects partially covered by a foreground piece in the rendering, reflection of smoke off a table surface, and shadows from objects can all be handled via compositing.

FIGURE 13.19 *The final image of the zeppelin with the smoke puffing from the end of the control gondola.*

To get you started in this field, I'll give you the basic procedure on how to add a smoke puff to a photograph of a person smoking over a table, which reflects this smoke puff. Keep in mind that this is an example illustrating the basic techniques and not a step-by-step tutorial. There are no files provided on the CD to accompany this example.

1. To begin, a photograph of a person holding a cigarette, but without much visible smoke is required. Load this photo as a background image in trueSpace as a reference while you work.

2. Create an irregular polygon that fits over the reflective area of the table in the photograph. Paint this polygon a black reflective material. The polygon will act as the table's surface, which the particle smoke can reflect off.

3. Add the particle smoke puff and paint it with a white or slightly gray matte shader to separate it from the background. Also change the background photo image to a complete black background color. Verify that the outer edges of the black reflective polygon are not noticeable against the black background by checking the materials; otherwise, this will appear in the photo when you go to composite. In addition, take note that the lighting of the scene should match the lighting in the photograph.

4. Render the image, and use a Gaussian Blur on the rendered image to make the smoke appear realistic and heighten the realism of the reflection. Layer it over the photograph.

TIP

In the compositing tutorials and examples, white and black background colors were used because they were the opposite colors of the atmospheric effect. However, other colors can be more suitable and should be considered. In the television/film industry, actors are often shot against blue or green screens and a different background is inserted afterward via other methods, including CG visual effects. Blue and green colors stand out well and don't blend in with people's skin and clothes that often. Clothes and objects against a blue screen cannot contain blue or other similar colors, such as purple. If they're shot against a green screen, green color cannot be used, or these colors will be transparent.

You now have a 3D animated puff of smoke in a photograph, which reflects off the table. Shadows aren't necessary for this atmospheric effect, but adding them can be done by using a white background and white matte painted polygon.

Compositing effects is a rewarding area worth adventuring into on your own.

OBJECT GENERATION FOR ATMOSPHERIC EFFECTS

On occasion, producing convincing atmospheric effects—especially atmospheric effects that are required to interact directly with objects, such as electrical bolts striking nearby houses or trees—requires adding 3D geometry to your scene. Although other 2D techniques can be implemented—using procedural texture to create lightning, for example—the end result probably won't be convincing. Imagine a cataclysmic scene in which lightning bolts erupt throughout the locale, striking and damaging objects, windows get blown out, and sparks fly. Now consider having to use filters, procedural textures, or alpha maps of lightning (covered later in this chapter), and aligning all these bolts with objects so the entire scene looks realistic. This tedious process could be achieved quickly if the lightning bolts were actual 3D objects that could be combined with other geometry.

Generating atmospheric effects using objects has become an easier process in trueSpace4 with the introduction of a slew of plug-ins aimed at this area that make both modeling and, particularly, animation faster and easier. Electrical and lightning bolt creation is one of those atmospheric effects made easier by the use of plug-ins.

LIGHTNING BOLTS WITH VERTILECTRIC

An easy way to create lightning is with Blevin's VertiLectric plug-in. Take a peek in the plug-ins/Vertilectric directory on the CD. A limited 30-day fully functional version of VertiLectric is contained in vlectric.zip. Copy the file to a new directory in your trueSpace tSX folder, unzip it, and install the plug-in in the eXtensions panel in trueSpace. When you first use VertiLectric, the plug-in will request a key. You'll find the key information located in key.txt, included in the vlectric.zip file.

For this tutorial, we'll create some simple cloud-to-ground or ground-to-cloud lightning where lightning sparks create several branches.

1. With trueSpace fired up, create a new scene, open a Front view and the VertiLectric plug-in (see Figure 13.20).

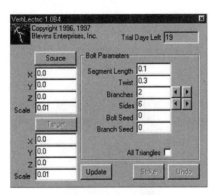

FIGURE 13.20   *The VertiLectric interface with the settings for the lightning bolt we'll generate.*

2. The default Scale setting for the source and target will create a fat bolt that isn't suitable for this tutorial. Change the Source Scale and Target Scale values to 0.01.

3. You'll notice that it's possible to enter the source and target positions of the bolt numerically in VertiLectric. However, you'll find it easier to handle the positioning interactively. Rotate the Perspective view so it more closely matches the Front view.

4. Click on the Source icon, and a small sphere will appear. Position this toward the lower portion of the Front view.

5. Click the Target icon and move it to the upper area of the Front view. Also shift it slightly left or right of the source sphere for a more realistic, chaotic lightning effect.

6. Leave the Segment Length at 0.1. In general, you'll find it best to keep the Segment Length below 0.4.

7. Keep the Twist default number at 0.3. Twist determines how twisted the bolt will become. A value of 1.0 produces zany bolts that will take over a minute to generate on most systems.

8. Set the Branches to 2 by either typing it in or using the arrow buttons next to the corresponding field in VertiLectric. You'll notice four branches are created. The two main branches each have an additional branch. Each main branch has one fewer branch than the branch number you specify. Specifying four branches, for example, gives you four main branches, each with three offshoot branches.

9. Click the Strike button to generate the bolt (see Figure 13.21). If the branches don't look good, you can click Undo and Strike again until the branches are in a position that's to your liking. Take note that when you undo, the bolt won't disappear in the view you're working in until you hit the Strike button again.

FIGURE 13.21   *The bolt generated by VertiLectric.*

10. Retain the Sides at 6. If you move the camera closer, you might want to increase the sides to get a smoother look.

If you decide to create more bolts, you can use the Bolt Seed and Branch Seed functions. By reusing a seed number, source, and target, you can replicate bolts exactly.

So, there you have it—the geometry of a lightning bolt. Follow the same shader application and Glow filter advice as described in the neon lighting tutorial earlier in this chapter and your lightning bolt is complete. Play around with VertiLectric, and you'll find that you can create more than just electrical bolts and lightning, such as tree trunks and branches that could be struck by the lightning.

LIGHTNING, TWISTERS, AND OTHER EFFECTS WITH 3D ENERGY

Often you'll find multiple tools that enable you to create the same atmospheric effect. 3D Energy by Alain Bellon is similar to VertiLectric because at its core it generates lightning bolts. While arguably slightly more difficult to use than VertiLectric, this is easily offset by the plug-in's advantages. It provides greater control and more possibilities for object generation, plus built-in glow and star highlight post-processing effects.

TIP

Bolts are made of cylinders so the lower the segment length and the higher the number of the sides, the more organic a look you will attain. Of course, this means VertiLectric will use more memory and take longer to create bolts due to the larger amount of polygons it needs to generate.

You'll find a special limited demo version of 3D Energy, available only with this book, in the CD's /3denergy directory. Here's how to use it:

1. Create a new scene in trueSpace and open the 3D Energy plug-in.

2. Make two spheres and scale them down to 0.075 meter for x, y, and z. Shift one sphere so it's above the other sphere by at least four meters (see Figure 13.22). These will serve as the start and end of the lightning and can be deleted once the lightning bolt has been generated.

3. Go to the Lightning section of the plug-in (see Figure 13.23). Change the Geometry options to the following settings and hit Enter after entering every numerical value in the numerical input fields.

   Faces   =   10
   Elements   =   45
   Top Size   =   0.0300
   End Size   =   0.0100

   Elements is the key to your lightning bolt because the number entered represents the amount of cylindrical floors, the same as VertiLectric's segments.

4. Let's add a dynamic shape to the lightning in the Dynamics part of 3D Energy. Use these settings to control the amount of oscillations, the oscillation noise, and the strength of the oscillations:

   Cycles   =   1.50
   Wiggle   =   9.00
   Strength   =   10.00
   XYZ   =   Active

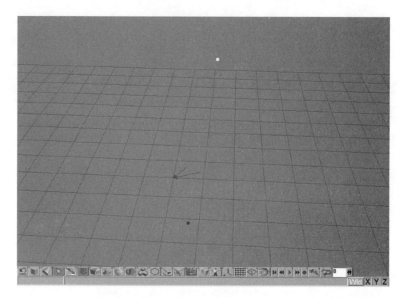

Figure 13.22 *The two spheres that serve as the start and end points for the lightning bolt.*

Figure 13.23 *The Lightning section of 3D Energy's interface.*

5. Select the top sphere and click the Select Start button. Highlight the lower sphere and click on the Select End button. Finish it with a click on Make Arc.

6. Paint the bolt with a white color, Constant Reflectance shader.

7. Zoom into your lightning bolt so the bolt tips aren't visible and render your image to file with no antialiasing.

In case you're wondering how to handle lightning branches, the branch aspect of the plug-in is missing in this limited version. Lightning bolts wouldn't be complete without that glow, but unlike

VertiLectric, we don't need to use an external tool like the Glow 'n Sparkle filter to handle glow. Here's how to add glow within 3D Energy:

1. Click on the ElectroGlow button (see Figure 13.24).

FIGURE 13.24   *We can apply the lightning glow directly in 3D Energy's ElectroGlow section.*

2. Load the image you rendered of the lightning bolt or load bolt01.jpg from the /3denergy directory on the CD.

3. In the ElectroGlow preview window, click and hold on the double bars covering the preview and drag the Preview window out of the plug-in boundaries. The full image appears.

4. Click and drag on the bolt in the image to grab the color for the Color Picked option.

5. Set the Glow color to light blue (R183, G183, B255).

6. Change Start/End Size to 10 and Opacity to 100.

7. Electric Style should have both Min Size values set to 8 and Max Size both set to 14. Intensity Delta equals 0.50.

8. Keep the Tol(erance) setting at the default of 5. If the glow doesn't appear or isn't powerful enough, increase the Tol(erance) setting.

9. Click on ElectroGlow and once the effect has been generated, save the image (see Figure 13.25).

Glow animation and StarLites are available in the full version. 3D Energy can produce intriguing results, including nonlightning objects, such as tornadoes or magical effects in a fantasy scene. If a tornado sounds appealing to you, there's a tutorial covering this in 3D Energy's help file.

FIGURE 13.25   *The lightning bolt generated with 3D Energy.*

WATER EFFECTS PLUG-INS

Plug-ins that aid in the creation of realistic water effects have become extremely powerful and popular tools in other programs. Arete's Digital Nature Tools was used in the creation of digital water in several recent films, including *Titanic, A Devil's Advocate, The Fifth Element,* and *The Truman Show.* LumeOcean, part of the LumeTools collection of plug-ins, was used in the computer game, Riven. Although there are no current plans for these plug-ins to be converted to trueSpace, trueSpace users now have several plug-in options of their own.

Alain Bellon, the man behind ThermoClay and 3D Energy, plans to release a new plug-in, Fluid Reality, that is geared toward realistic water effects creation. Fluid Reality creates animatable waves, water drops, splashes, object impact effects on water, wakes, and more. Creating some of these effects by using trueSpace's deformation and animated texture maps can be an overly complex and unwieldy process, with good results being hard to attain. Using a plug-in like Fluid Reality can help tremendously when trying to create realistic water effects.

Although Fluid Reality is still in development and a preview couldn't be made by press time, this is one plug-in you should consider for water effects. You'll find sample scenes that you can experiment with and preview animations generated by Fluid Reality in the plugins/fluidr directory.

Another plug-in that aids in the creation of water effects, such as waves and ripples, is FCreator from Urban Velkavrh. FCreator produces objects and animated objects based on mathematical formulae and gives you complete control over the formulae. Its capabilities aren't limited to animated wave geometry. Tornadoes, the creation of large water drops, and other atmospheric effects can all be created. The latest version, 3.0, adds an all new interface, making it simpler to implement geometry-based atmospheric effects, among other things. Added functionality in this latest version, include vertex coloring, UV mapping, and definable variables based on the mathematical formulae. While FCreator may appear daunting at first, take some time to learn it. The easiest way to begin is by using the presets and the included wizard, studying the formulae and adapting it to get the results you want. The shareware version of FCreator 3 can be found in the plugins/fcreator path on the book's CD.

USING SHADERS TO CREATE ATMOSPHERIC EFFECTS

Using shaders to create atmospheric effects can produce highly realistic results without the high-speed hits that other techniques, such as particle systems, cause. For example, you could map video footage of an explosion onto a plane or cylinder in trueSpace. In front of a camera, you could add several planes or a single plane with procedural snow or rain shaders to simulate weather. For these effects to come off convincingly, though, care must be taken when applying the effects shaders and integrating them into the scene. Potential problems include the transparency levels and the lighting interaction between the scene and effects-mapped objects, which have a flat 2D appearance in some instances. If the shaders and their application aren't handled properly, the atmospheric effect will stick out like a sore thumb.

PROCEDURALS AND TEXTURE MAPS

The foundation for shader-based atmospheric effects are either procedural materials or texture maps.

As you remember, procedural materials are textures calculated mathematically. The trueSpace4.1 patch enables users to program their own shaders with the C programming language. Even if you don't have programming knowledge, watch the Web for procedurals from your fellow users. With all the new possibilities shaders provide in trueSpace4, plus the capability to animate shaders easily, many atmospheric effects can come to life.

TIP

Unlike texture maps, procedural textures tend to require more processing power. However, texture maps frequently consume large amounts of memory; procedural shaders do not. Further slowdown is caused when there isn't sufficient RAM for all the texture maps, particularly the case with high-resolution textures, and the hard drive's swapfile is constantly used as a substitute to RAM. Always take this into consideration when dealing with shader-based atmospheric effects.

Simply painting your own textures in an image-editing program or using procedural image-generation tools and plug-ins is an excellent method of creating atmospheric effects. Many standalone procedural generation programs, such as DarkTree Textures from Darkling Simulations, can generate texture maps for use in trueSpace. Atmospheric effects, such as cloud backdrops, can be generated with trueSpace plug-ins such as Michael Gallo's Infinity, which creates more convincing clouds than trueSpace4's native cloud shader and also handles infinite ground and skies. Then simply apply the generated texture map to an object in trueSpace. Demos for both plug-ins are included on the CD. Some of these procedural texture engines are more powerful or better geared toward atmospheric effects than trueSpace's own native procedural shaders.

Gradient maps, also known as ramp textures, are good examples of atmospheric effects produced through texture maps. Photoshop, Kai's Power Tools, and many more image tools enable you to create a gradient map, where the color shifts from one color to the next. A gradient map could be applied to a cylinder, with one end shorter than the other, and made semitransparent using trueSpace4's plain transparency to give an afterburner effect on a jet engine, plane, or a spaceship. Transparency is often the key to shaders with atmospheric effects.

USING ALPHA MAPS

Alpha maps, also known as transparency maps, derive their name from the alpha channel an image contains. You can use the alpha channel information for a single color or a specific area of an image as an alpha map, or use the entire image's alpha channel. Great uses of alpha maps are fire and smoke effects, including explosions, shockwaves, sparks, and fireworks. The atmospheric effect can be applied in trueSpace with the background color of the alpha maps becoming transparent. This also means the shape of the object where the alpha map is applied won't be distinguishable, which is important when creating a convincing atmospheric effect.

NOTE

On the PC, the most ideal format for handling alpha channels is the Targa (TGA) file.

There are several great CDs available that contain footage of explosions and other pyrotechnic effects for compositing into your trueSpace scenes. The most popular of these include Visual

Concepts Entertainment's (VCE) Pyromania 1 through 3 and Pyromania Pro, used in professional broadcast work, and ArtBeats's excellent ReelExplosions and ReelFire collections. (Check out Netter Digital's visual effects for *Babylon 5* for examples of what can be done with ReelExplosions and 3D scenes.) These collections cost between $100 to $400, but are well worth it. However, you'll still find some good-quality collections at low costs, like Exodus Multimedia's FireCD and even the occasional free explosion clips from Web sites, such as Dub's trueSpace F/X Page (**http://www.concentric.net/~Eswan/**). To get you started, though, you'll find a few clips on the book's CD in the artbeats/explosion directory.

EXPLOSION ALPHA MAPPING

So that you can customize them, many of these pyrotechnic sequences lack alpha channels but have been prepared so you can add transparency easily. In the past, this meant that adding an explosion sequence to your animation was a two-phase process. First, one would create an alpha channel in Photoshop and apply the alpha map in trueSpace. With the new wrapped mask shader in trueSpace4, this is not necessary because it automatically creates an alpha channel from the image supplied. Let's take a look at how the explosion would be applied in trueSpace4. You'll find an explosion sequence from Artbeats' ReelExplosions (hotf_000.tga–hotf_053.tga) in the /explosions directory on the book's CD. We'll be using a single frame, hotf_014.tga.

FIGURE 13.26 *A frame of the Hot Flash explosion from Artbeats.*

1. Open trueSpace, create a plane, and universally scale it larger.

2. In the Color section of the Shaders panel, get the texture map and pick hotf_014.tga. trueSpace will pick up the color information, but it still needs the transparency information.

3. Pick the Transparency: Wrapped Mask shader and again, load hotf_014.tga. This Targa file lacks an alpha channel; however, trueSpace4 has automatically created an alpha channel from the image and is using it. The image itself remains unaffected, though.

4. Pick Caligari Phong as the Reflectance shader and crank up the Ambient Glow so the alpha map appears bright, more closely resembling an explosion.

5. With the plane highlighted, paint the object, and there's your explosion in trueSpace.

TIP

To have an entire explosion sequence in your trueSpace animation, pick hotf_001.tga in a directory with the rest of the alpha-mapped explosion frames. Toggle the Anim option on in both the Texture Map and Wrapped Mask shaders. Make a keyframe where the explosion sequence finishes and select the last Targa file in the sequence, hotf_053.tga, for both the Texture Map and Wrapped Mask shaders. At the frame where the explosion sequence should finish, use the Paint Over Existing Material tool on the object where the explosion sequence should be mapped on to.

There's plenty to explore with alpha maps. You can use alpha maps of shockwaves, fire, smoke, and much more. Also try applying them on different geometry and use multiple objects, such as multiple planes with explosions, to increase the believability. Tinkering with the shader settings will also open up more possibilities.

FOG

Fog is perhaps the most frequently implemented atmospheric effect in the world of 3D graphics. Nearly everywhere around us a low degree of fog is present, mostly outside, even if it isn't clearly visible. Implementing a low level of fog in your 3D graphics scene can heighten the realism and take away from the sharp and clean look 3D-rendered images sometimes have. When it comes to adding atmosphere and mood, thick fog can greatly enhance these aspects of your scene. A sense of mystery and not knowing what lies beyond dense fog can develop a fantasy world or reveal the progress of a crime at a crime scene or a detective's hunt to solve the crime.

Fog is considerably different in trueSpace4 than in past versions, and it might take a while to grasp and use fog effectively. One of the frequent criticisms of fog in trueSpace versions 1 through 3 was that it wouldn't appear in the reflection of reflective surfaces and the quality of reflective surfaces was greatly diminished. Gladly, this is not a problem in trueSpace4, and ground fog has also been added. To check out the fog options, go to the Scene Render Options panel and right-click the Fog button in Foreground Effects shader.

Regular fog affects other objects and the scene with the fog coloring. The distance of the fog from the view and the amount of fog is set by the Fog's Distance. Even if the fog is far away, it will still have a subtle effect on objects in the foreground. The problem with regular fog in the initial release of trueSpace4 was that the background was not affected. A background image or color would appear in its entirety, making dense fog impossible.

Ground fog is rather powerful and creates a noticeably uneven fog around the floor of the scene and base of objects. The fog becomes more dense as it stretches into the distance, to the point where the fog is entirely opaque, creating background haze. A background image is affected in this case, unlike regular fog. Remember, because the background fog cuts off sharply and is opaque at that cutoff point, it is important to have a background that closely matches the fog color for realism. Enclosing your scene in a room without windows can take away the background haze portion and create some incredible-looking ground fog, great for a some nightclub scenes if it's kept subtle, and replicating smoke seeping into a room and more.

You don't have to restrict yourself to using trueSpace's Fog feature. Using a large amount of tightly packed semitransparent planes placed over an environment to replicate ground fog or placing the texture in front of the camera are a couple of other possibilities. Both these methods would be further enhanced if a cloud or gradient semitransparent shader were used.

A free plug-in from Richard Robinson, Volumetrics Fog tSX, is included on the CD. This plug-in quickly creates fog, even volumetric clouds, by using partially transparent textured planes packed closely together.

VOLUMETRIC LIGHTS

Light shining in an atmosphere with a relatively high amount of dust, mist, or fog can become visible, particularly if the light is a focused beam. This phenomenon is known as *volumetric light*. Volumetric lighting is a popular tool among traditional cinematographers and 3D CGI artists to invoke mood and atmosphere. A great example of the power volumetric lighting can have is the signature shot from *The Exorcist*. Max von Sydow's silhouetted character arrives at the house, a beam of light flooding toward him from an upstairs window. The contrast between the visible light, the silhouetted environment, and Max von Sydow creates an eerie feeling that subtly reveals the film as a whole.

Studying how visible light is used in film (*Blade Runner)* and television (*The X-Files* and *Millennium*) will aid you greatly when implementing volumetric light in your scene. Overuse of volumetric lighting is not good, however, especially with the attraction it tends to garner in an image or animation. Always consider the use of volumetric lighting in your work. Does it enhance the scene's mood and atmosphere? Is its use logical?

Volumetric lights have the tendency to work best in high-contrast scenes as the primary light source surrounded by darkness, heightening the dark, eerie mood of an image. Old architectural structures, such as castles and cathedrals in Europe where fog and mist are common, are ideal locales for using volumetric lighting. This is further supported by the high dust content that we generally envision with an old locale.

TRUESPACE4'S VOLUMETRIC LIGHTS

Although trueSpace4's new Volumetric lighting features might seem difficult to get results from initially, they are actually quite simple once you get the hang of them (see Figure 13.27). You can attain high-quality results (such as this chapter's opening image) fairly quickly. To boost you up the learning curve, let's take a brief look at the volumetric settings before heading into a tutorial (see Figure 13.28).

FIGURE 13.27   *trueSpace4's Volumetric Lighting.*

Several volumetric light settings can be accessed and altered by right-clicking on the Foreground Volumetric shader in trueSpace4's Scene Render Options panel.

The key to any scene with volumetric light is the Fog Density option because it determines the density of particles in the visible light and whether the light will even be visible in a scene. As a result, the value you use for Fog Density varies drastically for each scene and can also be affected by the other volumetric and light settings. Due to this, I highly recommend you set all other volumetric settings to 0 and maintain the default Samples setting of 25. Manipulate the volumetric fog density in the scene until the light becomes visible, and you have the desired look.

The quality and time it takes to render volumetric lights is determined by Samples. The higher the number, the better quality the volumetric light will be, but the slower the rendering will be. The quality of the volumetrics is also affected by the rendering quality (low, medium, high) and the visibility settings (Scanline versus RayCast). The Noise parameters control the noise, or the breakup of volumetrics and visible particle appearance in the volumetric light. This can add some nice detail to the volumetric lights, but the rendering times can become considerably slower, even with low noise settings. The Attenuation options manipulate the fog density of the volumetrics, changing the lightness and darkness of the volumetric light and its shadows at various points, and even affecting the light on nearby objects.

One of the best ways to familiarize yourself with a new tool is to begin tinkering in a basic scene, which we'll do now. Five scenes, volum01.scn to volum05.scn, on the CD's scene/volumetric path display the tutorial at various points.

1. Create a new scene and add a plane. Scale the plane beyond the view and paint it with a dark gray texture.

2. Delete all the current lighting in your scene.

3. Add a spotlight and move it to the top-right corner of the view. Rotate the spotlight so it points toward the center of the view.

4. Set Spotlight Intensity to 1.0, Linear Falloff with distance, toggle on Volumetric, and Raytraced Shadows in the Spotlights Light panel.

5. The Foreground Effects shader in the Scene Render Options panel needs to be changed to Volumetric. Also right-click on the Volumetric button to open the volumetric options.

6. Set Fog Density to 0.1, Samples to 25. Change the rest of the volumetric options to 0.

7. Render the image, and there's the volumetric light (see Figure 13.28).

FIGURE 13.28   *Plain volumetric light.*

8. trueSpace4's volumetric lights produce great shadow streaks. Add a cube on the plane, in the center of the spotlight's field of view, to see this effect. This is one of the advantages to using trueSpace's native volumetric light rather than faking the volumetric light. Replicating shadow streaks can be a difficult and tedious task.

9. Time to add some chaos! Set Noise Amplitude to 0.1 and render the scene.

10. The volumetric light vanished. Not to worry, though—increase Fog Density to 2.0 and rerender. The volumetric light is back with plenty of visible noise (see Figure 13.29).

11. The noise doesn't look realistic, so smooth it out by setting the Noise Scale to 0.5. To compensate for this additional setting, let's raise the Fog Density to 3 to make the volumetric light remain clearly visible. Check out the results in Figure 13.30.

12. Shift the Noise Gain to 1. The output (see Figure 13.31) would fit well in a room with people smoking, though lowering the Fog Density to 2.0 or less would create a more realistic look.

FIGURE 13.29 *Volumetric light with added noise.*

FIGURE 13.30 *The noise has been blended together to form more subtle noise gradations.*

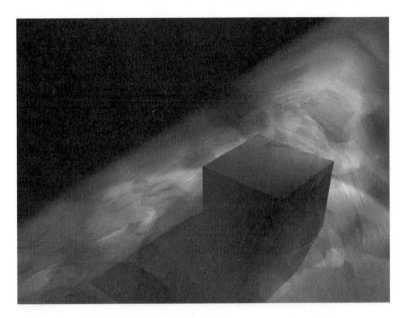

FIGURE 13.31   *Some major turbulence thrown in.*

13. Change the Noise Gain back to 0.0 before continuing.

14. Hike the Surface Attenuation value to 0.2 and render (see Figure 13.32). You'll notice the volumetric light itself hasn't changed; rather, the effect the volumetric light has on the cube has changed. This is great if you'd like the volumetric light primarily to make the fog and dust visible, with the light playing a less significant role in the scene.

15. Some artifacts, random unwanted lines, should have appeared in the volumetric light. To solve this problem, double the Samples to 50 (see Figure 13.33). Render again, though be prepared that this will take longer.

16. Revert the Surface Attenuation to 0.0 and raise the Volume Attenuation to 0.2 so the volumetric light appears dimmer farther away from its source. See Figure 13.34.

FIGURE 13.32 *The light has less effect on the cube in this example where the Surface Attenuation has been raised.*

FIGURE 13.33 *The short, artifact streaks that appeared behind the cube in Figure 13.31 have now vanished with the Samples set at 50, instead of the default of 25.*

FIGURE 13.34 *Increasing the Volume Attenuation causes the volumetric light to become dimmer farther away from its source.*

17. Let's go back and try the Source Attenuation option we skipped. With the noise implemented, it's difficult to get the volumetric light to appear, no matter what adjustments are made. Change the Noise and Volumetric Attenuation back to 0, the Fog Density to 0.1.

18. Set Source Attenuation to 0.2 and render. Although the other volumetric options are difficult to implement, when you use Source Attenuation, the payoff is notable, as shown in Figure 13.35!

Handle volumetric lights a step at a time and implement them early on in your scene to avoid later problems. Otherwise, keep on experimenting and unraveling this powerful new tool in trueSpace.

TIP

Volumetric light does not penetrate 3D objects such as a cube. It will, however, penetrate a plane. This is important to remember if you plan on modeling a window and would like the visible light to flood through. Visibility Determination also determines how well the volumetric light penetrates a plane. If Visibility is set to RayCast, the volumetric light won't penetrate as well as Visibility set to Scanline.

FIGURE 13.35   *While perhaps difficult to see in this figure, the increase in source attenuation has created superb volumetric light falloff.*

FAKING VOLUMETRIC LIGHTS

Although trueSpace4 has good volumetric lights, they're not always the best tool for the job. In some instances, they might be too slow, or perhaps you'd like to use other Foreground shaders, and multiple foreground shaders cannot be used in the initial release of trueSpace4. Volumetric lights have been faked with 3D graphic programs for years. The most recognizable examples have come from Using LightWave 3D, Amblin Imaging, and Foundation Imaging; these have created some of the most recognizable examples in their visual effects for *SeaQuest DSV* and the first few seasons of *Babylon 5*, respectively.

Painting multiple cones with semitransparent color or color gradient is the most common method for faking volumetric lights. Simply texture one cone with a high ambient shader and create a second cone, a little longer than the first. Paint the second cone with the same shader, but less bright and more transparent. Using a large amount of tightly packed semitransparent planes with a light shining above is another method. Yet another technique is to use trueSpace's unique Paint Vertices tool on a cone rather than painting the whole object, thus forming a split light ray effect.

SUMMARY

The power of atmospheric effects and advanced lighting is limitless. With some swirling visible light and lots of distant glows outside a window, a still life can suddenly transform from an uninteresting scene into an image infused with life and a dynamic look. Atmospheric effects excel at revealing the state of a scene, such as a flak exploding around a pilot cowering in the cockpit of his plane during World War I. Danger is apparent, but a close-by bank of clouds may suggest hope. Contemplate whether an atmospheric effect could better tell the story you're depicting through an image or animation, not just improve it visually.

CHAPTER 14

PREVISUALIZING PYROTECHNIC EFFECTS

by Frank Rivera and Oliver Zeller

Thick fog enveloped the Empire State Building, a light drizzle hitting the sidewalk on a gloomy Saturday morning in 1945. A roar from the engines of a B-25 bomber echoed through New York's streets as it emerged from the fog. Within moments, a deafening explosion erupted, flames leapt through windows, sparks flew, flaming debris plummeted to the city streets, and thick black smoke shrouded top floors of the massive 365,000-ton Empire State Building.

This historic event is a classic example of a special effects sequence and is a key element in an upcoming animation by Frank and me.

To create a believable special effect, such as this bomber crashing into the Empire State Building, requires a variety of effects. (Oliver covered many of these in Chapter 13, "Atmospheric Effects and Advanced Lighting.") For example, an alpha-mapped explosion composite over a plane that has crashed into the building would make a rather boring, unrealistic special effect. Rather, we need to implement other effects to make the main effect more convincing by including debris, damage to objects, smoke, fire, and more.

In this chapter, we will break down effects and techniques needed to bring the bomber crash and explosion to life and create a simplified version of the effect. Specifically, we will cover

- Previsualization and planning
- Using transparency shaders and image maps
- Hiding objects
- Creating thick, black smoke with particles

PREVISUALIZATION

Due to the complexity of many quality special effects, such as our bomber example, the first step should be to previsualize the effect sequence. Previsualization involves making lower-quality test versions of animation sequences. Previsualization is a great method for breaking down the necessary elements of an animation. It is particularly useful for determining many aspects of special effects without adding effects to a more complete scene that has extra overhead due to complex geometry, textures, and so on. It is often used in films, such as *The Fifth Element*, where a futuristic New York City, mostly implemented via the use of miniatures, was roughly previsualized with 3D computer graphics.

When collaborating on a project that will undoubtedly use new techniques or tools, it's a good idea to open the lines of communication and beat all your ideas until everyone involved has a good picture in their heads. The next step is to test the techniques by using some sort of medium that is visual so that all can have a look and comment on the effect. This process is an important part of previsualization (or what Oliver and I like to call "pre-vis") and is vital in keeping the creative process moving forward and moving smoothly.

THE EXPLOSION

Saying kablooie visually has always been a lot of fun for those of us with a love for detonating fuel drums, blazing structures, erupting lava pits, and your general run-of-the-mill fireballs. Basically, to create an explosion, you start by creating the initial blast. Usually, it consists of a bright flash followed by a fireball.

The first thing we did was mock up a rough draft of the building. After constructing the basic structure and façade, we concentrated our efforts on the impact scene. We had a couple of ideas, but we didn't know which would work best, so we set out to create a couple of render tests to see whether what we visualized was possible.

We identified and marked the area where the collision would take place with brightly colored cubes, roughly in the shape of what would become the impact crater, as depicted in Figure 14.1. This made our collaboration over the Web and the task of adding all the elements of the explosion to the correct location a snap.

FIGURE 14.1   *Identifying the impact crater with markers helped us move the elements of the explosion into place.*

To create the animated explosion caused by the B25-D Mitchell's collision with the Empire State Building, we applied a series of numbered images depicting each frame of the explosion to two spheres that will represent the fireball placed at our newly identified point of collision, as illustrated in Figure 14.2. During the animation, the spheres won't be seen—only the textures applied will be visible.

NOTE

It's important to note that if this weren't a pre-vis, we would create the spheres to the size equal to the volume of the explosive images we would be using. In fact, the scale of all the objects would be constructed around the general volume of the textures that would be used in those scenes. Because this is only a pre-vis, we weren't too concerned. For more information on texture volume, please see the Surfacing chapters.

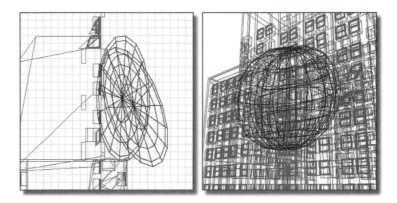

FIGURE 14.2   *The panel on the left displays the sphere's position in front of the building's façade from a Top view, and the right panel displays their position from a Perspective view.*

After the spheres were set in place, we switched to the Top view and applied a spherical UV mapping to each sphere, making sure the seam wasn't facing the camera. We then flattened each of the two spheres to about half their width along the same axis as the UV seam and rotated the spheres so the flattened areas opposite the UV seam were perpendicular to the camera's point of view. Flattening the spheres makes the applied fireball texture map appear to billow outward toward the viewer.

APPLY TEXTURES

The next step was to apply textures to the surfaces of the spheres. Some commercial explosion sequences, such as those by Artbeats and VCE (found on the resource CD), include separate alpha channel masks. In trueSpace4, Frank usually uses the same image to force transparency until only the explosion is visible. If the opaque black background of the image or the geometry of the spheres is visible, it will ruin the effect. If you have images that have an alpha channel but for some reason they won't show up in trueSpace, we have provided you with an action file for Photoshop that can be used to convert long sequences of images to images that will work in trueSpace. Simply follow these instructions. It's important to note that this action script creates an alpha channel from black areas in an image and saves it as a 32-bit image.

1. Open Photoshop. Open the Actions panel by choosing Window>Show Action, if it isn't open already.

2. Left-click the little arrow in the upper-right corner of the Actions window to open the drop-down Options menu. Select Load Actions.

3. Load AlphaChanne.ATN from the resource CD's Actions folder.

4. Click the little arrow in the upper-right corner of the Actions panel, and select Batch from the drop-down menu.

5. In the Batch panel's Source field, select Folder and choose the destination where your images will reside.

6. Select AlphaChannel from the Action field and set Destination to Save and Close. Click OK.

All the images the folder you selected will have their alpha channel re-created to work with trueSpace4.

Use a Transparency Shader

To create a fireball that looks good in trueSpace, it was necessary to eliminate the background colors of the pyrotechnic images. To do this, we turned to trueSpace's transparency shaders.

In previous versions of trueSpace, it was necessary to use an alpha channel to isolate the undesirable parts of a bitmapped image; this is no longer necessary with version 4. The new shaders in trueSpace4 make it possible to adjust the overall opacity of a bitmap texture, as well as offer the capability to define a RGB value that can be treated as transparent.

The Shader Choices

The use of transparency is vital if the images and overall effect are to blend seamlessly with your scene. So before we get into the actual mechanics of how a pyrotechnic effect can be achieved in trueSpace, we must review the six transparency shaders available to us in trueSpace4. Use Figure 14.3 as a guide.

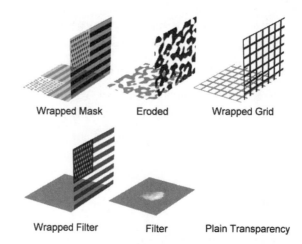

Wrapped Mask   Eroded   Wrapped Grid

Wrapped Filter   Filter   Plain Transparency

FIGURE 14.3   *trueSpace4 has six transparency shaders. Plain, Eroded, Filter, Wrapped Filter, Wrapped Grid, and Wrapped Mask.*

- **Eroded:** A procedural shader that adds spotted invisibility to a surface. You can adjust the Scale option to adjust the overall size of the opaque surfaces. Smaller values create small patches, and larger values create large patches. The allowable Scale values are 0 to 10. You can also control the amount of transparent material on the object's surface by adjusting the Coverage option. Acceptable Coverage values are 0 (transparent) to 1 (opaque). This tool also has a Fuzz feature that is used to create a fuzziness in and around the boundaries between the transparent and opaque areas. Acceptable Fuzz values are in the range of 0 (contrast between areas) to 1 (fuzzy blending between areas).

- **Filter:** Treats a color as transparent. For example, in the left panel in Figure 14.4, the image of the explosion is surrounded by the color black (RGB 0,0,0) to have trueSpace treat the black portions of the image as transparent; the transparency color of the Filter was set to RGB 0,0,0 via a right-click on the Transparency sphere to bring up the color selection cube.

FIGURE 14.4 *The left panel depicts how many pyrotechnic images appear with a black background. To define the color black as transparent in trueSpace4, the Transparency Filter is used to make the color black transparent. This result is depicted in the right panel.*

- **Plain Transparency:** Applies a uniform opacity value to the entire image. To open the Opacity settings panel, right-click on the Transparency sphere. Acceptable values are from 0 (totally transparent) to 1 (opaque).

- **Wrapped Filter:** Used to select an image map as a transparency mask. trueSpace4 adjusts the transparency according to pixel brightness. The brighter the pixel, the more transparent it appears. Darker pixels are more opaque. Right-click the Transparency sphere to select the image to be used as a Wrapped Filter.

- **Wrapped Grid:** Applies a transparent surface broken up by intersecting lines. Right-click the Transparency sphere to open the parameters panel. You can adjust the proportions of the grid by using the Scale option in the parameters panel. Acceptable Scale values range from 0 to 10. The Width and Height values control the size of the transparent areas between the grid lines. Use small values to make these areas narrow, and large values to increase these areas. Acceptable values for Width and Height are 0 to 1. You can adjust the width of the grid lines by using the Grid Size parameter, which has acceptable values from 0 (thin) to 1 (thick). You can adjust the opacity of the grid lines by using the Transparency setting. Acceptable Transparency values range from 0 (opaque) to 1 (transparent).

- **Wrapped Mask:** Works similarly to the Wrapped Filter shader except in reverse: Brighter areas are made more opaque, and darker areas appear more transparent. Right-click the Transparency sphere to select the image to be used as a mask filter.

NOTE

To view transparency in your scenes, you must use the High Quality setting in the Render Options panel.

NOTE

When the sequence of images being used is an AVI file, the rate at which the frames will be cued is determined by the base rate of the AVI file itself. For example, assuming the final trueSpace animation is 30fps and the AVI file's base rate is 15fps, each AVI frame will be repeated twice for every frame in the final trueSpace animation. If the trueSpace animation has more frames than the AVI file being used—the trueSpace animation is 30 frames and the AVI being applied as a texture is only 20 frames, for example—then the texture will repeat three times. This will also occur if you are using sequentially numbered images and there is a break in the sequence.

ADD A WRAPPED FILTER

For our pyrotechnic visualization, we will use the Wrapped Filter, which uses a pixel's brightness to determine its opacity. This will treat the black background of the images as transparent. The bright portions of the fireball will become semitransparent, making the object in the background visible through the fireball for a touch of reality.

For trueSpace to use an AVI file or series of images as a texture, we must ensure that the Anim option in the Transparency Wrapped Filter panel is checked. If Anim is enabled, trueSpace cues up each frame of the animated sequence for each frame of trueSpace animation.

After we select the series of images by using the Wrapped Filter, the rest of the sphere's properties needs to be adjusted for the best visual impact. The Transparency Wrapped Filter shader works by evaluating the brightness of the pixels, not only of the image being applied to the object, but also of the overall brightness of the object itself. Take a look at Figure 14.5. The spheres are visible, essentially ruining the effect. To correct this problem, the overall brightness of the object must be kept to a minimum.

FIGURE 14.5 *The left panel illustrates how an object's color can ruin the effect when using the Transparency Wrapped Filter shader. The right panel depicts the same scene with the spheres' colors set to black, making the spheres transparent.*

An easy way to fix this is to apply the same bitmap used for the Wrapped Filter with the Color Texture Map shader. This technique has two benefits. First, by adding a texture map shader, you can set the overall color of the object to black, thus eliminating the ghostlike effect depicted in the first panel of Figure 14.5. If the texture map used has an alpha channel, the color you select will be visible in those areas. Second, the additional brightness added by the texture map will make the explosion look fuller. The panel on the right in Figure 14.5 illustrates the appearance of the two spheres that have only the Transparency Wrapped Filter shader applied. Figure 14.6 depicts the same spheres with the Transparency Wrapped Filter and the Color Texture Map shaders applied. Notice how the explosions look fuller and more colorful, while still allowing the background to slip through.

FIGURE 14.6   *This image depicts four test frames of the pyrotechnic effect. The fireball was created by using two spheres texture mapped with a sequence of images. The Transparency Wrapped Filter and Color Texture Map shaders were used in conjunction to create the effect.*

A note of caution: Objects that have the Transparency Wrapped Filter shader applied will cast shadows, including the transparent areas, unlike shadows of the Wrapped Grid or Plain Transparency Filter with a 0 Opacity setting. Therefore, you will have to disable the Cast Shadows option in the Object Render Options panel. To do so:

1. Select the object.

2. Right-click the Object tool to open the Object Info Panel.

3. Click the Render Options button in the lower-right corner to open the Object Render Options Panel.

NOTE

A set of excellent explosions for use in your own pyrotechnic effects is provided by Artbeats and VCE on the resource CD.

Lighting Considerations

During the explosive sequence, the addition of interactive lighting can play a crucial part in pulling off the effect. The B-25 bomber is fueled; therefore, our explosion will be a brightly colored fireball. To mimic this, we added a couple of Omni lights with 0 Intensity to the scene. At the point when the plane explodes, we increased the light's intensity and made them flicker at certain points in the animation by using cues from the animated fireball textures. This made the fireball look to have an immediate impact on the surrounding surfaces in the scene.

The Aftermath

There's more to an explosion than a fireball. To be effective, the sequence must also portray the aftermath realistically: the bombed-out building and the flying debris.

The Building

Creating the illusion of destroying a structure is simple. The technique we used was to have two separate versions of the structure's façade: one intact and one destroyed. The intact façade is visible to the audience prior to and during the initial bast. In our animation, one second into the blast the original façade is replaced by the one that was modeled to look as if the explosion had destroyed it.

We first constructed the building. When we were satisfied with the preliminary results, we made copies of the walls where the collision would take place. By using a little Boolean magic and some point editing, we mangled the copied walls to fit the shape of the area where the B25-D Mitchell hit the building.

This is only a pre-vis, but to further complete the illusion, you could texture map the copied components to look charred. You could also add jagged chunks of debris to the surrounding area for added effect.

In trueSpace3.1 and 4, you can use the Visibility option in the Render Options panel to hide objects until just the right moment. For example, our pilot and plane are on a collision course with the Empire State Building. The actual point of impact doesn't take place until frame 42, so we made the copied version of the building's façade hidden until frame 42. At frame 42, we reversed the visibility settings of the copied and original versions. That is, we made the copy visible and the original hidden.

DEBRIS

At the moment of impact, we wanted to have some debris jet out from the point of collision and zip past the camera. We added a few particles behind the point of impact until frame 42. At the moment the plane smashes into the building, a burst of particles erupts from the impact point with some heading right for the camera. The particles fanned out and each set of particles were of different sizes and textures.

You can create these various sets of particles by following the Exploding Debris particles tutorial in Chapter 13, "Atmospheric Effects and Advanced Lighting."

To complete the effect, you can change the texture of the particles over time as they erupt from the explosion. For example, you can initially make the particles appear white hot. As the particles rush outward, you keyframe their color from white hot to yellow, then to orange and red, and then finally to black.

In addition, we can mix the particle debris with larger pieces of modeled debris for the final animation. These could even be cut-up pieces of the plane or building that have been deformed by using the Mesh Forge plug-in and its modifiers such as bend and twist.

You will find a short pre-vis animation on the resource CD; the filename is boom.avi.

BLACK RISING SMOKE

Immediately after the impact of the B-25 into the 78th and 79th floors of the Empire State Building, the fuel tanks ruptured, creating a fuel geyser sputtering fuel more than five stories high. An explosion billowed outward, flames spread throughout the floors, and thick black smoke rose out of the impact crater from the burning, mashed remains of the bomber. The fuel accounts for the black shade of smoke that began enveloping the 78th and 79th floors and hid the street and plane from the observation deck moments after impact. Smoke slowly rose upward within the next couple of hours and dissipated.

Due to the dynamic nature of the smoke, we will need to use particle systems to mimic it in our animation. Particle systems provide more control than mapping animated alpha maps. Handling the particles will be complex, far more so even than managing the particles in Chapter 13's tutorials.

Due to this complexity, we will need to generate several different particle systems to better simulate the smoke. This will also mean some particle systems will overlap after they have been layered together during the composite process. This should add further depth to the smoke and provide superior control over aspects such as transparency variation between the different particle systems.

NOTE

We recommend that you go over the first two particle tutorials in Chapter 13, "Atmospheric Effects and Advanced Lighting," before continuing. These tutorials cover the basics of particle generation with the Primal Particles plug-in.

PARTICLE SYSTEMS FOR SMOKE

To begin, we need particles to shift and rise out of the impact crater and windows on those two floors. By using a particle emitter, we can have the smoke billow through the windows and hole in the building and rise upward. To accomplish this without having the particles clash with the building, the particle emitters will need to be the same shape as the hole or an opened/smashed window. We'll concentrate specifically on smoke billowing from a window, but we'll throw in a twist: Although most of the glass got blown out by the plane's impact, we shall leave a piece of broken glass attached to the window frame to increase realism.

1. Make a rough version of a building; it can be as simple as some cubes or an early version of a model you're creating, such as the Empire State Building model in Figure 14.7.

FIGURE 14.7   *A very early version of the Empire State Building. The open window will be the source of our smoke.*

2. Create a circular polygon with 12 sides to serve as the particle shape.

NOTE

Because we're working with a large building and we're zoomed out, the particle settings might appear extreme. The basic shape of the building in the form of cubes, including a rough window from which the smoke billows, is included on the CD as esbform.scn. You might want to use this as a basis while going through the tutorial.

3. For later use, determine approximately where the plane crashes into the building and position the circle there. Because this is only a test, you can use two cubes to represent the impact point.

4. Open the Primal Particles plug-in, and with the circle selected, click on the Selected Object function in the Particles>Kind section of Primal Particles.

5. Choose an area close to the impact crater and create a basic window or use the scene on the CD, window.scn.

6. Attach a shard of glass to the window frame. To make the shard, make a sphere or cube. Next, push and pull its vertices to make a jagged edge or use a vertex randomization plug-in, such as the Noise function in MeshForge (included on the CD). Position the "roughed-up" primitive over the glass of the window object and use trueSpace's object subtraction tool. Remember to copy or save the roughed-up primitive because we'll need it later. This is an excellent technique for creating damage on objects and one you will likely use frequently in special effects scenarios like this one.

7. Now let's create a particle emitter by making a plane and quad dividing it twice. Position and rotate the emitter so it fits in the window and alter its XY dimensions so it closely matches the dimensions of the window glass. This is important because the particle emitter will act as the source of the smoke.

8. Verify that the particle emitter is selected by using the Object Intersect tool and make sure Delete Edges is off in the Booleans panel (right-click on Object Intersect to bring up this panel). Object Intersect the glass pane with the roughed-up primitive from Step 6. Now our particle emitter covers the space where glass was once present and from which the particle smoke will generate.

FIGURE 14.8 *The window and the highlighted particle emitter. Note the glass shard (top-right corner of the particle emitter) and the shape of the particle emitter.*

TIP

If Delete Edges is on when you intersect, subtract, or union objects, the extra polygons you create by quad dividing the particle emitter will disappear. Remember that the extra vertices the added polygons provide are necessary because particles generate from vertices on a particle emitter.

You can also add extra polygons by using the Add Vertex and Edge tool.

9. In Primal Particles Interactors group, click on the Emitter's Selected button with your emitter picked in trueSpace.

10. In the Particles group, keep the count at 100.

11. Also in the Particles group, set the size to 0.3.

12. Change the Flow Rate to Stream in Primal Particles Flow group so the particles generate in a steady stream.

13. Skip the Lifespan and Lives setting. For this test, we'll have the particles animate for two seconds. These and other settings can be tweaked later for a longer animation.

14. Lower the Power Rate a little to 75% so the particles generate with a little less force than the default setting. Keep Jitter at 0%.

15. Set the Flow X, Y, and Z Angles to Average, Feeble, and Weak, respectively. Because the particle emitter was rotated to 90 degrees on the y-axis, the x-axis now points upward, the z-axis outward, and the y-axis across. This is why the strongest angle setting is on the x-axis, because the particles need to drift upward to more closely represent the smoke surrounding the building. You can also use trueSpace's axes tool to identify the change in the particle emitter's axes.

16. Turn the middle row of XYZ knobs in the Flow group to Mist on all axes to create a more realistic, varied-particle density.

17. Change the X, Y, and Z Directions to +, +/-, and +, respectively.

18. In the Effects group, turn the Rotation knob to Twist.

19. Set the Strength of the x-axis in the Gravitation/Wind group to weak and the Direction to Negative to add a subtle appearance of gravity affecting the rise of the smoke. Strength for the y- and z-axes should be off.

20. Toggle the Expand/Contract option off in the Expansion section of the Effects group.

21. Because we've already set the emitter, go to the Recording group and enter 60 in the Frames field.

22. To finish it off, click on the Create Particles icon and preview the animation in Primal Particles. See Figure 14.9.

> **NOTE**
>
> Because we will have particle systems coming out of every window and the impact crater, keeping the particles to a low count is important. For the later figures in this chapter, we will increase the particle count to 250 to give a better sense of depth, which can also be improved by compositing the same smoke twice to give better-looking thick smoke. During previsualization, though, it's best to start with a low particle count and then increase when combining with other particle systems and effects.

Now that we have the particle smoke finished, we need to render and composite it over the scene. This is done the same way in the step-by-step tutorial in the Composite section of Chapter 13. A quick summary is:

1. Hide everything but the particles.

2. With a complete white background, render out your black particles.

3. Use the Gaussian Blur filter in PhotoShop or a similar program to give the particles a vaporous appearance (see Figure 14.10).

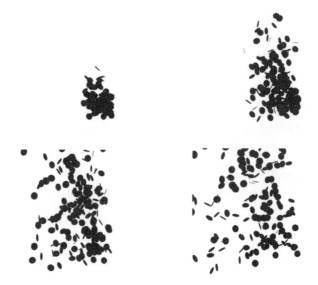

FIGURE 14.9   *Rendered particle layers without the Gaussian Blur filter applied.*

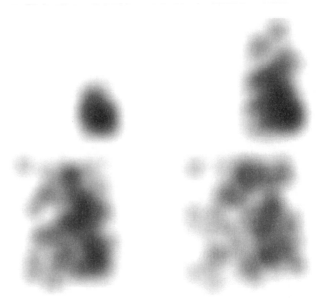

FIGURE 14.10   *Rendered particle layers with the Gaussian Blur filter applied. They'll look better applied over another image.*

ADDITIONAL EMBELLISHMENTS

Figure 14.11 shows the smoke coming out of the window. It doesn't look like much, but we're on the right track. From here, there are many aspects that need to be added.

FIGURE 14.11   *A previsualization example of the smoke we created in the tutorial, rising from the window.*

To begin, we can copy the particle systems to come out of other broken or partially open windows and from inside the impact crater or even specific parts of the plane wreckage, varying the strength, thickness, and other aspects of each particle system. Copying the particle systems for a previsualization is good, but for the most part, some variation between each particle system produces a more convincing effect.

The smoke drifts upward slowly and shrouds the top of the Empire State Building; more particle systems with emitters surrounding the top of the building could simulate this. However, these emitters would need to be positioned so that the emitters producing smoke from the windows and impact hole would have the particles blend together. Handling this can be another previsualization test.

One solution would be to create a plane that surrounds the building and hollow out the section where it intersects with the building. Insert edges and vertices to the plane and use this as an emitter for the ring of smoke surrounding the top of the building. Unfortunately, we were quickly reminded when we did the test that when the particles drift outward, they drift in only one direction, which would mean particles on one side would drift into the building. If you set them to drift in both directions, particles would enter the building, and no smoke was reported inside the building above the 80th floor. Depending on the camera position, this might not be a concern, but if it is, trueSpace4's collision detection would need to be upgraded to handle animated objects or the next version of Primal Particles, which repulses particles from objects, would solve this problem. For now, separate emitters are the best solution, although care needs to be taken so your rendering machine can handle the animation.

Another point becomes apparent during this special effects previsualization. The smoke coming from the impact crater will not only give extra depth to the explosion test you previously did, but it will also provide a black backdrop for the explosion, which should improve the look of the fireball. Normally, smoke comes after the explosion; however, additional research uncovered that the smoke actually flooded out of the hole before the explosion and fire erupted from the crashed bomber. Now we can have the black smoke appear before the explosion erupts, so when the fireball billows out, it will be against black. This will require all the elements to be handled via compositing so the explosion can be layered over the particle smoke, with perhaps some subtler, additional layers of smoke added between and over the explosion layers.

Further study of special effects and historical incidents reveals the detail that an impact of a plane such as this has. There is structural damage to the building and the plane. The heat of the subsequent fire and explosion partially melted some of the walls in the building and metal frame of the plane. Also evident are scorch marks on the limestone from the smoke and heat, and black-and-white blast patterns, the white blast pattern having been caused by the disintegration of the limestone. Sparks and falling, flaming debris are visual pieces that, when combined and integrated properly, create a convincing and complete special effect. We've only started to scratch the surface here with a rough version of the initial explosion and some smoke coming from a window, both of which still need work and need to be combined, along with other effects.

By using simpler geometry and previsualization, we have sped up the test process and gained a better idea or reinforced our initial thoughts of what techniques will work well in this situation. It also reinforces what may or may not be necessary. For example, we can confirm that small shards of glass around a window frame or remnants attached to the window frame don't add a damaged look. Instead, it appears that adding several sharper glass fragments around the entire inner edge of broken window frames or using larger, rougher pieces of broken glass will aid in giving the building a damaged appearance.

SUMMARY

Special effects add impact, excitement, horror, and much more when imple-mented well. The key to creating that convincing special effect is to layer detail on detail and seamlessly meld the effects together. The latter is not an easy task and requires experimentation that one does when previsualizing.

Previsualizing pyrotechnic effects in trueSpace is not unlike previsualizing pyrotechnics for film. Attention to detail is vital. The more details you put into your effects, the better chance you will have of pulling off the illusion.

Now, go blow something up!

CHAPTER 15

RADIOSITY

by Arnold Gallardo with Frank Rivera

Creating images that are virtually indistinguishable from real photographs has always been the "Holy Grail" of computer artists. For those of us working in 3D, the key is not so much modeling the perfect object, but giving it the best surfacing, lighting, and rendering characteristics. With the addition of the Radiosity rendering option in trueSpace4, the quest just got a little easier. Simply, radiosity is a rendering technique that calculates diffuse lighting interreflections between surfaces, which heightens the realism of your scenes. Understanding and effectively using such a powerful feature, however, takes study and practice. In this chapter, we will

NOTE

For an explanation of basic illumination and light interaction issues, as well as how they relate to rendering and radiosity, see Chapter 11, "Rendering Precursor, What Are Your Options." If you're new to the subject, a quick review might be useful before continuing.

- Examine the theory behind radiosity

- Outline how a radiosity solution is processed

- Discuss the Radiosity panel parameters

- Look at the modeling techniques best suited for use with radiosity

- Walk through a typical radiosity workflow in trueSpace4

- Practice the use of radiosity

RADIOSITY BASICS

Radiosity is defined as the total amount of radiation (light energy, for our purposes) leaving a point on a surface per unit time per unit area. This amount of radiation being exchanged is computed for all visible surfaces in the scene. However, before any computations can start, the properties of each surface must be evaluated to determine how light interacts with an object's surface and how that object modifies the light that hits it. In essence, how light interacts with objects must be addressed before any calculations of its transfer take place.

VIEW INDEPENDENCE

Radiosity is a *view-independent* method of global illumination. As stated in Chapter 11, its calculations do not consider the viewpint or camera position like ray tracing calculations do. For an environment to be view-independent, all the visible geometry in a scene must be accounted for in terms of polygonal face orientation, geometry placement, and, most importantly, surface properties and how they relate to the other objects in the scene. Because these parameters must be known for all surfaces and objects, view-independent solutions are memory hogs. However, a processed "solution," once finished, can be viewed in numerous perspectives without recalculating the environment. All the application has to do is regenerate the new point of view to the monitor.

RADIOSITY SOLUTION CALCULATION, SIMPLIFIED

How does trueSpace calculate a radiosity solution and compute all the light exchanges for visible surfaces in your scene? You don't really need to know this to use trueSpace radiosity, but for the sake of completeness, first, it assesses the geometry in your scene. Next, it overlays a *mesh* (think of it as a grid) on the scene as a way to pinpoint the location of light exchanges. (More on this later in the section about radiosity surface discretization.) You determine the initial size of the mesh's blocks with trueSpace's Quality setting in the Radiosity panel (see Figure 15.1).

NOTE

Ray tracing is *view-dependent*; the generation of an image depends upon the camera's position. Because it requires the light rays to be traced from the eye and from the light, when the eye (camera) is moved, a new set of calculations must be done.

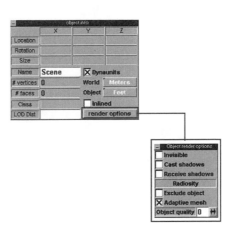

FIGURE 15.1   *The Quality setting in the Radiosity panel, where you set the size of the mesh blocks.*

Next, it evaluates the light shot (transferred) from the grid (which represents a piece of an object in your scene) into the environment. To further pinpoint the light exchanges, the process is repeated with a finer and finer grid until all light is accounted for (the solution reaches 100 percent), the solutions reach the Converged (convergence criterion) value you set in the Radiosity panel, or you tell trueSpace to stop. The operation of subdividing the grid into a finer mesh is called *substructuring*. This shooting of the energy from the lights into the environment is akin to asking each light the questions, "How much energy are you giving out? In what color and direction are you sending it? Are there any other surfaces obstructing your view?" The surfaces are then asked: "How much light have you received and are any surfaces obstructing your view of the lights?"

An analogy I often use to describe this process is the "bathroom analogy." The energy from the overhead light is distributed into the environment made up of tiles. In the room is an unseen traffic cop making sure everything moves along smoothly. The cop asks the light to bathe the environment. Then the cop asks each tile how much light it receives, from what angle the light is coming, and how bright the light is. The cop then proceeds to ask all the tiles the same question until all the light is accounted for. Then it asks the tiles adjacent to and near the area of the first tiles receiving the most light, "How much light did you get from that bright tile over there?" If this tile is too bright, all other tiles like it are also found and are asked to "act" like light sources. This process continues until all the energy is distributed, and the cop has asked all the surfaces.

This question-and-answer session that takes place when you shoot a radiosity solution can be time-consuming, especially if any specularity or reflections must be calculated. The end result, though, is worth the effort. Remember, although the calculations are lengthy, trueSpace has to make them only once, no matter how many times you change the camera's viewpoint.

HYBRID RADIOSITY

Although view-independent, radiosity unfortunately does not account for specularity, transparency, and reflections such as ray tracing. What would be ideal is a combination of the two. This merger of radiosity and ray tracing is what Caligari calls *hybrid radiosity*.

Hybrid radiosity renders your scene in two passes. The first is a radiosity solution pass that handles diffuse indirect illumination. The second pass is for transparency and specular reflections.

Hybrid radiosity has several advantages. There is no need to calculate for the shadows because radiosity takes care of them; the ray tracer pass is normally faster than standard ray tracing because it does not need to compute the shadows. If you need simple reflections, you can use environment maps or textures that simulate the reflections. But for accurate specular reflections, the ray tracer is ideal and more suited for the job.

We will look at the workflow and what's involved later in this chapter, but first let's look at the related panels.

THE RADIOSITY PANEL

Before you can shoot a radiosity solution, you must set a few parameters in the Radiosity panel. Right-click on the Radiosity tool to open the Radiosity panel, which is where you set the radiosity parameters, as well as load, delete, and save existing radiosity solutions (called LWR files)(see Figure 15.2). Let's look at each of the panel's parameters more closely.

NOTE

The first mistake many beginners make when shooting their first complex scene's radiosity solution in trueSpace is that they fail to enclose their scenes. Not doing so will likely cause the radiosity solution to take longer to complete. By simply enclosing your scenes in a simple cube primitive, the solution will complete more quickly. The cube isn't part of your scene—it's just a container that holds the lights, cameras, and objects that make up your scene. Think of it this way: How much longer would it take you to bake a pie in an oven with the door open than if the oven door were closed?

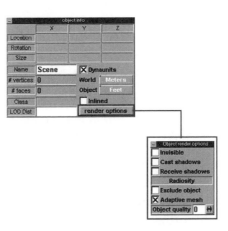

FIGURE 15.2   *In this image, you can see the Radiosity panel (left) and the Object Render Options panel on the right, which can be found in the Object Info panel. On the right side of the Radiosity Options panel, you set the radiosity parameters. On the left, you load, save, and delete LWR files of radiosity solutions.*

TIP

You can use radiosity in your animations. In fact, using radiosity can speed up animation render times. As stated previously and in Chapter 11, radiosity is a global illumination method. Because a lot of the work is done during the radiosity solution stage, flybys can usually be rendered faster by using hybrid radiosity than just ray tracing alone. A word of caution, though: Objects that are animated must be excluded from the radiosity solution. See the following warning.

QUALITY

Quality sets the radiosity *meshing's* (grid's) initial resolution for all objects in the scene and controls the subsequent substructuring-level settings for all the objects in the scene. This parameter directly affects the look and extent of a radiosity solution. It also affects how quickly the solution is processed. Acceptable values range from 1 to 9. A setting of 1 produces very coarse meshing and is ideal for checking light placement and its effect on geometry placement. A setting of 9 is ideal for final rendering and works well if you have a fast machine. The default of 5 is a good compromise, but it is a bit coarse for most scenes. You will know when your mesh is too course when triangular bands appear on surfaces. In some cases, the trouble areas look as if their face normals have been flipped. If the mesh is not dense enough, you will get light and shadow artifacts. Light might reach outside from below an object, and shadows might cause dark spots close to an object's edge. These artifacts are called *light* and *shadow leaks*, respectively. We discuss these artifacts a bit more in depth later in this chapter.

Quality is not, however, the only way to set radiosity meshing in trueSpace4. The Object Render Options panel offers a better and more efficient method. Here you can set the radiosity meshing for objects individually instead of globally for all objects, thereby optimizing the processing database. By setting objects with high significance to the scene to have high-resolution meshing and objects in the background to have moderate to low meshing, you can minimize the scene's memory needs and processing time.

To access the Object Render Options panel, right-click the Object tool. You will find the Render Options button in the lower-right corner (see Figure 15.2). The lower half of the Object Render Options panel is related to radiosity and the object currently selected. Here is a quick rundown of each of the options.

- **Adaptive Meshing:** Enables you to control the type of sampling used to simulate light diffusion. When this option is enabled, trueSpace creates an invisible triangulated mesh across the object's surface. This allows for much greater accuracy of diffuse reflections during the radiosity calculations. Adaptive meshing should normally be used on large, flat surfaces, such as walls and floors, because they are what often exhibit the effects of diffused light.

Adaptive meshing is primarily used for objects that receive significant shadows. A dense mesh is required to capture those shadows accurately. You can set an object's mesh either by increasing the object's Quality setting (this creates a uniform dense mesh) or by using adaptive meshing (this refines the mesh only in the area where it is needed). When the Adaptive Mesh option is disabled, trueSpace uses the object's existing geometry to map the radiosity diffusion. This speeds things up with regard to the selected object. However, this method does not simulate light accurately. For more complex objects, I suggest you disable Adaptive Meshing on objects with high polygon counts.

- **Exclude Object:** Enables you to determine whether an object is included or excluded from radiosity computations. For example, an object contains a large number of polygons, slowing the radiosity simulation. In such a situation, the object can be marked as being excluded from radiosity solution (speeding the radiosity solution).

Because of the complex nature of radiosity, it is sometimes necessary to specifically set the radiosity parameters for individual objects. That's where the Object Quality setting comes in.

- **Object Quality:** Similar to the overall Quality setting found in the Radiosity panel; enables you to specify the mesh sampling for the selected object. Acceptable values are 0 to 9. A lower setting performs fewer radiosity calculations on the surface of the object, resulting in quicker computation for that particular object. However, a lower setting results in the introduction of triangular artifacts into the scene. The highest setting of 9 removes artifacts, but the solution will take longer to finish.

WARNING

Objects that are animated, such as characters, must be excluded from the radiosity solution. Only stationary objects in your animations can use radiosity. You can exclude an object from a radiosity solution by selecting the object, right-clicking the Object tool to open the Object Info panel, clicking the Render Options button, and checking Exclude Object. The object will be ignored when you shoot the radiosity solution. Because the object is not being considered by radiosity calculations, you might have to take extra care when lighting the object; otherwise, the object might not blend well with the rest of a scene.

TIP

A Quality setting of 0 means an object doesn't have per-object quality assigned and is affected by the Global Radiosity Quality setting. To switch off per-object quality for the selected object, simply set Object Quality to 0.

TONE MAPPING

Tone Mapping is a fancy name for the process of translating the calculated luminance values of a radiosity solution into the limited tones of the video display. This translation is sometimes necessary because the calculated values in a

TIP

You can change the tone mapping setting anytime, and you don't have to reshoot the solution. Simply make the change and rerender the scene. For example, you just shot a solution and rendered it to screen. You find that the scene's highlights seem a little dark on your monitor. You can increase the Tone Mapping setting and rerender the scene without reshooting the radiosity solution. Remember, you don't have to reshoot the radiosity solution if you move the eye view, camera, or change the Tone Mapping settings in the Radiosity panel. However, because of the way radiosity works, any changes made to an object's geometry or surface texture—or if you add, change, or delete a light source—will require you to reshoot (recomputate) the radiosity solution.

NOTE

Tone Mapping is not a solution to inadequately processed radiosity scenes (dark scenes), nor is it a solution to overly processed scenes (light scenes). The solution in such instances is to change the light intensities in the scene and preferably use light attenuation in all the lights. Radiosity works with real-world units and scale, so the lights should behave the way they do in real life, that is, with attenuation.

radiosity solution might exceed the capability of the monitor to show all the possible calculated tones. When luminance values are translated into the visible range, some of the calculated values are clipped. By changing the Tone Mapping parameter, you specify which sections of the calculated values can be discarded. Values range from 0.01 to 10, and the default is 1.

In the majority of your scenes, you can keep Tone Mapping around 1 to 2. Setting Tone Mapping above 1.0 affects the highlight distribution as well as the upper lighter grays more than the shadows. Settings lower than 1.0 affect the middle grays and the shadows but also turn highlights gray (see Figure 15.3).

In other words, leave the default of 1 alone in most cases. If the scene is too dark, you're better off adjusting the light intensities in the scene rather than changing Tone Mapping, which could only lead to flat and bland scenes due to the lack of contrast. Tone Mapping in trueSpace is like a window of limited range that, if moved, affects both ends—the highlights and the shadows—and it is much more noticeable in the middle grays.

CONVERGED

The Converged parameter limits the amount of calculation that trueSpace does when processing a radiosity solution. Remember that all the surfaces have to be asked how much light they are receiving and reflecting back into the environment. A converged value of 75 percent means that the simulation stops after 75 percent of the radiosity solution has been shot.

By adjusting this value, you are essentially telling trueSpace to abort the process when a percentage of the radiosity solution has been completed. You will often find it is not necessary to wait until 100 percent of the energy in the scene is accounted for because the visual impact of those last bits of energy isn't significant. As mentioned in the following Note, you must sometimes shoot the radiosity solution over 80 percent or more for satisfactory diffuse reflections.

FIGURE 15.3 *Changing the Tone Mapping setting drastically changes the look of your radiosity rendering. These scenes were rendered with Tone Mapping set to 1.0, 1.5, and 0.85, respectively.*

NOTE

You can abort a radiosity solution anytime by pressing the Escape key or by double-right-clicking your mouse in the workspace.

NOTE

The calculation of diffused light is accurate only after the solution has reached 80 percent or so. For best results, Caligari suggests being patient. I think it's good advice. Go grab a bite to eat or a cup of coffee because the result is well worth the wait.

TIP

Set Iterations to 0, and trueSpace does not update the screen during the radiosity solution. I prefer setting Iterations to 0 because it speeds up the radiosity solution and gives me the option to evaluate the scene whenever I want by rendering the scene. Setting Iteration to 0 causes trueSpace to ignore the Do parameter altogether.

It's important to note that setting the Converged value less than 100 percent limits the amount of *color bleeding* (the partial reflecting of a surface's color along with its light) and the generation of indirect diffuse illumination in the scene. This severely limits the advantage of using radiosity because most of its effects would be minimized if the Converged value were set too low.

In practice, you're better off leaving Converged set to 100 percent and evaluating the amount of processing by stopping the solution periodically and rendering the scene to see how it looks.

ITERATIONS

The Iterations parameter controls the amount of visual feedback you get while a solution is processing. By default, trueSpace4 does not automatically show the result of radiosity solution progress. Iteration controls the interval between screen renderings. Values range between 0 and 1000. A setting of 1 means that trueSpace renders to the screen at every iteration step (every time the grid is made finer). A value of 2 updates the render after every two steps, and so on.

DO

The Do parameter controls the kind of iteration that is processed and shown in trueSpace during a solution. This parameter contains two options: Lights Only and Iterate.

LIGHTS

The Lights Only option tells trueSpace to calculate the effects of each light in the scene for the radiosity solution. When rendering, trueSpace shows the effect of each light consecutively, so the scene changes as each light's contribution is calculated and shown. This option is good for checking the contribution of each light in the scene, but by nature it is an incomplete radiosity solution. When Do is set to Lights, the Iterations parameter will default to 1 to show the effect of each light present in the scene. In practice, you should leave the Do parameter set to Iterate and change it to Lights only when you want to evaluate the effect of a particular light in a scene.

ITERATE

The Iterate option shows the effects of the lights, as well as object-to-object inter-reflection. This option is slower and more intensive than Lights Only because it computes both the object and the light contribution. Iterate calculates the effect of all the lights and geometry in the scene and produces a complete radiosity calculation.

WORKING WITH RADIOSITY

As you can see, there isn't much to the Radiosity panel. We will cover the last three options, Delete, Load, and Save, in a minute, as well as some modeling considerations, but first let's look at setting up a scene for radiosity.

SCENE CONSIDERATIONS

Creating a scene that will use radiosity is different only in two respects. You will probably want to use light sources suited to radiosity (Area and Sky lights), and you will want to enclose your scene so that the radiosity solution can run its course quickly and efficiently. The rest of the task usually undertaken to get a scene to look right should still be followed. For example, you still have to consider light placement and light intensities, the surfaces of your objects and their placement, the camera angle, and so on.

Let's look at these two light types specific to radiosity.

RADIOSITY-SPECIFIC LIGHTS

The Sky and the Area light types have been designed specifically to work with Radiosity rendering for greater realism in lighting effects. Each creates wide-area lighting that would otherwise be difficult to achieve by using the standard lights projector, infinite, local, and spot. You can use the Area light type in ray-traced renderings, but you will derive the most benefit from using this light type in radiosity renderings.

SKY LIGHT

The Sky light source is used to simulate illumination from the sky during radiosity calculations. The sky is modeled as an unseen hemisphere of infinite radius positioned above the center of the current scene. The position of the sun is determined by the direction of the arrow that points from the disc at the end of

NOTE

Although you can enable shadow-casting with a Sky light, Caligari recommends you avoid doing so because the computation time involved will slow radiosity calculations dramatically. Use the infinite light source to create shadows cast by the sun.

NOTE

When using Area lights in ray traced or ScanLine/RayCast renderings, the penumbra is not computed properly.

NOTE

Area lights are accounted for only during the initial first steps of radiosity solution.

the light object. Adjust this light's color attribute to change the mood of the scene or to reflect a different time of day. For example, Caligari suggests adding a reddish-orange hue to simulate a twilight setting.

The Sky light simulates the illumination only from the sky, not from a sun. You should use an infinite light source for this purpose. The two complement each other. You can set the Sky light to a particular lighting scheme to specify how the illumination is distributed over the sky by changing the light's Type setting, accessible from the Lights panel. Here are the three Options in the Lights panel that pertain to the Sky Light type:

- **Overcast:** An overcast sky means that the brightest part of the sky is directly overhead. The direction the Sky light's arrow points doesn't matter.

- **Intermediate:** An Intermediate sky offers illumination that is partially determined by the direction of the sun (the direction the Sky light's arrow is pointing).

- **Clear:** The Clear sky setting means that the brightest portion of the sky is determined by the Sky light's directional arrow.

AREA LIGHT

The Area light simulates illumination emitted from a rectangular area as opposed to the usual single point. In Wireframe mode, the area light appears in your scene as a plane with a single line emerging perpendicular to the plane. This line represents the direction the light will be emitted from. The light source can be scaled to widen the effect of the area light. Area lights are also supported in ScanLine and ray trace renderings.

In a radiosity solution, Area Lights are treated as any other surface radiating light energy. They are subject to the same Object Quality settings that apply to standard polyhedrons.

Let's try a simple exercise to illustrate how Sky lights work.

1. Load Skylight.scn and do a solution until the solution reaches 90–92%. The Sky light in this scene is set to clear (see Figure 15.4). The shadow areas

are lighter due to the Sky light filling in the shadow areas. Clear Sky lights spread out the color of the sky in objects in the scene.

FIGURE 15.4 *The clear Sky light.*

2. Change the Sky light setting to Overcast and process a solution. The shadow areas now have the high-contrast look and have darkened up. Notice the absence of the blue hue compared to the Clear skylight setting (see Figure 15.5).

3. Change the Sky light setting again to Intermediate and process a solution. This Sky light setting is the setting for simulating partly cloudy skies (see Figure 15.6).

The Sky lights can also be used in interior situations, but their effect would be unnatural in a well-lighted interior. Sky lights, however, can be used at night to create ambient lighting from buildings and even moonlight.

NOTE

When using the shadow casting option with Area lights, the size of the Area light has a direct impact on rendering time. Area lights of increased scale take longer to compute due to the increased distribution of shadows.

Unlike other light sources, they are always visible in the rendered image.

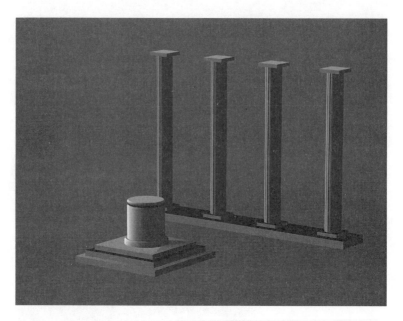

Figure 15.5 *The overcast Sky light.*

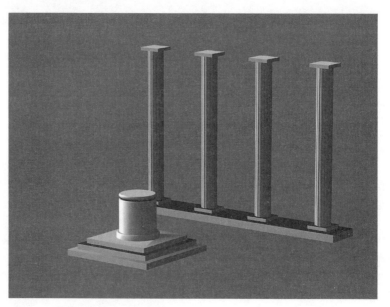

Figure 15.6 *The intermediate Sky light.*

FASTER SOLUTIONS

During the writing of this book, lots of questions were posted in newsgroups regarding how slow-shooting a radiosity solution can be when shooting complex scenes. The solution to this problem is remarkably simple: Enclose the scene in a cube primitive, including all the lights illuminating the scene. You will have to use a camera to view the enclosed scene, but that is a small price to pay for a fast, efficient solution. If you already have a camera in the scene, enclose it within the cube primitive, too.

To see for yourself what a difference this can make, let's try an experiment.

Load the Studio88.scn file from the resource CD. This scene was created by Arnold Gallardo so it's an unbiased test. Left-click the Radiosity tool. Watch the percentage of the radiosity solution that completes in one minute. Press Escape to stop the solution. On a Pentium II 266MHz machine with 64MB of RAM, the solution arrived at 38 percent in one minute. This scene was shot in the open air (for lack of a better word)—that is, all the objects, lights, and camera were placed in a scene just as you would if you were going to create a ray-trace rendering. Let's speed the solution a bit.

Reload the scene Studio88.scn. trueSpace will ask whether you are sure you want to delete the radiosity solution; answer yes. Now add a cube primitive to the scene and set its surface properties to

Color: Plain Color/White RGB 255.255.255

Transparency: None

Reflectance: Matte

Displacement: None

In the Shader attributes panel, set the following sliders as follows:

Ambient: 0.3

Diffuse: 1.0

Scale the cube primitive equally in all three axes until the cube encloses all the objects in the scene, including the camera and lights. Don't make the cube bigger than it has to be and check its position in all the views to ensure everything is in the cube. Left-click the Radiosity tool to shoot the solution. Before the scene has had a chance to render for a minute, you should notice that the radiosity solution has gone further this time in under a minute. Pretty cool, huh?

You can also use this technique when you use a Sky light. Don't worry about whether the Sky light's energy will soak right through the cube primitive, as long as you don't set it to cast shadows. Remember, setting a Sky light to cast shadows will bring your radiosity solutions to a crawl. You will have to simulate shadows cast by the sun by using a shadow-casting area, local, or spot light.

Now that you know how to speed up your radiosity solutions, let's look at saving and loading these solutions.

SAVING, LOADING, AND DELETING SOLUTIONS

In most cases, radiosity solutions are embedded with the geometry, meaning the luminance values are stored along with the geometry. This technique of calculating and storing luminance values with the geometry makes the radiosity calculation easier because the luminance values need not be mapped into the surfaces after computation. The location, as well as the occlusion information, is easily obtained from the scene geometry. All you need to do is make the stored luminance value be evenly distributed across a surface to create shading. Not evenly distributing the luminance value across a surface would create "plaid" or "blocky" shading.

However, this technique limits geometry and light movement in a scene, and if anything is moved or altered in a scene, it is necessary that the solution be recomputed again. Even light intensity and meshing changes require recalculation because they affect the stored luminance values.

The radiosity solution files in trueSpace4 use the suffix .LWR. LWR stands for Lightworks, the company that developed trueSpace's rendering engine. The stored solution files are generally huge and take time to save or load. The size of the LWRs is proportional to the number of surfaces in a scene.

In scene files (SCNs) for which you've processed a radiosity solution, be sure to save the LWR when the radiosity processing finishes because trueSpace does not automatically save the LWR file with the SCN information. Also, saving LWR files enables you to have different versions of a particular solution for a single scene. Just be sure to name the LWR something that links it to the correct SCN file because the LWR file's information cannot be used for any other scene.

NOTE

You don't always have to use ray tracing to create reflective objects. Phong shading with radiosity offers a good compromise, as well as a good result (see Figure 15.7).

Once an LWR is saved, it can be loaded again and again without any additional processing. One advantage of saving LWR files is that you can change the light settings in a scene to evoke different moods or times of day, save LWRs for each, and then load them later.

Deleting an LWR is a straightforward process, and trueSpace4 prompts you whether you need to save or delete a solution. When trueSpace4 detects a change in the SCN settings—whether it is a light intensity change or geometry that has been moved or added—the program prompts you to ask whether the radiosity solution should be deleted or left as it is. If you choose to leave it as it is, trueSpace renders the SCN by using the old solution information; the rendering will not reflect the changes that have been made. The rendered SCN would still look like the old scene, and any geometry changes would be ignored and not be rendered.

NOTE

Radiosity solutions can also be used with environmental maps to create simulated reflections. If ray tracing's explicit exactness were necessary, a very reflective Phong shading setting would be more than adequate to save rendering time. Radiosity could also be used with the anisotropic shaders. However, they do produce some visible banding and artifacts due to the nature of the shader. Anisotropic shaders reflect specular light in one direction and a bit of diffuse light in another direction. Using anisotropic shaders also can make some hidden geometry visible, especially if the geometry is tripled or tessellated.

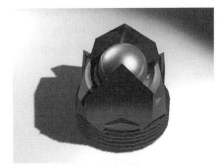

FIGURE 15.7   *A comparison of a radiosity rendering with Phong shading (left) and the same scene ray traced.*

MODELING CONSIDERATIONS

How you model is not much of an issue when you use local illumination techniques or ray tracing, but it can make or break a radiosity solution. In radiosity, you need to limit the number of polygons in a scene because each surface is taken into consideration and adds to the amount of memory needed to process the solution.

Radiosity by nature prefers to deal with quadrilateral polygons because they make the radiosity grid easier to set up and subdivide. Tessellated polygons often create radiosity artifacts that are noticeable as dark triangles or linear streaks. The best modeling techniques for radiosity are

- **Extrusion:** If possible, extrude shapes and forms instead of editing points and polygons. Extrusion from a spline preserves quads more than using other techniques, such as Boolean operations, point editing, and NURBS.

- **Lathe:** Lathing also creates and preserves quadrilateral polygons. When making hemispherical objects, it is best to lathe.

- **Macro/Sweep:** When constructing glasses, vases, and similar objects, create the cross-sectional shape and then use the Macro/Sweep tool to form the object. The profile this tool makes uses quadrilateral polygons.

- **Deformation tools**: If you must use the deformation tools, quad divide the object before doing the deformation to create quadrilateral polygons.

- **NURBS:** NURBS modeling in trueSpace4 always comes out tessellated. So quad subdivide the object before performing any NURBS cage manipulation. That way, the created triangles form 30- to 45-degree angles that render with fewer artifacts and faceting. Be forewarned, quad subdividing a NURBS object will increase its polygon count significantly.

- **Sweep/Bevel:** Use Sweep to create additional faces, and Bevel for additional edges. This technique creates and preserves quadrilateral polygons even if they are subdivided.

Geometry Placement Considerations

Geometry placement in scenes destined for radiosity rendering requires careful thought. Remember in trueSpace4 that all the surfaces in the scene are computed—even the undersides of things. This creates problems in certain situations where the objects occlude and compete for the radiosity calculation. This situation could result in missing shadows, floating objects, or a myriad of radiosity artifacts that cannot be solved even with adequate meshing.

Try an example:

1. Load radgeo1.scn and perform a radiosity solution.

2. Process the solution until it reaches 99.75%. Render the Camera viewport. Notice that one of the bow compass legs' shadows is missing (see Figure 15.8). This is due to the conflicting surface information that trueSpace has with this kind of geometry setup. The bottom of the paper and the top surface of the table underneath it confuses trueSpace on where the shadow is to be computed. One solution is to elevate the paper higher than the table, but this solution makes it look like the paper is levitating above the table. Another solution is to explicitly indicate trueSpace geometry and shadow boundaries.

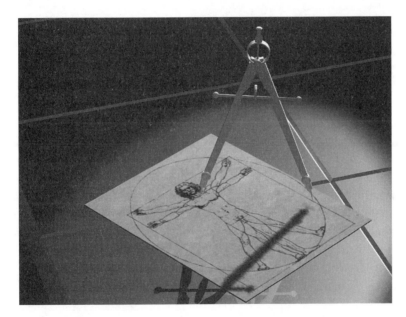

FIGURE 15.8   *Notice that one of the shadows from the legs of the compass is missing in this solution.*

3. Now load the radgeo2.scn and do another solution until it reaches 99.75% and stop it. Render the Camera view and observe that the shadow of the other compass' leg is now present (see Figure 15.9). trueSpace is not confused by the two surfaces anymore. The surface under the paper and the top surface of the table are now seen as unimportant because the surface area where the paper lies is now explicitly indicated through the use of subtractive Boolean operation.

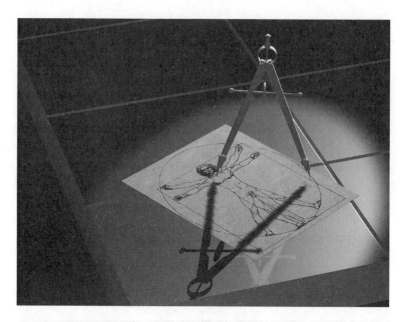

FIGURE 15.9   *The paper was subdivided into smaller surfaces so that the substructuring and the subsequent adaptive subdivision would be detailed enough because the quality of these depends upon the geometry and scale, as well as the Quality parameter.*

When occluding objects create radiosity artifacts that are not alleviated by increasing the meshing, explicitly indicating the geometry position by creating new polygons through Boolean subtraction is the best solution without increasing the radiosity database. This technique is, however, limited to objects that are stationary in the scene. If the object is moving, it is better to exclude it in the radiosity processing and use local illumination or ray-tracing techniques to create shadows associated with the object. This technique minimizes meshing-related artifacts and properly dictates the formation of patches and any subsequent adaptive subdivision.

GEOMETRY SCALE

Geometry scale is very important in radiosity because the calculations are performed using real-world coordinates and assumptions. If you light a room the size of a stadium with a 100-watt bulb, the room would be very dark, and a 2,000-watt floodlight would wash out an 8-foot by 10-foot room. Try to place a 60-watt bulb in a dollhouse or a penlight in an amphitheater, and you will see how important geometry scaling is.

ScanLine and ray tracing do not need properly scaled objects because they account only for local illumination and also because, by nature, they are view-dependent. As long as the geometry is properly occluded and the light's intensity is high enough, the rendering would come out fine. In radiosity, if either the light intensity or the scale were wrong, the radiosity solution would look wrong, either too dark or too bright.

Also since the radiosity meshing is tied to the scale of the geometry, improperly scaled objects would have coarse meshing, thereby creating radiosity artifacts, or would create floating images. Radiosity artifacts such as shadow leaks would occur, making improperly scaled objects look dark and dirty. Take a look.

1. Load the geoscl.scn and run a radiosity solution until it reaches 85%.

2. Observe that the scene is fairly dark and almost indiscernible (see Figure 15.10). This is due to two things: geometry scale and incorrect light setting.

FIGURE 15.10 *This image has very high contrast due to the darkness in the recessed areas, and the only illuminated parts are those that are within the reach of the lights. This is a demonstration of wrong geometry scale.*

3. Increase the light intensity to 1.74 and do another solution. Stop the solution when it reaches 85%. The top and the floor area near the center are illuminated well, but the corners are still dark.

4. Load geoscl2.scn. This scene's geometry has been scaled down but the light intensity has not been changed.

5. Do a solution and stop when it reaches 54 steps at 85%. Notice that the whole scene is now much more open, and the dark areas have been lighted, although some are still dark (see Figure 15.11). Processing this solution to 100% would open these areas some more.

Increasing the light intensity also would solve this problem, but that would make the scene highly contrasted, and properly scaled geometry works very well with light intensity changes.

FIGURE 15.11 *In this image, you can see that the dark areas have opened up some more, which is primarily due to using the proper scale and light intensity setting for the environment.*

The illumination of the scene is also drastically affected if the geometry's scale is wrong in relation to the light source's location to the object. Area lights begin to behave like point-source lights. A distant area light functions as a point source when placed in a large environment, and point-source lights would behave like area lights because they now light up a larger surface.

GEOMETRY THICKNESS

One assumption that is rarely discussed is the lack of real material "thickness" in a radiosity solution. This means that the geometry does not have thickness and object surface properties associated with thickness are not accounted for. By having the surfaces behave as ideal-diffuse, the actual thickness of a geometry in trueSpace is irrelevant.

NOTE

Ray tracing also can simulate luminaires, but it lacks the warmth that radiosity lends to an environment.

However, in certain cases, it is necessary to model geometry that has an inner and outer geometry. This is especially important when simulating luminaires. Luminaires are lights with associated structural supports and light refractors and reflectors.

Figure 15.12 illustrates this point. The image on the left shows the way the glass' color bathes and changes the environment. The luminaire geometry also helps in the shape of the light distribution in the environment. trueSpace, however, would not compute any glows that occur on the glass' surface because this shader is ignored by the radiosity renderer. The lens flare and the glows must be simulated as a post process by using the built-in Glows and Lens Flare Effects option. The image on the right shows the glow and lens flare well, and the proper camera placement hides the fact that glows and lens flares in trueSpace are post-rendering processes. (The luminaire simulation in this case, however, is for visual purposes only and is not physically accurate.)

 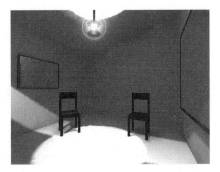

FIGURE 15.12   *Because trueSpace's radiosity does not take geometry thickness into account (left), the lens flare and glow of a luminaire must be added with post processing (right).*

RADIOSITY WORKFLOW IN TRUESPACE4

Although you could model your objects, add some lights to the scene, apply radiosity, and hope for the best, you probably won't be happy with the results. You're much better off planning ahead, using a consistent strategy, and assessing your progress frequently. There are numerous ways of optimizing the radiosity workflow in trueSpace4, but I find this one to be efficient:

1. **Erase all lights.** Removing all lights in a scene not only approximates the real-world habit of bringing in and setting up one light at a time, but it also clearly demonstrates the effect of each light in the scene. You can easily see how each light affects and models the geometry and the environment.

2. **Decide and position the key light.** As you remember from Chapter 12, the key, or main, light establishes the light direction, mood, time of day, and location of your scene. Plus it controls the subsequent placement and characteristics of additional lights in the scene.

3. **Add fill-in lights if necessary.** The "if necessary" part is the key. Although you need fill lights to open up dark areas in a scene when you render with local illumination, those dark areas might open up after considerable solution-processing time when you use radiosity. There is a difference between adding fill lights for cinematic effect and for overcoming the limitations of local-illumination methods. In most cases, fill lights are usually positioned opposite the key light and are three-quarters to one-half the intensity of the key light.

4. **Set individual object quality for each object.** Setting the quality of each object optimizes the speed and memory required to process the solution. Initially set the meshing for each object to 2.0 to accelerate the radiosity-solution processing during the first few trial runs. After you're comfortable with the lighting, you can increase the mesh quality of the objects that need it.

5. **Perform an initial evaluative radiosity solution.** Process an initial solution with a very coarse meshing of 2, and evaluate the light intensity settings, geometry placement, and shader settings. Please note that this coarse quality setting can cause minute details, such as subtleties in specular reflection and intricate shadow boundaries, to be absent in your initial trial renders.

6. **Evaluate the scene.** Assess and inspect the scene by moving and changing the camera point of view. Look for improper or wrong geometry placement, wrong material shader settings, and errors in light intensity settings, which are the most obvious problems. Make the necessary changes.

7. **Perform additional evaluative solution processing.** Subsequent processing of different solutions will demonstrate whether the changes you made worked and will also make the evaluation process easier and faster. Once you're happy with all your changes, you're ready to process for the final solution.

8. **Set object meshing to high.** Change object meshing, as well as the Radiosity Options panel's Quality setting, to 9.0. Also check the Quality setting in the Object Render and Radiosity Options panels.

9. **Assess geometry to be excluded.** In the Object Render Options panel, exclude the unnecessary objects from the radiosity solution processing, such as those objects that are not static (animated).

10. **Process a final radiosity solution.** This final step is probably the longest and most time-intensive one, but take heart. If the evaluative solutions are done well, this step will not need to be redone.

The steps shown here are guidelines only. You don't have to follow them strictly, but you should always evaluate your radiosity solution to minimize visible artifacts. Artifacts in radiosity cannot be avoided unless you are willing to wait for much longer computation times. Make sure you always remove all existing lights in the default scene, as well, to prevent unnecessary lights from showing up in the solution. Unnecessary lights increase the number of light-to-surface and surface-to-surface light calculations, which in turn increase processing requirements. Remember, the memory needs of a scene are proportional to the number of lights and surfaces in the scene.

Let us turn this workflow into an actual scene file to have a feel for it.

1. Load trpzrm.scn to start the tutorial. All the unnecessary lights have been removed. This scene has two key lights: the sunlight (Spot light) and the torchiere lamp light. Notice that the color of the key light approximates the time of the day (morning), while the torchiere point-source light approximates the warm color of an incandescent bulb.

2. Select the individual objects and set Object Quality to 2.0 in the Object Render and Radiosity Options panel under the Object Tool-Object Info panel.

3. Set the Radiosity Quality to 2.0, the Tone Mapping to 1, the Converged at 100, and the Iterations at 0 in this scene.

4. Run a solution by using these parameters until the solution reaches 65%.

5. Render and evaluate the scene. Look for radiosity-rendering artifacts, floating objects, wrong light settings, and face-normal problems. Notice that the ball on top of the table is floating (see Figure 15.13).

FIGURE 15.13   *The scene rendered at a 65% solution.*

6. Because this scene will eventually be animated, the ball should be excluded from the radiosity processing. Go to the Front view and select the polka-dot ball and lower it until it touches the table's upper surface.

7. Move the camera around the scene and render. This gives you the visual feedback necessary to evaluate whether the radiosity parameters currently applied to the scene are adequate or proper. Notice that the shadow

boundaries from the sunlight (Spot light) and the wall area where the torchiere lamp stands are also jagged.

8. Because this meshing resides on the house object, the meshing Quality on that object must be increased. Because the shadow of the chair's legs also falls on the house, its meshing must be set to a high resolution. Set the Object Quality of the house object to 5.

9. Run another solution and evaluate the scene again. Do this as often as possible to evaluate the scene before doing a final solution processing.

10. Set the final meshing of the house object to 9, and do the same for other objects in the scene that are affected by the lights in the scene, such as the chairs. Alternatively, you can universally set the meshing in the Radiosity Options panel. This, however, is not efficient because some of the obejcts do not need to have a high mesh setting. Remember that by setting the mesh quality individually for important objects, such as those that receive shadows, you can leave low the mesh quality of the other objects in the scene that do not need it. Use the object's individual mesh quality setting when possible. This makes it easy to control which objects suck up your PC's resources during the radiosity solution's calculation phase.

11. Exclude the polka-dot ball from the radiosity processing by clicking on the ball and accessing the Object render and Radiosity Options panel. Click on the Render Options and click Exclude Object.

12. Do a final radiosity solution processing. The meshing level, if your computer can handle it, should be set at 9, or 7, at least. This is the final step before rendering a still or a series of frames for the animation. Save the LWR once the solution reaches the 87–95%. Figure 15.14 illustrates the final render.

In this scene, both the ball and the camera are moving while the rest of the environment stays the same. This is a good example of how a radiosity solution functions as an environmental shader.

This section demonstrated one approach to a radiosity workflow. This makes the whole process smooth by constantly evaluating the scene for errors and correcting them prior to commiting the long computer time for a final radiosity solution.

FIGURE 15.14 *The final render of our workflow exercise.*

NOTE

Step 4 provides an evaluation solution, and there is no need for the solution to reach higher than 65%. If there are colors involved, the solution should be processed around 95–98% for the color bleeding to be visible. The 65% level is an arbitrary number and can be any number as long as sufficient iteration has been performed and the energy sufficiently distributed from the lights into the surfaces.

CORRECTING RADIOSITY ARTIFACTS

The chances that your first radiosity solution will give the results you want is low. The inherent demands of an unbiased global illumination calculation coupled with the unpredictability of the meshing refinement requires that the calculated results be evaluated visually. In other words, you're going to have to look at your scene and tweak it.

Most radiosity artifacts are caused by meshing resolution and light intensity issues, with the majority being meshing related. The meshing is either too large or the underlying geometry is triangulated, in which case the substructuring causes some elongated meshing to form and spawn weird shadow or light artifacts. The four most common radiosity artifacts are

- Light leaks
- Shadow leaks
- Floating objects
- Mach bands

Light Leaks

Light leaks are light-shadow boundary errors that result from inadequate meshing. Light leaks normally show up as light spikes that extend over the dark areas of the shadow or shade in a solution.

Some light leaks, however, occur as a result of both meshing resolution and geometry placement. The geometry placement coupled with meshing creation induces a weird structure that often is visible as light streaks.

Light leaks can be prevented by having an adequate meshing resolution, as well as by manually subdividing the affected polygonal face. Light leaks are preventable by using a finer mesh, as well as by explicitly indicating geometry placement. Don't go overboard, however; arbitrarily setting the meshing quality of an object too high without analyzing the scene is costly in terms of calculation time. You might need to do several solutions with different meshing resolutions to find the appropriate meshing quality setting. This tutorial will give you a feel for the process.

1. Load the litlk.scn file and process a solution until it reaches 97%. The red and white light leaks around the base of the drum are very obvious (see Figure 15.15). These are usually caused by inadequate meshing.

Figure 15.15   *Notice how the light leaks out at the base of the cylinder.*

2. Click on the base geometry and set the meshing to 9 and run a solution. You will notice that the light leaks have been drastically reduced, although they are still there (see Figure 15.16). The best solution here is to explicitly indicate the occlusion of the geometry by doing a Boolean operation.

FIGURE 15.16   *This solution is better, but still not perfect.*

3. Click on the drum object and lower the geometry into the base about 0.030 inch. This need not be precise; it needs only to be lower than the base object.

4. Make a copy of this object. Click on the base and do a Boolean subtract operation. This would make a circular outline on the base geometry while retaining the drum object. You can also do this operation by right-clicking on the Boolean operation panel and checking the Keep Drill box.

5. Do another solution and process until it reaches 85%. Render the Camera window and observe that the light leak is not there, even if the meshing level is low (see Figure 15.17). Explicit geometry setup helps lower the radiosity-processing needs. It lets you manage complex geometry better.

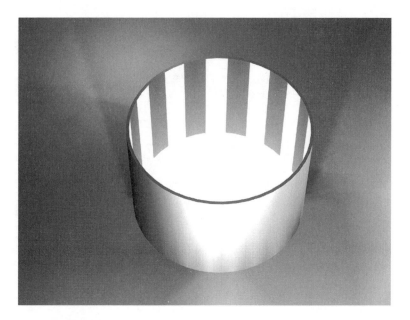

FIGURE 15.17 *Adding the Boolean operation creates the best solution for stopping light leaks.*

SHADOW LEAKS

Shadow leaks are the opposite of light leaks. They also occur because of wrong or inadequate meshing, as well as geometry placement. Shadow leaks manifest by creating dark spikes that extend over the lighted areas of the scene. Shadow leaks by their nature are more noticeable than light leaks because they look dark and out of place, as you will see in the following tutorial. If shadow leak happens in a light-shadow boundary, it is even more obtrusive.

1. Load shwlk1.scn and process a solution until it reaches 85%. Render the Camera view. Notice that on the floor, the shadow boundaries are jagged and it has spikes (see Figure 15.18). These spikes are called shadow leaks.

2. Select the wall object and change the meshing parameter to 9. Delete the existing LWR file and do another solution until it reaches 85%.

3. Render the Camera view and notice that the shadow leaks have been minimized, if not removed, by increasing the meshing (see Figure 15.19).

FIGURE 15.18   *Notice the jagged look of the shadows.*

FIGURE 15.19   *Notice how clean the shadows look now.*

Shadow leaks cannot be solved by explicitly indicating geometry because, by nature, they are more of a meshing issue than light leaks in trueSpace4. In other radiosity renders, both light leaks and shadow leaks are meshing-related issues.

Shadow leaks could also be due to geometry placement. Geometry that is not explicitly indicated can and does exhibit shadow leaks.

FLOATING OBJECTS

A floating object does not have visible or adequate shadow and looks like it is levitating when rendered. The reason for this is that the meshing missed the shadow boundary by being too coarse. Here's how you can fix it.

1. Load the fltobj.scn and set the meshing parameter (Quality) of the "wall" object to 5. Run a radiosity solution and stop at 85%. Notice that the torchiere and the chair are floating in this solution render (see Figure 15.20). This occurs because the meshing missed the shadow boundaries due to a very coarse grid.

FIGURE 15.20   *Floating objects lack adequate shadows to anchor them in the scene.*

2. Select and change the meshing quality of the wall object to 5 and do another solution. Render the Camera view. In this instance, the meshing

grid did catch the shadow boundaries and made the chair and the lamp's shadow visible. It made them look that they are firmly standing on the floor (see Figure 15.21).

FIGURE 15.21 *Making the meshing grid finer solved the floating objects problem in this scene.*

A finer mesh cannot solve all floating object problems in a radiosity solution. If the object is relatively small and is far from another object that accepts its shadow, for example, no amount of meshing would trigger the creation of a penumbra, much less an umbra.

The solution here is either to move the small object closer to the other object or to ray trace the image, which, hopefully, will provide the offending object a shadow. But the best solution is to use a finer mesh to capture shadow boundaries.

MACH BANDS

Named after Ernst Mach who studied the phenomenon, Mach bands are intense perceptual visual artifacts in areas with light and dark shading. In scenes with high light/dark contrasts, your eyes' retinal receptors exaggerate the tonal changes across the scene. You perceive the light tones as more intense when viewed next to a dark region and vice versa. This enhancement of the light and dark region results in a perceived light band, called a Mach band, that runs along the geometry. These Mach bands are very visible at acute and right angles. Take a look.

1. Load Machbd.scn.

2. Run a solution by clicking the Radiosity button on the Render panel until it reaches 92%.

3. Render the Camera view or do a Render Scene. Note the light bands (Mach bands) under the cube (see Figure 15.22). They are caused by the eyes intensifying edge contrasts between the light and dark areas. There is no easy solution for Mach bands, but they can be alleviated by increasing the meshing to minimize the creation of dark and light areas along the edges of geometry.

FIGURE 15.22   *The Mach bands are very evident in this rendering.*

4. Go to the Render panel and do a Render to File. Set these parameters: Save as type AVI and name it "mach band test.avi." Enter 352×240 NTSC MPEG1 for the resolution. This should make the aspect ratio just right for the camera moves on a cubic subject. In the Animation, select All Frames. On the AVI Compression, select Cinepak, and have the Compression Quality at 100%, and check off the Key Frame and the Data Rate. Press OK to start rendering the AVI to a file.

5. View the AVI after it finishes. Notice that the Mach bands also appear with other colors but are very noticeable with white. The file mach band.avi is located on the accompanying CD-ROM for you to view if you do not want to render the file.

Mach bands in radiosity are normally created in situations where the mesh is too coarse; coarse meshes enhance the contrast between vertices. A higher-resolution mesh can eliminate Mach bands because the tonality change across vertices would not be distributed across a wider area instead of jumping across two adjacent radiosity elements.

SUMMARY

Radiosity is one of the myriad of tools trueSpace offers to create more realistic renderings and animations. You should treat radiosity as a sophisticated built-in radiosity shader, rather than a rendering technique such as ray tracing or ScanLine. Radiosity, if treated this way, offers more possibilities than if you view it as a rendering method. It has limitations and advantages, but rendered radiosity output is well worth the effort. If you follow the workflow I outlined, radiosity will be less of a burden and will open up new worlds.

trueSpace Cinematography

by Frank Rivera

There is a lot more to creating great imagery in trueSpace than modeling, texture mapping, and rendering a scene—so much more. How your audience will view your imagery is as important as the objects in the scene. As you will see, the placement of the camera, or rather the framing of the APOV (Audience's Point of View), can be used to focus the audience's attention effectively. It can be used to control the mood of a shot and its composition, and it can take on the role of a character in your story.

NOTE

In trueSpace, any object can be used as a camera. To avoid confusion in the discussions, I will use APOV (Audience's Point of View) to refer to what the viewer sees.

This chapter covers

- The Camera tool
- Thinking like a cinematographer
- Lighting
- Framing shots
- Perspective
- Depth of field
- Creating more depth
- Camera movement
- Following the action
- Using different objects as cameras
- The Look At tool
- Following a set path
- Complex camera moves
- Making the camera part of the action
- Motion blur

THE CAMERA TOOL

trueSpace's camera tool is very simple to use. Essentially, you point it in the direction of the subject you want to capture. Using the tool itself is a breeze; here is basically all there is to trueSpace cameras.

The Camera tool adds a new camera to the scene. The camera can be moved and rotated, but not scaled; scaling the camera actually zooms in the camera target. A scene may contain more than one camera. To use the camera's viewpoint, select the Camera, and then select the View From Object tool.

That's about it for the physical use of cameras in trueSpace. This tool's simplicity shouldn't be taken for granted; it is a powerful means of communicating with your audience.

Thinking Like a Cinematographer

When setting up a shot for an image or animation, you must consider many things, tackling the same issues that a traditional cinematographer must. In that spirit, let's approach the subject from the perspective of a cinematographer, a trueSpace cinematographer.

Cinematography means to write with light. Therefore, it has a lot more to do with what the audience sees rather than the art of film making. The cinematographer, also known as the director of photography, is responsible for each shot's composition, lighting, and camera movement. If you are the sole person working on your animation, you will perform both the director's and the cinematographer's roles. This is usually the case, but for the remainder of this chapter, I would like you to isolate yourself from the role of the director and assume the role of the cinematographer.

The key elements a cinematographer must consider:

- Lighting
- Framing shots
- Perspective
- Focal length
- Depth of field
- Creating more depth
- Camera movement

Let's examine how each contributes to making a shot portray a certain mood or emotion.

Lighting

Chapter 12 discussed lighting your scenes in trueSpace, but let's look at how a cinematographer might use light. After all, the most important tool to change visual meaning is light. Four elements of light have a direct impact on your scenes.

- **Lighting quality:** Lighting quality can be split into two categories, hard and soft. Hard gives sharp, clearly-defined shadows. Soft creates a more ambient, subtle illumination. Consider the example in Figure 16.1.

Figure 16.1   *An example of how hard light and soft light can be used to change a scene's mood.*

- **Light source:** The *key light* provides the dominant light in the scene, whereas the manipulation or softening of shadows is performed by the *fill light*. In Figure 16.3, the room is illuminated with two lights. The light coming from the right is the key light. This is the shadow-casting light. The second light does not cast shadows and is placed behind the chair to soften the shadows cast by the key light. It produces an effect similar to a softer light.

- **Lighting direction:** The careful placement of lights can be used to create a sense of adventure and drama. An example of dramatic lighting is in the classic horror films where the character's face is lit from underneath. Figure 16.2 shows how the position of a key light can affect the mood of a shot.

- **Light color:** Color is mainly used in the objects and characters you create; the lights simply highlight them. However, colored lights can also add mood to a scene. The use of colored lights can be seen in the motion picture *Total Recall.* Remember all those shades of red used in the shots of the Mars planet surface. Take a peek at Figure 16.4. In it, the color lights change our interpretation of how we see the scene.

The lights in both scenes are identical in their locations and intensity. Changing the color of the lights from white to blue changes the scene from daylight to moonlight. By changing the light's color we have, in effect, changed the time of day the image represents. What time of day would the image project if we changed the light's color to orange?

Figure 16.2   *An example of using a light's position to change the mood of a shot.*

Figure 16.3   *An example of using secondary lights as fill light for a scene. The shadows cast by the key light are softened by placing a non-shadow–casting fill light behind the chair.*

FIGURE 16.4 *An example of using colored lights to change how the viewer will interpret the scene. In the first panel of this image, the lights project a white color. In the second panel, the lights have had their color changed to blue, which changes the scene to one of moonlight.*

FRAMING SHOTS

Good camera placement can help tell your story. The placement of the camera and the framing of the shot can make a scene more interesting. Below are the different types of shots and their use.

- **Extreme long shot:** For purposes of framing the environment. This is often used as an establishing shot, taking in the general area before any character or action is focused on.

- **Long shot:** Individual characters and objects have presence, but the general environment is still dominant. An example is a long shot used to capture hot-air balloons being inflated at the fairgrounds.

- **Medium shot:** A character is framed from the waist up, making gestures and expressions clear to the audience.

- **Medium close-up:** A character is framed from the chest up, used in intimate conversations.

- **Close-up:** Individual parts of an object are framed, such as a character's face, the hands opening a door, and so on.

- **Extreme close-up:** Individual parts of an object are framed, such as a character's eyes or a fly on the edge of a cup.

This is a general look at camera placement. A lot more details should be considered if you want to make your shots more interesting.

PERSPECTIVE AND FOCAL LENGTH

One such detail is perspective. Even very large objects appear smaller the farther away they are from us. Our eyes feed us information about the objects around us. Their surfaces not only tell us what an object is made of, but also its mass and distance. Although objects might be far away, we can approximate their size and the space between them. This is called *perspective relation.*

Unlike our eyes, we can directly change the focal length and depth of field in trueSpace without a need for a subject. For example, look at the room you're in. Do not focus on any one object and blur your surroundings. You can't—instinctively your eyes grab hold of something in the room to focus on. This ability to focus and not to focus on a given object gives us different possibilities of rendering perspective relations.

The camera's *focal length* can be used to alter perspective relations in a shot. The best way to understand focal length is to think of it in terms of the lenses a traditional camera uses. There are three types of lenses that convey different perspective relations.

- **Wide angle:** The depth is longer than normal, and a wide-angle lens distorts straight lines toward the edges of the screen. This alters our perception of the space in the shot, making it appear as though there is more space than there is. A tiny room can appear large. This effect can be used in animations to make your planes, trains, and automobiles appear to be moving fast.

- **Normal:** No fooled perception with this setting. In trueSpace, normal is a setting of 1.0.

- **Telephoto:** Flattens the depth planes, making the visible space appear smaller. Distances can squash together, giving an alteration of perspective as noticeable as a wide-angle lens.

You cannot scale the camera in trueSpace, but you can adjust the focal length. You must use the Zoom tool to adjust the camera's focal length. It helps to have the Object Info panel open when you do this. The acceptable range for setting the focal length is 0.25 to 4.0, and the default is 1.0. You can manually enter the focal length value in the Z Size entry field in the Object Info panel. Figure 16.5 is an example of different focal lengths and their effect.

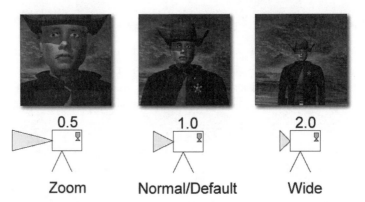

FIGURE 16.5   *Examples of different lens settings. The camera is two meters from the subject in each of these shots.*

Using a wide angle on close-up shots can have an odd effect. In Figure 16.6, a wide angle is used two meters from the subject. Moving the camera close distorts the image, causing a fish-eye effect.

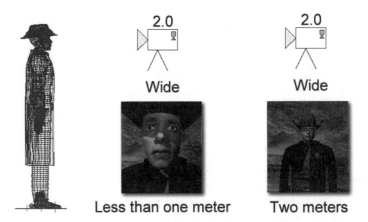

FIGURE 16.6   *The effects of using a wide angle on a subject from two meters and less than one meter.*

When creating an animation, it is a good idea to jot down the lenses used, and in what situations. That way, you can reuse the same lens for the same type of shot. This will give your film a look of continuity. A cinematographer wouldn't have it any other way.

DEPTH OF FIELD

The APOV represents the eyes of the viewer; actually just one eye. This can cause the images we create to appear flat. You can transform a flat image or animation into one with depth by using trueSpace's Depth of Field options. These options give you an effect similar to viewing the scene through an actual lens where objects outside the focal point appear blurred.

Depth of field is the measurement of focus accuracy, the range at which a shot is in focus. Outside the specified focus depth, the image will look less sharp, out of focus. For example, a wide-angle lens has a greater depth of field than a telephoto lens.

There are basically two types of focus:

- **Shallow:** Only one plane is in focus; the remainder is blurred.

- **Deep:** Everything is in focus; all planes in the frame are sharply defined. With deep focus, everything is clear and in focus. Deep focus was brought to new heights by Orson Welles in his film *Citizen Kane.* Take a look at the spatial relations between characters in the film.

> **NOTE**
>
> A lens transforms depth onto a flat surface (such as film) by gathering light waves of different lengths. The flat surface, in essence, becomes the focal plane. This is essentially what our eyes do.

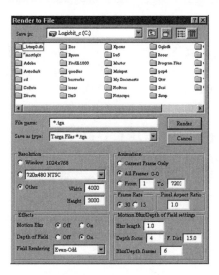

FIGURE 16.7 *A look at the Render to File dialog box.*

You can find the Depth of Field options in the Render to File dialog box (see Figure 16.7). The Depth of Field settings are grouped together with the Motion Blur options. The Depth of Field On/Off radio button located in the Effects area of the Render to File dialog box enables and disables the Depth of Field option. The three entry fields associated with the Depth of Field option are located in the Motion Blur/Depth of Field Settings area of the Render to File dialog box window.

- **F. Dist:** Sets the focal point of the image. This is the distance from the camera (or the object responsible for the APOV) out into the scene. At this distance, items will appear sharp and in focus.

- **Focus:** Used to set the amount of sharpness the objects outside the focal point will have. The larger the value, the more blurred the objects outside the focal point will appear.

- **Blur/Depth Frames:** Functions the same for both Depth of Field and Motion Blur. This essentially controls the quality of the out-of-focus effect. Setting it to less than 5 frames produces a kind of fanning effect, instead of the desired blur. Keep this value at 6 or higher for the best results. A value of 1 effectively turns the option off.

In Figure 16.8, the chair in the foreground is out of focus. This simple effect adds a sense of depth to the scene from what is essentially a flat image.

CREATING MORE DEPTH

When framing your shots, consider the space between objects in the scene and the actions they will perform. The use of space has everything to do with the visual aesthetics of the shot—how you want your viewer to perceive your imagery: flat and static, or with depth. The use of space isn't enough to suspend a viewer's disbelief, but combine it with motion, and you have something.

How we perceive an object being in the foreground, background, or somewhere in between is called *aerial perspective*.

Movement can contribute to this aerial perspective. We change perception depending on the movement of an object. For example, imagine a close-up shot of a frosty mug of beer in a bar. The mug

NOTE

Using Depth of Field and Motion Blur requires more than one frame. If you are working on an image, make an animation out of it.

NOTE

The Depth of Field option is global to your animation, but you're not out of luck. A technique called *pulling focus* allows different focal planes to be brought into the foreground or background. In other words, certain objects can be focused on at certain points in your animation. If you would like to have the focus change within your animation—during a flyby, for example—you can use a camera target and the Look At tool. If the Look At tool has been used, the focal point will automatically be set to the object being looked at. We will discuss this in detail later in this chapter.

is in focus, and patrons are sitting at the bar in the background. Although the patrons are blurred, if one were to get up and walk away, the viewer would focus on that action. The viewer feels that they are viewing a frosty mug, but the movement in the background changes things; they are now sitting at the bar in front of that frosty mug. That simple movement added more depth to the shot. Any trick you can use to pull more depth from your imagery should be used. Remember your audience is viewing 3D imagery on a 2D screen, so we have to try every trick possible to suspend disbelief. Another example can be found in a squirrel sitting on a park bench eating a nut. It's a great scene—everything is texture mapped and lit perfectly, right down to the trees in the background. To add more depth to the animation, consider adding a little sway to the trees in the background, another squirrel hopping across the grass far back in the scene, or shadows cast by the trees on the ground moving. The scene comes to life with more depth.

FIGURE 16.8 *An example of the dramatic effect the depth of field option can have on your imagery. In this image, the chair in the foreground is out of focus.*

The combination of movement and the use of aerial perspective is powerful. Take advantage of it.

CAMERA MOVEMENT

The freedom of camera movement in trueSpace is wonderful and can be used to add dramatic effect to your animations. Consider following a jogger with a camera. Although the camera keeps the character in the frame, the surroundings continually change, feeding the audience more information about the character's surroundings. This is called *mobile framing*. Camera movement allows your audience to know more about a shot.

Why move the camera? To give the scene a sense of depth. The rate of movement of all the objects in the scene shows the relative distance between the objects. Moving the camera also lets you follow the action. Camera moves can create a graceful transition between two shots or actions, called an *in-camera edit*.

As you can see, there are many reasons why you would want to perform a camera move. The standard types of camera moves follow; each is identified by a key word that can be used in your storyboards. In trueSpace, a camera looks down its own z-axis, the y-axis runs vertically up through the camera, and the x-axis runs horizontally. All the axes intersect at the point where the camera's lens meets the camera body. I suggest viewing the camera from the Top view as you rotate it. All movements of the camera are in relation to this fixed axis.

NOTE

Effectively noting camera moves in a storyboard is covered more in depth in Chapter 17, "Creating a Short Film."

- **Tilt:** Rotates up and down around its x-axis. This a common camera move but can add drama to a scene. Take the case where a pair of huge feet enter the scene; slowly the camera tilts upward, revealing a huge giant looking down onto the audience.

- **Roll:** Rotates clockwise and counterclockwise around its z-axis. This effect should not be overused, but it does have its place.

- **Pan:** Rotates around its y-axis, giving a panoramic view. This view is effective only if the camera maintains a constant height from the ground during the move. This move can be accompanied with a slow camera tilt, but the tilt should be in one direction only. Otherwise, your audience may become seasick. If you are trying for the look of an object floating on the surface of a body of water, use a slight tilt and roll: fast tilt, slow roll, fast roll, slow tilt, repeating as necessary.

- **Track:** Moves around in any direction on the ground. This can be accompanied by a tilt, a roll, a pan, or any combination.

- **Crane:** Moves around in any direction off the ground, including up and down. If you have ever seen a flyby animation, this is the type of camera move used. It is usually accompanied by a camera roll during the turns. Try to avoid the use of crane-like camera moves, if at all possible. They tend to make CG animation scream, "Hey, I was created on a computer."

- **Handheld:** Moves around as if the camera were held by a moving operator. The effect is that of shaky, erratic framing, in our case, deliberate. This is a wonderful effect that looks great for shots where a character is being chased or followed. It is assumed that this type of camera move will have the characteristics of the track method, but the crane method could also be used.

- **Reframing:** Follows a moving object, keeping the subject—a jogger or a car, for example—centered in frame. This is also called *mobile framing*. Reframing simply means the camera stays with the object throughout the shot. You should also specify how the camera is to be moved—handheld, track, pan, or crane, for example. When using this camera move, it is important to note that the audience will focus on the movement during the first few seconds of the shot. If the shot is long, the viewer will tend to watch the background and begin to starve for more information. You can use this to your advantage by placing clues of what is about to happen in the background.

You have complete freedom of movement in trueSpace, and sometimes this makes describing the type of camera move you want difficult to convey. The notation I use in my storyboards is simple and to the point. For example, in panel 2 of a storyboard, I might note a camera move by using two panels. One shows where the camera is looking at the start of the move and a second panel (panel 3) shows where the camera is looking at the end of the move. I then draw a line from panel 2 to panel 3 to show the team that both panels are part of the same shot. At first, this sounds like I have everything covered, but I don't. This illustrates only where the camera should point during the move, but it doesn't tell us how the camera got there. So I jot a simple note beneath panel 2, like this:

> Wide 2.0: Reframing 1meter/handheld/track

The "1meter" indicates the distance the camera is from the subject. If the camera view angle and the distance of the camera from the subject have changed, then under panel 3, I would note:

> Wide 2.0: 5feet

This is an unusual case. I usually wouldn't change the view angle during a shot because it is ineffective and distracting. Distance alone is a common change, so in that case I would note under panel 3: 5feet. Notice how I jot down only what has changed.

There are no rules chiseled in stone on how you notate camera moves on a storyboard. If you are working as part of a team for a studio, the method has probably already been decided for you. Keep in mind when creating your own storyboards that what matters is that you clearly state the move in a form that is easy to understand for everyone involved.

Whatever method or combination of methods you use, make note throughout your animation of the camera height and view angle used in each type of shot. It's a good idea to save your cameras as COB files for later use in your animations. For example, you can save a wide-angle camera and a camera used for close-ups as two separate COBs. Continuity in your shots makes the animation more enjoyable to us critics.

FOLLOWING THE ACTION

In trueSpace, you can follow the action in many ways. You can move the camera to a new location and keyframe its new position. You can have a camera follow an object or a specific path, or you can have a camera track an object as it moves. Let's look at these techniques more closely.

USING DIFFERENT OBJECTS AS CAMERAS

In trueSpace, any object can serve as a camera. To use an object as a camera, select the object, select the View From Object tool, and you're done. The view from the object is now the APOV. It is important to note when viewing from any object that you are looking down the object's z-axis.

NOTE

The axes of a camera cannot be displayed or manipulated. They are located in the center of the object with the z-axis pointing straight forward through the camera's lens with the y-axis pointing straight up.

You're not limited to a particular type of object. You can also use lights as cameras. This is extremely useful for pointing spotlights, eliminating any guesswork. Simply select the spotlight and select the View from Object tool. Rotate or move the spot into position.

Complex objects can also be used. Take the case of a space fighter made up of many subobjects. By placing the object's axis at the cockpit and orienting it so that the z-axis points out through the front window, you can give your audience a view from the cockpit as the space fighter engages some hostile enemies.

THE LOOK AT TOOL

The Look At tool automatically points the camera's z-axis at a second object's axis location. As the object or camera moves, the camera keeps the object centered in the frame.

NOTE

If the object is animated, you cannot change the position of its axis. You will have to orient the object's axis prior to animating the object.

To create a camera target, select the object to act as the camera and select the Look At tool. The cursor will change to a glue bottle. Select the object that will become the camera's target. The Look At button will appear depressed when the selected camera or object has been assigned a look at target. You can test the effect by switching to a Perspective view window. Try it with some simple objects:

1. Add a camera and sphere to the scene.

2. Select the camera.

3. Select the Look At tool and then the sphere. You should notice that the camera immediately points its lens at the sphere (your camera target).

4. Open a small window and set it to View From Object (camera view).

5. Switch the large window to the Top view and move the camera around. Notice how the camera stays focused on the sphere.

The Look At tool isn't limited to cameras. You can use it on any object you want. For example, I mentioned that you can use lights as cameras by using the View From Object tool for easy placement of spotlights, but this can become a tedious task for an animation. A simple approach would be to have the spotlight look at an object. The object can then be animated without having to worry about animating the spotlight as well. The spotlight will follow the object throughout the animation. It is important to note that if the Look At target (in this case, the camera target) were moved, the camera would appear as if it were no longer looking at the target. The screen gets visually updated if the camera is selected and moved or if the animation is played back. This doesn't mean that the camera isn't following the target; it just means the screen hasn't been updated to reflect the target's new position or rotation.

FOLLOWING A SET PATH

NOTE

During the course of an animation, you can have the camera look at another object, even with the Look At tool active.

Cameras can be made to follow an exact path, as well. Try it:

1. In a new scene, add a sphere.

2. Switch to the Top view. By using the Eye Zoom tool, zoom out so there's enough room around the sphere to place other objects.

3. Add a camera to the scene.

4. Make the sphere the camera's target by using the Look At tool as described previously.

5. Move the camera to the right near the edge of your screen.

6. Select the Path tool and click the center of the camera. Create a wide path around the sphere back to the camera's position with ten clicks of the mouse.

7. The Draw Path panel should be open. You will notice that there is a number in the segments field. This is the number of frames you create with each click of the mouse. To see the individual frame nodes, click the Frames radio button in the Draw Path panel.

If the animation group isn't already open, open it now. You have just recorded a path for the camera to take. To play the animation, click the Play button in the Animation group. The camera should circle the sphere, following the path and keeping its lens pointed in the sphere's direction.

COMPLEX CAMERA MOVES

We managed to get a camera to look at an object and follow a set path. What happens if the object the camera is looking at has a path of its own?

1. Rewind the animation by clicking the Return to Start button located in the Animation group.

2. Select the sphere and open the Draw Path panel again.

3. Click the center of the sphere.

4. With six clicks of your mouse, create a figure-eight. Click in the upper-right corner of the screen above the camera. Then click in the lower portion of

the screen below the camera. Click the center of the sphere again. Click in the upper-left corner of the screen and then down in the lower-left corner. Finally, click the center of the sphere again.

5. The sphere should move along its path. Let's look at what happens when both the sphere and the camera move. To see both animation paths, you will have to set Draw to Scene in the Animation Parameters panel. To open the Animation Parameters panel, right-click the Play button in the Animation group.

Play back the animation. Notice how the camera keeps track of the sphere as it moves around the scene. Because the sphere's path is shorter than the camera's, the sphere will end up back at its original position before the camera does. You can use this technique to create some interesting smooth complex camera moves.

You can take this even further by using invisible camera targets. Suppose you want the same camera path as previously, but you don't want the sphere visible. This is easily accomplished with the following steps:

1. Select the object.

2. Right-click the Object Info tool to open the Object Info panel.

3. Left-click the Render Options button located in the lower-right corner of the Object Info panel.

4. Check the Invisible option and uncheck the Cast Shadow option if it isn't already.

5. Because the Object isn't visible, you might as well uncheck the Receive shadow option.

The sphere will no longer be visible at render time.

If that is too much trouble, you can use a light with Intensity set to 0 as a camera target. Because lights don't render, all you have to do is give it a path to follow.

MAKING THE CAMERA PART OF THE ACTION

A simple method of getting the camera involved in the action is to glue a camera to an object. Suppose you are creating an animation of a crew of pirates. During a storm, you would like a view from the crow's nest as the ship fights its way across the open sea. After you have animated the ship crashing through waves, you can attach a camera to the top of the mast and view the scene from the camera's perspective.

Let's try this with the ship scene Caligari was so gracious to provide. In the location you installed trueSpace, you will find a folder called Scenes. Load up the scene called ship.scn. You will see the ship from the Perspective view.

1. Add a camera to the scene and place it atop the mast.

2. Rotate the camera so it points at the horizon over the bow of the ship.

3. Select the camera and enable View from Object.

4. Open a smaller view window and switch to the Perspective view.

5. In the small window, select the ship. Glue the camera to the ship's mast with the Glue As Child tool.

6. If the animation group isn't already open, open it now. The animation has already been recorded; all you have to do is play it. This is a simulation, so you will have to click the Start Simulation button.

You should see the horizon or grid beneath the ship move realistically as the ship makes its way over the waves. You can now create an elaborate scene where the ship is in a storm. After animating it, you can get multiple shots by placing cameras in different areas of the scene, providing different perspectives. You can then splice them together in a package, such as Premiere, to create a dramatic series of shots.

MOTION BLUR

Motion blur, like the Depth of Field effect, is global for the entire scene. Everything with motion is blurred, including shadows and reflections. This can create some stunning effects but can take a while to render (see Figure 16.9).

You can find the Motion Blur options in the Render to File dialog box. The Motion Blur settings are grouped together with the Depth of Field options. They share one parameter, the Blur/Depth Frames field.

The Motion Blur On/Off radio button located in the effects area of the Render to File dialog box enables and disables this option.

FIGURE 16.9   *An example of using Motion Blur in trueSpace. This character was animated. When Motion Blur was turned on, his limbs were blurred, giving the animation a realistic look.*

The Length field controls how much animation time will be displayed in a single frame. A setting of 1 to 3 is all you should need for a good blur.

The Frames field controls the quality of the blurring. This value is equal to the number of frames that will be rendered and combined together to form a single blurred image. I have found that a setting of 6 gives good results. Anything less than 6 causes the blurring effect to look fanned out, making the action look as though it starts and stops.

The results you get from Motion Blur are directly related to the smoothness and speed of the object's movement in the scene. A little experimentation is required to get the desired effect to fit your animation. I suggest rendering 10 frames of an important action sequence with Motion Blur on. A Length of 3 and Frames set to 6 is a starting point.

NOTE

If everything in the scene is moving, you can turn off antialiasing. The blurring effect will hide any jagged edges.

If for any reason you aren't getting a blur effect, it is probably because you forgot to turn on Motion Blur, a common mistake.

SUMMARY

As a trueSpace cinematographer, you play an important role in what viewers feel when they view your imagery. Like any good cinematographer, your aim should be to give the ideal picture of the scene, placing your camera so that the action can be recorded with the most dramatic effect. You must learn to use the camera as an observer and as the eye of your audience, giving them the best possible viewpoint of your story.

Frank Rivera 97

TAKING THE NEXT STEP

The Tomb

Photograph of the tomb of Khufu Circa 1900 (Frank Rivera, LOGICBL)

CHAPTER 17

CREATING A SHORT FILM

by Frank Rivera

The world of computer-generated imagery is an exciting one with unlimited possibilities. CG is used today in a broad range of situations, such as scientific visualization, art, the medical industry, and the entertainment industry, to name a few. In this chapter, we will look at the road to creating a short film in trueSpace4. We must now step back from the modeling and animation details of previous chapters to focus on the planning and management of your project or short film.

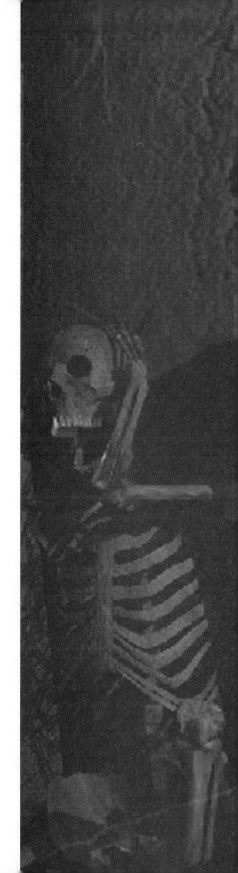

Specifically, we will cover

- Telling your story
- Creating a storyboard
- 12 key points to every storyboard
- An alternative to drawing storyboards
- Creating a master scene
- Managing your project
- Working with complex scenes

TELL A STORY

Every great animation has one important ingredient: a story. A story can take issues, events, and situations from life or can be totally made up and off the wall. All good stories have one thing in common: the actions, events, and environment all contribute to a narrative path that culminates in a reasonable conclusion. In life, events happen for no reason, issues are raised never to be resolved, and conflicts occur for no apparent reason. Why must all the events and actions in an animation's story guide the viewer to a final outcome, a resolution to an issue raised in the story? Because the goal of most animations is to entertain. If your story goes nowhere, viewers will be disappointed, and the animation will fail.

Certainly, you want them to be entertained, but what else should viewers feel after watching your film? The journey you take viewers on determines how they feel after seeing your animation. You have to decide what chain of events are to occur before reaching your film's apex. Is there a message you want to get across or just some laughs? Most stories deal with human emotion or moral decisions—we like to feel in control, we want to be assured that good will always triumph over evil, and so on. These make some of the best endings because it leaves the viewer with a feeling of fulfillment.

FIND INSPIRATION

Theoretical discussions are great, but where do you start a project? The cliché is with a storyboard. I say, however, the place every aspiring animator illustrator begins is with a bit of inspiration. I would be willing to bet that is why you're sitting here reading this book. Sometime ago, you saw a special effect in a movie or an image that lit a fire in your heart for 3D. Finding the inspiration for your next animation is a breeze and can occur anytime, anywhere—the next TV commercial to interrupt the NBA playoffs, a *Melrose Place* episode, or the next home-run Mark McGwire slams over the outfield fence. Inspiration breeds enthusiasm, and that's a formula for success, no matter how little experience you have.

A Story Without an Ending

Inspiration rarely comes as fully fleshed out storylines, but don't let that stop you. You don't have to start out with a complete story, just an idea. The animation I will be discussing in this chapter, *The Tomb*, began with an idea and a little inspiration.

Having always been fascinated with ancient Egypt, I wanted to create an animation that took place in or around the time of the last great dynasty. Once I gathered enough research materials (images of the people and places I would have to model), I sat down to think up a story outline—and think, and think, and think.

A day or two later, I was still sitting there staring at the blank page when my daughter rescued me by yelling, "Daddy! There's a show about Egypt on TV." I was about to dismiss the show as nothing I hadn't seen before when the commentator said, "Centuries ago, the tomb was pillaged by thieves."

FIGURE 17.1   *In this image from The Tomb, hieroglyphs morph into English text, revealing an ancient warning.*

That was it! A tomb robber pillaging an ancient tomb. I could see it: The scene starts outside at night during a storm (ancient Egypt wasn't arid back then). A torch light can be seen flickering in the distance. A man is digging in the faint light. Suddenly, the scene goes black; the next thing you hear is the chipping of block, rock falling to the ground. Light streams into the scene from a torch. Dust fills the air (an opportunity to create some visible light and haze).

You can't make out who is holding the torch; the light is too bright. The shadow of the man can be seen climbing in through the opening. The scene switches to the thief's perspective, and he eyeballs everything in the tomb. The flicker of the torch in his hand lends an eerie feeling to the scene. You can see the paintings on the walls, the pots and treasures left for the dead to take into the afterlife. The thief comes across a tablet. Beside the tablet is a skeleton in an unusual position. Inscribed on the tablet are hieroglyphs. The hieroglyphs morph into English text (for the sake of the viewers) (refer to Figure 17.1). "He who enters shall suffer a fate worse than death."

I had the makings of a story, but no ending yet. I eventually did find one (more on it later); but before I did, I began working with what I had so far.

Telling a good story can be somewhat intimidating and might seem like an impossible task at first; but like everything else, it can be broken into manageable chunks. This is where a storyboard comes in.

THE STORYBOARD

Storyboarding dates back as far as the time of Leonardo Da Vinci; he often used a series of doodles to illustrate his ideas. Centuries later, Walt Disney used storyboards to visualize ideas for his short films. In fact, storyboarding as it is used today in business is largely due to Mike Vance and Walt Disney who used storyboarding for business planning; they called this process *displayed-thinking*. Today it is used by programmers to help them lay out user interfaces, by architects to better visualize wayfinding (an architectural term that refers to the process used to orient and navigate), and Web page designers to help them construct better Web sites.

A storyboard as defined in the animation and film industry is a portfolio of sketches that illustrates a story's flow to a production team. A storyboard is what an artistic team collaborates with, it's what a director directs from, and it is used in set and costume design.

Storyboarding is an important step in the development phase of your short film, not only to yourself and your team, but to your clients as well. Like your animation, a storyboard is visual. When you provide your clients with a storyboard, they can follow the project visually, which in many cases can make things move more smoothly. Some things can be communicated better visually, and a storyboard is the instrument to do it. Let's look at creating a storyboard, from the simplest to one with great production value.

When most folks think of storyboards, they think of the expensive layouts produced by advertising firms on white board. Relax. A simple 8½×11–inch sheet of paper is just as good. You can use watercolor, ink, or crayons. You don't have to get fancy with your drawings, either. I often use stick people in my storyboards. Visualizing the steps required to create your animation is what you are after.

It will save a lot of time if you begin to create your storyboards after you have a story to tell or at least part of a story. A common method for writers is to start with an ending and build the story around it. Although it is possible to create storyboards as you brainstorm your plot, a general outline will help the process. Spend some time talking your ideas out with friends. This helps in more ways than one. The most obvious is that your friend can give you feedback on your ideas. Also, by talking your ideas out with a friend, you can piece them all together more easily. I find it useful to have an audience throughout the development process, and friends make a great audience. Don't limit your audience to friends. Friends tend to tell you what you want to hear. Try seeking out the opinions of other professionals. If you are having trouble getting a professional's opinion due to their busy schedule, enlist a friend of a friend whom you have never met. They will usually give their honest opinion if you ask for it.

A SIMPLE STORYBOARD

Once you have a couple of great ideas and a story, it is time to create the storyboard. Storyboards can contain a wealth of information to a production team, from the position of camera, lights, and characters, to the mood and look of the short film. No need to get that complex right away, however, because you can work up a simple storyboard in four steps.

1. Divide a piece of paper into six or eight panels.

2. In the upper-left square, write the title of the project.

3. In each of the panels, write a sentence or two describing the action.

4. In each of the panels, draw a picture to illustrate the shot.

KEY POINTS FOR EVERY STORYBOARD

Storyboards are serious business; entire careers have been built on them. Take a look at what serious storyboarding entails.

Often, the eye of the camera (what the camera sees) is used to create the panels of a storyboard. Therefore, you should consider the following when creating your panels:

- *Plan your story so that the visual images and the script can be clearly understood by reading your storyboard.* A storyboard isn't effective if it can't be understood.

- *Put your shots and scenes in an order that tells your story clearly.* A logical flow from shot to shot and scene to scene makes the film more enjoyable for the audience.

- *Considering what happens in a shot isn't enough.* You should take into account how fast or how slow you want the action to take place. Each shot's length should be in the range of three to seven seconds. If the shot or dialog is longer than five seconds, break it up into two or more shots.

- *Indicate how much of the background should be seen.* If everything in the scene must be in sharp focus, then you need to have greater depth of field. This should be noted on the storyboard so that when the scene is rendered, the appropriate Depth of Field can be set in the Render to File panel.

- *Make notes on the storyboard if the camera is looking down or up.* If the camera looks up at a character or figure, the character or figure will look more threatening. If the camera looks down, the character or figure will look insignificant.

- *If the camera moves in the scene, indicate the move by using two panels.* The first panel indicates where the camera starts, and the second indicates what the camera will see when the movement has completed. Draw an arrow between the two frames to indicate that they are part of the same shot. I use three panels for this purpose. The first panel is used to indicate where the camera starts, the second is a top view of the scene showing the placement of all the objects, camera, lights, and the path the camera is to take. The third panel shows what the camera will see at the end of the move. I then draw a line from panel one to panel three to indicate that the panels are all the same shot.

● *Break up long shots.* Use several shorter, more interesting shots in place of a single long, boring one.

● *Make sure your transitions are good and the scenes flow nicely together.* I recommend variations in your transitions. Don't make them all the same. Keep changing them to keep the audience engaged, but keep them simple. A transition can be a simple wipe, a fade out and fade in, a blur out and blur in, a white fade out and fade in, or a simple cut.

TIP

There is a rule of motion pictures that can be applied here. If it doesn't move, don't film it, or in our case don't record it. That means if your characters do not move in a scene, move the camera instead.

● *When your characters are interacting, use different perspectives and consider putting one character at a different angle from the other.* This simple technique can give the shot a more three-dimensional look and make it more interesting. What camera angle would best portray the mood of a scene may sometimes take precedence over the mood of the character. For example, a female character enters a scary, under-lit room. An establishing shot could be used to show her shadow entering the room with her right behind as some ominous music plays in the background. In this case, the camera's distant position is more effective in establishing the mood of the scene, whereas a close-up shot of her terrified look is more of a reaction to the scene's change in mood.

● *Use the depth of the scene to make the shot more interesting.* The movement of characters shouldn't be limited to left-right or vice versa. To make the shot more interesting and to add a third dimension, have your characters moving toward and away from the camera.

● *You can also use camera distance to convey mood and to establish context.* A long shot establishes location and displays mood. A midrange shot shows interactions between characters. A medium close-up shot communicates gestures. A close-up shot communicates expressions. An extreme close-up shot communicates a strong emotional impact.

● *There is always a physical or emotional response to every action.* Take advantage of this fact by isolating key elements during the action. For example, two characters are shown standing at a table talking. One accidentally knocks the ashtray off the table. Show the ashtray leaving the table's edge. Switch to the reaction of the two characters once they notice what's about to happen. Usually people bring their arms up in anticipation of the ashtray coming in contact with the ground as they watch it fall. Cut to a tight shot of the ashtray (top view) as it falls. Switch to a side view as the ashtray shatters. Cut back to the two characters at the table.

TIP

Never zoom the camera lens in or out. Instead, physically move the camera in or out. A zoom only magnifies an already flat image while moving the camera magnifies but maintains three-dimensional depth.

ASK BEFORE YOU DRAW

When creating a storyboard, always ask yourself these questions:

- Who will be the audience?

- How does the staging complement the story? Where are objects placed in the scene?

- How can you better visualize the main conflicts of the story?

- What resources do you have to work with?

- Is the time frame a factor? How much time do you have to complete the project? Can shots or scenes be integrated into one shot?

AN ALTERNATIVE TO DRAWING STORYBOARDS

Not every 3D artist can sketch drawings to use as storyboards, and in some cases a little more detail can help illustrate a shot more effectively. An inexpensive answer in both situations is MetaCreations' Poser, at least for storyboards that involve characters. Poser is a practical digital puppet program that can be used to create storyboards quickly. With Poser, you can choose from a variety of characters with different attributes, such as weight and height. Each of the characters can be posed easily. Poser enables you to work out the gestures required to tell the story effectively. You can then copy the characters into your storyboard. Figure 17.2 shows a portion of a storyboard created in Poser.

SILHOUETTES TO BETTER ILLUSTRATE YOUR STORY

Although a gesture or character's posture can be all that is needed for a shot to work, the positioning of the characters and camera also play an important part in how each of the panels of your storyboard is interpreted. In Figure 17.2, the action in each panel is clear. I accomplished this by silhouetting each of the characters prior to placing them in the storyboard. Figure 17.3 is an example of using silhouettes to clarify the action in panel 47 of the storyboard.

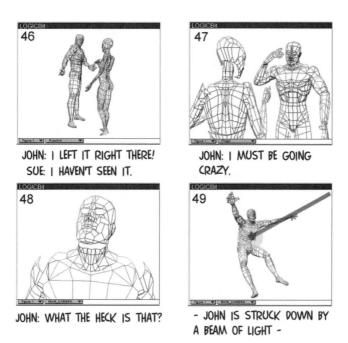

FIGURE 17.2 *An example of storyboarding with MetaCreations' Poser.*

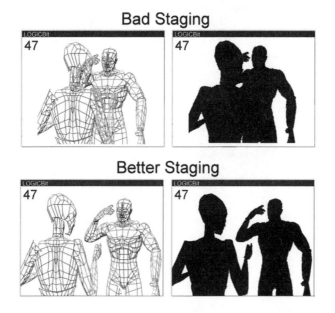

FIGURE 17.3 *Using silhouettes to improve how the action in a storyboard is interpreted.*

In Figure 17.3, the first two panels illustrate bad staging. In the top panels, it is difficult if not impossible to see each character's gesture or mood. The bottom two panels clearly show each of the characters' gestures. Silhouetting the characters was vital to ensure that all the members of the production team would interpret what each of the characters was doing in each of the panels.

THE TOMB STORYBOARD

Let's see how these storyboarding tips work in practice by examining the storyboard for *The Tomb*. What I knew about the story so far described what would be visible, and that was enough to determine the scenes I needed to create. It is also the basis of a storyboard: laying out which scenes constitute the story. Figure 17.4 illustrates the watercolor storyboard used in the making of *The Tomb*.

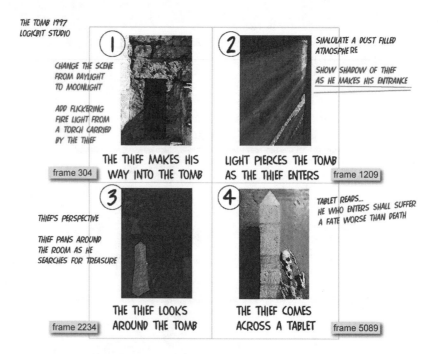

FIGURE 17.4　*The Tomb storyboard.*

The panels in the storyboard so far:

- Panel 1: A view of the tomb entrance
- Panel 2: Someone is entering the tomb

● Panel 3: The robber's view of things in the scene

● Panel 4: The tablet and warning

With as little as four panels, I had most of the story laid out. With a storyboard, you can achieve a better sense of what is going on in your project and you will be able to plan every step and manage your project more effectively. Let's take a closer look at managing your projects.

AFTER THE STORYBOARD: THE WORKFLOW

Once the storyboard has been finished, an animation script can be written. Animation scripts often do not tell the actors performing the narrative (if your story requires one) what the dialog will be. In most cases, the script is what determines which animation frame numbers the panels of the storyboard correspond to. This gives an approximate running length for the animation and helps determine how much time the project should take to complete. In a lot of cases, the script is used to create a storyboard, an approach best used for commercial ad campaigns.

I use my storyboard for everything related to my short film, from the shots, set design, camera motion, effects, and notes to the timing and dialog notes. You can get as detailed as you like. Remember that what counts is that the storyboard helps you and your team visualize the story's flow.

With your storyboard and animation script in hand, you're ready to begin development. The basic stages are:

● Modeling

● Animation

● Post Production

● Audio Recording

Let's look at the workflow a bit to get a general idea of where things fit in, and then we will look at some things you can do to keep the project in perspective and under control.

TIP

You don't have to draw every keyframe (a keyframe is where the action changes direction) when storyboarding your general scenes. That type of detail is mostly used with character animation or anything that needs to be put to timing, a subject covered in Chapter 10, "Character Animation."

TIP

After you have your storyboard and dialog, you can create a *leica reel.* A leica reel is a rough look at your animation. Essentially, the panels in your storyboard are played back like a film. This is a great way of working out the timing between shots. If your storyboard is made up of drawings, you will have to scan them into the computer. You can then import your images into Adobe Premiere to create your leica reel.

MODELING

After the story has been laid out, modeling and set design can begin. This isn't a rule carved in stone; I have modeled characters first and then created a story to fit their look. That approach is fine for personal projects, but if you're collaborating, you usually would want to settle on a story before starting any modeling. (Some tips on handling the modeling workflow are coming up.)

A lot of planning is required prior to modeling. I generally focus on the details of the model before I animate it. If it's a character, I use a detailed character sheet as a guide. All the objects that will be used throughout the short film should be modeled and texture mapped up front, so when the animation process begins, you can concentrate your efforts in that direction. This approach enables you to stay focused on the task ahead instead of being pulled in all directions during the animation phase. When I discuss managing complex scenes, you will see that prepping everything first makes animating and managing the project easier to handle.

ANIMATION

Technically, the visual illusion we perceive as motion is accomplished by displaying objects in varying positions in a sequence of images (stills). Anyone who has tried a hand at animation, however, knows there's much more to this phase. I'll give you some tips shortly. I also suggest you revisit Chapter 10, "Character Animation," for a review of modeling, character sheets, and character design in regard to characters and animation.

After the characters, sets, and character movements have been worked out, the scene is rendered and effects, such as motion blurring, can be applied.

POST PRODUCTION

In the post-production phase, you and your team apply all the editing and video effects to the animation. The finished animation is then put to tape or film. A high-quality video recording deck to record the animation without sacrificing image quality costs around $3,000, but a regular run-of-the-mill VHS deck will do for most projects, including corporate videos.

The editing is accomplished digitally and can be done with any of today's available off-the-shelf packages. Adobe's Premiere and a Miro DC20 or DC30 is all you need to put your animation to tape. The Miro boards are an inexpensive way to get your videos onto tape and usually are bundled with a light version of Premiere. All of today's packages support the most common effects, such as titles, fades, dissolves, and the capability to synchronize audio to video.

You're probably chomping at the bit right now, but hang tight; Terry Cotant will be discussing creating your very own 3D media studio in Chapter 18, "Creating Your Very Own 3D Media Studio."

AUDIO RECORDING

The next step in creating your film is to record the dialog and/or sound effects. This is often done first. Actors are hired and the dialog is recorded. The animation is then created in sync with the audio. This is an expensive method but yields the best results. An alternative is to place dialog text in with your leica reel for the animators to work from. A good animator doesn't need to hear the dialog and can merely read it to animate the characters.

MUSIC

If you have a little knowledge of music, you can use a package like Super Jam by Blue Ribbon Sound Works to create musical scores to add to your film. This is the package I used to create the soundtrack for *The Tomb*. If you do not have the skills to create your own music, consider hiring a professional musician. If budget is a factor (it always is), you can use sound and music from any of the many commercially available sound and loop libraries.

Called *samples*, these professional-quality sound libraries can be found at specialty stores, such as Sam Ash in New York and Los Angeles, that cater to professional musicians and recording studios. These libraries contain thousands of professionally sampled sounds and music tracks that can be used in your work royalty-free, many of which can be looped seamlessly.

DIALOG

Recording dialog is easy these days; just about every PC you buy comes with an audio card that is capable of recording sound. The problem is that most personal computers do not have what you need to record good-sounding dialog.

Unfortunately, you can't plug high-quality microphones directly into a standard Windows sound card. Instead, you need a mixer that can accept a low-impedance microphone. Connect the mixer to your sound card, and you're ready to go. A portable mixer works fine; Mackie makes a small mixer just for this purpose.

The problem with most PCs is that the quality of recorded sound when using the average sound card is not good enough for a short film. If you can spring for it, consider purchasing at least a 32-bit card. You can use a 16-bit sound card, but doing so might require some creative thinking on your part to capture good sound.

While I was recording the audio for *The Tomb*, I placed the microphone at one end of a cardboard tube made of heavy-stock cardboard. I pointed the other end toward the subject I wanted to record. As you can probably guess, the audio came out with a lot of bass. This was perfect—as a bass player, I think nothing sounds better than a note played on the F clef. Just the right amount of bass can shape mediocre sound into a deep, rich sound effect. The sound of the huge sliding stone was recorded this way. I stacked two bricks and slid one across the other for the effect. Without the added bass, the sound effect would have sounded like two wimpy bricks.

BUDGET

We are of the creative breed, which is probably why so many of us approach our work considering only its artistic value. We think about what kind of animation to create, how it will affect the audience, and who the audience will be. We dream up new and creative ways to incorporate stunning effects into our films.

But many of us forget about one little thing that always tends to pop up in conversation: the budget. The startup cost for creating a high-quality digital animation can, in my experience, run thousands of dollars. The cost can soar over 50 grand for a lengthy high-quality short, and if there is a client involved, things can get a little tight. How much the client is willing to spend determines the amount of resources you can harness to complete the project.

The best way to keep a client under control is through good communication from the start. Lay out the lay of the land up front. For example, when a client first contacts you with a project, get as much detail from the client as possible. Inform the client that you would need all their thoughts in writing before you can give a quote for the job. When you receive the information from the client, carefully weigh the project demands and the available resources that can be committed to it. Work out a detailed quote for the client and spell it out in a form easy for the client to understand. If the work is an animation, specify the cost per frame, per second, per minute. This way, the client can easily calculate how much any changes will cost. If there is modeling involved, you should quote the modeling separately from any animation, or at least specify how its cost figures into the total cost; that way, the client is aware that modeling involves a cost.

Be sure to state what changes will cost at different points of the project. For example, changing a character's look halfway through the project might require additional modeling and animation. The client should be made aware that any deviation from the approved project plan will increase the cost of the project.

If you communicate openly with your client, the relationship will start strong and finish strong. Communication is key to happy clients. Don't leave them in the dark, and get all your concerns out in the open before the work begins.

And if this isn't enough, something will always go wrong, so you will have to be prepared for the worst. PCs need to be repaired and updated regularly, incurring more expenses. Therefore, when considering a challenging project, carefully balance the cost versus the rewards, especially if you're one of those who creates for the sake of creating. Of course, don't let my experiences discourage you from pursuing your goals. This is a lucrative business; but remember that like any business, certain risks are involved.

MANAGING *THE TOMB* PROJECT

Now that you have a sense of the general workflow, let's consider some key points in the context of a real project. When we last looked in on *The Tomb*, I had just finished the general storyboard, and it was time to start creating the scenes.

CREATING A MASTER SCENE

When I begin a project, I usually start with a master scene. I create and texture map everything from the walls, ceilings, floors, and doors to the items on tables and the books on shelves. This has two advantages: It enables me to capture the feel of the shots that will take place in the scene, and I won't have to worry about continuity from shot to shot.

An example of bad continuity can be seen in the motion picture *As Good As It Gets*. Helen Hunt, Jack Nicholson, and Greg Kinnear are riding in a convertible on their way to visit Greg Kinnear's parents. Helen Hunt decides to pull over so she can give Greg Kinnear her full attention while listening to his story. In the scene where the decision to pull over is made, the convertible top is down. When they pull over, the top is up. Oops, someone lost track of the continuity.

The Tomb scene is pretty basic. We have some walls, a floor, ceiling, and some pots.

TIP

To get the objects in a scene all the same scale when modeling, I often use a silhouette of a man I created with the Spline Polygon tool and saved as a COB. I call him the scale guy.

After texture mapping all the objects, I save the scene with a 0 appended to the end of the filename to easily identify it as a master scene. I then add a camera to the scene, and, in wireframe mode, I move it around the room and perform some quick renders to get a feel for what things will look like. This is an important step because you might find that a texture that you thought would work well doesn't. It may look lighter than the rest or just too distracting to be used in the scene. This is an opportunity to make important changes before you dissect your master scene. After performing any necessary adjustments and when I am satisfied with the scene, I delete the camera and the default lights and save the scene.

Why use a master scene? The most obvious advantage is that if anything goes wrong, I have a perfect scene I can go back to. Also, if I get a corrupt SCN file, only the one shot is affected and not the entire project. Another advantage is where heavy animation is used. For example, stationary objects have been moved around. I wouldn't have to delete all the animation paths or keyframes; I could simply load up the master scene and move on. The real power of using a master scene comes in handy when working with many shots that take place in the same environment. (We will look at this in more depth later.)

MANAGING FILES

After the master scene, scene files start multiplying faster than rabbits. Keeping them organized is vital to mantaining your sanity and your project's deadlines. When working with a storyboard, I usually name my scenes after the panel they represent. This enables my colleagues and me to find scenes quickly on a hard drive or removable media. If, for any reason, I have to break a scene into smaller shots, I append an *a*, *b*, or *c* to the filename. For example, MyFil02a.scn and MyFil02b.scn are the SCN files for panel 2 of my storyboard but are made up of smaller shots.

When naming scenes with a number sequence appended to the filename, use a two- or three-digit format (MyFile02.scn or MyFile002.scn) depending on the number of scenes your project will have. This will keep all the files in sequential order when viewed on a storage device.

Project management starts with you. If you are part of a larger team, consider it carefully.

WORKING WITH COMPLEX SCENES

There's more to managing complex scenes than good naming etiquette. Let's look at panel 3 of *The Tomb*'s storyboard as an example. The first thing to do for any complex scene is to load up the master scene and save it with the panel number for the scene to be worked on, in this case the third scene in the sequence, scene03. In panel 3 of the storyboard, the scene calls for a thief's perspective of the tomb as he walks through it, eyeballing what there is to steal. This required an animated camera. I loaded a camera and created the path it would take as it navigates through the tomb. The scene could have then been saved, isolating it to a single file. Putting a complex scene like this in a single file can cause problems, though, especially if the scene has a high-polygon count.

I wanted to have one continuous shot showing the thief as he moved, but I had high-polygon-count pots everywhere. This meant that it would take forever to render each frame, putting me behind schedule. This particular shot worked out to be about 400 frames. With all the pots, walls, floor, ceiling, and high-resolution textures, one frame took about 30 minutes to render on a 200 mHz Pentium Pro and 256MB of RAM. Even if I used two machines, I wouldn't have been able to make the deadline, so I opted to dissect the shot and the scene.

REMOVE TO REDUCE

What I needed to do was reduce the number of calculations it would take to render a single frame. Logically, reducing the polygon count was the way to go. I loaded the scene and played the scene back in Wireframe mode from the Top view. In frames 0 to 70, all the jars and pots along the right and back wall weren't visible; therefore, I could delete those pots and jars, reducing the overall polygon count to a reasonable number. I deleted all the objects that wouldn't be visible during this segment of the shot and saved the scene as scene3a. I then rendered the scene. On average, each frame then took only nine minutes to render. I cut the render time per frame down by a third. When I was ready to render the next segment of frames, 71 to 190, I loaded scene3 again saved it as scene3b and removed nonessential objects from the other side of the room. I repeated this process until I had rendered all 400 frames. During post production, I used Premiere to splice the segments together as one continuous shot. Autodesk Animation Studio would also work.

SHADOW SUBSTITUTES

There may be situations where a shadow of an object not physically visible contributes to the shot by the shadow it casts. In this case, you have two options. You can leave that object in the scene or you can create a shadow mask. A shadow mask is nothing more than a low-polygon object you can use to create the same-shape shadow. A simple method of creating a shadow mask is from the Top view to lay the object down and trace around it with the Spline Polygon tool. Stand the object up and place it in the position of the original. Another option is to create a null object that casts shadows:

1. Select the object.

2. Right-click the Object Info tool to open the Object Info panel.

3. Left-click the Render Options button located in the lower-right corner of the Object Info panel.

4. Check the Invisible option and check the Cast Shadow option if it isn't already enabled.

5. Because the Object isn't visible, you might as well uncheck the Receive shadow option.

When the scene is rendered, the object will cast shadows, but that is about it. This can be a big help with extremely complex objects that only contribute shadows to a shot.

ISOLATE FOR SPEED

You can also improve the scene construction process and your modeling with a simple practice. A lot of users, including me, often build a scene piecemeal, modeling within the scene as we move forward. This can become irritating halfway through the scene's completion as the polygon count gradually climbs. You can avoid this problem if you model each object in a scene of its own. This will enable you to move quickly through the modeling process. A benefit of this approach is that you won't be forced to take shortcuts when modeling because the scene has become so complex that real-time feedback is slow. Moving along smoothly during the modeling project makes the modeling task much more fun.

In the case of complex objects, you can also benefit by constructing sections of the object separately. If scale is a concern, and it usually is, you can load a scale guy COB to ensure that the scale is kept uniform from scene to scene. When all the subobjects are modeled, you can load each into a new scene and assemble the final object.

As I said earlier, the advantages of creating a master scene are many. If, for any reason, things aren't working out in a complex scene, you could easily reload the master scene and repeat any of the steps necessary.

HOW DOES IT END?

I've left you hanging long enough. Before I tell you how *The Tomb* ends, however, let me recap. The story takes place in ancient Egypt sometime around the last great dynasty. A thief is breaking into a tomb. He enters the tomb and begins to search for valuables. During his search, he comes across a tablet inscribed with the text, "He who enters shall suffer a fate worse than death."

FIGURE 17.5   *The Tomb storyboard penciled by Mauricio Almeida LOGICBit Studio.*

I went with a funny ending, after a little help. While I was sitting and staring at yet another blank page, my wife burst in to my office saying, "I have your ending! I have your ending!" Through the door, I could hear the radio. "It's the Macarena," she explained. "The thief gets locked in the tomb, and the Macarena just plays on and on and on." I chuckled and thought, "Hey, that's pretty good. Everybody hates the Macarena."

This is how it turned out: The thief can be seen reading the tablet when a huge, heavy stone is heard sliding across the ground. The thief runs toward the opening in a desperate attempt to escape, but he isn't quick enough. He is shown standing at the door when the sound of drums begin to play. He turns with a puzzled look on his face. To his horror, the skeleton, which was once still by the tablet, is now standing. The drums are getting louder. The skeleton makes its way across the tomb toward the thief and stops as the Macarena starts to play. To the beat of the music, the skeleton starts to dance, *daa dada daa dada daa dada daa daa heyyy Macarena*! The torch is dropped to the floor as the thief lets out a terrifying scream, and the scene fades to black. Now *that's* a horrible way to go!

The animation turned out okay, considering my rush to get it done prior to Siggraph. The story is told without any dialog, and the story is by far the best part. Every time the animation played, I could see folks in the audience crack a smile when the skeleton began to dance to the tune.

What seemed like a difficult animation to produce was easy when I broke the story into manageable chunks. If you would like to view *The Tomb*, you will find a copy on the CD that accompanies this book. The filename is \chapters\TheTomb\TheTomb.avi.

SUMMARY

The field of computer-generated imagery is expanding rapidly. People are flocking to this new media by the thousands each year. We are visual creatures. The lure of expressing oneself so vividly and easily is difficult to resist.

When exploring the world of CG, keep in mind that your computer is just another tool; it can't create beauty or art—only you can. Your first work, like a painter's first painting, will rarely be exceptional, but with a little practice, the art of expressing oneself becomes child's play.

CHAPTER 18

CREATING YOUR VERY OWN 3D MEDIA STUDIO

by Terry Cotant

For the purposes of this book, a digital studio is a set of hardware and software systems designed to help you create digital content for a variety of media.

What does this mean to you? I will help you define what components you'll need to get the job done. This includes everything from using trueSpace4 well with other software; planning your strategies for going to broadcast video, printing, using multimedia CD-ROM; and even publishing for the Web. I'll also talk at a high level about overcoming many of the common bottlenecks to enable you to work more quickly and easily.

This chapter will

- Familiarize you with the concept of a digital studio
- Explain the common hardware and software used
- Help you define your individual requirements

TOOLS OF THE TRADE

The digital studio is a complex animal. There's no exact list of hardware and software that will be a perfect solution for everyone. Because individual requirements can be dramatically different from studio to studio, we'll help you build your own winning formula.

Digital studios often consist of certain core components, though. Because you're reading this book, we can rest assured that at some point in the game, you'll be producing 3D content. That's a great common denominator upon which to build.

The best way to define what you'll need is to consider what types of output you'll be producing. For instance, if you'll be doing animations for broadcast television, we can assume that you'll be concerned with editing video (and quite possibly audio), so nonlinear editing (NLE) might be a serious factor. When going to print, you'll need a color-calibrated monitor, software to convert to CMYK, and possibly a continuous-tone printer capable of doing match-prints.

As with most things, there's more than one way to approach a digital studio: with a realistic budget in mind or with a "money doesn't matter" attitude. I'll be assuming that we're dealing with the former because I don't know anyone who works with the latter. (If you do, please call me right away!) Our goal then is to assemble the best studio for the money, getting the components that will enable you to get today's job done (yet allowing for expandability).

HARDWARE CONSIDERATIONS

In a "traditional" studio, you'll often find several systems networked together, each with a specific task. Although this can add to the cost slightly, it allows for the most flexibility and usually allows a better overall workflow. It is possible to have one machine perform the rendering, NLE, output, and so on, but you might be overloading the machine, which can add plenty to the total "wait time." (Most machines in our budget may have a hard time keeping up rendering 3,000 frames of broadcast animations in the background while mixing and editing video.)

The issue at hand is how do we break up all that we want to do into logical systems? Until we decide everything we want to do, this may be a bit difficult. Therefore, we'll cover these system options individually, then show how some of them can be combined.

THE RENDERING SYSTEM

The first system is fairly easy because we can agree that we will need (at least) one machine as a rendering system. Even if you tend to model and animate on many machines (say, sharing our NLE machine), you will want one that is great at rendering.

Your first decision on the rendering machine is based on what kinds of rendering you will typically perform. If you do mostly print output, you will output single images. If it's broadcast video, you'll usually do animations consisting of many frames of output. Depending on the budget you have for this system, you might choose to go with a dual-processor Symmetrical Multi-Processing (SMP) machine. Today, the cost of an SMP machine is not that much more. Many vendors offer systems that are "SMP Ready," which means it has an empty place where you can add the second CPU when your requirements demand it.

RAM

The next decisions you make are based on removing common bottlenecks and increasing your rendering performance. 3D rendering is very memory intensive. Caligari lists 32MB of RAM as minimum, with 64MB recommended. This is true for most things, but if you're considering a machine that will be used solely for rendering (or at least most of the time), you'll want to invest more in memory. Many rendering boxes come standard with at least 128MB of memory, and 256MB isn't unheard of.

The best way to decide how much memory you'll need is to take a typical project and render it. Keep an eye on your hard drive activity indicator lights to see whether they are almost always on. If they are, it could be an indication that Windows is swapping to disk to make up for a lack of memory.

TIP

Windows NT supports multiple processors (Windows 95 and Windows 98 do not), so we will have that as a factor in our software list.

NOTE

Because you're using trueSpace4, you're very lucky: Many 3D rendering packages that support SMP do so by sending out different frames to different CPUs in the same machine. This is great for the broadcast video group, but if you're doing one very large frame for print, it won't do much for you. trueSpace4 works well for both groups because it breaks apart each frame into pieces that each CPU can work on. This enables you to get the most out of your SMP machine no matter what type of output you work on (even if this changes project to project).

To see how much Windows thinks you'll need for the task, use the Windows System Monitor (see Figure 18.1). You'll want to add items to view the total allocated memory, the amount of swapfile in use, and even the size of your swapfile. To do this, go to the System Monitor's Edit menu and select Add Item. From there, select Memory Manager in the Category column, then Allocated Memory, Swapfile In Use, and Swapfile Size. (You can hold down Ctrl and select them all to add them at once.) Once they're added, go to the View menu and select the Numerical Charts option, then Always On Top. Keep an eye on these values while rendering.

FIGURE 18.1   *The Windows 95 System Monitor.*

At the peak of activity, you may see the Allocated Memory exceed your physical memory. You can judge this along with the other values to determine the amount of memory required to render. Depending on the rendering process, you might simply be able to subtract your physical memory from the Allocated Memory and find out how much you need to add as a minimum. The Swapfile in Use and Swapfile Size should also give good indications about what's going on with the swapfile. Your goal is to virtually replace the swapping to disk with physical memory. Although this isn't always entirely possible due to how Windows works, you can get pretty close.

If you find out you're exceeding your physical memory only by 15MB, you might want to bump up to the next logical number, such as 32MB or 64MB more. (Some to grow on.) The factor you'll have to consider is how many physical slots you have for memory, and how many are currently filled. Hopefully, you have several open slots and can simply put new memory in. If they are all filled, you're looking at replacing some pieces with larger ones.

IDE VERSUS SCSI DRIVES

Once you've moved beyond the system memory, consider the next most common bottleneck: disk drives. Two types of disk drives must be considered—IDE and SCSI. Most systems use IDE drives of some sort, probably because the IDE interface is built into the motherboard on most computers. The other benefit to IDE drives is that they typically cost less than the same size SCSI. IDE, however, has a smaller limit to how many can be connected to your computer, compared with SCSI. With IDE, you can usually connect four drives at once (with the common dual channel IDE). This includes your IDE CD-ROM drive, too. With SCSI, you have the option to chain together either 7 or 15 disk drives at once, depending on whether you're using SCSI or Ultra-wide SCSI.

NOTE

Always consult with a system professional before attempting to replace internal components. Especially with memory, many systems require specific components. Some systems require sets of two pieces at a time to be added, while others can take one at a time. Memory modules are very susceptible to damage by static electricity and must be handled properly.

The other question about IDE versus SCSI is throughput. Simply put, SCSI has always been considered (and designed for) better throughput than IDE. Recently, however, newer styles of IDE drives have been getting closer to the performance you would get from SCSI. So, the first choice you can make up front is how important future expandability is to you. If you think you'll be requiring much more storage in the next year or two (as you pick up additional projects), you might want to start with SCSI. The second choice has to do with how much "system tuning" you want to be able to do.

Serious performance freaks will tell you that SCSI is the way to go because you can use Windows NT to stripe data across many disks. Without going into all of the gory details, this means that you're reading and writing data across many disks "at once," so you don't have to spend time waiting for one single drive to do the entire job. This is starting to get into RAID technology, which is even more complex, but has benefits of easily replaceable drives (on failure) and even better performance than simple striping. A final benefit for going with SCSI is that you can often get controller cards with lots of cache memory that can be another dramatic benefit in performance. Of course, this is an extra expense, but depending on your situation, it might be worth it. In the rendering game, time is money!

THE MODELING SYSTEM

Quite often, the modeling system is the same system as the rendering system. This seems natural because trueSpace4 integrates modeling and rendering so well. If you're lucky enough to afford it, however, breaking them into separate machines is a good idea.

I'm not suggesting you never do any rendering on your modeling machine. In fact, you'll quite often need to do some test renders as part of the modeling and animation process. Quite often in production environments, you are working with a predefined set of time constraints (often defined by someone else). With this being the case, you'll want to break your tasks into manageable groups. This way, you can model and animate one complete section and send it to the other machine to render while you move to the next set of modeling/animation steps.

So, what makes the rendering and modeling systems different? Quite often, the rendering box is very CPU and disk "heavy." Maybe it's a dual CPU box and has many SCSI disks so it can spread the various I/O tasks around better. It will often need large amounts of disk storage because your output will typically be very large. That's not to say your modeling machine won't need lots of disk space— some of your scenes can get pretty large themselves. But you might not need a large array of SCSI disks to get the performance you need. Maybe you can save money by going with some of today's large and fast Ultra DMA Enhanced IDE drives. Chances are, your motherboard already has the interface built in.

The modeling system is more concerned with real-time display in OpenGL or Direct3D. Because modeling doesn't require more than one CPU, it's often a single CPU machine, and that CPU can be in the medium to high end.

One thing your systems have in common is that they typically require a lot of memory. Of course, there's no exact rule for how much you'll need. Most people can model on machines in the 64MB for the low end to 128MB for average loads. You should consider that your scenes will have two main factors taking up lots of memory: geometry and textures. This memory topic goes for both your system memory and your video card memory.

VIDEO SUBSYSTEMS

The 8MB or 16MB video cards that are readily available today in the $200 range will often work for your modeling system's display. When you're dealing with the large amounts of geometry and textures that are found in high-end broadcast animations for TV and film, however, you should consider a video card that either starts out fairly large or that is easily expandable.

The 3D card business is evolving at a rapid rate. Newer technology seems to come into focus every day. For instance, some vendors are now taking advantage of compression for texture memory. The new S3 Savage card can have the equivalent of 200MB of textures displayed at once.

Currently labeled as the "biggest of the big," the MaxVision Titan II has two 3D Labs GLINT MX 3D chips onboard, the 3D Labs GLINT Gamma for video processing, and 96MB of memory (see Figure 18.2). Of course, it's priced at over $2,000.

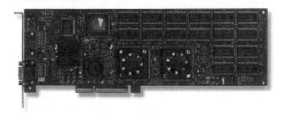

FIGURE 18.2   *The MaxVision Titan II with 96MB memory.*

How much is too much? Often our budget dictates this for us, but if you're more concerned with performance, it can require a bit of research to find out what's right for you. The first thing you'll have to do is figure out what your typical and high-end scenes are like. How many polygons do you usually push around in a scene? How much memory will you need for your textures? How important is instant feedback to you on very high polygon meshes? Once you get a good feeling for what you'll be asking of your video card, you should be able to match this with the details released by each 3D-accelerator vendor. You might also want to keep a close eye on magazine reviews—some of them even use trueSpace as a benchmark for 3D cards!

Some of the questions you'll want to ask while investigating what card is right for you are

- What is the card's fill rate in millions of pixels per second?

- How many millions of triangles per second can the card draw?

- Is it Microsoft DirectX 6-compatible for great Direct3D acceleration? If so, what new features does it support, such as hardware bump mapping, multitexture blending, and so on.

- Does it work well in Direct3D and OpenGL?

Another factor in your decision is quite often preference with a brand name. Several vendors, such as Diamond, Elsa, Hercules, and MaxVision, have a good lineup of cards ranging from inexpensive to ultra-high performance. If you've had good times with a vendor in the past and they offer the technology and configurations you're looking for, it's typical to stay with that which you're familiar.

THE EDITING SYSTEM

The editing system is used to assemble all of the rendered images, clean up images, add post-production effects, convert images to CMYK for print, or add your audio tracks for video. Also, this is where you get your work ready to go out to be used in the real world. In other words, whatever has to happen to your materials before other people see it or to get it to the appropriate media happens here.

The editing system is the box that will house your digital disk recorder or other hardware for going to tape. It's also the machine that could have your CD-R or Zip drive, continuous-tone printer, high-end audio card, and so on. Sure, you could simply spread these components to the other machines, but it's often quite an act to get everything to work well together in one single box. (Even if they do physically fit.) Imagine trying to fit a PCI SCSI adapter, PCI audio card, PCI or AGP video card, PCI broadcast video output card, PCI broadcast video capture card, network card, modem, and so on into one box. If you can get all of this to work without running out of Interrupts, it might require its own air-conditioning unit to keep cool enough!

So, as you can see, it makes more sense to break this into a dedicated system. To see what's required of this system, you must first have a good idea of what your final output will be. For instance, if you strictly work on print work but occasionally go to broadcast video, it might not be worth purchasing dedicated video hardware. Maybe you can find a good service bureau to render animation files when you need it, so you should only be concerned with a storage device to get them the materials. Chances are, they will accept the same media that the service bureau you use for print will accept. (CD-R and Zip disks are the most popular.)

Our main focus for this system will be the components you will need to produce your final media. What we have to be concerned with is to find the equipment that will offer the best output for each of your requirements (without exceeding your budget) and to get all of these items to work well together. Don't take this lightly—it's a very challenging task.

VIDEO COMPONENTS

If you're planning to go to video, you'll need a video output system. The system you select is based on several key factors:

- Cost
- Required quality
- Strict adherence to NTSC or PAL video

There are a few more decisions that will help you select what's right for you, and we'll cover them all in detail in the section on broadcast video output, later in this chapter.

When doing video work, you'll often need to capture video. This is typical when doing work such as rotoscoping and compositing. This might also influence which video output component you select because many have options for video capture as well.

Such video subsystems often require specific editing software, depending on which type of hardware you select. We're talking about nonlinear editing (NLE). As opposed to traditional (linear) editing, NLE means that you can edit all of your video internally on the computer. It also means that you have the freedom to work in the sequence you choose, as opposed to starting at the beginning of a tape straight through to the end, like in a traditional (linear) system. This offers superior capabilities and output quality, as everything happens digitally and in one "generation." (With traditional tape editing, you would experience a loss in quality with every generation throughout the process.)

NLE systems require some sort of digital disk recorder (DDR) to manipulate the media. This works hand-in-hand with your video capture and output subsystem, and sometimes it's even part of the same hardware.

For details on selecting NLE components, see the subsequent section on broadcast video output.

PRINT COMPONENTS

Most of the time when print is your final media, you will be concerned with preparing your files into certain formats and media that a service bureau can work with. The service bureau often produces the films that can be sent to a print house to have the final matter printed. This means that the main concern is often software related.

However, you'll need to keep in mind certain hardware components. The first is the type of media you need to share with the service bureau. Although the results vary for each place, most consider CD-R and Zip cartridges standard issue. CD-R stores 640MB per CD, and Zip cartridges store 100MB. Currently, Zip cartridges are a bit more expensive than CD-R, but you benefit by being able to use it over and over again. Also, CD-R drives are often a bit more expensive than Zip drives—two to three times more. The benefit of CD-R is that you can use it to create multimedia content, original CDs for duplication, and just about everyone today has a CD-ROM drive.

The other remaining piece of hardware for going to print is (take a guess?) the printer. Because there are so many types and brands of printers on the market, it's hard to select one that will work for everyone. However, the types of technology used can severely influence your decision. Continuous-tone printers (also referred to as dye-sublimation) are great for that photo-like quality. You won't see the little dots of ink as are found on laser and inkjet printers. The catch is that you pay for this benefit in the cost of the printer and usually in speed. On the other hand, inkjet printers are typically more cost-effective and produce good results for the money. They are quite fast printers these days, and often are good enough to give a basic idea of what your final output should look like.

If you're really concerned with accurate color reproduction, it might be worth considering a continuous-tone printer or simply working with your service bureau to get a good "proof." It's best to ask for a MatchPrint because this is supposed to accurately simulate the analog print process using a digital printer. It might cost some money, but that is better than being unhappy with your final print job or having to reproduce film several times.

For more information on going to print, see a following section on print media.

SOFTWARE CONSIDERATIONS

Let's take a look at what software you'll need for each of our basic systems. This might not be an all-inclusive list, but it covers the basics. Although brands are listed, there's obviously room for personal taste. In some instances, such as working with service bureaus, it's important to go with industry standards or at least have software capable of exporting to a standard format.

THE RENDERING SYSTEM SOFTWARE

Of course, the first thing you'll need is a copy of trueSpace4! Because the rendering system's primary function is rendering trueSpace scenes to various formats, you won't need to load this machine up with image editing, word processing, email, or NLE software.

You will need to make sure it has all the necessary add-ons that the modeling machine might have had to create the scenes. I'm not talking about plug-ins for modeling, but rather the custom material shaders, post-processing effects, textures, and so on.

THE MODELING SYSTEM SOFTWARE

For the modeling system, trueSpace4 is the starting block again. The other components you'll need on this machine revolve around how you use trueSpace.

This machine will require all of the tSX plug-ins you will need for modeling and animation, as well as custom material shaders, post-processing effects, and so on. Not only will you need to have the images used for textures, but this is typically the machine used to create such images. This means you'll at least need image-editing software, such as Adobe Photoshop or Paint Shop Pro, and maybe even Adobe Illustrator (or similar) for creating AI files to import into trueSpace.

Your list might also include specialty software used to create certain image maps, such as Darktree Textures, or libraries of prebuilt images, such as the Marlin Studios' "Seamless Textures You Can Really Use" CD or Pyromania Pro by VCE. You shouldn't forget your CDs full of useful prebuilt 3D objects, such as those created by Zygote or

> **WARNING**
>
> It's handy to consider networking our various machines together. There are even several network rendering plug-ins being developed that will enable you to start the render on another machine from your modeling workstation. With the proper network, you'll save yourself time from running media back and forth between the machines. You'll also save storage space because machines can simply access the files on other systems instead of maintaining their own instances of everything, such as textures, shaders, and so on.
>
> This also cuts out the "version problems" that can crop up. Imagine using a blue image map for your ship hull, and then changing it to red later. If you forget to update the rendering machine with the new texture, you might render the entire sequence before finding out it's the wrong version.

NOTE

Although Adobe products seem to be common and even are considered a standard in the print industry, many viable alternatives exist. For instance, Corel offers a good suite of software components that should perform the same tasks as their Adobe counterparts. This may be a cost-effective, "all-in-one" solution. Make sure, however, that if you intend to share files with others or service bureaus, you meet their requirements.

Viewpoint Data Labs. You may even need to draw upon the services of your editing system because you might require video files from the capture card for use as rotoscoped textures in trueSpace.

THE EDITING SYSTEM SOFTWARE

Because the editing machine is used to assemble your final results, it can be loaded with a wide variety of software. If you're going to do broadcast video, your NLE software will reside here. If you are doing print work, your image editing, layout, and color correction software will be here as well. If you're considering multimedia CD-ROM projects, various authoring packages and CD-R development software will be needed here as well. For Web development, this is where you'll need software such as HTML editors (or design packages), FTP software, Web browsers, and so on.

SOFTWARE FOR BROADCAST VIDEO

Let's first consider broadcast video. Your choice of nonlinear editing software may rely heavily on what you decided for video hardware. For instance, if going with components such as the DPS Perception Video Recorder or the Targa 2000 Pro, you can take advantage of features built into In:Sync's Speed Razor software. Speed Razor can talk directly to such hardware, enhancing performance and reducing wait times dramatically. The additional benefit is that you can often do real-time editing and audio previews. If you are using other hardware that does not offer such features, you might choose to go with an industry-standard program such as Adobe Premiere.

The important issue is to make sure you have video-editing software that will do the kinds of things you'll need to complete your project. If special effects or specialty or custom transitions are important to you, you should pay special care to the capability of the product you choose. If you will be integrating audio and it must sync critical (exact) times along your animation, you should ensure you're working with software that has a lot of audio tracks and can handle your timing requests.

SOFTWARE FOR PRINT

First, you'll need image-editing software here like on your modeling machine, but for a different reason. You'll need it here to be able to enhance and clean up images, do compositing, and other "post-processing" work.

This is where you'll need all of the whistles and bells—you'll most likely load this machine with all of the fancy image-enhancing plug-ins for effects such as drop shadows, glows, and so on. Don't forget that you'll need all of your coolest type-faces on this machine, too.

You also need page layout software. The two most common programs for this are Adobe's PageMaker and Quark's QuarkXPress. Your choice can rely greatly on your personal choice (do you like the Adobe look-and-feel from other Adobe products?) and compatibility with service bureaus and other outside services.

SOFTWARE FOR MULTIMEDIA/CD-ROM

When creating multimedia projects, you'll either be creating a custom interface (by using custom programming or HTML, for instance) or an authoring pack-age. A common authoring package is Macromedia Director. Such authoring packages enable you to create a workflow of what happens when buttons are pressed, when images are displayed, when animations are played, and so on. The end result is a standalone application that can be executed when the CD is inserted. More than likely, a runtime module will need to be distributed with your application. This module includes functions for all the behind-the-scenes work required for a dynamic multimedia presentation, but is typically free to dis-tribute with your projects.

The other component you will need is something to actually produce the media. This will most likely come with your CD-R drive. The typical application included with most drives seems to be Adaptec's Easy CD Pro. It's a very Windows95/98-based interface that allows creation of most (if not all) CD-based projects.

SOUND IS THE OTHER 50 PERCENT OF THE EQUATION

This brings us to the next important piece of software: the audio software. Chances are that unless you are strictly working with printed output, you'll need to do some audio work as well. This could range from simply applying various audio tracks to your video, creating or sampling your own sounds, or enhancing audio from external sources.

A typical, industry-standard program for this is Sound Forge by Sonic Foundry (see Figure 18.3). In fact, it's often thought of as "the" software for working with audio on the PC. So, while we discuss audio software solutions in general, we'll be look-ing closely at how Sonic Foundry's various components fit into your studio.

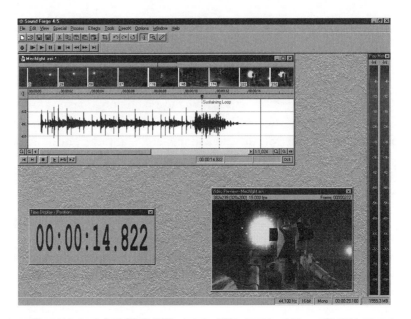

FIGURE 18.3 *The Sound Forge 4.5 interface.*

One of the many strengths of Sound Forge is the fact that it's very expandable to meet your needs. The main program, Sound Forge 4.5, offers advanced features that bring more professional audio capabilities to a personal studio than you could imagine, including

- Nonlinear audio editing
- Tons of high-end audio effects, processes, and tools
- Support for Microsoft AVI and ASF files for NetShow
- Read and write support for just about any file format out there
- Processing of audio files for use on the Internet
- Production of studio-quality audio for broadcast
- Playlists and region lists for CD mastering
- Support for DirectX Audio (that is, Noise Reduction, Acoustic Mirror, and XFX plug-ins)
- Batch Converter: previously a $199 product, saves tons of time when converting files.

- Spectrum Analysis: previously a $149 product, enables you to navigate easily through data and audio frequency

- MS NetShow 3.0 and RealAudio/RealVideo 5.0 support

As you can see, Sound Forge can be valuable in your digital studio, whether we're creating content for the Internet, multimedia CDs, or broadcast video. Its tools enable you to overcome serious issues, such as turning a 33-second clip into a 30-second clip with absolutely no change in pitch. Of course, it includes the effects you would expect, such as amplitude modulation, chorus, delay/echo, flange/wah-wah, noise gate, pitch bend/shift, reverb, and so on.

If the full Sound Forge 4.5 doesn't meet your budget constraints, there is a "lite" version—Sound Forge XP 4.5, available at a bargain price of $49.95.

Sonic Foundry also has an arsenal of other tools that are great to have in your toolbox. The first tool that comes to mind is Acid (see Figure 18.4). Acid (and its lower-cost variants Acid Music and Acid Style) is used to create looped music. It requires almost no knowledge of music theory or even instruments. You use Acid by working with digital sound loops (clips of sound that can be strung together to sound like continuous music) and "painting" them onto a sound track. You have full control over mixing the tracks and applying digital effects. Acid will automatically match the tempo and key in real-time.

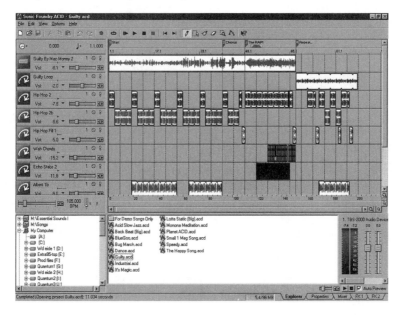

FIGURE 18.4 *The Acid interface.*

It's a great alternative to using (expensive) licensed music to accompany your work, and you can fit it to your exact timing requirements. There are hundreds of ready-made loops in many different instruments and styles, including

- Techno
- Rock
- Break Beat
- Funk
- Country
- Hip-hop
- Disco
- Alternative
- House
- Industrial
- Guitar
- Bass
- Synthesizer
- Drums
- Brass
- Scratching
- Sound Effects
- Ambient

Additional loop libraries are also available from Sonic Foundry, which will give you a wealth of material that you can use to kick your loop-based productions to the next level.

SOUND EXTENSIONS

Because we mentioned it's important to find audio software that's expandable to meet your future needs, we should talk about some of the extensions you might require for production.

You may be working with some older, noisy audio clips. Maybe you brought some in from an old analog tape or LP, or maybe your PC was a bit noisy while recording. Whatever the reason, it's common to need some sort of noise-reduction software. If you chose Sound Forge for your audio, it's an easy decision because the program's Noise Reduction plug-in is absolutely easy to use and produces fantastic results.

What if your audio sounds too "computerish"? Maybe you're producing a game that's supposed to happen in a grungy city alley. Maybe you want your audio to sound like it was recorded in a cathedral hall, not your basement. Whatever the reason, the Sonic Foundry Acoustic Mirror plug-in will save you. This software is a digital signal-processing tool that adds the acoustical coloration of real environments and sound-altering devices to existing recordings. Until now, adding reverberation to a sound meant settling with "canned" effects of artificial reverb units. In contrast, Acoustic Mirror imparts, and actually incorporates, the acoustical responses of a given environment onto a sound file. You can reproduce sounds such as large concert halls to the vintage sound of old tube microphones. It's a great tool that is often overlooked in the smaller studios.

WHAT CAN BE DONE IN YOUR DIGITAL STUDIO?

Here we'll explain what tasks your digital studio is suited for. In short, what's your return on investment? What types of projects should you feel comfortable accepting?

TODAY'S "ONE-MAN STUDIO"

Today, more than ever before, individuals have it within their reach (both in terms of budgets and capability) to produce artwork similar to what was thought only to be available to the "big boys." How can this be? It's due mostly to the rapid increase in hardware capabilities, prices dropping due to competition, and quantum leaps forward in software design.

Being on the creative side, this is great for us. Not only does it mean that we have better, faster "toys" to play with, but it means that the reality of competing with major studios is often left to how creative you are, instead of the size of your budget. This also means that the potential exists that you can become a major studio "overnight" if you play your cards right. That's the dream—basement to billionaire—right?

ROLES OF THE DIGITAL ARTIST

With all of these new capabilities, we quite often have to wear many more hats than ever before. In a smaller studio, it pays to become familiar with all areas of the creative process.

It used to be that if you were a 3D artist, you would have to be skilled at modeling, surfacing, and animating 3D objects. Now in addition to this, you have to be good at editing audio and video, producing media, marketing, and so on. What's the problem with this? You might become so involved in all of the low-level components that you can't seem to finish a project. Some people have enough time on their hands to do it all, but most people have to learn to delegate properly.

What's the rule on breaking apart the tasks properly? Unfortunately, there's no hard rule for this type of thing. It depends on what tasks you're best suited for and what you enjoy doing most. If you're very good at modeling, surfacing, and animating, but can't seem to get a killer idea to run with, look around. Maybe you're very good at creating the overall look and feel, but don't want to be bogged down editing video clips together. You'll have to discover how you work and learn how to run with it.

Whether it's a one-person studio or a large group, the basic rules still apply. You'll be asked to wear many hats. Of course, there's much more to each role, but this list should give you an idea of the high-level functions you'll be asked to perform.

- **Author:** Someone has to develop a concept and be responsible for creating a storyboard or some document describing the details of the project.

- **Art Director:** No matter what your final media, you'll have to have great art direction. Don't feel shy about going to someone who has a firm background here. Get other people's opinions.

- **Director:** If you are working on an animation, spend plenty of time considering the overall direction. This means breaking the project into the proper scenes, ensuring you have adequate camera angles, and making sure that everything has a consistent flow. If you're doing character animation, this might require someone specializing in this task or a ton of research.

- **Editor:** No matter how well the director and artists plan up front, there is undoubtedly going to be some editing required to get the final version ready for public consumption. If you're doing print, this means you're the one who composites everything, makes sure you meet the physical space constraints, performs color correction, and so on. If you're doing video, you're the one who assembles the list of clips on the timeline, puts the appropriate transitions between clips, performs blue-screening and compositing, synchronizes audio and video, and so on.

- **Producer:** Being responsible for the entire project at a high level is no easy business. It often means fitting everything into budgetary and time constraints, overseeing the work of the other components, working with outside services, and so on.

CREATING THE KILLER DEMO REEL/PORTFOLIO

One of the first things you'll want to do with your newly developed digital studio is create a demo reel or portfolio. This is the perfect opportunity to prove to the world (and perhaps yourself) what your studio can do.

With that decided, the question becomes what's the best way to create such a beast? How much do you include in your portfolio? What's a demo reel and what goes on it? How can you stand out in the crowd? These are all fantastic questions, and if you're asking them now, you're probably ahead of most people who don't even consider such things. (You'd be surprised.)

Whether we're talking about a demo reel or a personal portfolio, they are both your "ticket to success." If you're getting quality people to look at your stuff, you're halfway there. No pressure here, but what you do with such an opportunity can make or break your career as a digital artist.

The best way to start is to describe what you should *not* do on a demo reel or portfolio:

- **Do not simply make it a compilation of everything you've done.** Nobody wants to sit through your biography. Chances are you'll be showing a lot of older stuff, and that's no good. It's the digital equivalent of sitting through Aunt Martha's summer vacation slides.

- **Do not show static, unrelated material.** This appears to be too "random" and makes you look unfocused.

- **Do not bore your audience to death by doing the same thing they've seen on the 1,200 other reels they've just looked at.** Your goal is to get their attention and stand out from the crowd. If you look like everyone else, why should they pick you?

- **Do not reproduce someone else's concepts or artwork.** Not only do you have to worry about copyright and licensing issues, but they want to see *your* work, not a re-creation.

- **Do not do generic spaceships or other boring space scenes without being creative.** Everyone sends in space scenes, so if this is your major interest, you had better stand out by a mile.

Now, what *should* you do?

- **Think long and hard about what to show someone.** Make sure the pieces you choose are your absolute best work.

- **Tell a story.** Show them that you're capable of getting and keeping their attention. Make sure everything you show them has a consistent look and serves a purpose.

- **Be creative!** Think of something that's so original, it will stick in their minds when they leave and make them want to search for your reel when they come back.

- **Use their emotions—be funny, sad, or scary.** Chances are they will want to convey some similar emotions in their work, so this shows that you're capable.

- **Make sure the transitions between clips are smooth.** It's okay to use effects and transitions, but don't go overboard. They don't care whether you just bought the latest transition for your NLE, but they want to know you can produce seamless material.

- **Make sure your delivery materials are high quality.** If it's printed work, use heavy stock and a process that reproduces color (if appropriate) well. If it's video, make sure you're giving them broadcast-quality resolution and high-quality tapes. Packaging also counts: Don't let someone else destroy your material before it gets a chance to be seen.

- **Make it short and to the point.** If you have something to say, don't spend another 15 minutes of "fluff" getting to the point. Figure that the people who review demo reels and portfolios sift through tons and tons of this stuff, and if they feel their time is being wasted, they may hit the Stop button before getting to what you really wanted to show them.

- **Be persistent, but not annoying.** If you haven't heard anything, contact them to make sure they received the reel. Don't call every day for their decision, but don't be a stranger, either. (Don't look desperate.)

What's the bottom line? Give them what they want: Be creative, look good without looking like everyone else, and know how to convey your point in an efficient manner.

PRODUCTION WORK

Okay, so you have someone interested. Then they ask you what kinds of things you can do. Personal abilities aside, let's take a look at some of the things your studio is able to produce.

With desktop computers and packaged software, you're able to seriously compete with the big boys. Sound too good to be true? There must be some reason to purchase $100,000 dedicated workstations, right? Today, the difference between what you have and what they have is measured in performance, not capability. For instance, if you're using PC hardware that can produce NTSC broadcast video, it's the same coming from you as it is coming from an expensive dedicated video workstation. High-end machines might be able to generate real-time 2500-pixel-wide images without working up a sweat, and your trusty PC might have to wait a few minutes, but as long as you do a good job of selecting your components, you should be able to produce the same type of output as the other guys. Because planning is such an important factor, the next sections focus on what to consider while making these important decisions. They will help you select the components you'll need to compete.

INPUT DEVICES: WORKING WITH THE REAL WORLD

This section discusses the types of devices you'll need to bring in materials for use in your productions. We will discuss when and why you need each component and, perhaps more importantly, how to make the right decision for your studio's particular needs.

WHAT'S THE GOAL?

On nearly every project you tackle, you're going to need real-world input; it might be scanning images to be used for custom textures, some line art of characters you're going to model, or video you've shot on your camcorder that you will composite with your trueSpace graphics. Your goal here should be to decide up front what types of input you'll need on a day-to-day basis and what level of quality you will need.

This also might present more choices for how you can get your daily tasks done. For instance, do you take a picture on your analog camera and then scan it in on your flatbed scanner? What about digital cameras? What about PhotoCDs?

FLATBED SCANNERS

Flatbed scanners of some type are considered "standard issue" in the digital studio, no matter whether you're doing broadcast video, game development, Web production, or print work. Why? They're fairly versatile, multipurpose devices. You might use one to digitize your hand-drawn storyboard (drawn on napkins, of course), bring in an existing company logo, or scan high-resolution textures to be applied to your objects in trueSpace.

So that's easy; just get a scanner, right? Wrong. Of course, there are only about 500 to chose from at your local computer store. They range in price from under a hundred dollars to several thousand. What's the difference? There are a few basic aspects to consider when buying a scanner:

- **Interface:** Typical choices are either parallel port or SCSI. If you have chosen to go with SCSI for your disk drives and have an extra SCSI ID left on your chain, this would make an excellent choice. If you want a quick and easy connection or don't have any other SCSI devices, stick with the parallel port type. The SCSI interface, however, tends to transfer the data back to the system much faster than parallel. If you go with parallel, don't worry about losing your printer connection. Most scanners have a printer pass-through in the interface connector.

- **Size:** Yes, size does matter here. Most people can get away with the "standard issue" 8.5×14–inch scanning area. If you tend to work with oversized material, the B-Sized scanners let you bring in material up to 12.2×17.2 inches.

- **Resolution:** There are a few things to consider when looking at the resolution figures. They are often broken into two segments: optical and software. Optical resolution is the physical resolution that the scanner operates at. The software resolution figure is higher because the scanner's internal software does some interpretation on the incoming data, providing a higher resolution. Be aware, though, that at extremely high software resolutions, you might experience *pixelization*, similar to the digital zoom found on camcorders. If you don't know how much you'll need, consider the type of work you'll do. If you're doing print work, go for the high numbers because you'll need to scan at least as high (preferably higher) as the output method. If you're working with desktop playback of video, one of the typical consumer-level ($100 to $200) models should suffice.

- **Color Depth:** Most scanners operate today with 36 bits of color. Of course, if you're very dependent on realistic color reproduction, you'll want to make sure you have a great color range. Some older scanners didn't have such high capacity.

- **Passes:** Most scanners today operate by scanning the image in one pass, but older technology required that the image be scanned multiple times: one pass for red, one for green, and one for blue. This, of course, led to very long scanning times.

TABLETS

Tablets are often overlooked by 3D artists but are considered mandatory by 2D artists. Why would a 3D artist need a tablet? Creating or editing texture maps in a 2D image-editing package (Photoshop, for example) are dramatically easier and more precise when using a tablet. Even some 3D paint packages, such as 4D Paint by Right Hemisphere, recommend you use a tablet. The most common input device on a tablet is a pressure-sensitive pen. By using a pressure-sensitive pen, you can create more natural effects. Just like the analog equivalent, you can make the digital pen create heavier lines, depending on how hard you press. Many even have erasers so you can flip the pen over and erase.

VIDEO CAPTURE

Need realistic, animated clouds for your background in trueSpace? How about playing your client's existing TV commercial on a 3D TV in your trueSpace scene? Chances are you can find a million reasons to manipulate video on your computer. But for nearly each of these reasons, you can find a different method of capturing the video.

TIP

One thing to note is that the tablet usually uses a COM device in your computer. This means that you might have to be careful on your computer's configuration. If you have a modem using COM2 and a serial mouse using COM1, where do you put the tablet? The best solution is to get a PS/2 connector mouse (if your motherboard supports it) and put the tablet on the unused COM port.

Your options might range from an inexpensive daughter card for your graphics adapter, an external piece of hardware connected to your system, or a dedicated digital disk recorder component. Each of the options offers different quality and, of course, cost factors.

So, how do you decide what's the best video input device for your studio? First consider what type of output you'll be doing. (Remember, garbage in equals garbage out.) If you want to capture high-quality stills from video to be used in print work, maybe Play's Snappy device would work well and be most cost effective. If, however, you'll be producing high-quality broadcast video, you'll need to have an equally high-quality capture device.

To decide on the hardware, you'll have to do some research on input capabilities. Standard NTSC video is defined as 720×480 pixels and runs at approximately 30 frames per second. Some of the video-capture devices capture at only 640×480 pixels and not all can capture a full 30 frames per second. If you will be capturing at 640×480 and output 720×480, the first thing you'll notice (besides some skipped pixels on each side) is that the images will seem stretched due to the change in aspect ratio. Suddenly "round" objects seem to look stretched. If you don't capture at 30 frames per second, you could skip directly over several important frames, and the result could appear to be very "jumpy" motion.

If true broadcast-quality video isn't ultimately important to you, just make sure that your input device and output device are "matched" for resolution and frames per second.

One of my favorite options today is still the DPS Perception Video Recorder's AD-2500 daughter card. This is a full-length PCI card that attaches to the side of the main PVR-2500 unit. The benefits of this approach are that the capture card is "automatically" matched for the PVR's broadcast-quality output, it captures 720×480 pixels in real-time, and 30 frames per second (technically, 60 fields per second). So with this combination, you'll be sure to capture video that looks good and won't skip a beat. As you'll find with the PVR solution, it works well because the data does not have to cross your PC's bus at all: It gets stored directly on the PVR's dedicated A/V SCSI disk units. (More about that in the Broadcast Video Output section, as follows.)

FILM AND PHOTOCD

Maybe you're working on a project that requires input of physically huge objects. Of course, attempting to get an image of your car by placing it on the flatbed scanner can achieve less-than-desired results, so why not take a picture of it, and then scan it in?

Depending on a few factors, you may choose to take a picture with your standard, analog camera, get the film developed, and then scan the image by placing the photo on your flatbed scanner. Another option is to use the analog camera, but when processing your negatives, ask for a PhotoCD in addition to, or instead of, photographs. What's the difference? Well, depending on whether you get "professional" or "standard" PhotoCDs, there may not be too much difference, except that you can save a step in the process. Whenever you skip a step, you also skip customization options. When scanning your photos yourself, you choose the area of the photo to scan and the resolution. By going to PhotoCD, you don't have to worry about damaging a physical photograph, but the files are all the same resolution, which produces large files in the process. Professional-level PhotoCDs are even larger, providing very good color and image quality (but you usually have to use professional-grade cameras and film).

Whatever the process, you should always consider one thing: lighting of the real-world objects. If you take a picture of your shiny red sports car in the middle of the afternoon while the sun is bright, you will run into problems when trying to place this image in a dark alley. Also, you may end up with "hot spots" on objects that don't match the lighting in the 3D environment. The bottom line here is to use light that best matches the end result in your virtual world.

OUTPUT: THE END RESULT

Everything else has been leading up to this section. No matter how much time you've spent scanning texture maps, designing characters, laying out the storyboard, and animating your environments, it doesn't matter unless you can show someone else. Here we'll discuss various types of output you'll be concerned with and the techniques to get the most out of it.

TIP

A change was implemented in trueSpace4.0 to "automatically" calculate the pixel aspect ratio based on the resolution (and ratio) that you are rendering to file. This is different than how tS3.x and prior worked with Pixel Aspect Ratio, as you used to have to calculate it by hand. Due to the requests of .users, trueSpace4.1 now works like tS3.x and prior.

For clarification, here's how TS3.x and prior worked: If you need to render to NTSC broadcast video, you will use a resolution of 720×480. The aspect ratio of this format is different than the square pixels shown on a computer monitor, say at 800×600. (720÷480 = 1.5, where 800÷600 = 1.333) Because you normally output to the computer screen, trueSpace3.x considered this "1.333" number to be its baseline, so this is considered to be a trueSpace Pixel Aspect Ratio of 1.0. To calculate the proper Pixel Aspect Ratio when using 720×480, you would take 1.333÷1.5, which gives you 0.888.

In trueSpace4: If you rendered to a resolution of 720×480, tS4 would automatically (internally) calculate a new aspect ratio, so then the Pixel Aspect Ratio of 1.0 becomes this new reference. The issue is that when you require custom aspect ratios (say, letterbox format), it can be more difficult to calculate. Therefore, tS4.1 uses the method that tS3.x and prior used. Figure 18.5 shows the trueSpace4.1 Render Scene to File dialog box, showing NTSC settings.

OUTPUT TO BROADCAST VIDEO

Broadcast video is probably the most popular, yet least understood media among digital creators. There seems to be some shroud of secrecy, some mysterious methods only the "pros" know about. The term "broadcast-quality video" seems to be defined differently depending on whom you ask. We'll define the term and explain how you can produce video projects so appealing that you'll have a hard time distinguishing it from what you see being broadcast today.

WHAT IS BROADCAST VIDEO?

The term "broadcast video" is defined by the Society of Motion Picture & Television Engineers (SMPTE). The standard format defined by SMPTE for use in the United States is called NTSC. The SMPTE specification that defines digital processing for NTSC video is called "CCIR 601." Believe me, this is a very in-depth document.

Interestingly enough, there's still much debate over how to interpret this document. Many suggest that the specification calls for a digital resolution of 720×480, while others claim 720×486. To be honest, if you bring either of these to a station, they will both be "broadcast legal." There's also a misconception that television is broadcast at 30 frames per second. In all reality, it's broadcast at 29.97 frames per second. This is known as NTSC "Drop-Frame" rate. Sound like we're splitting hairs? It makes a difference in calculations when you're trying to synchronize audio and so on.

The true test is in how clean the video signal is. If you buy a solid product such as the DPS Perception Video Recorder (PVR) or Hollywood Video Recorder, you know that you'll be putting out a very clean signal. The PVR works with 10-bit video encoding, and performs CCIR 601 4:2:2 processing. The HVR is very similar, except that it works with uncompressed D1 video. The D1 video format is basically the cleanest digital video you can work with (although the PVR's hardware compression is barely noticeable, even by a trained eye).

For more information on digital disk recorders, see the following section.

HOW TO RENDER TO VIDEO FROM TRUESPACE

To produce great-looking video from trueSpace, you'll need to consider a few things. First, the aspect ratios of computer monitors and television sets are not the same. Depending on the version of trueSpace you are using, you might have to make some changes to the Pixel Aspect Ratio setting when rendering to file.

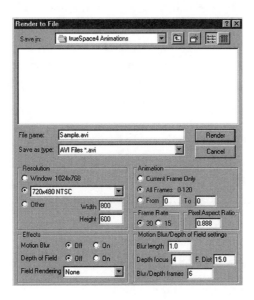

FIGURE 18.5   *The trueSpace4.1 Render Scene to File dialog box.*

An additional consideration you might have is in what file format to render to from trueSpace. If you're using a digital disk recorder (DDR), chances are that it will either have a special codec that you can use to render to AVI files or you can render directly to its dedicated disks. If you are not using a DDR and simply have

If you are not using a DDR, you might want to plan to boost the playback system with plenty of hardware to try to overcome these inherent bottlenecks. Consider fast CPUs, a lot of fast memory, a high-output disk controller, dedicated, fast disk drives, and so on.

Another thing you should look for are "A/V" disk drives. "Standard" drives go through a process called *thermal calibration* that causes frames to be dropped upon playback. The "A/V" drives are built for playing audio and video files and do not go through this process.

a "video output" device, it will rely on the throughput of your entire system to keep up with the frames.

This means that you are suddenly open to plenty of serious bottlenecks. If your system decides it's a good time to do some system tasks or your screen saver kicks in, you might not be able to play back your video without serious pausing or skipped frames. You still have the problem of having to push large quantities of data very fast from your disk drive to memory and back out across the PCI bus. If you're planning to use uncompressed files of some sort, your system might have a hard time keeping up. This may require you to use a codec to compress your frames into an AVI file. This might not be perfect because your computer still has to spend time uncompressing it, but it can help.

DIGITAL DISK RECORDERS

Throughout this chapter, I've made plenty of mention about digital disk recorders (DDRs). If your studio must produce broadcast video to make money, consider getting a DDR. The savings in time and the boost in quality will be more than enough to get a return on your investment.

Before we get in depth into the various DDRs, what are your alternatives?

- **Output directly to videotape**: There are several issues with this approach, including errors and normal wear-and-tear on the analog videotape. This can cause you to have noise or even skipped or "blending" frames.

- **Frame-accurate tape decks:** This is a very expensive option because they were built strictly for high-end analog editing situations. With this type of deck, you can render a frame of your animation and output this to the deck, move forward to the next frame, render again, and so on. Besides being a very tedious process, it can also cause tremendous wear on the deck. Even though they are built to do this function, it's something that may cause you to replace the heads, which is expensive maintenance.

With desktop video production and 3D animation becoming more popular, many very good DDRs can be found on the market. The good news is that with such competition, they keep getting better, faster, and cheaper. It would be impossible to list every option available today. Many of the popular models are discussed in the following sections. Think of this is a starting block instead of an all-inclusive list.

DPS PERCEPTION VIDEO RECORDER (PVR)

The PVR (PVR-2500) is a full-length PCI card that runs in both Intel and Alpha Windows workstations (see Figure 18.6). The PVR uses 10-bit encoding for high-quality CCIR-601 4:2:2 video. Its raster size is 720×480.

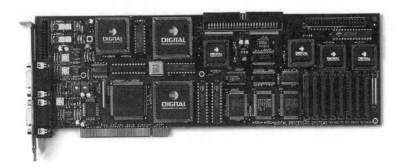

FIGURE 18.6   *The PVR-2500 card.*

One of the most powerful features about the PVR is that it contains its own dedicated Fast SCSI-2 (50-pin) interface. This means that when you send images to the PVR, it interprets them, performs hardware compression, and stores the image on the PVR's drive without having to go back through the CPU/memory/PCI bus. This also means that when playing back your video, your CPU simply sends the commands to the PVR, and it performs the task without involving your system. (It takes them directly from its drive and sends them out its dedicated video output connectors.)

How do you render to the PVR? How do you work with images if they're on a dedicated hard drive? If you're using Windows 95/98, you can render to an AVI file from trueSpace and choose the DPS PVR codec. This codec interprets each rendered frame and sends it to the PVR directly (as opposed to being rendered to your system drive). If you're using Windows NT, you can simply render a series of bitmap images to the PVR drive. (A special drive letter will appear for the PVR drive, usually P:.)

Another outstanding (and time-saving) benefit is that the PVR uses the DPS Virtual File System (VFS). This enables you to read or write in any of a number of standard RGB bitmap image formats, and the PVR's VFS converts them to be available in the other formats. It doesn't actually copy the files. For example, say you want to render to a series of TGA files, but some of your post-production software reads only BMP files. After you've written the TGA files to the PVR drive, they also appear in a different directory as BMP files.

The PVR has an automatic entropy circuit. This is used to determine the optimum amount of video compression on a frame-by-frame basis. You also have complete manual control over the compression/quality level settings.

You can count on an average of four minutes of video per 1GB of storage. If you have seven hard drives of 9GB each, that's over four hours of video! What's more is that the PVR can span multiple hard drives without skipping a frame of video.

All of this wouldn't add up to much if you couldn't get absolutely clean output. The PVR has a breakout cable set that includes output for composite, S-Video, and component (Betacam/MII). If you're going to broadcast, chances are you'll be using component connections to a high-quality Betacam-SP deck.

If you want to be able to capture video, you can get the optional AD-2500 daughter card (see Figure 18.7.). Although this is another full-length card, it does not require a PCI connection. It attaches directly to a special connector on the PVR card. It will, however, take the physical space of a card, so plan accordingly. (Place your PVR in the PCI slot that might be shared with an ISA slot.) This card performs just as easily as the PVR. It can capture in real-time, full 720×480, and at the full-frame rate. This means you don't have to have any special frame-accurate video deck for the capture process.

FIGURE 18.7   *The AD-2500 capture card.*

This newly captured video is immediately converted to a series of digital files on the PVR hard drive. This means you can use it in your NLE software to mix your animations with video or for compositing and rotoscoping situations.

DPS HOLLYWOOD VIDEO RECORDER (HVR)

The HVR (HVR-2800) is a set of cards—two PCI and one ISA—designed to work with Intel and Alpha Windows NT workstations (see Figure 18.8). The HVR is 100 percent uncompressed, providing a reasonably priced D1-quality system. The HVR consists of three cards: a luminance processor (PCI), a chrominance processor (PCI), and a genlock timing/serial D1 interface (ISA). An optional fourth card adds a real-time alpha channel (4:2:2:4 mode). The individual cards are interconnected by a ribbon cable that transmits parallel 10-bit video data between the boards.

FIGURE 18.8   *The HVR-2500 cards.*

The luminance and chrominance boards are connected to separate chains of SCSI drives via the onboard Fast-Wide SCSI-II controllers. This unique architecture enables the HVR to be operated in either 10-bit or 8-bit processing modes, depending on hard drive preferences and recording time considerations. The drives are configured as striped pairs to achieve the required bandwidth. Up to three pairs of drives may be used per channel. For virtually unlimited storage, an external RAID system can be used.

The HVR uses the DPS Virtual File System, as mentioned in the previous PVR section.

DPS PERCEPTION RT FAMILY

Also of note from DPS is the Perception RT series, which consists of two main products: the PRT-4200 is its core, whereas the PRT/3DX-4200 adds a new component (see Figure 18.9).

FIGURE 18.9   *The Perception 4200 Real Time with all components.*

The PRT-4200 is a fully integrated, dual-stream, real-time video editing system. (Whew!) Real-time video? This means that with the onboard SCSI controller, two streams of video can always be played at any compression level with minimal CPU and PCI overhead. Real-time transitions are performed in hardware, which is CPU independent. Of course, it still implements the DPS Virtual File System to give third-party applications such as trueSpace access to the media in multiple graphics formats. The PRT-4200 also comes with a new I/O breakout box, including all of the audio and video connections. That's right—audio. In addition to two channels of real-time video, you have one stereo channel of real-time audio recording. Hardware components even ensure audio/video synchronization.

The PRT/3DX-4200 is essentially the same as the PRT-4200, except for one new piece of hardware. This new component is a new PCI card that attaches to the PRT-4200 core system via an internal Movie-2 bus connection. This card is a real-time 3D effects processor. It allows you to instantly manipulate the size, position, perspective, and rotation of live video images. Two video streams, dual-image buffers, and shadow/border generator enable five layers of video to be processed in real-time. Over 200 real-time 3D DVE transitions and scrolling/rolling titles become available.

TRUEVISION TARGA 2000 PRO

The TARGA 2000 Pro is a single, full-length PCI card that enables you to record high-quality video and audio to disk digitally (see Figure 18.10). The TARGA 2000 Pro is capable of CCIR 601 resolution and frame rates, and CD- or DAT-quality audio is onboard as well. Both composite and S-Video output formats exist. For audio, there are two unbalanced input channels sampled at 48kHz (configured as left and right stereo channels with 20k Ohm input impedance) and two unbalanced output channels (configured as left and right stereo channels with 600k Ohm impedance).

FIGURE 18.10   *The TARGA 2000 series.*

A benefit to the TARGA 2000 Pro is that you use the same card to work with audio and video. The downside is that it records this data directly to your system drive(s). This means that all of the traffic for audio and video has to cross your PCI bus. To ensure you don't have any loss of frames or synchronization issues, it's recommended that you store the data on dedicated A/V hard drives. Most likely, you'll want to connect them to a dedicated, very fast SCSI adapter of your liking. It would also be beneficial to make sure you have lots of fast memory and a fast CPU.

TRUEVISION TARGA 2000 RTX

The next generation of TARGA 2000 cards is the TARGA 2000 RTX. This product delivers dual-stream architecture and real-time effects processing. The onboard alpha channel support enables a real-time CG track. It uses lossless component YUV image quality, 1.5:1 compression in single-stream mode, and better than 3:1 in dual-stream mode.

The TARGA 2000 RTX ships standard with Truevision's Breakout Box, providing professional connections, such as component RGB and YUV, and balanced audio input/output. Also included in the RTX model are balanced CD and DAT audio via XLR connectors, as well as the unbalanced RCA connector pair.

EDITING YOUR ANIMATIONS: NLE

Here, we'll take a serious look at using a nonlinear editing package. If you're going to video, you'll be editing or combining various video clips, synchronizing with audio, or even applying post-production effects and transitions. The NLE program is where it all comes together.

IN:SYNC'S SPEED RAZOR MACH 4

Speed Razor Mach 4 is the industry's leading nonlinear video editing and compositing software for Windows NT. It was designed to meet the demands of high-end post production, television broadcast, and video/film production environments. It includes a full range of video editing, real-time audio mixing, and video effects compositing features.

Speed Razor Mach 4 comes in two versions: RT and S. RT is optimized for real-time video effects editing with dual-stream video-capture hardware. S is optimized for single-stream, traditional DDR boards.

Like trueSpace, Speed Razor is widely known for its leading interface design and real-time capabilities. In fact, the new version takes advantage of multiprocessor speed, provides significantly faster screen redraw, and dramatically reduces render time for software effects. Let's take a quick look at the interface as shown in Figure 18.11.

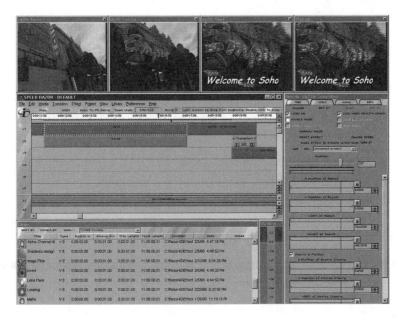

FIGURE 18.11   *The Speed Razor Mach 4 interface.*

Across the very top of the screen, you'll see four preview windows. From the left, they are

- Trim In
- Trim Out
- Video Effect and Transition Source/Result Images
- Playback Preview

These let you see various aspects of video and effects at the same time, saving you time from having to jump back and forth to check the status of everything along the way.

The "main" window in the middle with the timeline is the Composition window. This is where you do the layout for video and audio on the project timeline. It really is as easy as dragging clips from the library onto the timeline and adjusting their position. The same goes for creating transitions and effects. You can quickly create a simple "wipe" transition by dragging it between two clips of video on the timeline.

The Item Info window is to the right of the Composition window. This is where you go to scale any image clip, composite video effects, trim items, mix audio in real-time, and get information for any item in the project.

The Library is along the bottom-left side of the screen by default. This is where you organize your video, audio, and other media items that you will use in your project. This Library also is the home for the effects and transitions to be used in the open project, and is the place you'll get your materials from to drag onto the timeline.

The VU Meter window is the audio monitor. It enables you to check the volume levels of your audio as it plays during capture, editing, and output, and to maintain sound within the safe boundaries of digital playback. There is even an automatic "clipping" control that will notify you when any part of your audio is oversaturated.

So at a high level, here are the steps you would take to do a fairly straightforward video project using several animation clips created in trueSpace4:

1. Start a new project. Add to the Library all of the media clips necessary for your project. This includes all of the video created by trueSpace4, audio clips for the background music and narration, and any transitions or effects you'll need to use between the different shots.

2. Drag clip #1 onto the timeline in the V1 row.

3. Drag clip #2 onto the timeline in the V3 row, making sure there is some overlap from clip #1's ending to clip #2's beginning. The amount of time they overlap is the amount of time your transition will take.

4. Drag a transition (say a wipe of some sort) from the Library to the timeline in the V2 row. Place it near the section where clip #1 and clip #2 overlap.

5. By default, the transition knows that the top clip is the "in" and the bottom is the "out" due to how they are arranged along the timeline.

6. Add your various audio clips in the A1 and A2 sections at the bottom of the timeline. Optionally, you can view the waveform of the audio if you need to do some specific timing.

7. Save the project.

8. Viewing your results depends slightly on which kind of hardware you use. Most likely, it's as easy as pressing the Play button.

PRINT MEDIA

When going to print with your digital artwork, you'll find it's like entering a whole new world. There are so many buzzwords in this industry, it seems that they have us 3D geeks beat. But with enough patience and some insight, you might be able to squeak by without being branded a newbie.

First, what we're talking about here is going to print in a publication such as a book, magazine, or even a poster. The issue at hand is that you must put your digital files through a lot of conversion and create output via analog printing processes. (Not exactly the same as saying "print" to your inkjet printer.)

LEARNING THE LINGO

The most typical printing process for trueSpace artists will be some "four-color process printing." Four colors, you say? Aren't we all used to 16.8 million colors? Yes, and that's exactly the point. The digital world works in RGB mode, which depends on a light source to create color. The printing world works in CMYK mode, which is based on the light-absorbing quality of ink that's printed on paper. When (white) light gets cast on semitransparent inks, some of the light spectrum is absorbed. Color that's not absorbed is reflected back to you.

In the CMYK theory, cyan (C), magenta (M), and yellow (Y) pigments should combine to absorb all color and produce black. In reality, these colors combine to get a little less than black, so they must be combined with black (K) ink. (K is used instead of B because it can be confused with blue.) So, cyan, magenta, yellow, and black are the four colors in four-color process printing.

There's a certain problem, though, when taking digital artwork to CMYK. There are significantly more colors in the RGB spectrum than there are in CMYK. When you output from programs such as trueSpace4, you are creating RGB files. Therefore, you need to convert to CMYK by using an image-editing package such as Adobe Photoshop. Easy, right? Wrong.

By simply converting from RGB mode to CMYK mode, you're using the program's default conversion process, and this might not work for everything. For example, while producing the cover for the Caligari pluSpack1 CD, I had an image that was filled with cool neon blue water. After converting to CMYK, this water became a very harsh violet color. Only after a lot of hand massaging via Photoshop's Curves Adjustment tools was I able to get an acceptable image (see Figure 18.12).

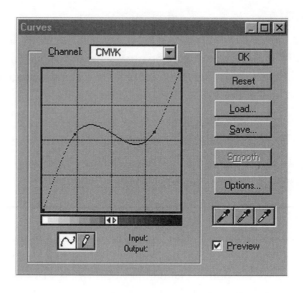

FIGURE 18.12   *Adobe Photoshop's Curves Adjustment dialog box.*

COMMON OUTPUT FILE FORMATS

In the print world, you have to remember that there's quite a mix of computers and analog equipment being used. You might be working with people who have a combination of Macintosh and Windows computers, or maybe (gasp!) just Macintosh. This means that you'll have to be very careful selecting files that translate well across these boundaries.

For various reasons, the TGA, TIF, and PSD (Photoshop Document) files seem to be the best supported formats. The TGA format is very simple because there are not many options, and it's pretty much just a set of RGB numbers. The TIF format is great because it enables you to use lossless LZW compression. Good news for people going to print: trueSpace4 now creates TIF files directly. This may save you a lot of conversion work.

Finally, you may find a place that uses Photoshop quite a bit. If they are going to have to adjust the work once they get it, they might request PSD files. This is helpful in some instances because you can retain your various "layers" of images that you have composited (while the other formats are flattened versions).

RESOLUTIONS AND LINE SCREEN

How do you go about generating output from trueSpace4? The first thing you'll need to know is the actual dimension of the piece. The second thing you'll need to know is either the line screening or dpi resolution.

Say, for instance, you are to create an image that's 4 inches wide by 3 inches tall. If you happen to know the dpi for this job is 300, then it's easy to calculate your render size. Simply take the width and height in inches and multiply this with the dpi to get your rendering sizes. In our example, 4 inches×300dpi = 1,200 pixels wide, and 3 inches×300dpi = 900 pixels tall.

What if the service bureau that's creating your film doesn't work in dpi and instead gives you a line-screening number? Without going in depth and describing why they give this to you instead, simply go by the general rule of thumb that you double the line screening numbers to get your dpi. Therefore, a line screen of 150 should work with 300dpi.

CREATING PROOFS

A *proof* is exactly that: It's supposed to closely match the print process before you actually take your material to the press. Some inkjet printers do a fairly good job of producing proofs. Note, however, that what's involved here is accurately reproducing the colors (inks) used in the print process. To achieve this, you'll have to use a color calibration system that's been tuned to the inks used in the print process.

TIP

The easiest way to correct these issues is to open your newly created CMYK image and go to the Adjust Curves dialog box. Once you have this tool open, find the area with the problem, and see which of the C, M, Y, or K areas it fits best in. Pull down the Channel box and select this channel. With your mouse cursor, move over to your image and left-click. Your mouse will turn into a dropper, and you'll quickly see on the Curves graph where the color in question is located. Go back to the curve and left-click where you noticed the color. This gives you a new point on the curve that you can use to adjust the color. You might have to add another point on the curve in order to get it where you want it. By dragging the points around and shifting the color, you will find the combination that more closely resembles your original RGB work.

More than likely, you'll have to work closely with a service bureau to get very accurate proofs produced. This extra step is going to be worth it. This could save you the very expensive step of having to halt a print run due to color problems. One of the best proofs to get is called a Matchprint. If you take your files to a service bureau and ask them to produce a Matchprint, you'll receive back a continuous tone print, full size, representing to the best of its digital abilities the final print job.

Be prepared to get several proofs done, especially when working with a new printer or service bureau. It's going to take time for you to get used to how their systems are calibrated. It might be that you look at the proof and notice that some colors are too dark or too washed out, some got converted to CMYK improperly, and so on. It's just a matter of correcting them and getting another proof produced.

CREATING SEPARATIONS

After you are happy with your proof, you need to create *separations*. These are the individual pieces of film—one each for C, M, Y, and K—that will be combined and used in the actual (analog) printing process. Essentially, you are producing a black-and-white print of each of the C, M, Y, and K channels. This is printed on transparency film. The most common way to do this is to have your service bureau print them from the actual file they used when producing your proof.

The film process is a fairly expensive one, which is another reason it pays to make sure you're totally happy with a proof before getting to this point. If you go to press and have to make changes, it means throwing out this set of films and paying for another full set after you've corrected the problem.

After you have the film, you should be set to get your job printed. It's best to send the printer a quality proof along with the films. This is a good thing to do so they have a concept of how you imagine the print will turn out. It's easy for them to mistakenly use too much or too little ink on the run. If they have something to compare it with, it should help you get what you're after—an accurate print job.

PUBLISHING FOR THE WEB

You'll find that creating artwork for the Web seems to be a combination of many other styles of publishing. Because, of course, there are many 2D images involved, it's very similar to print media. Now there are also plenty of animations, either as animated GIF files, embedded AVI files, or some type of streaming video technology. This means that some of your processes might be similar to how you produce animations for broadcast television or film.

IMAGES

The most common image formats on the Web are JPG, GIF, and PNG. All of these image formats were selected due to their portability and potentially small sizes. More and more, static (nonanimated) GIF images are being replaced by the other two formats. This is most likely due to their better color capabilities and competitive file sizes.

ANIMATED GIFS

An easy way to add some interesting flare to your Web page might be to add a few animated GIF files. These files give the appearance of being animated because they can store multiple frames in one file, and popular Web browsers know how to read the files and play back the frames one on top of another properly (similar to an animated flip book). There's one more thing that makes GIFs popular for the Web: It's possible to mark part of each image as transparent. This means that you can place your spinning corporate logo on your Web page and still see the background image beneath it.

The best way to create animated 3D GIF files is to render your animation to an AVI file. There are several programs that will be able to read an AVI file and convert it to GIF animations for you. You may opt for a tool that simply does conversions, such as Microsoft GIF Animator, or go all out and purchase a product such as Ulead's GIF Animator 3. GIF Animator 3 actually resembles a mini video-editing package. It has options for creating cool transitions and effects between frames in your animation, and greatly simplifies the entire process.

VRML

VRML has been around for some time in its various forms. Although it's been seemingly pushed aside in popularity votes, there are still plenty of users and Web sites using VRML. If you want to create a truly 3D Web environment instead of generating 2D artwork simulating a 3D environment, VRML might be worth considering. Because we all know that your favorite 3D package already has VRML built in, you'll be ahead of the game should you need to use it.

I'M AN ARTIST, NOT A PROGRAMMER!

If you're developing Web content, chances are you'll at some point be involved in creating the actual pages. This might require some knowledge of HTML and even JavaScript.

Even if you're not the primary HTML or JavaScript developer, you should be aware of how things work and what has to be done to get the desired results.

For instance, many Web pages today do *mouseovers*. This means that different images can appear on the Web page when the mouse pointer is over a graphic or when it has left the graphic. Such a use may be the look of a "pushed-in" versus a "raised" button on your Web page interface, or changing a "tool-tip" graphic as the mouse passes over your page's various components. Whatever the function, you need to be aware of this at design time. In this instance, it means you might have to generate twice the amount of graphics.

If you are one of the lucky people creating the HTML and JavaScript for your pages, you'll have to be even more concerned with such fancy designs. We've all been to sites that look visually stunning, but clearly lacked planning or a technical design.

Luckily, there are tons of tools appearing all the time to help relieve most of the technical headaches. Microsoft FrontPage seems to be a leader in the field of Web page design, layout, and coding. Other software on the market is available if you want to start building Web sites with streaming audio and video. This is great for us, because it means there will be new ways for us to create cooler and more imaginative Web sites filled with 3D goodies.

SUMMARY

It's clear that whatever your media, you will able to tackle the job by using today's desktop technology. For the first time, affordable desktop PCs running affordable software are able to produce simply outstanding work.

This means that several things are underway. First, the creativity envelope will be forced to accelerate at an enormous rate. It also means that the consumer of yesterday is the producer of today. This is a dramatic change from how things used to be—only the limited few had such power as to shape minds and convey your personal stories. We shall soon see how many hidden "Spielbergs" there are out there. Now if there's not anything interesting to watch, it may be your own fault!

Hitting even closer to home is the fact that smaller studios are able to take on very cool and important projects. It's getting to the point of who's truly more creative—not necessarily who's got the biggest, most expensive machines—gets the work. This spells an awesome opportunity for success. Creating a great digital studio is your first step in this direction.

Part VII

Appendixes

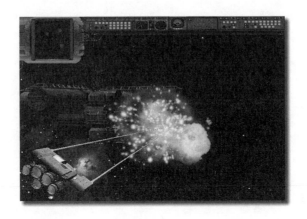

APPENDIX A

CREATING GAMES

by Frank Rivera

First and foremost, trueSpace is ideally suited for the creation of 2D imagery used for sprites and 3D game objects (it does export to the DirectX and the DXF formats). Second, I receive a lot of email with questions regarding trueSpace, game design, and game graphics. Third, with the addition of Python scripting, games can now be coded and played right in trueSpace4. In this Appendix, I won't go into the programming aspects of game creation, but I will cover game design, graphics, palette, and target platform issues.

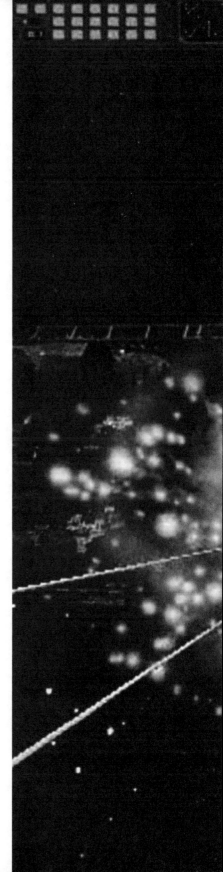

I have been creating my own games and creating game art in trueSpace for a few years now. It is a very fun and satisfying hobby when I can find the time to fit some programming into my busy schedule. I have more individual game graphics than I have actual finished games simply because I love to create in trueSpace—so much that I quickly move on to other trueSpace-related projects before sitting down to write some code.

Before we get into game creation, go ahead and take a few moments to explore the two games, Solar-X and SolarRay, I have provided on the resource CD. The imagery in both these games was created entirely in trueSpace (except the explosions). Solar-X is a Wing Commander-type game, except it plays at a higher resolution and the cockpit is little more complex with readouts, communication panels, and a drop-down information, task, and mission panel. I originally created this game in early 1995 for the Solaris platform so a group of my friends and I could blast one another from the comfort of our desks; I ported the code to the DOS platform in 1996. The game requires a joystick to play, so dust that bad boy off. SolarRay is a first-person 3D-perspective game. The game is a bit of a challenge but fun to play. Who doesn't like spending the afternoon blasting bad guys? After you have had your fill of firing ion cannons and plasma rifles, we will discuss some game creation concepts and how the imagery was created for these games.

Games Are Serious Business

Today's games are booming with dazzling graphics and sound. The game designer today is afforded almost unlimited resources with the recent advances in graphics, sound, the computational power of today's PCs, and, of course, 3D software such as trueSpace4.

Video games have evolved over the years to the point of almost unimaginable complexity. Just about every game written today is graphically intensive. This is where you come in. All kinds of gaming imagery can be created in trueSpace— simple backdrops, 2D sprites, 3D sprites, and 3D objects that can be animated by a 3D engine. The types of games you can create graphics for are many—first-person 3D walk- and fly-throughs, sports games, sideview one-on-one combat, scrolling adventures, fantasy, and roleplaying games (RPG), to name a few.

It wasn't that long ago that the targeted market of video game manufacturers was children between the ages of 6 and 18. The industry didn't start to take off until the mid-1980s when the popular 8-bit (one-byte color depth) image formats began to be used; but when the 16-bit (two-byte color depths) formats were introduced in 1991, the industry really took off. Thanks to Nintendo and Sega, the industry's retail sales soared to $560 million in 1992 and continued into 1993. In 1994, the industry's sales dropped to $410 million but were still higher than the movie industry's revenues that year.

GAME DESIGN I: REFINE YOUR IDEA

So why do we play computer games? I know that my love of game programming is second only to playing them. In fact, I've spent many hours playing Wing Commander when I could have been doing something more productive, but of course, you can't write games without a good feeling for what makes them so enjoyable.

Back to the question. It's hardly something you can easily describe, and nearly impossible to put into a design schematic. You can't take a poll because game players have a wide range of opinions on what they think a successful game should be, but as Bill and Ted would put it, "Excellent." Is an excellent game one that is fun, exciting, or enthralling? Probably a bit of all of these things.

Let's assume that you know how to program and you know how to program games. Now you want to put that knowledge to use by creating a game that you can position in the shareware market. As a programmer, your first response is probably to sit down and type

main()

but that's jumping the gun. I can't emphasize enough how important the design phase is. Don't get impatient and jump into coding. If you have a new idea for a game engine, then this is an exception. In this case, you'll probably want to write a small test program to make sure your technique is going to work. I'll assume that you're writing a game for which there is already a standard technique—a side scroller, shoot-em-up, an overhead RPG, and so on.

What Kind of a Game?

The type of game you decide to create will depend a lot on the resources available to you. If you're not an artist yourself, you'll need to do something that does not need a lot of bitmapped art. This might be a polygon-based flight simulator, an arcade game, or a tile-based war game—all of which trueSpace is suited for. For your first game, the type you create should appeal to *you*. If you don't like war games, don't try to write one. At the very least, plan on something that you're sure you are capable of doing rather than something that is a little beyond your reach or technical expertise. If you decide to create a side scroller, you probably already have a good feel for how the basic mechanics work; if not, play a few—there are tons of them out there. The best advice I can give the beginner is to start with a small, simple game as your first project. You will learn a lot your first time around.

Plot and Playability

In late 1994, Doom took the gaming world by storm. One of its most attractive features was its simple nature. Go from entrance to exit and kill everything on the way. Yea! Baby! Kill them all and let God sort them out!

Since then, about 50 games have been developed with exactly the same premise. Although technology has progressed by leaps and bounds, the plot hasn't changed. If it moves, blast it; if it doesn't, blast it anyway.

Total carnage and whooping the big boss at the end is no longer good enough or adequate justification for playing a game. Gamers want more! Of course, they still want to maim and destroy (who doesn't?), but now they want to do other things along the way. Give your game an interesting plot. Here are some thoughts to get your creative juices flowing.

Interactivity

It's no fun reading a story if it doesn't interact with the gameplay. A plot isn't just an excuse to have aliens land in New York. Players need to know the background and act (interact) accordingly. For example, if a big mothership drops off aliens, then the mothership should keep appearing until the player destroys it, and players should have to wade through aliens to get to it. When the mothership has been destroyed, the aliens disappear from all levels. This forces players to develop priorities. Let players tackle lots of tasks in whatever order they feel best. This is called "an evolving plot" and "multiple mission paths." This takes a lot more work and thought on your part, but it will boost the game's playability. Try to have the plot evolve according to the player's actions. If a specific secret is discovered, have it lead to the development of a different plot, which in turn takes players to a different mission or level later in the game. You can even have the ending change depend on how much extra stuff players collect, accomplish, or kill along the way.

IMMERSIVENESS

A bit of advice: Your game should never, ever stop with a cut scene. All the plot-developing points should be built in. This may seem like a trivial point, but consider this: You're walking down a corridor. You have 11 shots in your weapon, and you know that slimy critter is going to jump out at you any second. You approach a corner, you inch closer to the wall as you make your way around to get a better look, *cut scene*! This gives the player a feeling of losing control and is called "gaming whiplash," which is a feeling of being yanked from a virtual environment. The player is walking down a corridor doing their thing and suddenly they lose control as the game cuts to something completely different. This essentially ruins the game.

If your game is mission based, don't stop the action with a cut scene or a point where players have to read text, such as, "For your next mission...." Instead, make players go through a door to activate a communications panel. Then have the mission commander give players their new instructions. Place a lot of objects in the room so that they can walk around and inspect things while they are listening to the mission brief. When done, have the opposite door open to the new area of the game. Never take control away from the player. The added immersiveness will keep the game interesting.

MISSIONS AND PUZZLES

Missons and puzzles are perhaps the greatest elements a game needs. Give your players a set of objectives and puzzles for every level. Give them power grids to activate or destroy, enemy patrols to creatively avoid, doors and latches that work in strange ways, and timed countdowns to beat before the whole level blows. Add fun things to do, and the game's playability is extended.

LEVEL EVOLUTION

Have your levels evolve over time. For example, your player has just docked on a lonely space station and is aware that the station is protected by a genetically enhanced beast. They're no threat to your weapon-toting player—not at first any-way. As time goes by and the plot thickens, the genetically altered creatures start to get bigger and meaner and more of a challenge. Have the creatures split open as another escapes from its old carcass. Have it become more intense as the game progresses, to the point where going in any direction is a struggle. This adds a strong climactic element to the game. Tie this element to your plot, and you have a recipe for a terrific game.

AN IDEA WITH POTENTIAL

You're full of enthusiasm and a vision for your game—time for the all-important reality check. Does your idea have potential; is it different? This is difficult to answer, and I can't give you a formula that ensures a game idea has potential. The best I can offer is to tell you that most successful games focus on one mood and put all their resources into bringing that to the player.

Ask yourself what the best thing about your game will be? If you answer cool graphics, then your game is probably condemned to rot on a shelf. If it's an adventure, the answer should be story or setting. If it's an RPG, the answer should be exploration. If it's a shooter, the answer should be action and excitement.

From here, you need to define how the game is going to make the player feel. For example, a good war game makes you feel like you are commanding real units. A good war game makes you surprised when the enemy slips through your defenses and makes you feel pride when you draw your opponent into a carefully con-structed trap. Many games suffer from a form of schizophrenia; they seem to get confused whether they are trying to be funny, mysterious, or exciting. Not that a game can't be all of these, but balancing multiple moods is a trick few have mas-tered. You need to pick a mood and put most of your effort into promoting it.

GAME DESIGN II: IMPLEMENTATION

After you've established the basic goals of your game, get more specific. Remember always to keep the goals in mind for each element of the game. Start with a broad idea of how the game will play and focus on the individual elements. You are, of course, limited by whatever the current technology can handle, so keep that in mind. Make a habit of writing everything down. If you've got mul-tiple designers working on the game, set some time aside to brainstorm. (This works great around a pizza. People like to sit and talk while they eat.) Sketch some of the screens if it will help you visualize later. When you've got more than one person working on the project, visuals are critical. At this stage, you should make all the important design decisions and write them down so that there is no miscommunication.

GRAPHICS

The graphical appearance of a game is the first impression a user gets. Although game play is the ultimate measure of how engaging a game is, weak graphics often kill a potentially successful game. For this reason, it's important to take the time to create stunning imagery that is sure to catch the attention of the players. If you will be working with others, then it is your responsibility as a graphic artist to create the best imagery you can to help tell the story and make the game more engaging. No one else has a better understanding of the role the imagery will play in your game. Any insight you can share with the other game developers on your project with regard to the image creation process will serve to ease the development cycle and improve the overall visual appeal of the game.

Before you begin any actual graphics creation, it's important to decide exactly what you need in terms of game graphics. You should already have the game's plot, characters, mood, and so on laid out before progressing to this stage. The next step is to take what you know about the game and assess the graphical content required to make it a reality. This consists of making decisions regarding the game's graphical elements. A good place to start is with a list of the graphics you will need to create for the game. This will help with your game's continuity. For example, you will need backgrounds, foregrounds, animations, and short animated sequences of characters, enemies, intros, cut scenes, status bars, buttons, title screens, credit screens, option screens, individual objects, tiles, maps, and miscellaneous objects. (Please note that this list doesn't take into account every genre or the special needs of the target system.) Your game will also need a consistent look or style.

SUBJECT MATTER AND GRAPHICS STYLE

Subject matter dictates the graphics style of imagery used in the game. Graphics style is basically the look of the images. For example, a child's game would more likely have a cartoony look, but a game targeted to teenagers and adults would probably use a more realistic or stylized approach. After selecting a graphic style, keep all the graphics consistent throughout the game and remember that a more consistent style results in a more absorbing and realistic game.

TARGET AUDIENCE

The target audience for your game can greatly impact its image requirements. Games for children typically use graphics with bright colors, whereas games aimed at teenagers and up use a more toned-down palette. The graphics pretty much depend on the game itself. Many teens and young adults are attracted to games with realistic violence and a lot of gore. I personally love gory graphics, and I don't think they're any different than special effects in movies. Gore has its place, and, in some games, it adds to the excitement.

Movies are a good example of how the target audience dictates graphic detail and content. Children gravitate toward cartoons where the characters contrast well with the background. There are varying levels of detail that are typically associated with a target age group. Older kids usually are more interested in cartoons that more closely model life and reality. Similarly, adults prefer movies with human-like actors.

It is sometimes possible to aim primarily for a particular target audience while also including elements that appeal to other audiences. For example, consider any of the popular Disney animated movies; they clearly target children but always include plenty of humor that usually only adults can appreciate.

SETTING AND MOOD

Perhaps even more important than the target audience of your game is its setting and mood. Where is your game taking place, both in time and in location? If it's a space game set in the future, your graphics might include metallic colors, whereas a gothic game might have dark, gloomy imagery.

Colors are important because it is the colors that effectively dictate the mood of the game. It's simple to see the effects of color with a little experiment. In Figure A.1, a character is placed on a black background and on a white background. How does one image differ from the other? To further see the effects of color and mood, consider the dimmer switch on a light. Have you ever dimmed the lights in a room and noticed the immediate change in mood? Whether the mood is interpreted as gloomy or romantic, it is altered nevertheless. This lighting technique is used frequently in game imagery and can be equated to altering the brightness of the textures used.

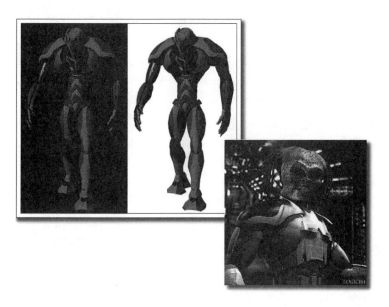

FIGURE A.1 *Color plays an important part in establishing the mood of your characters, a scene, and the overall mood of a game. Background colors play an important role in how the mood of the scene or character is interpreted by the player.*

GAME WINDOW SIZE

The first major decision regarding the game's imagery is the size of the game window. This will decide the size of the images you will need to create for sprites, control panels, and so on. The game window is the rectangular surface on the screen where the game's imagery will be displayed. There are several standard sizes used, 320×200 (considered low resolution), 320×240 (also known as mode X), 320×400 (mode Z), 640×400 and 640×480 (high resolution), and 800×600 and 1,024×768 (super-high resolution). With the exception of games destined for the PC, the game's resolution will be decided by the type of system the game will be played on. You will be limited to a fixed window size that depends on the target platform. If you are creating a game for the PC platform, then you have control over the size of the game window. The only potential limitation on the game window is the performance factor. If you will be creating a game for one of the console platforms, then the maximum resolution your game will play is 640×480 or less. We will look at some other console platform issues in a bit.

You might wonder how performance could be related to the size of the game window. In games with animation, the game window is usually constantly redrawn with every frame of animation. The amount of time it takes to redraw the game window is based on the window's size. Therefore, the larger the game window, the longer it takes to redraw or refresh the screen because there is more to draw. Therefore, you need to weigh the game window size against the performance of the game. I've found that a game window size in the range of 200×300 to 600×480 yields decent results on the PC as a target platform.

Another issue with regard to game window size is available video RAM. On the PC platform, a screen width of 600×400 pixels using a 1-byte color depth (256 colors/8-bit) will take up 240KB per video page. Usually two or more video pages are used to eliminate flicker, a technique called *page flipping*. That means the video card must have at least 480KB of available RAM.

Take this same window size but increase the color depth to 2 bytes (high color/16-bit) and the minimum video RAM required to 960KB, with Truecolor the player would need at a minimum of 1.92MB of video RAM. Today, 2MB video cards are commonplace, and there are techniques a programmer can implement to reduce the need for physical video RAM, such a creating a virtual buffer from conventional system RAM for the purpose of storing sprites and graphics.

PALETTE

Another area you will have to be concerned with is the palette. A palette defines what colors the images will use. In the case with 256-color images and games that use an index into a color palette, not using the same palette sometimes causes an undesirable psychedelic effect. If you are doing work for someone or as part of a team, there may be cases where the palette has already been chosen, but the artist usually is the one who creates the palette. Creating a palette is a challenge. As you can imagine, a single palette must be able to work with all the colors necessary for the game's imagery. For games and game systems that are limited to 256 colors, this can be a laborious task. We will look at some palette issues for each system in "Target System Concerns," later in this appendix.

IMAGE FORMAT

Graphic format is another issue that must be decided. The format is usually decided by the programmers because they are the ones writing the game code. Some systems require a specific format. I personally prefer the PCX format for

256-color games and images because they load very quickly compared to many of the other 256-color image formats. Some target platforms require the use of specific tools. For example, when working with the Sony Playstation, you will likely be working with the DXF file format and the Art tool. The Art tool is where the bitmap graphics are applied to the 3D surface of the object. This tool saves the files in a specific format especially for the Sony Playstation.

PAINT PROGRAM CONCERNS

Whether you create your own graphics or hire an artist, you will need a graphics utility at some point in the graphic development process. Even if you don't need to change the content of the graphics, you often will need to resize or change the transparency of a color. Besides a copy of trueSpace, a nice graphics editor is the most important tool for developing and maintaining games graphics.

Creating video game graphics is a specialized skill. Game artists are consistently working within severe limitations, whether it's the game resolution and/or the game palette. Although a paint package can do little to help with hardware limitations of the target system, a 2D paint package is essential for working around the limitations of the palette, resolution, and color depth.

An ideal paint program needs to have excellent palette control, the capability to select and/or move any portion of a bitmap image from one location on a canvas to another, and the capability to zoom in tight.

PALETTE CONTROL

A color palette is a group of colors available to an image. All 256-color images have an associated color palette that defines the colors the image contains. Good palette control means you can copy, modify, and create colors or ramps of colors with a minimum of keyboard fuss.

When working with 256-color images, you have the ability to specify which colors make up the 256-color palette. Tweaking the color palette to fit the particular color needs of an image is referred to as *palette optimization*. Using the palette optimization tools of a good paint program can yield good results with just 256 colors.

When working with images created in trueSpace, you will need a paint package that performs *dithering*, a process in which the colors in an image are reduced to a lesser amount of colors. This is carried out by using different patterns of the lesser colors to represent the colors lost.

Bitmap Moving and Positioning

You must be able to grab any part of an image and place it (with precision) anywhere on any canvas. You should also be able to specify a single color or group of colors to be treated as transparent (colors not included in a selection).

Transparent colors are colors in an image that aren't drawn. The significance of transparency is that it allows the background behind a sprite to show through. Sprites are discussed later in this chapter.

Zooming In

You must be able to zoom in tight without any loss in tool flexibility.

A Recommendation—Autodesk's Animator Pro

One of the best tools game artists can have in their arsenal is Autodesk's Animator Pro. It has some of the best palette utilities for dealing with 8-bit image files I have come across and has all the features discussed previously. I would suggest picking up a copy. It is an old DOS application that can be a challenge to find, but I have seen it on store shelves, and the Internet has plenty of information on it.

Background Graphics and Textures

Background graphics are any graphics that appear behind the main objects or characters of the game, such as a wall or trees. A background image isn't just a static image that never changes. In fact, the background can be animated, too. In some side-scroller games, two or more backgrounds are used, each having transparent areas. An example is using an image of a set of mountains in the distance and one of a group of trees. By laying the trees over the mountains, we have an interesting background, but it is still static. We can apply a technique called *parallax scrolling*, and here is how it works. As the character walks right, the background image of the trees is scrolled left. To give the scene a sense of depth, the mountains are also scrolled left, but at half the speed as the trees, making it appear as though the mountains are far in the distance and the trees are close to the character. This is a common technique used in many side-scrolling games.

Using textures in games is very useful, primarily because they take up relatively little space because they are tiled repeatedly to create a larger image at runtime. I have provided 30 or so spaceship hull textures and 30 sprites on the resource CD for your use and experimentation. The game SolarRay located on the resource

CD uses these textures for the walls and doors, and the Solar-X game uses them for the hulls of the ships.

Libraries of royalty-free textures exist that also make a good resource. One of these libraries is Tom Marlin's seamless texture collection. You will find a few samples on the resource CD that accompanies this book, along with 300 of my own custom textures.

SPRITES AND ANIMATED IMAGES

What is a sprite, you ask? Sprites are movable bitmap objects on a video game field. The term was coined by Atari in the 1970s. Figure A.2 illustrates a sprite, a background, and the sprite placed over the background.

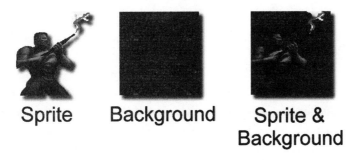

FIGURE A.2 *The image on the left is a bitmap image used as a sprite. The image in the center is of a background tile. The image on the right depicts the sprite placed over the background tile.*

The animation frames for an object or sprite in game lingo are referred to as *phases* or the *phase of an animated sequence.* The phases depict the movements the object goes through, independent of positional motion. We looked at this in Chapter 10 when we had the Franky character walk in place using seven keyframes. The phase of a sprite or 3D object can mean different things, depending on the object or sprite. For example, an animation of a door opening might have four or five frames. On the other hand, the phases of a spaceship's rotation, such as those in Solar-X, might have as many phases as eight to ten frames or individual images.

It is also possible for objects to change phase in more than one way. Depending on the angle the spaceships are viewed, separate sets of images depict that object in the appropriate position. For example, as viewed from the cockpit of a starfighter, an enemy ship below the ship I'm piloting would be seen from above, so I would display an image of the enemy ship from above. Still depending on the angle I'm viewing the ship (on the right), I would display an image of the enemy ship, depicting it from the top view with a different angle than if I were viewing it from above and to the left. This is a simplified explanation because the angle the enemy ship is traveling would also have to be taken into account.

In Solar-X, the sprites were created in trueSpace by using a black background as depicted in Figure A.3. If you have ever played Wing Commander, then you have seen 3D sprites. All sprites are 2D; a 3D sprite is a 2D image that depicts an object in 3D space. Depending on the angle the object is viewed by the player, the appropriate image is displayed onscreen. For example, the ship in the top panel of Figure A.3 required ten separate images. To create the 10 sprites needed to cover all the angles that will be used by the sprite engine, a camera was added to the scene and placed at a height slightly above the object. The axis was moved to the center of the object. This made rotating the object easy.

Looking at the ship in Figure A.3, you might think that the camera was moved around the object to get the shots needed, but that method proves fallible. The best approach is to rotate the object around its own x-axis, not the camera. This will enable you to keep the proper perspective and scale of the object as it rotates. When I started coding this program, video cards had a limited amount of RAM, so I opted to use 10 images to represent one full 360-degree rotation at eye level. Each of these images depict the object at angles equal to 0, 36, 72, 108, and so on. To accommodate viewing the ship from above, another 10 images were created. The camera was fixed on the object by using the Look At tool and then moved along the y-axis until the camera's view of the ship was from above at a 45-degree angle. The camera was then moved so that the ship was viewed from below for a total of 30 sprites.

Besides the ships in Solar-X, I used sprites for characters the player interacts with and receives communications from. In Figure A.4, you can see three characters each at a different stage of dialog. This set of images was stored on a hidden page in video memory. When one of the sprites was needed, it was fetched and placed into position.

To create the cockpit of the starfighter in Solar-X, I stored the cockpit as a separate image in video RAM. While the player viewed the active video page, sprites were placed into position on a hidden page. When all the spaceships, planets, space stations, and stars have been updated to the hidden page, the cockpit is placed over these images, and the dials in the cockpit are updated by placing the appropriate sprites into position over the cockpit image (see Figure A.5). Finally, the hidden page is made the active page, and the process starts over again.

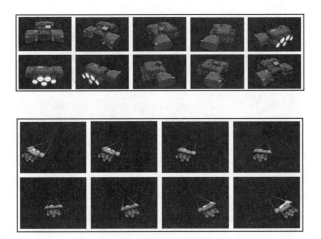

FIGURE A.3   *An example of two ships and the sprites used in the game Solar-X.*

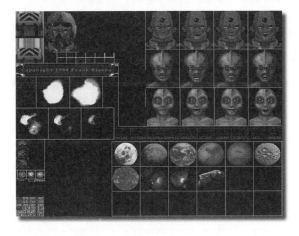

FIGURE A.4   *This is an image of sprites placed in a hidden page of video RAM.*

LOW-POLYGON OBJECTS

When creating 3D models for real-time 3D games, you need to create models that contain as few polygons as possible. This is called *low-poly modeling.* Because a great number of polygons will slow down the interactive experience for the player, you need to make up for the lack of detail by creating the detail using texture maps. These texture maps have to simulate the missing 3D features so that the object looks like an object that takes up actual 3D space. Figure A.6 illustrates how an object with fewer polygons isn't necessarily less convincing.

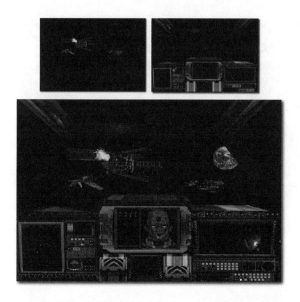

FIGURE A.5   *The completed updated image displayed to the player.*

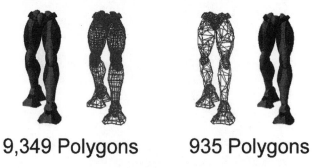

FIGURE A.6   *In this image, the legs of this character started out with over 9,000 polygons. For a 3D game, the character would have to be remodeled with a lower poly count.*

THE CODE

Writing the code will probably be the most time-consuming part, depending on the complexity of the project and the number of people involved.

So, where to start? Now that you have your game laid out, should you start to write **main()**? Perhaps you will want to start building the low-level functions first. If you're creating the type of game where the engine is basically the game, such as a flight simulation, you will probably want to start with the low-level functions first and build up. On the other hand, if you're creating a strategy or puzzle game, it's probably better to start by writing a text or simplified version of the game to see how it plays.

I prefer to build from the middle out, rather than create from the top down or bottom up. I begin by writing my header files and my main functions. I then build the low-level functions and gradually work my way toward the middle tier. On occasion, and when the game is complex, I first write all the header files before writing a line of code. This isn't a bad idea—thinking about the data you will need forces you to consider everything carefully, in a way that isn't possible when you're just thinking about the algorithms in your head abstractly. You should also consider the tools you have at your disposal. For example, if you're writing a tile-based RPG game from scratch, you will want to write a map editor first.

EVALUATE AND MODIFY

You've spent every night of the last nine months hunched over your keyboard, swilling Jolt Cola with Bush blasting through your stereo speakers and candy wrappers all over the floor. You have written what seems to be a complete and working game. Now enters the toughest phase of your project, assuming you stuck to your design. Now it's time to put it to the test. Of course, you would have tested it a bit yourself, checking for obvious bugs, but now you need to turn it over to someone outside the project. You need someone who can look at the game with a fresh view, find those bugs you have overlooked, and point out which features are annoying and which items don't make sense. This can be frustrating at first because you may feel the game is finished, but it is not.

It's easy to get annoyed when people find problems with your code, but you have to roll with it if you want your game to be a success, at least enjoyable. It's all a part of the process. I know how frustrating it is when you write what you think is a final, perfect version, and a day or two later some kid emails you a list of bugs, misspellings, installation problems, and so on. Don't freak out because this is a vital phase of the project, so don't try to cut corners or worse, cut this phase short. I've seen many games over the years that could have been excellent but were rendered nearly unplayable or highly annoying due to a little quirk.

Another aspect that needs to be tested is the interface. A good interface is essential, as with any software package. In a game, the best interface is the one that you see the least of. A truly intuitive interface will feel as if it's not even there. It should be fairly obvious for someone to figure out, but more importantly, it should make mundane tasks, such as pulling up your inventory easily and quickly. If there's a task that players are going to be doing a lot, don't make them go through multiple menus; try implementing a hot key. Keep in mind that it's a game, so it's supposed to be fun. If you want to make the game challenging, then bump up the AI or add more puzzles—don't make the player find an orb to save the game. Don't leave out a pause feature or limit the capability to save inventory items. Lastly, try to include options, such as difficulty level, keystroke combos, and so on. The player should never feel tied down by the limits of the program. Of course, you can't please everyone, but try to avoid forcing the player into a linear path or leading them by the nose. Also, consider adding little things like a secret level or joke. Anything to make the player chuckle or say "cool" will make the game more fun.

TARGET SYSTEM CONCERNS

There are many game systems today: Sega Genesis, Sega CD, Sega Saturn, Super Nintendo, Sony Playstation, and the PC platform just to name a few. Each of these systems has its own set of graphics-related hurdles that must be understood before you can create graphics for these systems.

SEGA GENESIS

Creating imagery for the Sega Genesis game system is a bit of a challenge. First, you are limited to specific palette numbers. The numbers 0, 16, 30, 44, 58, 72, 86, and 100 can be used in any combination for the red, green, and blue colors in a 256-color palette. In order to get other colors, you need to dither these colors when you create the imagery. Also, the top color in each of the palette registers is considered transparent, so you actually end up with 16 fewer colors to work with. A color register is a group of 16 colors in one vertical strip. Second, the lines on a TV spread or bleed horizontally, not vertically, so you need to take this into account when creating your palette. Because there is no vertical bleed, you need to use two pixels of the same color vertically. Another bummer is when creating backgrounds; you are limited to 4 registers of 16 colors each, with the first color being transparent.

Other than these few palette limitations, you have free range to create imagery any way you desire, as long as the cartridge has enough storage space for them.

SUPER NINTENDO

The Super Nintendo game system has its own graphics challenges, but they are easily conquered with a little persistence. This system also uses a 256-color palette, but you are not limited to the colors you create. The big limitation is that you can use colors only inside a single 16-color register for each 8×8 grid of the image. A color register is a group of 16 colors in one vertical strip. For example, colors 1–16 are in the first register, colors 17–32 are in the second register, colors 33–48 are in the third register, and so on. Figure A.7 illustrates this best.

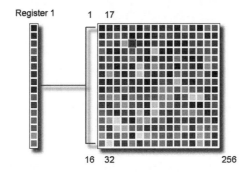

FIGURE A.7 *On the Super Nintendo game system, the color palette is divided into registers of 16 colors each.*

SEGA CD

With regard to game image creation, the Sega CD game system is similar to the Sega Genesis system except that with the CD, a lot more imagery, including animated sequences and screen layers, audio files, and game code, can be created.

SONY PLAYSTATION

The Sony Playstation is more fun to create graphics for than most of its counterparts in the game console industry because you are usually creating 3D graphics. You also have good palette freedom. The most difficult part is having all the tools required. There is a special Art tool for sticking the bitmap graphic onto your 3D objects. It's fairly easy to use and has a short learning curve, but it also requires an extra monitor, hardware, and, of course, software.

SEGA SATURN

Personally, I wouldn't want to create graphics for the Sega Saturn. An unusual thing about this system is that there are no art tools to make applying the bitmap graphics to the 3D objects easy. Furthermore, it uses a four-point polygon system where two of the points overlap. It's a bear to make the graphics look right. It's like taking a square image and folding it into a triangle. This distorts the graphics (a big no-no in my book) and must be taken into consideration when creating the images. You have to stretch them out on one side, so when it is applied to the object, the image looks correct.

PC

The PC is my favorite platform. The PC is the most versatile of all the target systems. Many games still stay within a 256-color palette, but most PC games today use Highcolor and Truecolor modes. Highcolor can display 65,536 colors simultaneously, and Truecolor can display 16.7 million colors. With the Highcolor mode, each pixel occupies two bytes (16 bits) of video memory. The two bytes representing each pixel contain a red, green, and blue color component. Bits 0–4 represent the blue color component, bits 5–10 the green, and bits 11–15 the red. With Truecolor, each pixel occupies either three bytes (24 bits) or four bytes (32 bits) of video memory. The data stored in these bytes directly determines the pixel color instead of serving as an index into a color palette. For this reason, Highcolor and Truecolor modes are called *direct-color modes*, whereas 256 color modes are called *palette-based mode*.

The best part about designing for the PC is that you are not limited to a cartridge's memory limitation. Today's PC game can encompass five CDs and consume up to 100MB of hard disk space.

These are a few of the basics for the major game systems. Once you learn their little eccentricities, you can create images that use these systems to their fullest.

SUMMARY

The goal of this appendix was to inspire those of you who want to create games with trueSpace and to give you enough background information so you will have a better idea of what is involved in creating game imagery for your own games.

SHADING FORMULAS

by Frank Rivera

Here are some formulas for surface materials you can use immediately, or on which you can add your own spin. I tried to include the toughest materials I could think of, with some unusual surfaces thrown in.

For best results, use the ray-tracing option. Results may vary, depending on the lighting setup used. Season to taste.

TRANSPARENT OBJECTS

Transparent objects are everywhere, so it's no wonder that they end up in our imagery. Nothing looks as impressive as perfectly rendered glass.

DRINKING GLASS

Here is the formula for believable glass. This formula was also used to create the glass window panes in Chapter 5's Figure 5.11.

Reflectance: Glass
Color: Plain (RGB: 255,255,255)
Transparency: N/A
Displacement: N/A
Facet: Auto
Ambient Glow: N/A
Diffuse: N/A
Shininess: 1.0
Roughness: 1.0
Mirror: 0.2
Transmission Coeff: 1.0
Reflectance Coeff: 1.5

WATER DROPLETS

This formula is ideal for beads of water on shiny surfaces, such as that of a car or the dew that forms on a cold glass of iced tea on a warm day.

Reflectance: Dielectric
Color: Plain (RGB: 255,255,255)
Transparency: N/A
Displacement: N/A
Facet: Auto
Ambient Glow: 0.0
Diffuse: 0.0
Shininess: 1.0
Roughness: 1.0
Mirror: 0.3
Transmission Coeff: 1.0
Reflectance Coeff: 2.0

CLEAR PLASTIC

Try this formula for tape and CD cases, shampoo bottles, and Plexiglas.

Reflectance: Glass
Color: Plain (RGB: 255,255,255)
Transparency: N/A
Displacement: N/A
Facet: Auto
Ambient Glow: N/A
Diffuse: N/A
Shininess: 1.0
Roughness: 0.5
Mirror: 0.3
Transmission Coeff: 1.0
Reflectance Coeff: 1.02

CERAMICS

Whether you're working on a Mayan civilization or an Egyptian tomb, use these formulas as a starting point for all your ceramic surfaces.

FINE CHINA

Try this formula when surfacing dishes, coffee cups, and fruit bowls.

Reflectance: Phong
Color: Plain (RGB: 250,250,255)
Transparency: N/A
Displacement: N/A
Facet: Auto
Ambient Glow: 0.54
Diffuse: 0.33
Shininess: 0.68
Roughness: 0.83
Mirror: N/A
Transmission Coeff: N/A
Reflectance Coeff: N/A

GLAZED POTTERY

Apply this material to bowls and pots for a glazed look.

Reflectance: Phong
Color: Plain (RGB: 208,136,113)
Transparency: N/A
Displacement: N/A
Facet: Auto
Ambient Glow: 0.5
Diffuse: 0.6
Shininess: 0.46
Roughness: 1.0
Mirror: N/A
Transmission Coeff: N/A
Reflectance Coeff: N/A

PORCELAIN

Give your bathrooms just the right amount of specularity and diffuse color. Adjust the color to the desired shade.

Reflectance: Phong
Color: Plain (RGB: 248,250,250)
Transparency: N/A
Displacement: N/A
Facet: Auto
Ambient Glow: 0.5
Diffuse: 0.6
Shininess: 1.0
Roughness: 1.0
Mirror: N/A
Transmission Coeff: N/A
Reflectance Coeff: N/A

METALS

These formulas are ideal for, hmmmm, let me guess.

CHROME

Use this formula for hot rod bumpers and chrome trim on everything from cars and boats to tricycles.

Reflectance: Glass
Color: Plain (RGB: 255,255,255)
Transparency: N/A
Displacement: N/A
Facet: Auto
Ambient Glow: N/A
Diffuse: N/A
Shininess: 1.0
Roughness: 1.0
Mirror: 0.75
Transmission Coeff: 1.0
Reflectance Coeff: 1.5

GOLD RING

Gold jewelry looks great with this formula.

Reflectance: Conductor
Color: Plain (RGB: 255,180,60)
Transparency: N/A
Displacement: N/A
Facet: Auto
Ambient Glow: 0.32
Diffuse: 0.15
Shininess: 1.0
Roughness: 0.0
Mirror: 0.3
Transmission Coeff: N/A
Reflectance Coeff: N/A

SILVERWARE

Here is the formula used in Chapter 5 for creating silverware.

Reflectance: Mirror
Color: Plain (RGB: 249,245,255)

Transparency: N/A
Displacement: N/A
Facet: Auto
Ambient Glow: 0.0
Diffuse: 0.3
Shininess: 1.0
Roughness: 0.15
Mirror: 0.5
Transmission Coeff: N/A
Reflectance Coeff: N/A

POLISHED ALUMINUM

This formula is ideal for polished aluminum. The surfaces it is applied to look physically light, if that's possible.

Reflectance: Conductor
Color: Plain (RGB: 255,255,255)
Transparency: N/A
Displacement: N/A
Facet: Auto
Ambient Glow: 0.32
Diffuse: 0.15
Shininess: 1.0
Roughness: 0.0
Mirror: 0.3
Transmission Coeff: N/A
Reflectance Coeff: N/A

FLESH

This formula is an ideal starting point for mimicking human flesh. This texture uses the Rough displacement shader.

Reflectance: Phong
Color: Plain (RGB: 255,215,185)
Transparency: N/A
Displacement: Rough (Scale: 0.1; Amplitude: 0.015;
Detail: 1.0; Sharpness: 1.0)

Facet: Auto
Ambient Glow: 0.5
Diffuse: 0.7
Shininess: 0.12
Roughness: 0.32
Mirror: N/A
Transmission Coeff: N/A
Reflectance Coeff: N/A

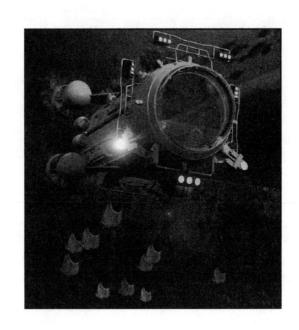

GETTING YOUR WORK VIEWED BY THE MASSES

by Frank Rivera

Getting your work viewed by others in and out the 3D community is relatively easy. There is always a contest, Web site, or magazine willing to view your work and place it in an article, on a video cassette, in a Web site gallery, or even on the front cover of an online magazine. Here you will find a few of the magazines, video producers, and Web sites seeking good material.

CONTESTS

Winning a contest can be a rewarding experience. In some cases, the rewards go beyond the feeling of accomplishment you feel when you win—you can also win graphics cards and software.

3D ARK

The International CG Art & Animation Contest sponsored by 3D Ark is open to professionals and nonprofessionals. You may submit work created as an individual or in a collaborative effort.

Categories include

- Best Character Design, Realistic and Nonrealistic
- Best Character Animation, Short and Long Films
- Best Technical Model, Architectural and Object-Oriented
- Best Noncharacter-Oriented Animation
- Best CG Image, Most Visually Stunning
- Best Character or Objects in an Environment

All entries are judged on creativity, originality, and degree of difficulty. Additional recognition is given to the most original and most difficult entries.

Special notes on submissions:

- **Best Character Design, Realistic and Nonrealistic:** Submit various images in any pose from various angles. Shots should include a front, back, side, and perspective angled view. The character or object should be rendered against a black or white background, preferably with an alpha channel in TGA format at 640×480.

- **Best Characters or Objects in an Environment:** For those who have modeled either characters or technical objects and want to submit images in which they have placed these items into a scene.

- **Best CG Image, Most Visually Stunning:** For those who want to enter complete 3D scenes. Scenes may involve landscapes and architecture.

- **Best Character Animation, Short and Long Films:** A short film entry must be at least 15 seconds and no longer than 59 seconds. A long film character animation must be at least 60 seconds long.

> **NOTE**
>
> Animated submissions may include a soundtrack, but you must own the rights.

- **Best Noncharacter-Oriented Animation:** Open to space battles, abstracts, and so on. Submissions must be at least 15 seconds long.

3D Ark is a great resource; check it out at **http://www.3Dark.com**.

CALIGARI

Caligari holds a contest every month to see who can create the best imagery with trueSpace. The winner wins a graphics accelerator card. Runners-up receive Caligari software or Tom Marlin's "Seamless Textures You Can Really Use" CD.

There are two categories:

- Best Still Image

- Best Animation

All entries are submitted via email. To qualify, the image or animation must be created in trueSpace. You may use other programs to create texture maps, crop and scale your rendered images, and assemble animation clips into one animation. You may also use trueSpace plug-ins. Still submissions should must be no larger than 800×600 and in the JPEG format with "high-quality compression."Animations should be less than 2MB in the AVI, FLC, or MOV format. You must submit a text file with the same name as the image or animation. The text file should include your name, address, phone number, email address, and any notes you think are important in regard to your submission. Send submissions to **gallery@caligari.com**.

> **NOTE**
>
> By submitting your artwork, you authorize Caligari to use it in promotional materials and materials related to Caligari products, without compensation. You are given credit for your artwork, so be sure to include your name with your submission.

For more information, visit Caligari on the Web at **http://www.caligari.com**.

INTERNET RAY TRACING COMPETITION (IRTC)

To enter the Internet Ray Tracing Competition, create an image that is your interpretation of the topic for the current competition. IRTC strongly suggests making a single entry per round, but the organizers will accept more.

NOTE

IRTC recommends that you submit a Zip archive containing some or all the source files used to create your submission for public use. Organizers strongly believe in the sharing of information, but they do understand that you may have a need to protect your work, so it is not required—it's just a polite request.

You may use any rendering program you like to create your submission. You may not use paint and image-editing applications to alter the image after it has been rendered.

Your image must be 800×600 or smaller, but IRTC recommends you use 800×600. The JPEG file must be less than 250KB and must not be a progressive JPEG. All images must be original.

You must include a specially formatted text file explaining how you made your image and, if possible, a Zip archive file containing the source files for them. IRTC has a template text file and an example text file available on its site; the address is **ftp.irtc.org/pub**. Send your entries via FTP to **ftp.irtc.org/pub/stills/incoming** or via email at **irtc-submit-stills@irtc.org**.

The following is an example of the text file that must accompany your submission; all elements must be included. Tokens—such as "EMAIL:"—are required.

EMAIL: <your@email.address>
NAME: <your name>
TOPIC: <the topic of the competition you are entering>
COPYRIGHT: I SUBMIT TO THE STANDARD RAY TRACING COMPE-
TITION COPYRIGHT.
TITLE: <the title of your image>
COUNTRY: <the country you are a citizen of>
WEBPAGE: <your web address>
RENDERER USED: <povray 2.2, 3DS, trueSpace, and so on>
TOOLS USED: <font3D, torpatch, povsb, and so on>
RENDER TIME: <time your image took to render>
HARDWARE USED: <Pentium, Sparc, SGI, and so on>
IMAGE DESCRIPTION: <anything you choose to say about your image>
DESCRIPTION OF HOW THIS IMAGE WAS CREATED: <description of
what techniques you used, and so on>

The competition is open to everyone, including beginners. The contest is truly about what can be learned from one another, not about winning. You have to respect that. Professionals and skilled artisans are encouraged to share their wisdom. Images created on SGI machines with SoftImage don't impress these guys. The little guy rendering his heart out on what he can afford is what they like to see.

Acceptable tools include scanners, digitizers, and motion-capture devices. Any rendering program is acceptable. You may use objects and textures downloaded from the Internet or purchased commercially, but it is not encouraged.

A submission must contain a JPEG image file with the JPG extension. Your submission must contain the specially formatted text file with the TXT extension. All files of a submission must have the same name. Please use eight-character filenames.

FTP submissions must be sent to **ftp://ftp.irtc.org/pub/incoming**. Transfer your text file in ASCII mode. Transfer your JPEG and/or Zip files in Binary mode.

Send submissions via email to **irtc-submit-stills@irtc.org**.

You can submit via the Web; point your browser to **http://www.irtc.org/cgi-bin/irtc_submit_stills**. Simply follow the prompts.

For more information, visit the IRTC at **http://www.irtc.org**.

NOTE

Your entry will be renamed if it conflicts with an already existing entry's name. To ensure your name is unique, look to see what names people have already used. A common name collision avoidance technique is to use your initials as the first few characters of your filenames.

WARNING

Do not insert your text file into the body of your message.

3D DESIGN MAGAZINE

3D Design sponsors the annual Big Kahuna Design and Animation Contest.

Categories include

- Character Design
- Commercial Animation
- Non-Commercial Animation
- Interactive 3D (VRML, Games, and the Web)
- Architectural Visualization
- Print Graphics
- Scientific and Medical
- Industrial and Mechanical
- Best Logo and Corporate ID
- 3D Cartoon

- Fantasy World

- 3D Film and Video Compositing

Submissions are accepted in the following formats:

- Betacam

- Betacam SP or VHS (No S-VHS) NTSC format only

- JPG

- TGA

- TIF

- BMP

- PICT

- SGI

- RGB

- PSD

- AVI

- MOV

File submissions are accepted on floppy, Zip, and Jazz disks only.

NOTE

There is a limit of three separate entries per person, no more. If more than three entries are received, only the first three received will qualify.

Entries must be sent to:

Big Kahuna Design and Animation Contest
3D Design Magazine
525 Market St. Suite 500
San Francisco, CA 94105
415-278-5300

For more information, visit **http://www.3D-design.com**.

MASS MARKET VIDEOS

WARNING

You must send a printed copy of the submission form located on 3D Design's Web site, or you will not be qualified to win.

If you have created an animation, then you would probably want to submit it on video cassette where it would look its best. The following company is always willing to take a look at your work, and if it is used, you will receive royalties for each copy sold.

Odyssey Productions

Odyssey Productions, the creators of the Mind's Eye video series, is always looking for new content for its videos. As part of Odyssey's pursuit of great content, computer animations of any style or type are seriously considered for submission, and there is no specific deadline for your submissions. If your animation is included in one of the Odyssey videos, you share in the royalties. Half of all the net revenues are shared by the animators.

I personally think this is the best route to take if what you seek is exposure to a mass audience outside the CG community. If your submission makes it on a tape, your work will be admired by millions of people around the world, including me. I have every copy Odyssey has produced. They're great fun to watch.

Animators are requested to send either VHS or $\frac{3}{4}$-inch viewing copies of their work to:

Steven Churchill
ODYSSEY PRODUCTIONS
4413 Ocean Valley Lane
San Diego, CA 92130
phone: 619-793-1900; fax: 619-793-1942
email: **odyssey@odyssey3D.com**

> **NOTE**
> Odyssey Productions requests that you contact it prior to sending your submissions.

For more information, visit Odyssey Productions at **http://www.odyssey3D.com**.

Magazines

If you do 3D, then you likely subscribe to one or more of the popular 3D magazines. They always seem to have a contest or two, but what you might not be aware of is that online magazines have a larger audience, and getting your work up on one of those sites will get your work viewed by hundreds of thousands of people every day.

Sci-Fi Channel's *Science Fiction Weekly*

Science Fiction Weekly is always seeking artwork submissions for its cover. A major prerequisite is that the art must contain an element of science fiction. Art selected will run on the cover of one issue and be included in the magazine's galleries.

NOTE

If your work is chosen for the Sci-Fi Weekly cover, the words "Sci-Fi Weekly" will be superimposed on your image. They do it very well, so as not to alter the context or beauty of the image itself. They make it blend as if it were part of the original image. Visit the gallery to see how some of the cover images were altered.

If you have a Web site, *Science Fiction Weekly* will link to it or your email address.

To submit artwork, you must contact the magazine first via email at **scifiweekly@scifi.com**.

For more information, visit *Science Fiction Weekly* at **http://207.25.144.246/sfw**.

If you check out the galleries, you will find a couple of images created by me and some other trueSpace users. Making the cover of *Sci-Fi Weekly* is a great way to have folks outside the 3D community view your work.

WEB SITES

Web sites are a wonderful resource for getting information and getting your work viewed by others. Besides the sites mentioned earlier in the book, be sure to check out these as well.

3D CAFÉ

Submissions must be 3D-rendered images. The image must be submitted by an individual author or authors, not by a company. The image must be 577 pixels wide in *nonprogressive* JPG format. The image filename must be eight characters long with no spaces and must not contain any text on the image. *3D Café* accepts the best of the best only, so you may want to submit several images separately to increase your chances.

You must include a text file with your submission, containing the image title, a brief description of how you created the image, a list of the software used, your name, and your email address.

For more information visit *3D Café* at **http://www.3Dcafe.com**.

THE *INSIDE TRUESPACE* WEB SITE

The premiere *Inside trueSpace* Web site is where you will find advanced modeling, surfacing, and plug-in use techniques, plus custom shaders, tutorials, objects, textures, plug-ins articles, reviews and interviews. The book you are holding in your hand doesn't end at the back cover.

No rules or guidelines other than the image must be rendered in trueSpace; simply email your submission to **LOGICBit@aol.com** or FTP your submission to **ftp://ftp.logicbit.com/incoming**.

For the latest trueSpace tutorials, tips, and techniques, visit the *Inside trueSpace* Web site at **http://logicbit.com/InsidetrueSpace**.

WHAT'S ON THE RESOURCE CD

The resource CD is packed with over 500MB of content with over 300 textures, royalty-free clips of explosions and other natural phenomena from Artbeats worth several hundred dollars, and over 30 plug-ins and filters including special versions from popular developers Alain Bellon and Brendan Hack not available elsewhere. Image/animation editing, compositing and texture generation program demos, and a full version of Autodesk's Animation Player, along with the latest Indeo codec, and also provided. Rounding out the resources on the CD are two sample games with graphics created using trueSpace, images submitted by trueSpace users, and scene/data files accompanying each chapter's tutorials.

ACTIONS

The action folder contains a Photoshop action script you can use to convert stubborn alpha channel images to a format that works well with trueSpace 4.x. View the readme file in the Actions folder or Chapter 14, "Previsualizing Pyrotechnic Effects," for information on how to use this script.

ADOBE

In this folder, you will find a trial version of Adobe Premiere 5.0, Adobe Photoshop 4.0, 5.0, and Adobe After Effects 3.1. Unzip each and follow the direction in the readme files.

ANIMATOR

This is a freeware version of Autodesk's Animation Player. This player will play any animation by using any of the codecs you have installed on your PC. A great feature of this player is it will automatically loop the animation you are playing. It also has a lot of other features you may find interesting. Please read the readme file and license agreement before installing.

ARTBEATS

This folder contains a wonderful sample of clips from Artbeats Digital Film Library which are used in films such as *Starship Troopers* and *Spawn*, television series such as *Babylon 5*, and games including Fallout 2. These clips of explosion, fire, water, and sky effects were shot on 35mm film. All these are royalty-free clips in quicktime format at NTSC resolution worth hundreds of dollars. Check out the readme file for any last-minute details. There is also a wonderful Quicktime-to-Targa converter included. To view the clips, Quicktime for Windows 3.0 has also been added.

BITMAP GENESIS

This folder includes a demo version of Bitmap Genesis. Bitmap Genesis is a great landscape-generation tool that produces highly realistic textured landscape scenes for trueSpace complete with trees, lights, and cameras. Bitmap Genesis is currently being ported to a tSX in order to take advantage of some of the new features of tS4. Please review the BGREADME.txt file for last-minute details and product information.

CHAPTERS

This folder contains all the exercise files used in the book. Each chapter is contained in its own folder and contains the actual scenes, COBs, and animations used to create the exercises. For example, in the Character Modeling chapter, I demonstrate how to create a humanoid character with metaballs. Not only is the finished character included, the scene containing the character with the metaball structure intact is also included for your experimentation and review.

CODECS

The latest version of the Indeo codec can be found in this chapter. This folder contains what I think is the best general-use video compressor available today. View the readme file during installation for some last-minute information.

NOTE

You will need to install this codec to view the exercise animations.

DARKTREE TEXTURES

An incredible standalone procedural texture generator (dumps bmps and tgas for use in tS). The executable contains additional notes.

EXPLODER

This folder contains a standalone program that generates an animated exploded COB version of any object you import from trueSpace. The Zip file contains a readme file listing some notes not found in the help files.

GAMES

In this folder, you will find two games containing graphics created in trueSpace, Solar-X and SolarRay. Each game is contained in its own folder and has been stripped of a lot of game logic. They are still playable and are included only to show how images created in trueSpace can be used to make games.

SolarRay has an install program and also two disk images if you prefer to save the game to disk. Solar-X is zipped up and can be unzipped into any directory and then played. Solar-X takes up around a hundred megabytes of disk space, so be sure you have enough room before you unzip it. Each game has a readme text file to get you started. Solar-X displays the hotkeys upon startup so you may want to jot the information down before proceeding. Solar-X also requires a mouse, so dust that bad boy off if you want to blow things up. SolarRay is menu driven and uses either a mouse or keyboard as input. Solar-X is a very simple game; point your weapons at the enemy and blast away. SolarRay, on the other, hand is a little more involved. Here are some tips to get you started.

THE STORY

SolarRay is the code name for an elite task force of which you are the sole member. The year is 2104 and our understanding of the universe and the development of technology has increased exponentially. We have colonized most of the planets in our humble solar system and remarkably have kept peace with one another for hundreds of years. Unfortunately, from time to time, a madman commits crimes against humanity in one of our colonies. This is where SolarRay is called on to neutralize the situation.

On an asteroid in the belt of Orion, the SDD (Solar Defense Department) abandoned a six-square-mile genetic lab called Xbase. 17 years have passed since your escape from this military installation (Escape from XBase). Now, you must return to destroy it, and the madman whose genetic experiments are a threat to the security and well-being of planet Earth and its colonies.

The object of the game is to destroy the space station by detonating the nuclear reactor that powers it. Proceed down corridors by eliminating all occupants on each deck and neutralizing all force fields between you and your objective. The mastermind behind the genetic experiments taking place on this space station will intercept you when you have reached the station's core. Good luck!

HINTS AND TIPS

I have included some hints as follows to help you get through the station, but have intentionally left out some important facts so that a challenge will still remain.

- Save the game often as you move along.

- Deck 1: Loading Bay and Storage Hangar: Lots of men working; don't make them aware of your presence.

- Use the [J] key to jump the pit filled with land mines.

- Kill the power to the force fields to gain access to the transporter.

- Deck 2: Cryonics Lab: twisting corridors designed to confuse. Kill the power to the force fields to proceed. Locate the transporter to the next level.

- Deck 3: Abandoned Research Level: (Guards still patrol so be aware.) This is the gateway to many decks, but you will have to find the passcards and secret doors to accomplish your mission. Find the radar pack on this level; it's in a wall.

- Deck 4: Power Station1: Destroy power transformers and recover the passcards. Avoid the force field trap or you will have to start over (it has its own power supply; you must destroy it). Blast all the power cells, but first find the cell that powers the force field protecting the door.

- Deck 5: Many hidden rooms. Find the rocket launcher.

- Deck 6: Avoid setting the silent alarm, NOT! You will beam to another level and back again to reach the transporter to the lower levels.

- Decks 7 through 28 will have to be explored!

- Suicide: Running into mines intentionally or walking through force fields will dump you to DOS, not the menu.

NOTE

Save your present position as often as you can. The wrong turn can send you back to deck 1 or trap you behind a force field for eternity.

WARNING

Please do not use the first position on the save screen; it is buggy.

The preceding list seems short, but there are bonus levels and plenty of hidden rooms, and the levels are large and dangerous. Good luck.

Both these games were written for DOS, so please review the readme files that accompany the games for more information on playing them.

IMAGES

This folder contains some images submitted by trueSpace users. Images in the color panels can also be found here.

PLUG-INS AND FILTERS

This folder contains 36 trial versions of the coolest plug-ins and filters available today.

Axion:

- Flare and Glow Effects Demos for trueSpace and Photoshop. A powerful filter system for adding flares, glows, and sparkles to your renders.

Blevins:

- VertiLectric Dem—Object-branching plug-in useful for creating lightning, tree branches, and more.

Brendan Hack:

- Blur-N-Feather filter S/E—A special version only available with this book, this trueSpace filter Gaussian Blurs only selected objects, useful for creating vaporous particle effects and more.

- Meshsize—Calculates and allows the scaling of a polyhedron's surface area and volume.

- Roundit—Creates rounded cubes.

- TrueConez—Creates real cones without the extra face and vertices at the apex of the cone that trueSpace's native cones feature.

- TSXtruder—Makes heightfield objects by extruding targa image files from the top of cubes.

- UV Rip—This plug-in rips the UV map of a polyhedron and saves to targa format which can then be used as a template for painting textures.

Michael Gallo:

- Infinity Demo—Creates infinite planes great for simulating extensive sky and ground. Features a great layer system and procedural generator for producing clouds and more.

Primitive Itch:

- Art Director Demo—A material, texture, bump map, and image-management plug-in that far surpasses trueSpace's native material library.

- Gaffer Assistant—Gives the capability to adjust grouped lights all at once.

- Hair Plug—Creates straight hair and fur. Also ideal for grass generation.

- Layery—Shows or hides objects by using layers.

- MeshForge Demo—Stackable modifiers allow you to bend, twist, taper, add noise, and so on, to an object.

- MLB Pathfinder—Use this plug-in to fix incorrect filenames in material libraries.

- Primal Particles Demo—Particle Systems plug-in useful for creating fire, smoke, exploding objects, and much more.

- tSX Extender—Install plug-ins beyond the eight allowed by trueSpace.

- Unwrapper—Output an image of a mesh's UV space.

fs24

- UV Tweak—Change the position or scale of a mesh's UV space.

Quantum Impulse:

- ThermoClay S/E—Polyhedron-smoothing plug-in that makes sharp, cubical objects appear organic. Perfect for modeling creatures, animals, humans, vehicle hulls, and so on.

- Energy3D S/E—Great for creating electricity, lightning, sparks, tornadoes, glows, and sparkles.

- Space Time Morph S/E—Brings multiple-channel object morphing to trueSpace, most ideal for lip synching and facial expressions.

- Fluid Reality Preview—Exclusive preview scenes from a water-effects plug-in in development that dynamically creates ripples, waves, and more according to object interaction.

Urban Velkavrh:

- ETC Shareware—Object duplication plug-in that allows quick multiple copies to be made of an object.

- Fcreator Shareware—Generates, modifies, and animates objects based on mathematical formulae.

- Intruder Demo—A depth renderer that renders the selected object or scene with a visible representation of distance from the viewing plane.

- Shell Shareware—Creates a shell from an object, the fastest tS solution around for making hollow objects.

- Sunshine Shareware—Adds lights with sunlike properties based on Earth location, month, day, year, and so on.

- Treedo Shareware—A parametric tree generator.

White Dragon Studio:

- Primitives tSX—Includes all primitive shapes and input fields for each primitive's settings in one panel.

- Repositioner tSX—Retrieve object translation, rotation, and scale data and apply it to another object.

- Volumetric FOG tSX—Creates layered volumetric fog and clouds.

Binary Reality:

- Bitmap Primitives Demo—Creates geometry with optimized UV mapping by using grayscale images as heightfields on planes, spheres, and cylinders.

Paladin Studios:

- TextureBin tSX S/E—Thumbnail image viewer and editing tool. Includes several filters for altering images and textures directly in trueSpace.

TEXTURES

This folder includes 300 LOGICBit textures. Feel free to use them in your own work royalty free.

MARLIN STUDIO

This folder includes some examples of Marlin Studio's Texture collections.

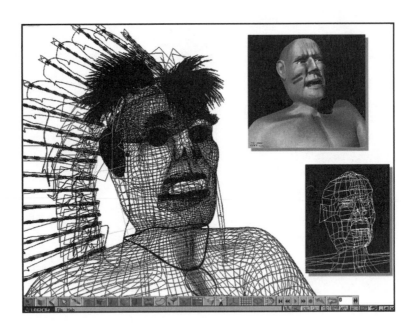

GLOSSARY OF 3D TERMS

SYMBOLS

3D: Three-dimensional. Having the appearance of length, width, and depth.

3DR: A 3D software interface (3D-API) from Intel. It supports Microsoft's GDI, DDI, DCI, and 3D-DDI.

A

A*: A heuristic approach to finding the shortest path in a tile-based game world. It is considered one of the fastest algorithms and is sufficient for most needs.

active picture area: The elements of a TV picture that contain actual picture data as opposed to sync data. The active vertical picture area is 487 lines for NTSC and 576 lines for PAL. The inactive area is referred to as blanking.

actor: A movable 3D object in procedural animation and kinetic animation.

AES/EBU (Audio Engineering Society/European Broadcast Union): The digital audio used by most forms of digital audio from CDs to D1.

aliasing: Defects in a picture caused by too low a sampling frequency or poor filtering. Usually called the "jaggies" or stairsteps effect.

alpha blending: Creating transparent materials with the help of additional information for each pixel.

alpha channel: The extra eight bits of information in a 32-bit image. Eight bits are used for storing the red color information, eight are used for the green information, and eight are used for the blue color information. The remaining eight bits can be used to store masking information for compositing. It is commonly used for communicating transparency.

ambient color: The color response of a surface to an ambient light source.

ambient glow: A surface property that creates the illusion of light emanating from an object.

ambient light: The stray photons that exist in a scene that do not come from an explicit light source. An example of ambient light is the light that you see in shadows that is not reflected directly from any object.

animate: To give motion to an object over time.

animated textures: Textures that provide the illusion of motion on a surface. This is accomplished by using an AVI file or series of numbered images as a texture map.

animation: A collection of images called frames that, when played one after another, create the illusion of movement.

antialiasing: A graphics procedure used to eliminate the stair-stepping effect, known as jaggies or aliasing, caused by pixels of contrasting colors next to one another.

artifact: Degraded image quality in portions of a digital video sequence.

aspect ratio: Width-to-height ratio of a picture. A theater screen is usually 1.85:1, wide-screen TV (16×9) 1.77:1, and currently normal TV (4×3) 1.33:1.

atmospheric effects: Effects that visually alter the environment to simulate conditions such as fog and depth cueing.

atmospheric shader: A process that algorithmically describes the behavior of the atmosphere between a surface and the viewer.

axis of motion: An imaginary line in 3D space, which an object is moved along.

axis of rotation: An imaginary line in 3D space, which an object is rotated around.

B

B-Frame (Bidirectional frame): The frame in an MPEG sequence created by comparing the difference between the current frame and the frames before and after.

B-Mode edit: Assembling footage in the order it appears on the source reels. Missing scenes are left as black to be filled in later by another reel. This editing technique requires fewer reel changes.

B-Spline: A spline curve that rarely passes through its control points.

bevel: A 3D modeling operation. A bevel removes sharp edges from an extruded object by adding additional surface area around the surrounding faces.

Bézier curve: Originally used for car body design, Pierre Bézier first described this curve in France during the 1960s. A Bézier curve is formed from two end points and two or more control points along the curve.

Bézier patch: A Bézier patch uses the Bézier curve algorithm to define the surface of a 3D shape. Bézier patches interpolate the curved surface of a three-dimensional object from the curve's control points.

Bilinear filtering: Eliminates pixelization or blockiness when textures are viewed up close.

bitmap: A 2D digital image where every pixel expresses a level of color. Examples are images stored in digital form for the World Wide Web, 3D texture maps, and family photos used for desktop wallpaper.

bits per pixel: A number representing the amount of color information of a pixel.

BMP (Windows Bitmap): A graphics format that enables Microsoft Windows to display images on devices with similar capabilities in a consistent way.

Boolean operation: A 3D modeling method where one object is modeled by adding or subtracting another object from its surface. The common commands are Boolean union, Boolean subtraction, and Boolean intersection.

bounding box: A simple representation of a 3D object as a wireframe hollow box. Useful when moving objects in scenes with lots of polygons.

BSP tree: A method used to subdivide space along planes to build a tree that is usable to do sorting, fast culling, collision detection, and so on.

bump mapping: A technique used to simulate rough or bumpy textures.

C

camera target: An object the camera will track through a scene.

Cartesian Coordinate System: A mathematical arrangement of spatial measurements where a point can be defined by the intersection of two or more coordinates.

child: An object that is linked to a parent object. *See hierarchical model.*

chrominance: The color part of a video signal. It also includes information about hue and saturation.

clipping: Limiting a drawing area to a rectangular area by cutting out its edges.

collision detection: A method of identifying the moment when a vertex or facet of a 3D object conflicts with the space occupied by a vertex or facet of another object.

color depth: The number of possible colors that can be shown in a particular image. For example, an 8-bit image can represent a total of 256 colors; a 16-bit image can represent a total of 65,536 colors.

component video: A video signal in which the luminance and chrominance signals are separated. This has higher picture quality at the expense of higher bandwidth.

composite video: The luminance and chrominance signals are combined in an encoder to create the common NTSC, PAL, or SECAM video signals. An economical form of analog video compression for broadcasting video.

compositing: Layering multiple pictures one on top of another.

compression: The reduction in size of a collection of digital information.

continuity pass: Consulting a detailed script to avoid discrepancies from shot to shot in a film or animated sequence.

Contrast: The overall difference between light and dark in an image.

Control track: A signal recorded on videotape to allow the tape to play back at a precise speed in any video tape recorder (VTR). Can be equated to the sprocket holes on film.

cross-section: A 2D representation of a 3D extrusion's basic shape. A planar sample taken from a 3D object.

CSG (Constructive Solid Geometry): The method of constructing complex objects by performing Boolean operations.

culling: The act of removing polygons that aren't visible on the screen.

D

D1, D2, D3, D5, and D16: Digital videotape format using the CCIR 601 standard to record 4:2:2 component video on 19mm tape. The first digital videotape format. The D2 format uses the 4 FSC method to record composite digital video and uses a cassette similar to D1 and 19mm tape. The D3 format uses a 4 FSC composite signal like D2, but recorded on 1/2-inch tape. The D5 format uses CCIR 601, 4:2:2 video on 1/2-inch tape. D16 is used to store film resolution images on D1 format tape recorders; it records one film frame in the space normally used for 16 video frames.

DCT (Discrete Cosine Transform): A popular method of video compression.

DDC (Display Data Channel): There are different DDC standards: DDC1, DDC2B, and DDC2AB. In the case of VESA, the Display Data Channel provides a serial data channel between the monitor and the graphics board. DDC support automatically transfers monitor data, maximum horizontal frequency, timing, and so on to the graphics board. Both the monitor and graphics card must support DDC to use any of this functionality.

DDR (Digital Disk Recorder): A digital video recording device consisting of high speed hard drives. Used to get video into and out of computers.

deformation: Applying a change to an object by pulling or pushing vertices, faces, or lattices.

depth cueing: An object's color is changed in relation to the object's distance from the viewer as to make objects in the distance appear to fade into the distance.

depth of field: The range of distance along the z-axis from the viewer. Used to set the focal point.

diffuse light: Light that is evenly reflected from an object's surface, regardless of the angle from which it is viewed.

digital Betacam: A digital video tape format (CCIR 601) to record 4:2:2 component video (compressed) on 1/2" tape.

digitize: Process of turning an analog signal into digital data.

digitizer: An input device used in CAD packages in much the same way as a mouse is used as an input device for a Windows software package. A device for scanning printed drawings and converting them to digital form.

Direct3D: 3D software interface (3D-API) from Microsoft for Windows95/98/NT, which uses DirectDraw.

DirectColor: A generic term for Truecolor, Realcolor, or Hicolor. Color information is passed directly to a D/A converter instead of using a lookup table to perform the translation.

directional light (aka distant light): A light source with direction but no point of origin. Also known as Infinite lights.

displacement shader: A shader that algorithmically describes the modification of a surface, either physically (surface displacement shader) or one that simply renders the displacement. The difference is really in the shadows cast by the object. An object that has a surface displacement shader applied will cast shadows that also reflect the surface bumps, but in the rendered method a sphere will cast a smooth surface shadow, regardless of the amplitude of the displacement shader applied.

dithering: A class of techniques for representing a large range of colors from a small palette. It's an approximation of colors not available in a reduced palette. Some areas of solid color in the original image become a mix of differently colored pixels, as is the case with 256-color image file formats. Every pixel in the original image is mapped to the nearest color value in the reduced palette.

double buffering (aka page flipping): A method of displaying animation in which an image is displayed from one portion of the buffer while the next image is being prepared in another. This technique produces smoother animations by eliminating flicker.

DVB (Digital Video Broadcast): A group of international standards for the broadcasting of digital video regardless of medium; for example, satellite and cable.

DVD (Digital Video Disk): A new format for putting full-length movies on a 5-inch CD by using MPEG-2 compression. It is said to be better than VHS in quality.

DVD-ROM: A format that can store 4.7GB on a single disc. It is expected to replace the CD-ROM eventually.

DVE (Digital Video Effects): A device or software application which digitally manipulates video to create a special effect.

E

edge numbers: Numbers printed every foot on the edge of 16mm and 35mm film that allow frames to be easily identified in an edit list.

EDL (Edit Decision List): A list of edit points and so on made during an edit session and saved to floppy disk. Allows an edit session to be repeated or modified at a later time.

environment map: A bitmap image used to simulate the surroundings of a highly reflective object.

extruding: A 3D modeling operation where a surface of an object is raised in the direction of the surface's normal.

F

face or facet: Three or more vertices joined to form a polygon. A collection of faces is referred to as a mesh. Each face also has a special vector tied to it called a normal. The normal defines which side of the face is considered to be the inside of an object and which is the outside.

field: One half of a complete video frame (picture) containing all the odd or even scan lines of a picture.

filter: An application that applies a visual effect to a video segment or image. Filters are also used to correct problems with an image—to perform color balancing, for example.

Flat/Faceted shading: A rendering process where an algorithm calculates one color for each polygon in the model, based on the texture used and its position relative to light sources. A single illumination level across all faces resulting in a faceted surface.

FLC/FLI: FLC is an acronym for flick, as in movie flick. Developed by Autodesk for animations, FLC files are resolution-independent bitmapped images. This file format uses a form of delta compression. The FLI format is a low-resolution format supporting 320×200 256 colors only.

fog: An atmospheric special effect that mimics the real world tendency of an object to fade by a certain amount as it moves into the distance. Usually a blending technique is used to simulate the fading and obfuscation of each pixel.

fps (frames per second): Frame rate measurement unit.

frame: Single video or animation image or two video fields; a single film image. There are 30 frames in one second of NTSC video.

frame rate: Number of images shown per unit time.

frame size: Width and height of a frame expressed in pixels.

G

geometric modeling: A method of modeling a 3D object where the object is constructed from geometric primitives.

GLINT: 3D processor from 3DLabs.

glow: A surface property that creates the illusion of light emanating from an object.

Gouraud shading (aka smooth shading): A rendering process. The colors are first calculated at each of the vertices in a polygon. Then the surface of the polygon is shaded to give a smooth transition between different colors at each vertex. The result is a smooth appearance.

graphics accelerator: A device used to increase graphics performance.

grayscale: Images that consist of a palette of different shades of gray.

H

HGC (Hercules Graphics Card): A video board providing bitmapped single-color graphics.

HiColor: Designates 15 bpp (bits per pixel) or 16 bpp graphics mode, which produce 32,768 and 65,536 colors, respectively.

hidden page: A graphics page that is not currently being displayed. See Appendix A, "Creating Games," for an example of its use.

hierarchical model: A group of linked child and parent objects. A child object can be moved independently of the parent object, but when the parent object is moved, the child object is affected.

hierarchy or hierarchical linking: The connecting of objects so that they move in relation to one another. In character modeling, the hand is linked hierarchically to the arm, which is linked to the body.

I

image mapping: Applying an image to the surface of an object.

index of refraction: The ratio at which light bends as it passes through a transparent object.

indexed color images: An image that contains a color table in the file. An indexed 16-color image contains a table with 16 color entries (four bits), whereas an indexed 256-color image will have 256 color entries (eight bits).

interlacing: A process in which the picture is split into two fields by sending all the odd-numbered lines to field 1 and all the even-numbered lines to field 2.

inverse kinematics: A method of hierarchically linking objects where the objects are constrained via joints to ease the posing and animation of characters. In an inverse kinematics environment, moving a character's fingertip in turn moves the wrist, which moves the forearm and bicep, making animation of characters intuitive.

J

JPEG (Joint Photographic Experts Group): A standard for compressing still images.

K

key light: The primary light source in a scene.

keyframe: A frame that defines the beginning or end of a motion, sequence of motions, or actions. A 3D application creates a series of transition frames between two keyframes. This process is called tweening, which is short for "in-betweening."

kinematics: The study of motion.

L

lathing: A 3D modeling operation that creates a new object from a 2D profile by rotating it around an axis.

line drawing: A method of producing images in which the starting and ending coordinates of a line are supplied by the CPU; the rest of the work drawing the line is then done by the graphics processor.

linear interpolation: An algorithm for generating in-between images from keyframes whereby the movement of a vertex is assumed to follow a straight line.

lofting: A 3D modeling operation where a stretched surface, often called a skin, is pulled over interior cross sections, sometimes called ribs.

LTC (Linear Time Code): Time code recorded on a videotape's linear analog track.

luminance: The black, white, and bright part of a component video signal. A portion of a video signal corresponding to the black and white base of a color video picture.

M

map/mapping: To project an image onto a surface of an object.

matte: A high-contrast image used to cut a hole in a background picture to allow the image the matte was created from to seamlessly fit in the hole.

mesh: A collection of faces, often called *patches*, that describe an object.

metaballs: A method of modeling that creates organic models by using primitives and indicating the amount of fusion between them.

metallicity: The surface property that determines how much of the surface's color is present in any of its specular highlights.

metamesh: The smooth surface of a metaball model.

metaprimitive: A primitive used in the creation of a metaball object.

MIP mapping: Creates three or more copies, called *MIP levels*, of a texture. Each level copy is a different size so the best fit can be applied to an object.

model: An object composed of one or more faces or patches.

modeling: The act or creating a 3D representation of an object.

morphing: A special effect where one shape is gradually transformed into another.

motion blur: Image fuzziness caused when the visible subject is moving faster than the shutter speed of the camera.

motion capture: A process used to record and digitize an object's motion through 3D space. Motion capture systems come in many forms, from magnetic systems to a series of cameras, lasers, and mechanicals. After the motion is recorded, it can be applied to 3D objects to give them lifelike movements.

motion path: A series of lines or a line drawn onscreen that represents the motion path of an object.

MPEG (Moving Picture Experts Group): A standard for compressing moving pictures. MPEG 1 uses a data rate of 1.2 megabits per second (Mbps). MPEG 2 supports higher quality with a data rate of 1.2 to 15 Mpbs. MPEG 2 is the format used for transmitting digital television. MPEG is "lossy" and MPEG compressed video is of lower quality than standard VHS video.

N

negative lights: Lights that have a negative intensity. The intensity of negative lights is added to the scene just as any other light source. The effect is a darkened area in the location of the light source. A light with a negative intensity of -0.05 in the same location as a light source with an intensity of 0.05 would yield no light.

noise: A mathematically defined pattern using variable degrees of randomness and used to generate color patterns in imagery.

normal: A vector tied to a 3D face that defines which side of the face is considered to be the inside of an object and which is the outside.

NTSC (National Television Standards Committee): The television and video standard in use in the United States. Five hundred twenty-five horizontal lines at 60 fields per second (two fields equals one frame). Four hundred eighty-seven of these lines are actually used for the picture. The remainder is used for sync, VITC, and closed captioning.

NURBS: Nonuniform rational B-spline. Unlike Bézier curves where their control points provide local control over segments of a curve near a control point, NURBS adds the capability to adjust a segment's tension and bias. The result is more complex (nonuniform) curves and better shape control.

O

object: An object can be a collection of points, splines and faces, or patches (spline modelers), or a collection of polygons (polygonal modelers), which can be manipulated as a whole.

object tree: A group of linked objects. A model containing object trees is called a hierarchical model.

omni light: A type of light that simulates lighting conditions similar to a bare light bulb.

onion skin: In today's software, a feature whereby the previous and/or next few frames of an animation are superimposed over the current frame. A technique borrowed from traditional cel animation.

opacity: The measure of an object's capability to block light transmission; the opposite of transparency.

OpenGL: A 3D software interface (3D API) based on Iris GL from Silicon Graphics.

orthographic projection: The view of a 3D scene without any perspective distortion.

overlay: An overlay takes two images as parameters and returns an image that is made by laying the first image on top of the second. Blending takes place where the images overlap and the image laid on top is partially opaque (neither fully opaque nor fully transparent).

P

PAL (Phase Alternating Line): The television and video standard used in Europe. Six hundred twenty-five horizontal lines at 50 fields per second (two fields equals one frame). Five hundred seventy-six of these lines are used for the actual picture, and the rest are used for sync, VITC, and closed captioning.

palette: A selection of colors from which to choose.

parametric surface: A surface that describes a small number of points and a mathematical function whose shape is determined by those points. For example, a bicubic patch.

parent: An object at the top of a hierarchy model. A parent of a child can be the child of another parent, depending on its placement in the object tree.

particle system: A system of defining states and rules of behavior for each particle or group of particles. A particle can be anything from a point to a primitive. Usually used for simulating and animating different phenomena such as rain, fire, smoke, bee swarms, and explosions.

patch: A patch is made of three or four splines (three or four connected points). A surface is made up of at least one patch but is usually made up of many.

path: A sequence of 2D points, typically used to draw images consisting of line segments or to define borders for geometric shapes.

perspective projection: The view of a 3D scene using perspective distortion.

perspective view: The view of a 3D scene where the objects are displayed with perspective distortion.

perspective-corrected texture mapping: A technique where texture maps are continually updated to match the perspective.

phong shading: A technique in which the color shades on a triangle are calculated by interpolating the vertex colors, additionally regarding the normal vector at each triangle.

photorealistic imagery: Any 3D scene or 2D graphic that resembles a real-world environment.

pixel: Short for Picture Element, also know as a pel. The basic unit from which a video or computer picture is made. D1 images are 720 pixels wide by 486 high.

pixel clock (aka pixel frequency): The number of pixels displayed per second in MHz.

pixel depth (aka color depth): The number of bits of color information per pixel. With 8 bits per pixel, 256 colors can be displayed. With 16 bits per pixel 65,536 colors can be displayed. With 24 bits per pixel, 16.7 million colors can be displayed. With 32-bit pixel depth, 16.7 million colors can be displayed with 8 bits used for an alpha channel.

point light: A light source that emits light omnidirectionally.

polygon: A three- or more-sided 2D shape from which 3D objects are created.

polygon fill: A routine used to fill polygons with color. Usually performed by special hardware (chip).

polygonal model: A geometric model constructed from polygons.

polygonal modelers: A modeling application in which surfaces are defined as a collection of squares or triangles called polygons.

primitive: A basic geometric shape: plane, cone, torus, cube, and sphere are examples.

procedural modeling: Generating objects from algebraic equations.

procedural shader: An algorithm that creates the surface of an object mathematically, rather than with a 2D image map.

R

radiosity: An imaging technique used to determine the distribution of illumination in an environment, usually a closed space.

rasterization: The act of rendering a 3D image to a 2D screen.

ray tracing: A way of rendering a 3D image that follows the path of every ray of light. The light beam may be absorbed or reflected.

RealColor: Normally designates a 15 bpp, 32,768 colors or 16 bpp, 65,536 colors.

Real-time animation: An animation sequence that is being created and displayed dynamically.

reflection mapping: Simulating reflections in objects by mapping a 2D image of the reflected object onto their surfaces.

reflectivity: The degree to which an object bounces light back from its surfaces.

refraction: The appearance of bending or turning that occurs when a light wave passes from air through another medium, such as water or thick glass.

rendering: The process of displaying an object with shading effects to appear three-dimensional.

resolution: Used to describe the size of an image, usually in pixels. Number of pixels displayed horizontally and vertically on a monitor. The higher the resolution, the crisper the images will appear.

RGB (red, green, blue): The primary colors of light. Analog component devices use separate red, green, and blue color channels in order to keep the full bandwidth, which in turn produces a higher-quality picture.

RGB color model: The additive mixing of the three basic colors (red, green, and blue) to create images.

rotoscope: A procedure used to remove an object from a shot. For example, removing cables and wires from a film sequence.

rotoscoping: A way of creating animation by tracing the movements of actors from film or video.

S

saturation: The amount of color content in an image. A color with a high saturation value looks very intensive. A color with a low saturation value appears to have less color content (takes on a gray tone).

scaling: The transformation of image data from one size to another.

scanline rendering: A scan line is a single horizontal line on a monitor. The process of converting a 3D scene to a 2D image one scan line at a time usually begins from the upper-left corner of the image.

scanned image: An image or illustration that was digitized with a scanner.

scene: A 3D environment including models, cameras, and lights.

shading: The interaction between light sources, the atmosphere, and surfaces.

shadow: The effect of a light source being blocked from illuminating an object's surface.

shininess: How shiny an object's surface is.

skinning: The stretching of a surface, also called a skin, over interior cross sections (ribs).

specular highlight: A highlight on a smooth surface caused by a light source; light that reflects nonuniformly in a specific direction.

specular reflection: The reflection of a light source off a shiny surface.

spline: A curve used to define the shape of a model and defined by the position of its control points.

spline modelers: A modeling application in which surfaces are defined as splines connected by points.

spotlight: A light source that projects a conical beam from its source.

supersampling: A technique of antialiasing where multiple samples of a synthetic image are generated for each pixel.

surface: The exterior of a three-dimensional object and the materials assigned to it.

surface normal: A vector associated with a surface describing the orientation of a surface.

surface properties: The characteristics of a surface material that determines its reaction to light.

sweeping: A 3D modeling operation used to extrude a surface from a group of faces.

T

texture coordinates: Describes a location within texture space. *See UV coordinates.*

texture mapping: The wrapping of a bitmap image or 3D volume texture onto a surface.

texture modulation: The technique of modifying a displayed texture to simulate lighting.

tiling: The technique of repeating an image over a large area.

transformation matrix: A method of performing all the transformations within a 3D scene; scaling, rotation, position, and perspective distortion are specified by a 4×4 transformation matrix.

transparency/transmitivity: A measure of an object's capability to transmit light through its surface.

TrueColor: Capability to display 16.7 million colors simultaneously. Lookup tables are not used to translate the color values.

tweening/in-betweening: The creation of a series of transition frames between two keyframes or reference images. This process is called tweening, which is short for in-betweening.

U

UV coordinates: Absolute definition of the coordinates used for the placement of an image map on the surface of an object.

V

vertex: A specific point in 3D space; a corner point where plane polygons join.

VESA (Video Electronics Standard Association): A consortium for the standardization of computer graphics.

VGA (Video Graphics Adapter—IBM): A standard resolution of 640×480 with 16 colors.

volumetric data/rendering: The representation of 3D information as a three-dimensional array of 3D pixels or elements called *voxels*.

voxel: The individual volume component of 3D volumetric data.

W

wireframe: A wire mesh representation of a 3D object.

World Coordinate System: A system of representing and recording the position of 3D objects in 3D space. An object's position is given by the x, y, and z coordinates at its center point.

X

x-, y-, z-axes: The three axes of the world's three-dimensional coordinate system. In some applications, the x-axis is an imaginary horizontal line running left to right. The y-axis is a vertical line, and the z-axis comes out of the screen toward you. Generally any movement along one of these axes is said to be moved along its axis. For more information on axes and coordinate systems in trueSpace, see Chapter 1.

Y

YUV color palette: Image information of individual frames comprised of one part brightness and two parts color. First used in television.

Z

Z-buffer: 3D depth information for each pixel. Each pixel's Z-buffer value is compared, and the one with the lowest value gets drawn.

zoetrope: A cylinder with slots carved out of it. A series of images are placed on the inner wall of the cylinder with each image being slightly different than the other. The cylinder is then spun, and as it spins, a viewer looks through the slots. The images inside the cylinder appear to take on fluid movement. This was the most sophisticated motion viewing device of its day.

INDEX

SYMBOLS

W

X-Z